Microprocessor and Digital Computer Technology

JEROME E. OLEKSY, P.E.

Electronics Technology Institute
Cleveland, Ohio
Formerly Design Engineer,
Allen-Bradley Systems Group

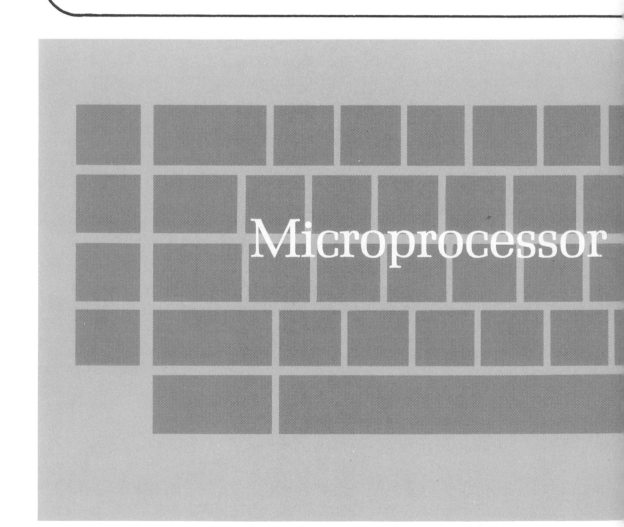

Microprocessor

GEORGE B. RUTKOWSKI, P.E.

Head, Electronics Department
Electronics Technology Institute
Cleveland, Ohio

and Digital
Computer Technology

Prentice-Hall, Inc., Englewood Cliffs, New Jersey 07632

and voluminous work. Computers will depend on humans for energy, body repairs, and reproduction.

Review Questions

1. How does a computer differ from a calculator?

2. Who first visualized a punched card scheme of programming computers?

3. Name three advantages modern computers have compared to the first-generation computers.

4. What is an IC?

5. What basic material is an IC made of?

6. What are the electronic switches used in second-generation computers called?

7. What is hardware? What is software?

8. What are usually easier, changes in hardware or changes in software?

9. What is an MPU?

10. Why are MPUs expected to grow very rapidly in applications?

CHAPTER 2

Numbers and Codes for Computers and Microprocessors

In this chapter we shall discuss number systems and codes that are commonly used with microprocessors and computer systems. Our familiarity with these number systems and codes will enable us later to understand how microprocessors and computers are programmed and how they work.

2-1 Binary and Decimal Numbers Compared

Because our familiar number system uses 10 characters, 0 through 9, it is called the decimal or a base-10 number system. It is generally assumed that this system evolved because humans naturally started counting by tens on their fingers. A system with 10 characters, however, is not well suited for modern electrical and electronic calculating machines. An electrical signal, such as a voltage, would require 10 levels or values to represent the 10 characters in our decimal system. Such a scheme would be far less reliable than one that requires only 2 levels, which can easily be obtained with switches. In Chapter 3, we shall see that transistors and FETs (field-effect transistors) are easily turned on and off and thus serve as very reliable switches. Therefore, a number system that is far more suitable for transistor and FET circuits is the *binary* or *base-2* number system. This system has only two characters, 1 and 0. The 1 and 0 can be represented by HIGH and LOW signals of a typical logic circuit. In the common TTL family* of digital devices, a HIGH

* The term TTL means transistor-to-transistor logic, which is discussed in detail in Chapter 3.

Binary numbers	Decimal numbers
0	0
1	1
10	2
11	3
100	4
101	5
110	6
111	7
1000	8
1001	9
1010	10
1011	11
1100	12
1101	13
1110	14
1111	15
10000	16
10001	17
10010	18
10011	19
10100	20
:	:
1001011	75
1001100	76
:	:
1100011	99
1100100	100

Figure 2-1. List of binary numbers and their decimal equivalents.

logic signal is typically in the range of 3.3–5 V, whereas a LOW logic signal is in the range of 0.5–0 V. Generally, regardless of logic family, the HIGH and LOW signals are represented by positive and less positive voltages, respectively. A portion of the binary number system, with its equivalent decimal values, is shown in Fig. 2-1. Obviously, the binary number system has the disadvantage of generally using more characters, which are called *bits,* to represent any given value than does the decimal system. This disadvantage, however, is insignificant when we consider the advantages that the binary number system has and the low cost per bit in modern computer-type circuits.

Often, when decimal (base-10) and binary (base-2) numbers are likely to appear together, their bases are shown in subscript to avoid confusing the two. For example, the number 11 might be interpreted as eleven in decimal or as three in binary if it is not more clearly defined. We can more specifically show that 11_{10} represents eleven in decimal and that 11_2 represents three in binary.

2-2 Binary-to-Decimal Conversions

The binary number system is *weighted.* This means that a character 1, in a binary number, represents a greater or lesser part of the number's value depending on its position in the number. The weight distribution of binary numbers is shown in Fig. 2-2. If not otherwise shown, a *binary point* is

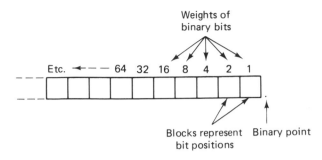

Figure 2-2. Weight distribution of binary number; weight doubles with each bit position to the left.

assumed to be at the far right of a binary number, just as decimal points are assumed to be to the far right of decimal numbers. The first binary bit to the left of the binary point carries a weight of 2^0 or 1. The second binary bit to the left of the binary point carries a weight of 2^1 or 2. Similarly, the third bit carries a weight of 2^2 or 4. Generally, then, as we move left from

Figure 2-3. Examples of how binary numbers are converted to their decimal equivalents.

Weight distribution

(A) Binary number →
$$
\overset{4}{1}\ \overset{2}{1}\ \overset{1}{1} = 4 + 2 + 1 = 7; \text{ thus, } 111_2 = 7_{10}
$$
Weights over 1's added

(B) Binary number →
$$
\overset{8}{1}\ \overset{4}{0}\ \overset{2}{1}\ \overset{1}{0} = 8 + 2 = 10; \text{ thus, } 1010_2 = 10_{10}
$$
Weights over 1's

(C) Binary number →
$$
\overset{16}{1}\ \overset{8}{0}\ \overset{4}{1}\ \overset{2}{0}\ \overset{1}{0} = 16 + 4 = 20; \text{ thus, } 10100_2 = 20_{10}
$$
Weights over 1's

(D) Binary number →
$$
\overset{32}{1}\ \overset{16}{0}\ \overset{8}{1}\ \overset{4}{0}\ \overset{2}{0}\ \overset{1}{1} = 32 + 8 + 1 = 41; \text{ thus, } 101001_2 = 41_1
$$
Weights over 1's

(E) Binary number →
$$
\overset{64}{1}\ \overset{32}{0}\ \overset{16}{0}\ \overset{8}{0}\ \overset{4}{0}\ \overset{2}{0}\ \overset{1}{0} = 64; \text{ thus, } 1000000_2 = 64_{10}
$$

(A) $11000_2 = 24_{10}$ (F) $111111_2 = 63_{10}$
(B) $11100_2 = 28_{10}$ (G) $1000110_2 = 70_{10}$
(C) $11111_2 = 31_{10}$ (H) $1100110_2 = 102_{10}$
(D) $100110_2 = 38_{10}$ (I) $1111111_2 = 127_{10}$
(E) $111001_2 = 57_{10}$ (J) $10101010_2 = 170_{10}$

Figure 2-4. Binary numbers and their decimal equivalents.

bit position to bit position, the weight of each 1 in that position simply doubles. The far-right bit of a binary number is called the least significant bit (LSB). The far-left bit of a binary number is called the most significant bit (MSB).

By knowing the weights in binary numbers, we are able to find the decimal equivalents of such numbers. For example, several binary numbers are converted to their decimal equivalents in Fig. 2-3. The weights are shown above each bit. The weights that are above 1s in the binary number are simply added to give the decimal equivalent of the number. More binary numbers and their decimal equivalents are given in Fig. 2-4. The reader should verify each equation for practice.

2-3 Decimal-to-Binary Conversions

Decimal numbers can be converted to their binary equivalents by a *successive division by 2* process. Figure 2-5 shows how binary equivalents of a few

Figure 2-5. Examples of how decimal numbers are converted to their equivalent binary numbers.

(A) Convert 35_{10} to its binary equivalent.

Solution:
$35 \div 2 = 17 \rightarrow 1$
$17 \div 2 = 8 \;\; \rightarrow 1$
$8 \div 2 = 4 \;\; \rightarrow 0$
$4 \div 2 = 2 \;\; \rightarrow 0$
$2 \div 2 = 1 \;\; \rightarrow 0$
$1 \div 2 = 0 \;\; \rightarrow 1$

Thus, $35_{10} = 100011_2$

(B) Convert 235_{10} to its binary equivalent.

Solution:
$235 \div 2 = 117 \rightarrow 1$
$117 \div 2 = 58 \;\; \rightarrow 1$
$58 \div 2 = 29 \;\; \rightarrow 0$
$29 \div 2 = 14 \;\; \rightarrow 1$
$14 \div 2 = 7 \;\; \rightarrow 0$
$7 \div 2 = 3 \;\; \rightarrow 1$
$3 \div 2 = 1 \;\; \rightarrow 1$
$1 \div 2 = 0 \;\; \rightarrow 1$

Thus, $235_{10} = 11101011_2$

(C) Convert 1492_{10} to its binary equivalent.

Solution:
$1492 \div 2 = 746 \rightarrow 0$
$746 \div 2 = 373 \rightarrow 0$
$373 \div 2 = 186 \rightarrow 1$
$186 \div 2 = 93 \;\; \rightarrow 0$
$93 \div 2 = 46 \;\; \rightarrow 1$
$46 \div 2 = 23 \;\; \rightarrow 0$
$23 \div 2 = 11 \;\; \rightarrow 1$
$11 \div 2 = 5 \;\; \rightarrow 1$
$5 \div 2 = 2 \;\; \rightarrow 1$
$2 \div 2 = 1 \;\; \rightarrow 0$
$1 \div 2 = 0 \;\; \rightarrow 1$

Thus, $1492_{10} = 10111010100$

decimal numbers are found with this method. In Fig. 2-5(A), 35_{10} is converted to its binary equivalent by first dividing it by 2. As shown, the result is 17 with a remainder of 1. The remainder is written off to the right and eventually becomes the LSB of the binary equivalent number. The 17 is moved down and, in turn, is also divided by 2. The quotient 8 is moved down to be divided by 2, and the remainder 1 is written off to the right. The result of dividing 8 by 2 is 4 with a remainder of 0. As before, the 4 is moved down for further division, and the remainder 0 is shown to the right. The last step of this process always results in a 1 divided by 2. Of course, 2 divides into 1 zero times with a 1 remainder. The last remainder 1 is the MSB of the binary equivalent number. That is, as shown, the remainders read upward become the binary equivalent number as written from left to right. The remaining examples of Fig. 2-5 can similarly be analyzed. The reader, as an exercise, should work for each binary equivalent number of the decimal numbers given in Fig. 2-4.

2-4 Fractions in the Binary Number System

Fractional values in decimal can also be expressed in a binary format. Examples of decimal fractions and mixed numbers with their equivalent binary numbers are shown in Fig. 2-6. Note that as fractional values can be expressed

Figure 2-6. Examples of decimal fractions and mixed numbers with their binary equivalents.

(A) $\frac{1}{2} = 0.5_{10} = 0.1_2$

(B) $\frac{1}{4} = 0.25_{10} = 0.01_2$

(C) $\frac{3}{4} = 0.75_{10} = 0.11_2$

(D) $\frac{1}{8} = 0.125_{10} = 0.001_2$

(E) $\frac{7}{8} = 0.875_{10} = 0.111_2$

(F) $\frac{1}{16} = 0.0625_{10} = 0.0001_2$

(G) $\frac{15}{16} = 0.9375_{10} = 0.1111_2$

(H) $\frac{11}{16} = 0.6875_{10} = 0.1011_2$

(I) $3\frac{3}{4} = 3.75_{10} = 11.11_2$

(J) $6\frac{7}{8} = 6.875_{10} = 110.111_2$

with decimal characters to the right of the decimal point, so likewise are such values expressed with binary bits to the right of the binary point.

The weight distribution of a binary fraction is shown in Fig. 2-7. As shown, a 1 directly to the right of the binary point carries a weight of $\frac{1}{2}$ or 0.5_{10}. The next bit to the right carries a weight of $\frac{1}{4}$ or 0.25_{10}, etc. We can see that, generally, the weight of each bit is one-half of the weight of the bit immediately to its left. Finding the decimal equivalent of a binary fraction therefore simply requires that we add the weights over the 1s, exactly as we did with whole numbers. Again, for practice, the reader can verify the equations of Fig. 2-6.

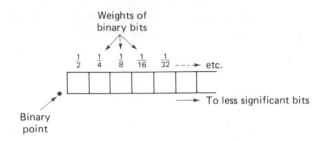

Figure 2-7. Weight distribution of binary fractions; weight halves with each bit position to the right.

We can convert any decimal fraction to its binary equivalent by a successive multiplication by 2 process. Figure 2-8 shows how binary equivalents of a few decimal fractions are found by this process. Note in (A) of this figure that when 0.8125 is multiplied by 2, the whole number part of the

Figure 2-8. Examples of how decimal fractions are converted to their equivalent binary numbers.

(A) Convert 0.8125_{10} to its binary equivalent.

Solution:

$0.8125 \times 2 = 1.625 \rightarrow 1$
$0.625 \times 2 = 1.25 \longrightarrow 1$
$0.25 \times 2 = 0.5 \longrightarrow 0$
$0.5 \times 2 = 1.0 \longrightarrow 1$
$0 \times 2 = 0$

Thus, $0.8125_{10} = 0.1101_2$.

(B) Convert 0.40625_{10} to its binary equivalent.

Solution:

$0.40625 \times 2 = 0.8125 \rightarrow 0$
$0.8125 \times 2 = 1.625 \longrightarrow 1$
$0.625 \times 2 = 1.25 \longrightarrow 1$
$0.25 \times 2 = 0.5 \longrightarrow 0$
$0.5 \times 2 = 1.0 \longrightarrow 1$
$0 \times 2 = 0$

Thus, $0.40625_{10} = 0.01101_2$.

(C) Convert 0.333_{10} to its binary equivalent.

Solution:

$0.333 \times 2 = 0.666 \rightarrow 0$
$0.666 \times 2 = 1.332 \rightarrow 1$
$0.332 \times 2 = 0.664 \rightarrow 0$
$0.664 \times 2 = 1.328 \rightarrow 1$
$0.328 \times 2 = 0.656 \rightarrow 0$
$0.656 \times 2 = 1.312 \rightarrow 1$
$0.312 \times 2 = 0.624 \rightarrow 0$
$0.624 \times 2 = 1.248 \rightarrow 1$
$0.248 \times 2 = 0.496 \rightarrow 0$
$0.496 \times 2 = 0.992 \rightarrow 0$
$0.992 \times 2 = 1.984 \rightarrow 1$
$0.984 \times 2 = 1.968 \rightarrow 1$
$\vdots$

Thus, $0.333_{10} \cong 0.010101010011$.

product is written off to the right and the fractional part is brought down for another multiplication by 2. This process is repeated until no fraction appears in the product or until the required degree of accuracy is obtained.

2-5 Octal and Hexadecimal Number Systems

As already mentioned, the binary system is suited for digital electronic circuits though not particularly suited for humans. On the other hand, the decimal number system is familiar to and therefore convenient for humans but is not practical for digital circuits. Furthermore, converting decimal numbers to their binary equivalents is a time-consuming process. Since humans are often required to instruct (program) computers in their own language (a

Figure 2-9. Decimal, binary, octal, and hexadecimal numbers compared.

Decimal	Binary	Octal	Hexadecimal
0	0	0	0
1	1	1	1
2	10	2	2
3	11	3	3
4	100	4	4
5	101	5	5
6	110	6	6
7	111	7	7
8	1000	10	8
9	1001	11	9
10	1010	12	A
11	1011	13	B
12	1100	14	C
13	1101	15	D
14	1110	16	E
15	1111	17	F
16	10000	20	10
17	10001	21	11
18	10010	22	12
19	10011	23	13
20	10100	24	14
:	:	:	:
63	111111	77	3F
64	1000000	100	40
65	1000001	101	41
:	:	:	:
127	1111111	177	7F
128	10000000	200	80

binary format called *machine language*), two more number systems become very useful. These are the octal (base-8) and the hexadecimal (base-16) number systems. For humans familiar with the decimal number system, octal and hexadecimal (hex) systems are easy to learn. Also, octal and hex numbers are very easy to convert into their binary equivalents, and likewise binary numbers are easily converted into octal and hex. Examples of equivalent decimal, octal, and hex numbers are shown in Fig. 2-9. If numbers of different bases must be used in the same text, their bases should be shown in subscript. For example, $19_{10} = 10011_2 = 23_8 = 13_{16}$.*

As shown in Fig. 2-10, binary numbers are converted to their octal equivalents by dividing each binary number into groups of three starting

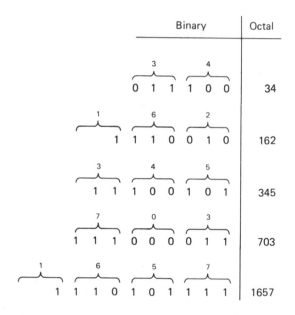

Figure 2-10. Examples of binary numbers being converted to their equivalent octal numbers.

with the binary point. Each group of three is then converted to its equivalent decimal character. The decimal characters form the octal equivalent number. Note that if the far-left bits of the binary number do not form a group of three, the missing bits are assumed to be 0s. When converting octal to binary, simply reverse this process. Octal numbers are used with minicomputers and with some computer-based industrial controllers.

Some binary numbers and their equivalent hex numbers are shown in

---

* Hexadecimal numbers are commonly identified with a suffix H or subscript H; that is, $13_{16} = 13H = 13_H$.

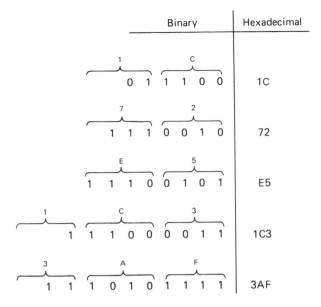

Figure 2-11. Examples of binary numbers being converted to their equivalent hex numbers.

Fig. 2-11. In this case, the binary words are divided into groups of four. Each group of four bits is then converted to its equivalent hex character. Then each group of the resulting hex characters becomes the hex equivalent of the binary number. Note again that if the left bits of the binary number do not fill in the last (most left) group of four, the missing bits are assumed to be 0s. Hex numbers are commonly used with microprocessors.

2-6 Arithmetic with Binary Numbers

In practice, we shall rarely be required to do arithmetic with binary numbers by hand; computers or microprocessor systems will do it for us. We should, however, be familiar with the mechanics of such arithmetic. Such familiarity will enable us to understand how certain computer circuits work and what some program instructions do.

Examples of several binary numbers being added are shown in Fig. 2-12. The addition process starts at the far right, that is, with the LSBs. In (A), the 0 and 1, in the LSB column, added give the sum of 1, as shown. The next column over adds 0 and 0, and their sum is 0. Next 1 and 0 are added, and again the sum is 1. So far no carries have been involved. Adding the 1 and 1 in the fourth column to the left results in a binary sum of 10 (equivalent to decimal 2). The 0 of this 2-bit word is placed in the answer row of the fourth column, and the 1 becomes a carry into the fifth column. Therefore, this 1 carry must add to the two 1s already in the fifth column,

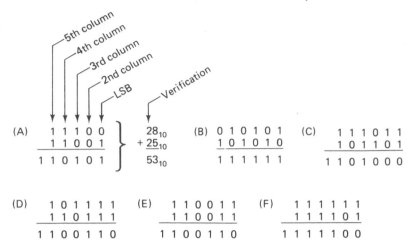

Figure 2-12. Examples of binary numbers being added.

resulting in a binary sum of 11 (equivalent to 3 in decimal). The right bit of this 2-bit sum, a 1 in this case, is placed in the fifth column of the answer row. The left bit is carried over to the sixth column. Since there are no sixth-column bits in the binary numbers being added, the 1 carry into the sixth column simply becomes the MSB of the answer. The remaining examples in Fig. 2-12 can similarly be analyzed. The answer of each example can be verified by converting its binary numbers to decimal equivalents.

2-7 Subtraction with Binary Numbers

As with the addition process, subtraction begins with the LSBs. When the bit in the minuend is smaller than the bit of the subtrahend in the same column, we borrow from the more significant bit of the minuend. Several

Figure 2-13. Examples of binary numbers being subtracted.

Decimal equivalents

(A)
```
  1101          13
 −1001        −  9
  0100           4
```

(B)
```
  10110         22
 −10100       −20
  00010         02
```

(C)
```
  11111         31
 −01110        −14
  10001         17
```

(D)
```
  0 10
  1010          10
 −0001        −  1
  1001           9
```
Minuends after all barrowings are completed

(E)
```
  0 10
  1101          13
  1011         −11
  0010           2
```

(F)
```
  0 1 1 0
  11001         25
  00111       −  7
  10010         18
```

Binary numbers	Their one's complements
0000	1111
0001	1110
0010	1101
0011	1100
0100	1011
0101	1010
0110	1001
0111	1000
1000	0111
1001	0110
1010	0101

Figure 2-14. Examples of binary numbers and their complements.

examples of subtraction are shown in Fig. 2-13. Examples (A) – (C) are quite simple in that no borrowing was required. That is, in example (A), 1 subtracted from 1 yields 0 in the 2^0 column. Then 0 from 0 in the 2^1 column yields 0, and 0 from 1 in the 2^2 column yields 1, etc. Examples (B) and (C) can similarly be analyzed.

Examples (D) – (F) in Fig. 2-13 involve a borrowing process. In the 2^0 column of example (D), a 1 must be borrowed from the 2^1 column in the minuend before subtraction can take place. This borrowing causes a 10_2 minuend in the 2^0 column. Subtracting a 1 from a 10_2 minuend results in a difference of 1, as shown. That is, any column that requires a subtraction of 1 from 0 also requires that we borrow from the adjacent (more significant) column. If the adjacent column also has a 0, it will have to borrow from the next left column. Therefore, if a 0 borrows from the left, it becomes 10_2. But if a 10_2 loans to the right, it becomes a 1; note the resulting minuend after this kind of borrow/loan process in example (F).

In most computers and microprocessor units (MPUs), the difference in two numbers is found by addition. In other words, the hardware, in an MPU or computer system, that performs the arithmetic is called the *arithmetic logic unit* (ALU) and typically is able to perform addition only. Therefore, special techniques are used to subtract binary numbers by addition.

Subtraction by addition can be performed by first *complementing* the subtrahend. A binary number is complemented by inverting each of its bits. Examples of binary numbers and their complements are shown in Fig. 2-14. These complements are also known as *one's complements*. If we add the one's complement of the subtrahend to the minuend, we get their difference less 1. A 1 is then added to this difference for a final answer. This process is best understood by examples; see Fig. 2-15.

Note, in each example of Fig. 2-15, that the subtrahend is first complemented and then the complement is added to the minuend. The result is an extra 1 (an overflow) in the far-left column. This far-left 1 is then carried down to the least significant (2^0) column and added to the previous answer. The final answer is the correct difference. This process is sometimes called the *end-around-carry* method of subtraction.

In the previous paragraph we learned that the sum of the minuend, the complement of the subtrahend, and 1 yields the correct difference between

(A)
```
 1101          1101
-1001         +0110
          }  1 0011
               └──→ 1
               0100
```

(B)
```
 10110         10110  ← Minuend
-10100        +01011  ← One's complement of subtrahend
          }  1 00001
               └──→ 1 ← End-around-carry of MSB
               00010
```

(C)
```
 11111         11111
-01110        +10001
          }  1 01110
               └──→ 1
               10001
```

(D)
```
 1010          1010
-0001         +1110
          }  1 1000
               └──→ 1
               1001
```

(E)
```
 1101          1101
-1011         +0100
          }  1 0001
               └──→ 1
               0010
```

(F)
```
 11001         11001
-00111        +11000
          }  1 10001
               └──→ 1
               10010
```

Figure 2-15. Binary subtraction problems solved with one's complements and the end-around-carry method.

Figure 2-16. Examples showing how to perform subtraction by adding with two's complements.

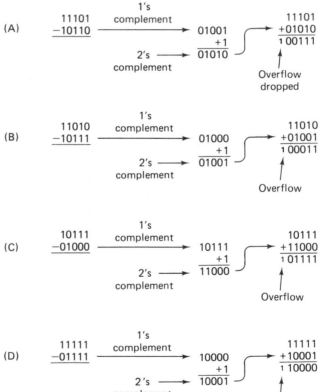

the minuend and subtrahend. We can just as correctly add the 1 to the one's complement of the subtrahend first. This changes the one's complement to a *two's complement*. The two's complement of the subtrahend added to the minuend gives the correct difference without the end-around-carry step. Several examples of subtraction with two's complements are shown in Fig. 2-16. Note in each example that the 1 carry out of the MSB (the overflow) is simply dropped.

If we compare binary numbers with their two's complements, we can observe a pattern; see Fig. 2-17. Starting at the right with the LSB of each binary number and then working toward the left one bit at a time, we can see that the two's complement is the same as the binary number above it up to and including the first 1. Note, however, that after the first 1, each two's complement bit is the inverse of the binary bit in the same column. Exactly the same procedure is followed when converting a number in two's complement form to binary.

Figure 2-17. Examples of how binary numbers are converted to their equivalent two's complements.

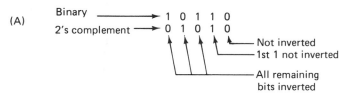

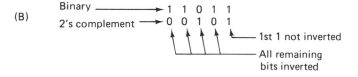

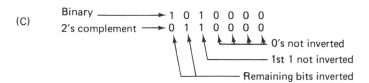

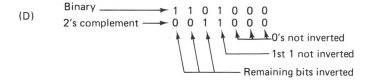

2-8 Signed Numbers in Microprocessors and Computers

Signed numbers must often be processed by microprocessor and computer systems. Numbers are treated as data by such systems. Data word size is commonly 8 bits in MPUs. Minicomputers are either 12-bit or 16-bit machines and thus can process 12- or 16-bit data words. Positive numbers are simply in binary format, whereas negative numbers are usually in two's complement form. Figure 2-18 shows several positive and negative decimal numbers with their equivalents in binary and two's complement forms, respectively. Also note the octal and hex equivalents of such numbers.

When a data word represents a signed number, the far-left bit is the *sign bit*. A 0 in the sign bit position identifies a positive number. A 1 in the sign bit position identifies a negative number. Note the sign bits with

Figure 2-18. Examples of equivalent signed numbers in decimal, binary or two's complement, octal, and hexadecimal formats.

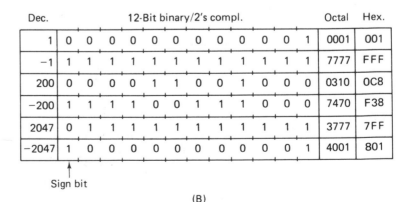

Dec.	8-Bit binary/2's compl.								Octal	Hex.
0	0	0	0	0	0	0	0	0	000	00
43	0	0	1	0	1	0	1	1	053	2B
−43	1	1	0	1	0	1	0	1	325	D5
64	0	1	0	0	0	0	0	0	100	40
−64	1	1	0	0	0	0	0	0	300	C0
127	0	1	1	1	1	1	1	1	177	7F
−127	1	0	0	0	0	0	0	1	201	81

Sign bit

(A)

Dec.	12-Bit binary/2's compl.												Octal	Hex.
1	0	0	0	0	0	0	0	0	0	0	0	1	0001	001
−1	1	1	1	1	1	1	1	1	1	1	1	1	7777	FFF
200	0	0	0	0	1	1	0	0	1	0	0	0	0310	0C8
−200	1	1	1	1	0	0	1	1	1	0	0	0	7470	F38
2047	0	1	1	1	1	1	1	1	1	1	1	1	3777	7FF
−2047	1	0	0	0	0	0	0	0	0	0	0	1	4001	801

Sign bit

(B)

each of the positive and negative quantities in Fig. 2-18. When subtracting numbers such that the minuend is smaller than the subtrahend, we expect a negative difference. In microprocessor and computer systems, a negative answer will be in two's complement form, which means that its sign bit will be *set* (logic 1).

Example 2-1

Using the two's complement of the subtrahend, subtract 01000100_2 from 00011001_2. Check your answer by converting these binary numbers into decimal equivalents and solve for their difference in decimal.

Solution

The problem:

$$\begin{array}{r} 00011001 \\ -\ 01000100 \end{array}$$

Using two's complement:

two's complement
of subtrahend
$\diagdown$ ┌─minuend

$$\begin{array}{r} \rightarrow 00011001 \\ \rightarrow 10111100 \\ \hline 11010101 \leftarrow \text{sum} \end{array}$$

↑
Sign bit is
set (1), which means that the
answer is negative.

Since the answer in two's complement is 11010101, the equivalent in binary format can be shown as -00101011 (the negative sign means that the answer is negative). Converting to decimal, we can show that

$$00101011_2 = 43_{10}$$

or

$$-00101011_2 = -43_{10}$$

Check:

$$\begin{array}{r} 00011001_2 = 25_{10} \\ -\ 01000100_2 = -68_{10} \\ \hline -43_{10} \end{array}$$

2-9 Binary-Coded Decimal (BCD) Numbers

The binary-coded decimal (BCD) system is commonly used in digital electronics. Like binary, the BCD system is weighted. Decimal numbers and their equivalent BCD values are shown in Fig. 2-19. Note that each decimal character is represented by a 4-bit word. That is, if a decimal number consists of

Decimal numbers	Equivalent BCD 8421		
0			0000
1			0001
2			0010
3			0011
4			0100
5			0101
6			0110
7			0111
8			1000
9			1001
10		0001	0000
11		0001	0001
12		0001	0010
13		0001	0011
.			
.			
25		0010	0101
26		0010	0110
.			
.			
38		0011	1000
39		0011	1001
.			
.			
43		0100	0011
.			
99		1001	1001
.			
123	0001	0010	0011
.			
256	0010	0101	0110

Figure 2-19. Decimal numbers and their equivalent BCD numbers.

two or three characters, its equivalent in BCD consists of two or three 4-bit words, respectively. The weight distribution of each 4-bit BCD word is exactly the same as in a 4-bit binary word. Thus, from left to right, the weights of the 4 bits are 8421. A 4-bit BCD word, unlike a 4-bit binary word, never represents a value greater than 9. For values greater than 9, more than one 4-bit BCD word must be used. As shown in Fig. 2-19, therefore,

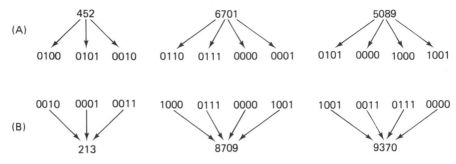

Figure 2-20. (A) Each decimal character of a decimal number is represented by a 4-bit BCD word; (B) each 4-bit word of a BCD number is represented by a decimal character.

the largest 4-bit BCD word is 1001. Figure 2-20(A) shows how a few decimal numbers are converted to their BCD equivalents, and Fig. 2-20(B) shows how a few BCD numbers are converted to their decimal equivalents. Generally, it is quite easy to convert decimal to BCD values and vice versa.

2-10 ASCII Codes

Every computer and microprocessor type has an *instruction set.* An instruction set includes a list of instructions (commands) that a programmer uses when preparing programs. Both instructions and programs are discussed further in later chapters. For the present, we can say that instructions in a program tell the computer or microprocessor exactly what to do in a detailed step-by-step procedure. Typically, the programmer types his or her program on a typewriter-like keyboard (terminal) of the computer or microprocessor system. Each numbered or lettered key that the programmer pushes must produce a series of digital bits (0s and 1s) that represent that number or letter. As we shall see, a computer or microprocessor, by itself, can only respond to (understand) a digital format of 0s and 1s. Commonly, therefore, numbers and letters are converted to a digital format called ASCII (American Standard Code for Information Interchange); see the table of Fig. 2-21. Typical keyboard terminals produce (output) a group of digital bits that contain the ASCII equivalent of each numbered or lettered key that is pushed. For example, if a given terminal uses 7-bit ASCII and its A key is pushed, the terminal's output will include the bit pattern 100 0001. That is, as shown in the table of Fig. 2-21, character A has an octal equivalent of 101_8 and a hex equivalent of 41_{16}, which converts to 1000001_2. Similarly, the number 5 is shown to have the hex equivalent of 35_{16}, which converts to 0110101_2 in 7-bit ASCII.

Printing character	7-Bit ASCII (octal)	7-Bit ASCII code (hex)	6-Bit trimmed ASCII (octal)	Printing character	7-Bit ASCII (octal)	7-Bit ASCII code (hex)	6-Bit trimmed ASCII (octal)
@	100	40	00	(Space)	040	20	40
A	101	41	01	!	041	21	41
B	102	42	02	"	042	22	42
C	103	43	03	#	043	23	43
D	104	44	04	$	044	24	44
E	105	45	05	%	045	25	45
F	106	46	06	&	046	26	46
G	107	47	07	'	047	27	47
H	110	48	10	(	050	28	50
I	111	49	11	)	051	29	51
J	112	4A	12	*	052	2A	52
K	113	4B	13	+	053	2B	53
L	114	4C	14	'	054	2C	54
M	115	4D	15	—	055	2D	55
N	116	4E	16	.	056	2E	56
O	117	4F	17	/	057	2F	57
P	120	50	20	0	060	30	60
Q	121	51	21	1	061	31	61
R	122	52	22	2	062	32	62
S	123	53	23	3	063	33	63
T	124	54	24	4	064	34	64
U	125	55	25	5	065	35	65
V	126	56	26	6	066	36	66
W	127	57	27	7	067	37	67
X	130	58	30	8	070	38	70
Y	131	59	31	9	071	39	71
Z	132	5A	32	: *	072	3A	72
[*	133	5B	33	;	073	3B	73
/	134	5C	34	<	074	3C	74
] *	135	5D	35	=	075	3D	75
↑ *	136	5E	36	>	076	3E	76
← *	137	5F	37	?	077	3F	77
Null	000						
Horizontal tab	011						
Line feed	012						
Vertical tab	013						
Form feed	014						
Carriage return	015						
Rubout	177						

Figure 2-21. Conversion table for ASCII (American Standard Code for Information Interchange); 7-bit and 6-bit codes.

Example 2-2

(a) Using ASCII code, show the 7-bit equivalents of the following characters: L, $, 7, and %. (b) Find the printing characters or instructions of the following 7-bit ASCII words: 1000100, 1011010, 1111111, and 1000011.

Numbers and
Codes for
Computers and
Microprocessors

(a)

Char.	Octal	Hex	7-Bit ASCII
L	114	4C	100 1100
$	044	24	010 0100
7	067	37	011 0111
%	045	25	010 0101

(b)

7-Bit ASCII	Octal	Hex	Char./Inst.
1000100	104	44	D
1011010	132	5A	Z
1111111	177	7F	Rubout
1000011	103	43	C

2-11 Parity Bits for Error Detection

Often, digital information must be transmitted over distances. These distances might be short, like between a computer and its terminal just a few feet away. On the other hand, the distances can be hundreds of miles, as is the case when a computer in one state services terminals in several other states via telephone lines. During such transmissions, errors can occur. Errors are caused by noise pickup by the transmission lines and many other factors. An error might be a logic bit that is transmitted as a LOW by the source device but is received or interpreted as a HIGH by the destination device.

Character	ASCII
A	0100 0001
C	1100 0011
3	0011 0011
4	1011 0100

Even parity bit

(A)

Character	ASCII
Q	0101 0001
S	1101 0011
8	0011 1000
9	1011 1001

Odd parity bit

(B)

Figure 2-22. Examples of alphanumeric characters and their 7-bit ASCII equivalents with (A) even parity bit and (B) odd parity bit.

Therefore, a parity bit is usually added to each digital word transmitted. The parity bit is either HIGH or LOW depending on the number of HIGHs normally in the word. For example, if the words to be transmitted are in 7-bit ASCII, a parity bit can be added after the seventh bit. Examples of ASCII words with even parity bits are shown in (A) of Fig. 2-22. *Even parity* simply means that the number of HIGHs in each 8-bit word (7-bit ASCII and one parity bit) is even. Odd parity on 7-bit ASCII is shown in (B) of Fig. 2-22.

As we shall see later, the source device has circuitry, called a parity generator, that adds the appropriate parity bit to each word transmitted. The destination device has circuitry, called a parity checker, that determines the number of HIGHs in each word received. Therefore, in either even or odd parity systems, if an error in one bit of a digital word occurs during transmission, the destination device can detect it.

Review Questions

1. Why is the binary number system used with digital computers?

2. What are the meanings of the terms HIGH and LOW as used when describing signals in digital systems?

3. Why is the binary number system called weighted?

4. Describe the weight distribution of a binary whole number and of a binary fraction.

5. What is the purpose of using a binary point in a binary mixed number?

6. Name four number systems that we must be familiar with when working with computer and microprocessor systems.

7. Describe what a one's complement of a binary number is.

8. What is a two's complement of a binary number?

9. Typically, what logic level is the sign bit of a positive number? Of a negative number?

10. What words do the letters in the term ASCII represent?

11. What is the purpose of using a parity bit?

Problems

2-1   Convert each of the following binary numbers to its decimal equivalent: (a) 0111, (b) 110100, (c) 01001001, (d) 10000001, (e) 11111111, (f) 10101010, (g) 01010101, (h) 100000000.

2-2 Convert each of the following binary numbers to its decimal equivalent: (a) 1110, (b) 100110, (c) 01110111, (d) 11111110, (e) 01111111, (f) 11100110, (g) 10000000, (h) 110011101.

2-3 Convert each of the following decimal numbers to its binary equivalent: (a) 12, (b) 31, (c) 32, (d) 105, (e) 254, (f) 300, (g) 2047, (h) 2048, (i) 5280, (j) 16,384.

2-4 Convert each of the following decimal numbers to its binary equivalent: (a) 15, (b) 62, (c) 64, (d) 152, (e) 511, (f) 512, (g) 756, (h) 1023, (i) 1024, (j) 65,536.

2-5 Referring to Problem 2-1, convert each of the binary values given to its octal equivalent.

2-6 Referring to Problem 2-2, convert each of the binary values given to its octal equivalent.

2-7 Referring to Problem 2-3, convert each of the decimal values given to its hexadecimal equivalent. *Hint:* Convert to binary and then to hex.

2-8 Referring to Problem 2-4, convert each of the decimal values given to its octal and hex equivalents. *Hint:* Convert to binary and then to octal and hex.

2-9 Convert each of the following octal numbers to its 8-bit binary equivalent: (a) 10, (b) 25, (c) 37, (d) 77, (e) 100, (f) 233, (g) 356, (h) 377.

2-10 Convert each of the following octal numbers to its 8-bit binary equivalent: (a) 45, (b) 64, (c) 177, (d) 200, (e) 277, (f) 300, (g) 333, (h) 366.

2-11 Which of the values in Problem 2-9 have binary equivalents with the eighth (far-left) bits set (HIGH)?

2-12 Which of the values in Problem 2-10 have binary equivalents with the eighth (far-left) bits set (HIGH)?

2-13 Convert each of the following hexadecimal numbers to its 8-bit binary equivalent: (a) 0A, (b) C1, (c) EB, (d) 7F, (e) 8D, (f) 49.

2-14 Convert each of the following hexadecimal numbers to its 8-bit binary equivalent: (a) 50, (b) A6, (c) BF, (d) 77, (e) 1D, (f) 35.

2-15 Which of the values in Problem 2-13 have binary equivalents with the eighth (far-left) bits set (HIGH)?

2-16 Which of the values in Problem 2-14 have binary equivalents with the eighth (far-left) bits set (HIGH)?

2-17 If the far-left bit of an 8-bit word is a sign bit, the sign bit being HIGH on negative values and LOW on positive values, which of the numbers given in Problem 2-13 are negative? Next to each, show its equivalent decimal value.

2-18 If the far-left bit of an 8-bit word is a sign bit, the sign bit being HIGH on negative values and LOW on positive values, (a) which of the octal numbers in Problem 2-10 represent negative values? (b) Which of the hex numbers in Problem 2-14 represent negative values? (c) Next to each, show its equivalent decimal value.

2-19 Work the following: (a) 1000 + 0111, (b) 1010 + 0101, (c) 0011 + 0111, (d) 1100 + 0100, (e) 1111 + 1111, (f) 01001110 + 00110111.

2-20 Work the following: (a) 1010 + 0110, (b) 1101 + 0100, (c) 1110 + 0111, (d) 0011111 + 00011101, (e) 00010000 + 00010001.

2-21 Show the one's complement of each binary value given in Problem 2-1.

2-22 Show the one's complement of each binary value given in Problem 2-2.

2-23 Convert each of the following hex numbers into binary and then show the two's complement of each; beside each two's complement, show its octal and hex equivalents: (a) 2B, (b) D4, (c) 00, (d) FF.

2-24 Convert each of the following octal numbers into equivalent 8-bit binary, and then show the two's complement of each; beside each two's complement, show its octal and hex equivalents: (a) 001, (b) 377, (c) 137, (d) 200.

2-25 Convert each of the decimal numbers of Problem 2-3 to its BCD equivalent.

2-26 Convert each of the decimal numbers of Problem 2-4 to its BCD equivalent.

2-27 Work the following problems by converting each subtrahend to its two's complement and adding it to the minuend; if any answer overflows into the ninth bit position, simply drop (ignore) the overflow: (a) 00001100 − 00000100, (b) 00011111 − 00001011, (c) 00001000 − 00001010, (d) 00000111 − 00111110.

2-28 Work the following problems by converting each subtrahend to its two's complement and adding it to the minuend; if any answer overflows into the ninth bit position, simply drop the overflow: (a) 00010111 − 00000111, (b) 01110100 − 00110000, (c) 00110000 − 01110100, (d) 00010111 − 00100000.

2-29 Since typically the sign (far-left) bit is HIGH on negative values, (a) which of the answers to Problem 2-27 are negative? (b) The negative answers in Problem 2-27 are in two's complement form. Convert each to binary and then to decimal.

2-30 Since typically the sign (far-left) bit is HIGH on negative values, (a) which of the answers to Problem 2-28 are negative? (b) The negative answers in Problem 2-28 are in two's complement form. Convert each to binary and then to decimal.

2-31 Convert each of the following decimal numbers to equivalent 8-bit binary or two's complement, whichever is appropriate: (a) +2, (b) −2, (c) +63, (d) −63, (e) +116, (f) −116.

2-32 Convert each of the following characters to its 7-bit ASCII equivalent: (a) G, (b) J, (c) Z, (d) !, (e) @, (f) &, (g) 4, (h) 9, (i) ;.

2-33 Convert each of the following characters or instructions to its 6-bit trimmed ASCII equivalent: (a) C, (b) L, (c) line feed, (d) carriage return, (e) O, (f) 0, (g) 2, (h) +, (i) =.

2-34 In the table of Fig. 2-21, fill in the 7-bit ASCII code (hex) and the 6-bit trimmed ASCII (octal) columns for instructions null through rubout.

2-35 Referring to the characters and instructions given in Problem 2-33, show the equivalent of each in 7-bit ASCII and add a parity bit to the far-left (eighth) bit position so that each resulting 8-bit word has odd parity.

CHAPTER 3

Programming

Due to overwhelming advances made in the manufacture of large-scale integrated circuits in the last decade, *programmed* logic is rapidly replacing *hardwired* logic. Circuits and systems which used to be custom-designed to meet specific operating requirements are now being handled by computers. Rather than change the *hardware* to meet new design requirements, the designer uses more or less standard computer systems and customizes the *software,* or programs.

Since standard components can be used for most applications, the development time for a new system is drastically reduced, thereby making the design more cost effective. Similarly, design changes are easily implemented by simply changing the program.

These advances have opened up opportunities for a "new breed" of engineers and technologists. Today's designers and service personnel must be familiar with *programming* as well as with hardware design techniques.

In this chapter we shall familiarize you with the important aspects of programming from the *computer's* point of view. You will learn how a computer's *instruction set* directs its operation. You will see how *flowcharts* make programming easier. Finally, you will learn the differences in various languages used in computer programming, such as *machine* language, *assembly* language, and *compiler,* or high-level, language.

3-1 Computer Programs

Although a computer is capable of handling remarkable tasks, by itself the computer can do nothing without first being programmed. The programmer, not the computer, actually solves a problem. By means of his or her program, the programmer tells the computer what to do, when to do it, and exactly how to do it. The program must therefore contain *instructions* as well as *data* to be operated on. The computer then simply follows the instructions to the letter, performing arithmetic operations and making logical decisions, until it arrives at a solution to the problem. Finally, it does whatever it was instructed to do with that solution, such as print out an answer to a math problem or fire a spark plug in an automobile engine.

It might seem, at first, that if the programmer must first solve the problem, why use a computer at all? Well the answer, of course, is speed. Once programmed, the computer can make thousands of calculations and decisions every second, thus making it possible to control systems where things are changing too rapidly for human control. For example, in a computerized automobile ignition system, the computer can be programmed to continually monitor engine temperature, revolutions per minute, throttle position, and crankshaft angle. It then decides on the precise instant to fire the spark plugs to obtain the best possible fuel economy and emission control. But remember, the program instructions tell the computer exactly what to do and how to do it.

We shall now study typical instructions and programming techniques.

3-2 Instruction Sets

The list of instructions that a computer can interpret is called its *instruction set*. Large, high-speed computers have very large instruction sets containing hundreds of possible operations. Others, intended for simple control purposes,

Table 3-1 Simple Instruction Set

Instruction	Description
LDA	(Load accumulator) Tells computer to load a word from memory into the arithmetic unit.
ADD	(Add) Tells computer to add a number in memory to the present contents of the accumulator.
SUB	(Subtract) Tells computer to subtract a number in memory from the present contents of the accumulator.
STA	(Store) Tells computer to store the contents of the accumulator into memory.
BMI	(Branch if minus) Tells computer to take its next instruction from a designated memory location if the number in the accumulator is negative. Otherwise, take the next sequential instruction.
HLT	(Halt) Tells computer to stop.

may have instruction sets of 16 or less. The Motorola MC6800 microprocessor, for example, has a set of 72 instructions, which by slight variations are expanded into almost 200 different operations. Generally speaking, the larger the instruction set, the more powerful the computer is.

An instruction set for a simple computer, which will be studied later, is shown in Table 3-1. Mnemonics, such as LDA and STA, are abbreviations of the operations.

The *accumulator* is a circuit inside the computer where the result of an arithmetic operation appears. It can be thought of as being similar to the circuit driving (providing) the numerical display on a pocket calculator.

Just how the computer knows where in memory to look for instructions or data will be made clear shortly. Now let's see how to write some simple programs.

3-3 Straight-Line Programs

Before the computer can begin to run a program, all instructions and data* must be loaded into the computer's memory. Memories will be studied in detail in a later chapter. For now, just consider a memory as a number of storage locations, such as boxes or bins, where instructions and data are stored. Each memory location is given an *address* so that the computer can find it. Figure 3-1(A) shows 16 consecutive memory locations whose hexadecimal addresses are 00 through 0F. The slips of paper in the various locations represent instructions and data. Of course in an actual memory the information is stored electronically in binary.

Instructions generally have two parts: an *operation code* (op code) and an *operand address*. The op code tells the computer *what* to do. The operand address identifies the memory location holding the data that are to be operated on.

Refer to Fig. 3-1(B). The instruction in memory location 00 tells the computer to load the accumulator with the *contents* of memory location 0A. Note that after this instruction is executed, the accumulator will contain the number 7. The next instruction tells the computer to add the contents of memory location 0B to the present contents of the accumulator. After execution, the accumulator will contain 13.

The next instruction causes the contents of memory location 0C to be subtracted from the accumulator. The accumulator will contain the value 5 after execution.

The instruction in memory location 03 stores the contents of the accumulator into memory location 0F. After execution, memory location 0F will contain the value 5. It doesn't matter whether location 0F had any previous data in it or not. The store operation erases any previous data, similar to

---

* Sometimes data are input to the computer during operation; such would be the case for variables like temperature, etc.

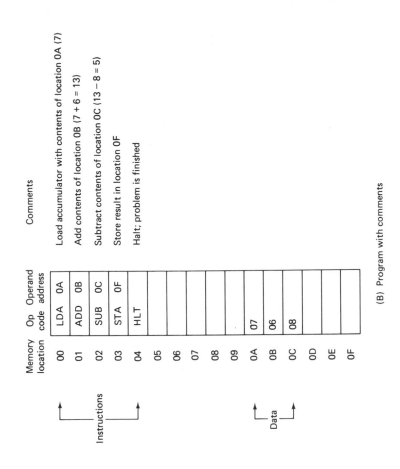

Memory location	Op code	Operand address	Comments
00	LDA	0A	Load accumulator with contents of location 0A (7)
01	ADD	0B	Add contents of location 0B (7 + 6 = 13)
02	SUB	0C	Subtract contents of location 0C (13 − 8 = 5)
03	STA	0F	Store result in location 0F
04	HLT		Halt; problem is finished
05			
06			
07			
08			
09			
0A	07		
0B	06		
0C	08		
0D			
0E			
0F			

Instructions

Data

(B) Program with comments

Addresses

Instructions

Data

(A) A computer memory acts like a set of numbered storage locations where instructions and data are kept

Figure 3-1. Memory loaded with instructions and data.

33

recording on magnetic tape. Any previously recorded data are lost. After storing, the accumulator will still contain the value 5. Storing does not alter the accumulator contents.

Last, we must tell the computer to stop. Note that no operand address is required here. The computer comes to a halt as soon as the instruction is decoded.

A few things should be pointed out about the program. First, the instructions *must* be loaded into memory in the correct sequence. Computers are designed to start at the first instruction and then look for following instructions in sequential memory locations.

Data can be loaded *anywhere* in memory, and the locations need not be sequential. The computer can obtain data from any memory location as long as the programmer tells it where to look; that is, he or she must tell it the correct operand address.

Let's examine another program.

We'll include a multiply (MUL) and a divide (DIV) instruction to our set and solve for R in the equation

Figure 3-2. Program to solve $R = AX^2 + (Y/2) - C$.

Mem. loc.	Op code	Operand address	Comments (accumulator contents)
00	LDA	0A	X
01	MUL*	0A	X^2 (multiply acc. by operand)
02	MUL	0B	AX^2
03	STA	0F	AX^2
04	LDA	0C	Y
05	DIV*	0D	Y/2 (divide acc. by operand)
06	ADD	0F	$AX^2 + (Y/2)$
07	SUB	0E	$AX^2 + (Y/2) - C$
08	STA	0F	$AX^2 + (Y/2) - C$
09	HLT		
0A	X		
0B	A		
0C	Y		
0D	2		
0E	C		
0F			

*Note: Two new instructions, multiply (MUL) and divide (DIV), were added to the instruction set.

$$R = AX^2 + (Y/2) - C$$

See Fig. 3-2. Note that the instruction in location 03 temporarily stores the value AX^2 into location 0F so that the accumulator can be used to form $Y/2$.

Once again, note that the instructions are loaded into memory sequentially in the order that they are to be carried out. Data can be stored in any convenient location. Of course only op codes, operand addresses, and data are loaded into the computer. The column marked Comments is shown for illustrative purposes only.

3-4   Flowcharts

The two programs we saw earlier were simple enough to follow by just reading through the program listing. They are called straight-line programs because the solution progresses in a straight line from beginning to end. However, most programs contain instructions which direct the computer to take its next instruction from a different location, depending on the outcome of some operation. To follow these more involved programs more easily, we use *flowcharts*. Flowcharts are simplified diagrams which guide us step by step through the program. Flowcharts use special symbols for each operation which act like signposts on a highway, guiding us to our destination.

Figure 3-3 shows the common symbols used in flowcharting. The oval symbol is used at the beginning or end of a program. Next, the rectangular

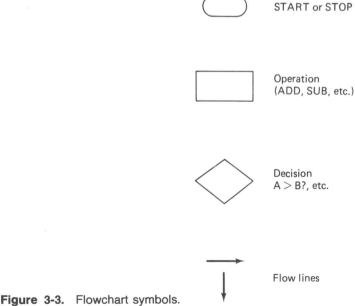

Figure 3-3.   Flowchart symbols.

box is used for any operation, such as ADD, SUB, etc. When in doubt, use the rectangular box.

The diamond-shaped symbol is a decision symbol. It is this symbol that makes flowcharts so valuable, because the diamond directs us to different routes when necessary. The types of decisions that a computer can make are usually simple mathematical decisions, such as $A > B$?, or $A = 0$?, etc. They are usually yes or no decisions.

Arrows indicate the flow of the program from beginning to end. Now let's look at some flowcharts.

Figure 3-4 shows the flowchart to solve the equation $F = A + B - C$.

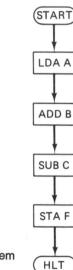

Figure 3-4. Flowchart for problem $F = A + B - C$.

Note that this is the same program shown in Fig. 3-1. Note also that the flowchart doesn't contain memory addresses, but rather it uses symbols A, B, and C to represent numbers to be used. Once the programmer has drawn the flowchart for the problem, he or she simply has to translate the flowchart into corresponding op codes and operand addresses.

Now let's look at a program using a decision box.

3-5 Branches and Loops

Figure 3-5 shows the flowchart for a program to compare two numbers A and B and store the larger number in memory. We start by loading the accumulator with one of the numbers, A in this case. Next we subtract the second number, B, from the first, calling the result C. The decision box

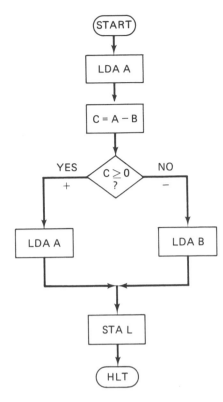

Figure 3-5. Flowchart for program to compare two numbers.

tests whether C is greater than or equal to zero. If the answer is yes, A must have been larger than or equal to B, so we want to store A in memory. Therefore we load A back into the accumulator and then store it in the memory location reserved for the larger number. The memory address is not given here, simply some *label* L, representing a location. Finally we halt.

Of course if A were less than B, C would be a negative number, so the NO route would be taken from the decision box.

In Fig. 3-6 we see the program written from the flowchart. Note that after A is loaded and B is subtracted from A, the instruction BMI (branch if minus) at 02 tells the computer to branch to location 06 for its next instruction if the current contents of the accumulator are negative. If the result is not negative, the computer will take its next instruction from the following location (03).

Remember that the variable A stored in location 0A and B in location 0B are *symbols* representing numbers to be used in the program. However, when actually entering the data, *numbers,* not symbols, are loaded into locations 0A and 0B.

Now let's look at a branch instruction to control a *loop.*

Mem. loc.	Op code	Operand address	Comments
00	LDA	0A	Load first number A
01	SUB	0B	A − B
02	BMI	06	If result is minus, go to 06
03	LDA	0A	A is larger; load A
04	STA	0E	Store A in 0E
05	HLT		
06	LDA	0B	B is larger; load B
07	STA	0E	Store B in 0E
08	HLT		
09			
0A	A		First number
0B	B		Second number
0C			
0D			
0E			Storage location for larger
0F			

Figure 3-6. Program to compare two numbers and store the larger.

The program whose flowchart is shown in Fig. 3-7 is used to calculate and print the values of X^2 for $X = 1$ to 100. Assume that the computer is connected to a hard-copy printer and will print the contents of the accumulator when directed to by the PRT instruction.

The program runs as follows: The initial value of X (1) is loaded into the accumulator. Next, X is multiplied by itself, yielding X^2. Then X^2 is printed. The next few instructions demonstrate how the computer makes decisions.

The current value of X is loaded into the accumulator and incremented. This updated value of X is then stored into memory, replacing the old value. Next the final value of X (101 in this case) is subtracted from the accumulator contents (current value of X). If the current value of X is less than 101, the accumulator contents will be negative after subtraction, that is, less than 0. At this point, a BMI instruction tells the computer to go back and repeat the loop again. However, after going through the loop 100 times, the accumulator contents will not be negative. This time the BMI instruction is skipped, and the computer halts. The program listing is shown in Fig. 3-8.

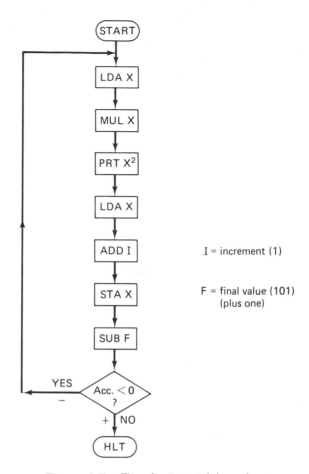

I = increment (1)

F = final value (101)
(plus one)

Figure 3-7. Flowchart containing a loop.

The power of the computer program is indicated by its ability to direct the computer to perform hundreds of calculations even though the program contains only a few steps.

Flowcharts need not be as detailed as the ones we've been using. Each block in those flowcharts corresponds to an instruction. But many times the blocks in a flowchart simply describe what operation or decision is to be performed in a general way. Thus each block may correspond to several instructions.

For example, the flowchart of Fig. 3-5 was used to compare two numbers. Let's take a look at a flowchart for a program to compare *three* numbers *A, B,* and *C* and print the largest. See Fig. 3-9. Note that not all the computer steps in solving the problem are shown, but the general flow of the program is clearly indicated.

Mathematical problem solving is only one use of computers. Due to the reduced cost of electronic components in the last decade, computers

Mem. loc.	Op code	Operand address	Comments
00	LDA	0C	X
01	MUL	0C	X^2
02	PRT		Print value of X^2
03	LDA	0C	X
04	ADD	0E	X + 1
05	STA	0C	Replace old value of X with new value
06	SUB	0F	X − 101; compare X to final value
07	BMI	00	If result is minus, go to 00
08	HLT		When result is positive, stop
09			
0A			
0B			
0C	X		Initial value = 1
0D			
0E	1		Increment
0F	101		Final value of X

Figure 3-8. Program to square all values of X from 1 to 100.

Figure 3-9. Flowchart for program to compare three numbers and print the largest.

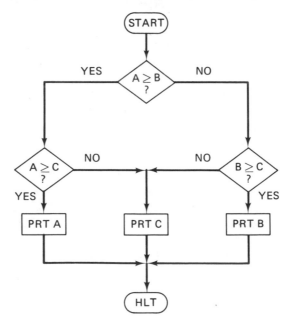

are being used more and more for *control* purposes. One example of a computer control system, which we'll be seeing in buildings and homes in the near future, is environmental control. For example, we might like the computer to maintain the temperature of a home within desired limits, around the clock.

Let's say we want the temperature during the night to be held at 60°F (15°C). Then at 6:30 A.M., we want the temperature to be raised to 68°F (20°C) and remain at that temperature throughout the day. Finally, at 11:00 P.M., we want the temperature to automatically be reduced to 60°F again for the night.

Our computer will need a *real-time* clock, that is, a clock that can keep track of (and possibly display) local time in hours and minutes (seconds optional). We'll use a 24-hr clock.

Also, the computer must have some sort of temperature-sensing element

Figure 3-10. Flowchart for home temperature control.

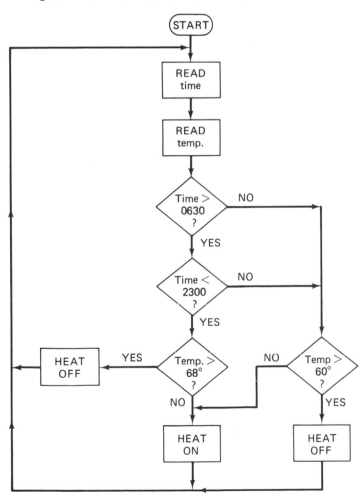

connected to it. In a later chapter, we'll discuss *interfacing* sensors and power control devices to computers. For now, we'll just look at the program.

Figure 3-10 shows the various paths the computer will follow and the decisions it must make.

First, the computer reads the time and the temperature. Then it makes its first decision. Is the time greater than 0630 (6:30 A.M.)? If not, it follows the NO route and checks if the temperature is greater than 60°F. If yes, it follows the YES route and turns off the heat. The heater can be either an electrical heater or simply a solenoid valve for a gas or oil burner.

After turning off the heat, the computer branches back to the beginning and repeats the loop over and over again. When the temperature finally drops below 60°F, the computer will turn on the heat. The dashed arrows in Fig. 3-11 show the path followed at 0500 and at a temperature of 58°F.

Figure 3-11. Path taken by computer at 0500 and 58°F.

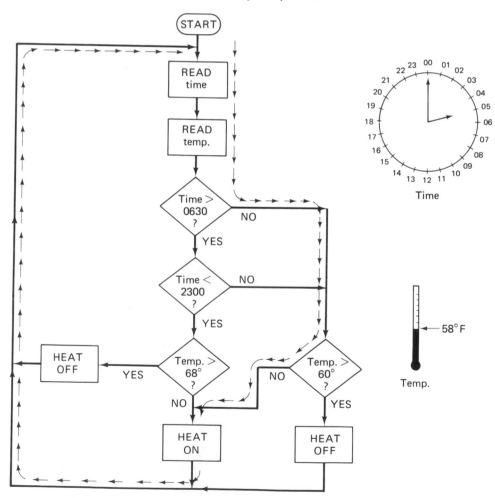

Try following the paths for different times and temperatures to make sure you understand what the computer is doing.

Of course, the home computer will also be doing many other things simultaneously, such as controlling the humidity and lighting in the home, monitoring the burglar and smoke alarms, recording telephone messages, and countless other tasks.

3-6 Computer Languages

Now that you are familiar with what a program is, let's discuss some languages used in communicating with computers.

Since the computer is a machine, it only understands *machine language*. Machine language consists of binary signals. Each instruction must therefore be *coded* in binary. Table 3-2 shows that each instruction of our simple

Table 3-2 Machine Codes

Instruction	Machine or Op Code
LDA	101
ADD	110
SUB	111
STA	000
BMI	001
HLT	011

instruction set has a corresponding 3-bit binary code. The binary code for each operation (instruction) is called the *op code*. Large instruction sets obviously need many more bits to represent each instruction. The MC6800, for example, has an 8-bit op code.

In addition to the op code, the operand address must also be stored in binary in the machine's memory. Figure 3-12 shows the entire program of Fig. 3-1 written in machine language. Note that the memory locations are also shown in binary.

The first instruction, with op code 101, located at memory location 00000 tells the computer to load the accumulator with the contents of memory location 01010. The contents are 00000111, or $7_{(10)}$. Compare each instruction with those in Fig. 3-1 to see the correspondence.

Simple computers, like the J-100 which you'll study later in this book, have provisions for entering the program in machine language via switches on the front panel.

Figure 3-13 shows that the switches are first set according to the binary word that is to be entered. Note that the memory address register shows

Mem. loc.	Op code	Operand address
00000	101	01010
00001	110	01011
00010	111	01100
00011	000	01111
00100	011	XXXXX
00101		
00110		
00111		
01000		
01001		
01010	00000111	
01011	00000110	
01100	00001000	
01101		
01110		
01111		

Figure 3-12. Machine language program.

Figure 3-13. Entering a program in machine language via switches.

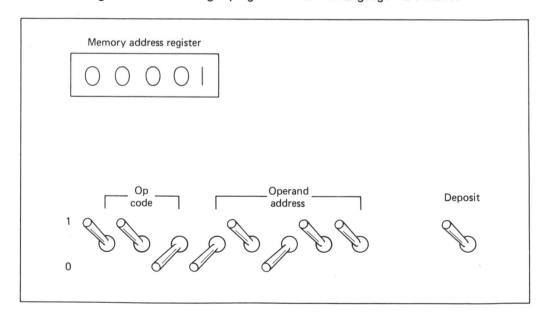

the location in memory where the word will be stored. When the deposit button is pressed, the binary word set up on the switches is stored into memory. Next the memory address register is incremented, and the next instruction word is set up on the switches and deposited. This process is continued until the entire program and all data are entered. Finally, the memory address register is reset to zero, and the program is run.

Obviously, this is a tedious and time-consuming procedure to follow if lengthy programs are to be entered. Thus easier methods of programming have been developed. First, rather than use toggle switches, keyboards can be used so that the programmer enters the program either in octal or hexadecimal code. Each key on a hex keyboard replaces four toggle switches. Likewise, programs written in octal or hex are easier to read and write than those using all 1s and 0s. Most microprocessors are programmed in hexadecimal code.

A step up from machine language is *assembly* language. Using assembly language, the programmer enters his or her program via a TTY (teletype) keyboard or video terminal. But rather than type in 1s and 0s, the programmer types mnemonic abbreviations of the instructions, such as LDA for load accumulator, etc. The computer then *assembles* the instruction into machine code. The process works like this:

Already stored inside the computer is a program called an *assembler*. When an instruction is typed in, the assembler program compares the mnemonic with a list of mnemonics already stored in its own memory. When a match occurs, the machine code for that instruction is obtained. Effectively, the assembler "looks up" the correct machine code for each instruction for the programmer, thus saving him or her time.

In addition to looking up the op code for the programmer, the assembler also keeps track of where data are stored. In other words, the programmer need not type in an operand address. A *variable* name is simply assigned to each operand, such as *A, B, L2*, etc. The assembler then assigns an operand address to each variable.

The programmer, of course, must tell the computer the numerical value of each variable. An assembly language program to square all values of X from 1 to 100 is shown in Fig. 3-14. Compare this program to that shown in Fig. 3-8.

Figure 3-14. Assembly language program to square values of X from 1 to 100; label BEGIN represents the address location of instruction LDA X.

```
                        X = 1
                        I = 1
                        F = 101
              BEGIN     LDA    X
                        MUL    X
                        PRT
                        LDA    X
                        ADD    I
                        STA    X
                        SUB    F
                        BMI          BEGIN
                        HLT
```

Note in Fig. 3-14 that the program first tells the computer that the initial value for *X* is 1, the increment *(I)* is 1, and the final value *(F)* for *X* is 101. The program listing then just makes reference to *X* or *I* or *F,* without specifying an operand address.

One more thing to note is the use of the *label* BEGIN. The word BEGIN identifies the *starting* address of the loop. The programmer need not specify a memory location; the computer will assign one. Note that the BMI instruction tells the computer to take its next instruction from the memory location (BEGIN) where the LDA instruction is stored if the accumulator contents are negative. Otherwise the computer goes on to the next instruction, HLT.

Finally, let's discuss some really powerful programming languages. Three commonly used high-level languages are BASIC (Beginners All-purpose Symbolic Instruction Code), FORTRAN (FORmula TRANslation), and COBOL (COmmon Business-Oriented Language).

COBOL, as the name implies, is a plain language method of programming the computer, often used in business applications, such as accounting. FORTRAN is a mathematics-oriented language, often used by scientists and engineers. BASIC is a simple but powerful language often used by hobbyists. When using any of these languages, the programmer does not tell the computer what to do each step of the way. He or she simply types in almost plain language statements describing the problem that needs to be solved, and the computer does the rest. These high-level languages are entered into the computer by means of TTY keyboards, punched tapes, punched cards, etc., which are described in Chapter 10.

10	LET A = 7
20	LET B = 6
30	LET C = 8
40	R = A + B − C
50	PRINT R
60	END

Figure 3-15. Program written in BASIC.

A simple program written in BASIC is shown in Fig. 3-15. The numbers (10, 20, 30, . . .) at the left of each line are called *statement* numbers. They are not memory locations but simply tell the computer the order in which the statements are to be followed. You probably recognized this as the program of Fig. 3-1.

The statement $R = A + B - C$ directs the computer to get the value of *A* from memory, load it into the accumulator, add the value of *B,* and finally subtract the value of *C* and store the result. The statement is far more compact than an equivalent machine language or assembly language statement. Since *several* operations are involved in that single statement, the computer must have some way of *translating* it into a number of op codes and operand addresses. The computer does so by means of an *interpreter* program. An interpreter is a program already stored in memory which takes each BASIC statement and translates it into several machine code statements. The process is shown in Fig. 3-16.

Another way of putting it is that the interpreter takes the *source* program, written in BASIC, and translates it into an *object* program in machine language. The program must be in machine language before the computer can execute it.

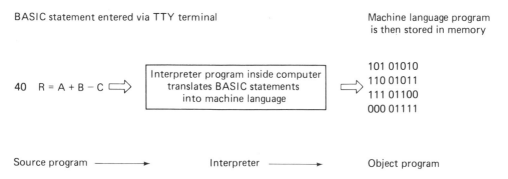

Figure 3-16. Interpreter changes BASIC into machine language.

FORTRAN and COBOL use similar programs, called *compilers,* to convert source programs into object programs. Compilers are faster than interpreters, but compilers usually require that an entire program be entered, either by means of punched cards or tape, before compiling can begin. Interpreters, on the other hand, can translate *each statement* as it is entered, by means of a keyboard, for example. The advantage is that each statement is analyzed by the interpreter to see if it contains any errors before it is translated and made part of the input program. If any errors exist (incorrect syntax, etc.), the computer will reject the statement and notify the operator by means of an error message printout.

Some BASIC symbols and operators are shown below.

Addition	$+$
Subtraction	$-$
Multiplication	$*$
Division	$/$
Exponentiation	$\uparrow$

Figure 3-17 shows the program of Fig. 3-2 written in BASIC. We have added the PRINT statement so that the computer will tell us the value for *R*. Once again, note the compactness of statement 50.

One last example of a BASIC program is shown in Fig. 3-18. Can you determine what the program does?

10	LET A = 4
20	LET X = 3.7
30	LET Y = 9.2
40	LET C = 7.5
50	R = A * X ↑ 2 + (Y / 2) − C
60	PRINT R
70	END

Figure 3-17. Program of Fig. 3-2 written in BASIC.

10	FOR X = 1 TO 100
20	Y = X ↑ 2
30	PRINT X, Y
40	NEXT X
50	END

Figure 3-18. BASIC program containing a loop.

Problems

3-1 Write a program using the format of Fig. 3-2 to add five numbers in locations 0A through 0E and store the sum in 0F.

3-2 Write a program using the format of Fig. 3-2 to solve the equation $R = A + B - C - D$. Store the result in location 0F.

3-3 Write a program using the format of Fig. 3-2 to square all even integers from 2 to 50, and print the result.

3-4 Write a program using the format of Fig. 3-2 to cube all odd integers from 1 to 99, and print the result.

3-5 Refer to the program of Fig. 3-19. Determine the contents of the accumulator after the instruction in each of the following locations is executed: (a) 00, (b) 01, (c) 02, (d) 03, (e) 04, (f) 05, (g) 06.

Figure 3-19. Program for Problems 3-5 and 3-6.

Mem. loc.	Op code	Operand address
00	LDA	0D
01	MUL	0A
02	ADD	0B
03	MUL	0D
04	ADD	0C
05	STA	0F
06	HLT	
07		
08		
09		
0A	3	(A)
0B	4	(B)
0C	5	(C)
0D	2	(X)

3-6 Refer to the program of Fig. 3-19. Change the instruction at memory location 03 to MUL 0B. Then determine the contents of the accumulator after execution of each instruction, as in Problem 3-5.

3-7 Draw a flowchart for the program of Problem 3-3.

3-8 Draw a flowchart for the program of Problem 3-4.

3-9 Refer to the temperature control flowchart of Fig. 3-10. Assume the system is operating, the temperature is 59°F, and the time is 0400. Assume also that the instruction in the decision box which reads *Temp. > 68°?* was erroneously entered as *Temp. < 68°?*. (a) Will the system operate normally between hours 0001 and 0630? (b) Will the system operate normally between hours 0631 and 2300? (c) Will the system operate normally between hours 2301 and 2400?

3-10 Refer to Problem 3-9. (a) Can the temperature of the system at any time drop much below 60°F? If yes, during what time period? (b) Can the temperature of the system at any time rise above 68°F? If yes, during what time period?

3-11 Using the instruction set of Table 3-2, rewrite the program of Fig. 3-6 in machine code. Use binary notation, and use 5-bit binary addresses.

3-12 Using the instruction set of Table 3-2, write a program to compare three numbers and store the largest. Use binary notation and use 5-bit binary addresses.

3-13 Write an assembly language program to calculate and print the squares of all odd integers from 1 to 99. Use the MUL instruction in addition to those listed in Table 3-1.

3-14 Write an assembly language program to calculate and print the cubes of all even integers from 2 to 100.

3-15. Write an assembly language program to compare two numbers *A* and *B* and store the larger.

3-16 Write an assembly language program to compare three numbers *A*, *B*, and *C* and store the largest.

3-17 Given the program of Fig. 3-20 written in BASIC, what value will be printed for *X* after the program is run?

```
10    LET A = 2
20    LET B = 4
30    LET C = 8
40    X = 4 * (A + B) / C
50    PRINT X
60    END
```

Figure 3-20. Program for Problem 3-17.

3-18 Given the program of Fig. 3-21 written in BASIC, what value will be printed for *Y* after the program is run?

10	LET U = 6
20	LET V = 3
30	LET W = 4
40	Y = ((U / V) * W) + 2
50	PRINT Y
60	END

Figure 3-21. Program for Problem 3-18.

3-19 Write a program in BASIC to solve the equation $Y = AX^2 + BX + C$ for $A = 2$, $B = 3$, $C = 4$, and $X = 5$.

3-20 Write a program in BASIC to solve the equation

$$Z = \frac{X + Y}{3} + W^2(X + 5)$$

Assign values for the variables.

3-21 Rewrite the program of Fig. 3-12 using hex numbers for all addresses, op codes, and data.

3-22 Rewrite the program of Fig. 3-12 using octal numbers for all addresses, op codes, and data.

3-23 Rewrite the program of Fig. 3-12 in assembly language. Assign the symbol A to the data byte in location 01010, B to the data byte in location 01011, and C to the byte in 01100. Use the symbol R to denote the storage location for the result.

CHAPTER 4

Discrete Parts and Gates for Computer Systems

This chapter contains important fundamentals on discrete components, logic gates, inverters, and buffers. The term *discrete components* refers to individual parts like diodes, transistors, light-emitting diodes (LEDs), etc. Knowledge of them is necessary if we are to understand how digital circuits basically work. Discussions here on gates, inverters, and buffers lean toward the popular TTL and complementary-pair metal oxide semiconductor (CMOS) families and processor applications. A microprocessor unit (MPU) cannot work alone. Among other things, an MPU requires *hang-on chips,* which are ICs such as the types discussed here. Also, we shall see how MIL SPEC (military specifications) terminology is used to simplify reading and interpreting digital circuit diagrams.

4-1 Diodes

Diodes are the simplest of electronic components. Each diode has only two leads, an *anode* and a *cathode*. The symbol of a diode and typical diode packages are shown in Fig. 4-1. Note in (B) of Fig. 4-1 that the diode is a junction of *P*- and *N*-type semiconductors. These semiconductors are either silicon or germanium and therefore form either silicon or germanium diodes. The size of the diode's package is a good indicator of its current carrying capability. Larger packages usually mean higher current capabilities.

Small diodes are used in large numbers in electronic equipment. In amplifiers and communications equipment, such as radios, TVs, and citizens'

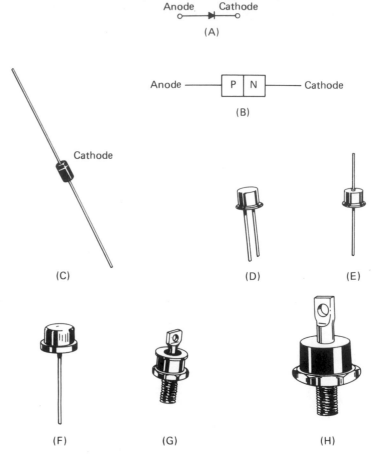

Figure 4-1. (A) Schematic symbol for a diode; (B) junction of *P*- and *N*-type semiconductors form a diode; (C) small-signal diode; stripe indicates end to which the cathode is connected; (D)–(F) are moderate-current diodes; (G)–(H) are high-current diodes. The diodes (E)–(H) have one lead connected to the case, which can be either the cathode or the anode as ordered by the user.

band transceivers, diodes serve as temperature stabilizers, signal detectors, and regulators, to name just a few. Also, small diodes are used in decision-making logic circuits within computers and automated industrial equipment.

4-2 Diodes as Unilateral Conductors

A unilateral conductor conducts current well in one direction but not well in the other. The arrow on the diode symbol points in the direction conventional current flows well, which means that electrons flow well in the direction opposite of the arrow.*

By noting the polarity of voltage across a diode, we can determine whether a diode will or will not conduct. Direct-current (dc) voltage across a diode is commonly called bias. When the diode's anode is more positive than its cathode, as shown in Fig. 4-2(A), the diode is said to be *forward-biased* and is able to conduct current well. If the applied voltage is such as to make the diode's anode more negative than its cathode, as shown in Fig. 4-2(B), it is *reverse-biased* or *back-biased* and does not conduct current well.

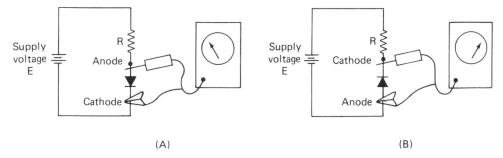

(A)   (B)

Figure 4-2. (A) Forward-biased diode acts like a short and has negligible voltage across it; (B) reverse-biased diode acts like an open and has the entire supply voltage *E* across it.

In other words, a forward-biased diode has low resistance, whereas a reverse-biased diode has high resistance. In *most* cases we can assume that diodes are ideal. An *ideal diode* is one that has zero resistance (acts like a short) when forward-biased and acts like an open when reverse-biased. If the values of the supply voltage *E* and circuit resistance *R* are known, we can estimate the circuit's current by Ohm's law:

$$I \cong \frac{E}{R}$$

4-3   Diodes as Rectifiers

An alternating-current (ac) voltage is one whose amplitude and polarity vary periodically as time passes. The continually changing polarity of ac voltage tends to cause current to change direction repetitively. When used in an ac circuit, the diode, or the circuit itself, is called a *rectifier*.

The simplest rectifier circuit is shown in Fig. 4-3(A). As the ac supply voltage repetitively changes polarity, the diode repetitively switches from

*Conventional current direction can be described as the direction of positive charge flow, while electron flow direction is the direction of negative charge flow.

being conductive (forward-biased) to nonconductive (reverse-biased). Thus, as shown in Fig. 4-3(B), each positive alternation of the supply voltage E puts a forward bias on the diode, causing it to act like a short for most practical purposes. All positive alternations therefore appear across the re-

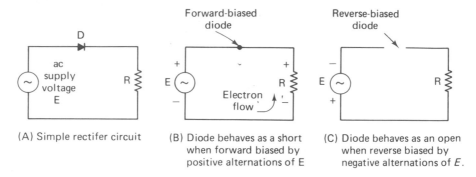

(A) Simple rectifer circuit

(B) Diode behaves as a short when forward biased by positive alternations of E

(C) Diode behaves as an open when reverse biased by negative alternations of E.

Figure 4-3. Diode behavior with AC applied.

sistor R. On each negative alternation, the diode is reverse-biased and acts like an open, as shown in Fig. 4-3(C), causing all negative alternations to appear across the diode D.

4-4 Diodes as Logic Circuit Components

In this age of computers and automation, digital logic circuits represent the largest and most rapidly growing segment of the electronics industry. Digital logic circuits are built with basic "building blocks" called gates. Among the most elementary of gates are AND gates and OR gates, whose symbols are shown in Fig. 4-4. Gates contain components such as resistors, diodes, and transistors. As we shall see while progressing through this text, logic circuit gates are classified in *logic families* such as DTL (diode-transistor logic), RTL (resistor-transistor logic), and TTL or T²L (transistor-transistor logic). At this time we shall confine ourselves to gates made with diodes and resistors.

Generally, regardless of the logic family, logic gates and circuits work with signals that have two voltage levels. Typically, these levels are about 0 V and some positive value. Frequent switching from one level to the other occurs during normal circuit operation.

Commonly, the term LOW or the letter L and sometimes the symbol 0 (zero) are used in reference to the near 0-V level. On the other hand, the term HIGH or the letter H and sometimes the number 1 (one) are used in reference to the more positive level.

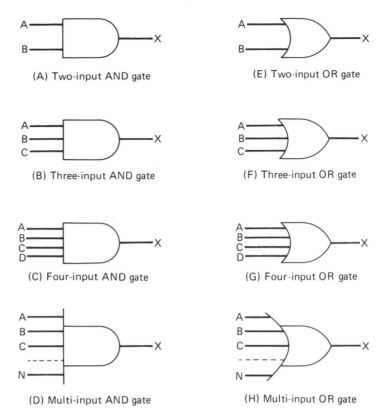

Figure 4-4. Symbols of AND gates and OR gates.

4-4-1 The AND Gate

Generally, the output signal of a logic gate is HIGH or LOW depending on the levels of its inputs and the type of gate it is. The AND gate's output is HIGH only when all its inputs are HIGH. This means that the AND gate's output is LOW if any one or more of its inputs are LOW. Thus in the case of the two-input AND gate of Fig. 4-4(A), its inputs *A and B* have to be HIGH before its output *X* can go HIGH. Similarly, then, input *A and* input *B and* input *C* must be HIGH, on the gate of Fig. 4-4(B), before its output *X* can go HIGH.

4-4-2 The OR Gate

An OR gate's output goes HIGH if any one or more of its inputs go HIGH. In other words, an OR's output is LOW only if all its inputs are LOW. For example, on a three-input OR gate, like that of Fig. 4-4(F), the

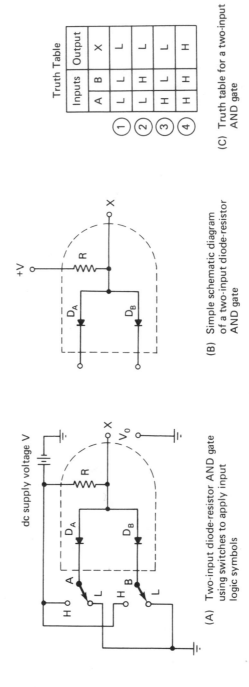

Truth Table

	Inputs		Output
	A	B	X
①	L	L	L
②	L	H	L
③	H	L	L
④	H	H	H

(C) Truth table for a two-input AND gate

(B) Simple schematic diagram of a two-input diode-resistor AND gate

(A) Two-input diode-resistor AND gate using switches to apply input logic symbols

Figure 4-5. Diode-resistor OR gate.

output X is HIGH if input A is HIGH *or* input B is HIGH *or* input C is HIGH *or* if any combination of these inputs is HIGH.

4-4-3 The Diode-Resistor AND Gate

A two-input diode-resistor AND gate is shown in Fig. 4-5. In part (A) of this figure, the input logic signals are applied to the inputs A and B with mechanical switches. In practice, however, input logic signals are more likely applied from the outputs of other logic circuits, as we shall see later.

The way any logic circuit works can be itemized on a *truth table*. A truth table for a two-input AND gate is shown in Fig. 4-5(C). It itemizes all possible combinations of inputs A and B and the resulting output X with each input combination. For example, when both inputs are L (LOW), as shown in row 1 of the table, the resulting output X is LOW. Two LOW inputs are caused if both switches are down in the L positions. As shown in Fig. 4-6(A), grounding both inputs forward-biases both diodes. Assuming

Figure 4-6. Two-input diode-resistor AND gate with (A) both inputs L; (B) input A logic L and input B logic H; (C) input A logic H and input B logic L; (D) both inputs H.

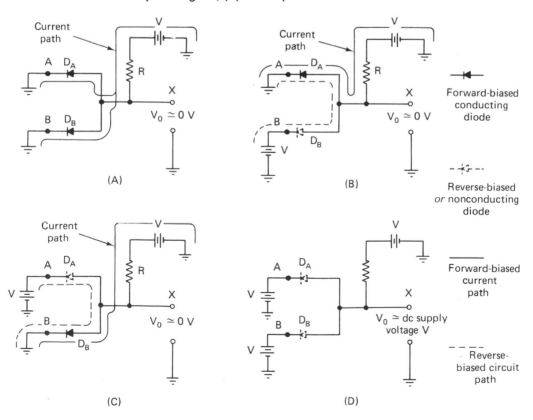

that the diodes are ideal, the output voltage V_o is 0 V or logic L because the output terminal X is effectively grounded through these conducting diodes.

If the switch at input B of the two-input diode-resistor AND gate is placed up in the H position while switch A remains in the L position, row 2 of the truth table indicates the resulting input and output signals. Diode D_A is forward-biased and conducts current in the path shown in Fig. 4-6(B). In this case, however, diode D_B is reverse-biased and nonconducting. That is, the HIGH logic signal at input B reverse-biases diode D_B through the conducting diode D_A in the broken-line circuit path shown. The forward-

Figure 4-7. Diode-resistor OR gate.

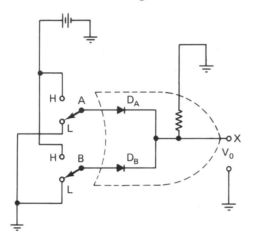

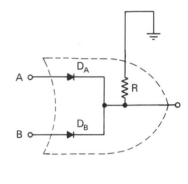

(A) Two-input diode-resistor OR gate using mechanical switches at its inputs

(B) Simple schematic diagram of a two-input diode-resistor OR gate

Truth Table

	Inputs		Output
	A	B	X
①	L	L	L
②	L	H	H
③	H	L	H
④	H	H	H

(C) Truth table for the two-input OR gate

biased D_A, behaving like a short, holds the output X at ground potential, which is at logic level L.

When input A is HIGH and input B is LOW, the equivalent circuit can be shown as in Fig. 4-6(C). In this case, diode D_B is forward-biased and conducts current in the path indicated. Diode D_A is reverse-biased by the HIGH logic level applied to input A through the conducting diode D_B in the broken-line circuit path. The output X is still LOW because the conducting D_B holds this output at ground (logic L) potential. Row 3 of the truth table indicates the input and resulting output conditions in this case.

Finally, when both switches are up in the H positions in the circuit of Fig. 4-5(A), the equivalent circuit can be shown as in Fig. 4-6(D). Now the anode and cathode of each diode are at the same potential, assuming that each input voltage V and the supply voltage V are equal. With no potential difference across them, the diodes are nonconducting. This causes no current through or voltage across resistor R, and the entire dc supply voltage appears at output X with respect to ground. Thus, as shown in row 4 of the table, output X is at logic H when both inputs are H.

4-4-4   The Diode-Resistor OR Gate

Two-input diode-resistor OR gates and their truth tables are shown in Fig. 4-7. As with the AND gate, the inputs A and B of the OR gate can be mechanically switched HIGH or LOW, but more commonly the H or L signals arrive from the outputs of other logic circuits.

As shown in row 1 of the truth table of Fig. 4-7(C), the output voltage at X is LOW only when both inputs are LOW. With both inputs LOW, there is no source voltage, as shown in the equivalent circuit of Fig. 4-8(A), and the voltage at X must be 0 V or logic LOW.

When input A is LOW but input B is HIGH, corresponding to row 2 of the truth table, the equivalent circuit in Fig. 4-8(B) applies. As shown, the input V_{in} (logic H) applied to input B forward-biases diode D_B, admitting current in the path shown. Diode D_A, however, is reverse-biased by V_{in} via the conducting diode D_B. Thus, the input V_{in} is passed directly to output X via the conducting diode D_B.

When input A is HIGH while input B is LOW, as shown in row 3 of the truth table, the circuit of Fig. 4-8(C) illustrates the situation. In this case D_A is forward-biased and conducting while D_B is reverse-biased and nonconducting. That is, input V_{in} applies a reverse bias voltage across diode D_B through the conducting diode D_A. The output X is HIGH again because input A and output X are directly connected via the conducting diode D_A.

When both inputs are HIGH, as in row 4, both diodes conduct as shown in Fig. 4-8(C). In this case, both of the HIGH inputs are directly connected to the output X through their respective conducting diodes.

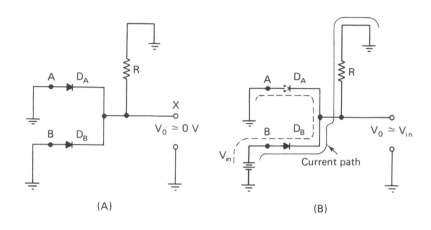

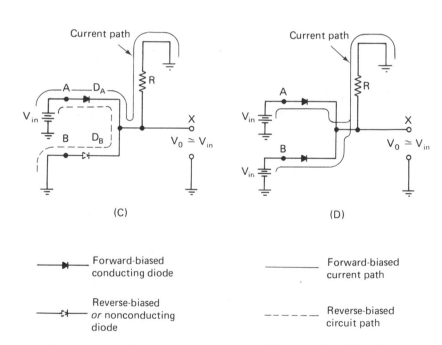

Forward-biased conducting diode	Forward-biased current path
Reverse-biased *or* nonconducting diode	Reverse-biased circuit path

Figure 4-8. Two-input diode-resistor OR gate with (A) both inputs L; (B) input A logic L and input B logic H; (C) input A logic H and input B logic L; (D) both inputs H.

4-5   Transistors

Invention of the transistor triggered the rapid growth of the electronics industry. Before transistors, electronic circuits were large, bulky, and unreliable. They consumed considerable power (energy) and therefore generated too much heat, which contributed to deterioration of other circuit parts and materials. With transistors, circuits became much smaller, more efficient, and far more reliable. The higher reliability of transistor circuits compared to vacuum tube equivalents is an extremely important advantage. In a properly designed circuit, the transistor is much less likely to become defective than a tube. The high reliability of modern electronic devices and circuits has made possible the development of today's complicated digital systems.

The techniques used to manufacture transistors led to developments that made it possible to mass-produce very small and highly reliable electronic circuits commonly known as integrated circuits (ICs).* ICs have transistors, diodes, resistors, and all interconnecting leads formed on a single piece of semiconductor material.

4-6   Transistor Packages

Individual (discrete part) transistors are available in a number of package types, as shown in Fig. 4-9. Generally, the larger packages contain transistors that are able to conduct larger currents. The packages in Fig. 4-9(A) are typical of transistors that are required to conduct small currents, up to about 200 mA. These small-current transistors are frequently found in digital circuits and systems. The larger packages in Fig. 4-9(B) contain transistors capable of carrying up to a few amperes. Such larger transistors are used in some types of *peripherals* associated with digital computers and microprocessors. Peripherals are discussed further in later chapters. For the present we should know that peripherals often are instruments with which computers and microprocessors communicate. Teletype terminals, tape drives, video displays, digital-to-analog (A/D) converters, etc., are examples of peripherals. Each of these larger transistor packages is designed so that it can easily be mounted on a *heat sink.* As shown in Fig. 4-10, a heat sink is a piece of metal with fins that can draw heat from the transistor package and transfer it to the surrounding air. Regardless of the package type, each has three terminals called its *base, collector,* and *emitter,* though with some larger packages, the case serves as the collector terminal. Terminal identifications on common package types are shown in Fig. 4-11.

---

* The Institute of Electrical and Electronic Engineers (IEEE) defines an IC as "a combination of interconnected circuit elements inseparably associated on or within a continuous substrate."

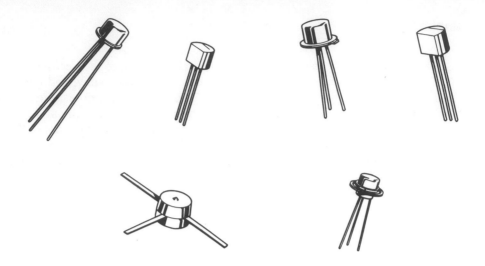

(A) Typical packages of low current transistors

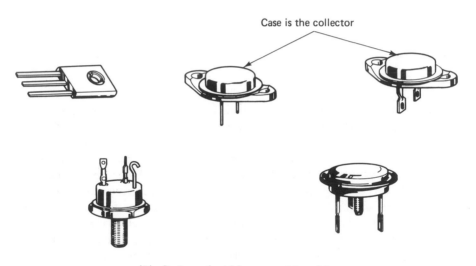

Case is the collector

(B) Packages for higher current transistors

Figure 4-9.

Figure 4-10. Heat sinks.

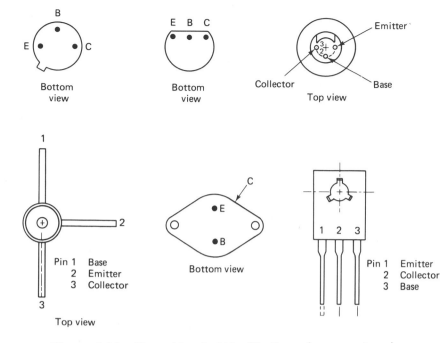

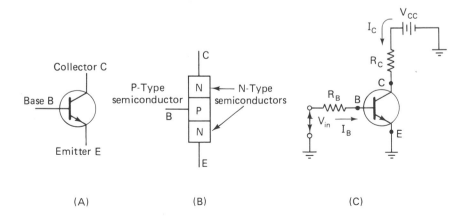

Figure 4-11. Pin and terminal identifications of common transistor packages.

4-7 *NPN* and *PNP* Transistors

Regardless of current ratings, transistors are available in two basic types. As shown in Figs. 4-12 and 4-13, these are *NPN* and *PNP* types. The arrow is always on the emitter *E* lead of the transistor symbol and points outward

Figure 4-12. (A) Symbol for the *NPN* transistor; (B) basic construction of the *NPN* transistor; (C) *NPN* transistor in a typical digital application.

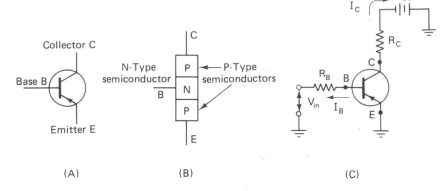

Figure 4-13. (A) Symbol for the *PNP* transistor; (B) basic construction of the *PNP* transistor; (C) *PNP* transistor in a typical digital application.

on the *NPN* transistor symbol and inward on the symbol for the *PNP* transistor. As shown in Fig. 4-12(B), the *NPN* transistor has its base *B* lead connected to a *P*-type semiconductor material which is formed between *N*-type materials of the collector *C* and the emitter *E*. Of course, then, a *PNP*-type transistor consists of an *N*-type base *B* material between *P*-type collector *C* and emitter *E* materials; see Fig. 4-13(B).

We should note in Figs. 4-12(C) and 4-13(C) that either an *NPN*- or a *PNP*-type transistor is used depending on the polarity of the available supply V_{CC}. As with diodes, a dc voltage applied to a transistor is called *bias*. As shown, the *NPN* transistor is biased so that its collector *C* is positive with respect to its emitter *E*, whereas the *PNP* transistor is biased with its collector negative with respect to the emitter.

In typical digital applications, input signal voltages V_{in} are applied to the base, through resistor R_B, to control the collector current I_C. On the circuit of Fig. 4-12(C), if we increase V_{in} from zero to more *positive* values, an increasing current I_B flows through R_B and across the forward-biased base-emitter diode junction. This I_B flow causes I_C to flow through resistor R_C. This collector current I_C is larger than I_B by the factor β or h_{FE}; that is,

$$I_C \cong \beta I_B \qquad (4-1a)$$

$$I_C \cong h_{FE}I_B \qquad (4-1b)$$

The factor β is called the beta of the transistor, which is essentially equivalent to h_{FE}.* Transistor manufacturers usually specify h_{FE} values with their prod-

* The factor h_{FE} is called a hybrid parameter and is the forward current transfer ratio of the grounded or common emitter configuration.

ucts. With the *PNP* transistor in Fig. 4-13(C), a larger *negative* input V_{in} causes a larger base current I_B which consequently increases the collector current I_C. In both circuits of Figs. 4-12(C) and 4-13(C), negligible current I_C flows when $V_{in} = 0$ V. If I_C is increased to the point that the drop across R_C becomes equal to the V_{CC} supply voltage, I_C will not increase further even if I_B continues to be increased.

4-8   The Transistor as a Switch

Transistors work mainly as switches in digital electronic circuits. An input signal V_{in} can make a transistor turn on and act like a short (between its collector and emitter terminals), while an absence of an input signal can make it act like an open. Figure 4-14 shows how an *NPN* transistor is frequently used as a switch. When a signal V_{in} of about 5 V is applied to the

Figure 4-14.   (A) A transistor as a lamp driver; (B) input equivalent of the lamp driver circuit when V_{in} is positive enough to forward-bias the emitter-to-base *(EB)* junction; (C) input equivalent of the lamp driver circuit when $V_{in} = 0$ V (input *X* is grounded).

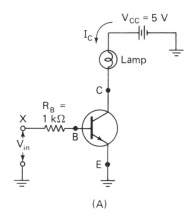

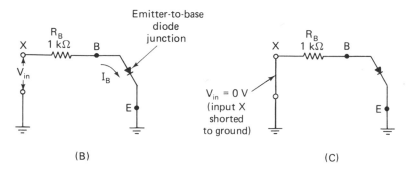

input X, the transistor turns on; that is, it virtually acts like a short or a closed switch. The resulting current I_C causes the lamp to light. When the input signal $V_{in} = 0$ V (input X grounded), the transistor turns off and for practical purposes acts like an open, causing the lamp to go out. In this application the transistor, or the circuit as a whole, is called a lamp driver. In this circuit, the lamp will go out when input X is open. Normally, however, input leads are never left hanging open, permanently, in digital circuits. A 0-V input signal is obtained by pulling the input lead down to ground potential.

As shown in Fig. 4-14, if the input voltage V_{in} is positive enough, typically about 5 V, it will forward-bias the base-emitter diode junction and cause base current I_B to flow. As mentioned before, it is this base current I_B that actually turns on the transistor and admits collector current I_C. The transistor is therefore called a current-controlled device. The resistor R_B is necessary to limit I_B to safe and practical values. If R_B is too small, I_B might be large enough to destroy the transistor, or it might *load down* the source of input signal V_{in}. If R_B is too large, the current I_B might be too small to fully turn on the transistor. Of course, if the transistor does not turn on fully (hard) and act like a short, the lamp will not light to full brilliance. In usual digital applications, a transistor is expected, at certain times, to turn on hard and act like a closed switch. At other times it is turned off and must act like an open switch. When turned on hard, the transistor is said to be *saturated;* when turned off, it is said to be *cut off.* The important feature of a transistor is that it can be used as a switch that can be turned on or off with an input voltage V_{in}.

Other circuits using *NPN* transistors as lamp or display drivers are shown in Fig. 4-15. The circuit of Fig. 4-15(A) is a lamp driver that is more suitable to *interface* (work) with TTL family digital devices for reasons

Figure 4-15. (A) More sophisticated lamp driver circuit; (B) a transistor as an LED (light-emitting diode) driver.

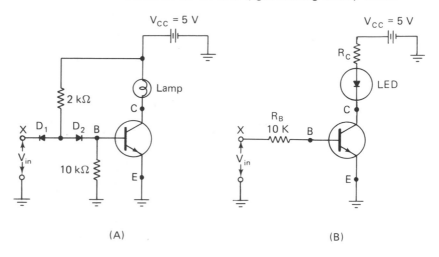

(A)   (B)

we shall see later in this chapter. For the present we can say that it offers less *loading* on the source of input signal V_{in}. The circuit of Fig. 4-15(B) uses a *light-emitting diode* (LED). As its name implies, the LED emits light when conducting a forward-biased current. Typical LEDs require about 10–20 mA, depending on size. The resistor R_C is necessary to limit the current through the LED. If the resistance R_C is too small, the LED will illuminate brightly, become hot, and possibly be destroyed. If R_C is too large, the LED will be too dim.

Another type of LED display circuit is shown in Fig. 4-16. In this

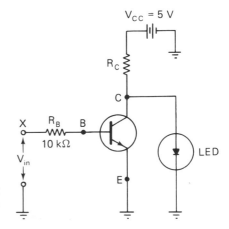

Figure 4-16. LED driver circuit lights the LED when $V_{in} \cong 0$ V.

circuit the LED lights when the input signal is LOW ($V_{in} \cong 0$ V), whereas in the previous circuits the LED lights when the input is HIGH (V_{in} is a positive value). Using common terminology, therefore, we can say that the circuits of Fig. 4-15 have active HIGH inputs, but the circuit of Fig. 4-16 has an active LOW input.

4-9 The Field-Effect Transistor (FET)

Field-effect transistors (FETs) are very common components within some types of ICs. Where low power (energy) consumption is very important, such as with battery-operated digital equipment, FETs are used almost exclusively. As are junction transistors,* discussed in previous sections, FETs are mainly used as voltage-operated switches. Also like the junction transistor, an FET has three terminals. They are called the gate *G*, drain *D*, and source *S*. These are somewhat analogous to the base *B*, collector *C*, and emitter *E*, respectively, of the junction transistor.

---

* Junction transistors are also called bipolar transistors, whereas FETs are sometimes called unipolar transistors.

4-10 Construction and Behavior of the Field-Effect Transistor

Parts (A) – (D) of Fig. 4-17 show basically how the FET is constructed. As shown in Fig. 4-17(A), the manufacturing process starts with a piece of lightly doped semiconductor. A lightly doped semiconductor has few charge carriers, which makes it a poor conductor in the absence of external influences. As we shall see, a portion of this lightly doped material serves as the *channel* of the FET. The number of charge carriers in this channel and its ability to conduct current are increased when an electric field is applied.

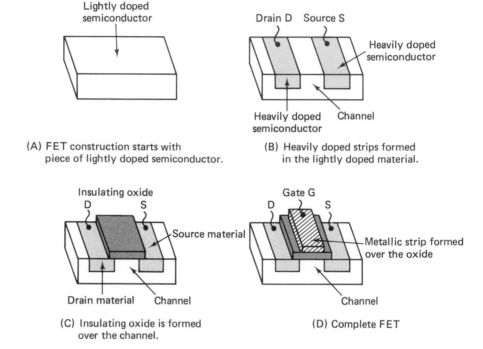

Figure 4-17. Construction of the field-effect transistor (FET).

As shown in Fig. 4-17(B), heavily doped semiconductor strips, which are good conductors, are formed in the channel material. Leads called the drain *D* and source *S* are connected to these areas. The channel is between these drain and source materials. Next, an insulating oxide is formed over the channel as shown in Fig. 4-17(C).

Finally, a metal strip is formed over the oxide, and a gate *G* lead is connected to this metal; see Fig. 4-17(D). The gate *G* is thus insulated from the semiconductor materials. While current cannot flow through the oxide, an electric field can easily penetrate this oxide and the channel. Because of its insulating oxide, this type of FET is also called a metal oxide semiconductor

(A) Schematic symbol for the
N-channel metal oxide semiconductor
field effect transistor (MOSFET)

(B) Schematic symbol for the
P-channel metal oxide
semiconductor field effect
transistor (MOSFET)

Figure 4-18. Enhancement mode MOSFETs.

field-effect transistor (MOSFET) or an insulated gate field-effect transistor
(IGFET). Schematic symbols for the MOSFET type of Fig. 4-17(D) are
shown in Fig. 4-18.

When the proper polarity of voltage is applied across the gate and
source of the MOSFET, an electric field penetrates into the channel and
attracts (induces) charge carriers into it. The channel's conductivity is thus
enhanced. In fact, this type of MOSFET is further classified as an *induced
channel* or *enhancement mode* MOSFET.

Just as junction transistors are available in two types, *NPN* and *PNP*,
MOSFETs are made in two types: *N*-channel and *P*-channel. *N*-channel
types rely on negative charge carriers (electrons) as current carriers, whereas
P-channel types rely on positive charge carriers (holes). Electrons are attracted
into the channel of the *N*-channel MOSFET when its gate is made positive
with respect to its source. Thus the *N*-channel MOSFET becomes more
conductive when we apply a positive gate-to-source voltage. Holes are attracted into the channel of the *P*-channel MOSFET when a negative gate-
to-source voltage is applied, and thus its channel becomes more conductive.
If we apply 0 V on the gate with respect to the source of either the
N-channel or *P*-channel MOSFET, the channel is not conductive and acts
like an open switch for most practical purposes.

The circuit of Fig. 4-19 shows how an *N*-channel MOSFET can be

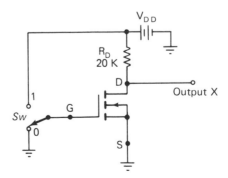

Figure 4-19. Inverter circuit with
a pull-up resistor
R_D and *N*-channel
MOSFET.

Discrete Parts and
Gates for
Computer Systems

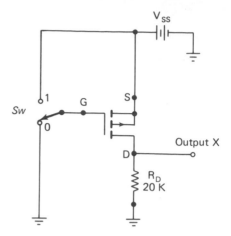

Figure 4-20. Inverter circuit with a
pull-down resistor R_D
and a *P*-channel
MOSFET.

used in a logic inverter circuit. When the switch Sw is down in the 0 position, the gate-to-source voltage is 0 V, and the MOSFET is not conductive and acts like an open compared to resistance R_D. Therefore, practically all the V_{DD} supply voltage appears across the MOSFET and at the output X with respect to ground. Thus a LOW logic input (0 V) causes a HIGH logic (positive voltage) output. On the other hand, when the switch Sw is up in the 1 position, the gate-to-source voltage is positive. This turns the MOSFET on, causing it to act like a short compared to the resistance of R_D. Thus the voltage across the MOSFET and at the output X to ground drops to nearly 0 V. In this case, a HIGH input (V_{DD} voltage) causes a LOW output (nearly 0 V).

In much the same way, the *P*-channel MOSFET in Fig. 4-20 works as an inverter. Note that the drain is biased negatively in this case. Therefore, when the switch Sw is down in the 0 position, the gate is negative with respect to the source. For example, if we use a 10-V V_{SS} supply, the gate becomes −10 V with respect to the source when Sw is down in the 0 position. Such a negative gate-to-source voltage turns on the *P*-channel MOSFET, causing it to act like a short. This pulls the output X up to the V_{SS} potential.

If the switch Sw is thrown into the 1 position in the circuit of Fig. 4-20, the gate is pulled up to the V_{SS} potential, and the gate-to-source voltage becomes 0 V. This turns the *P*-channel MOSFET off, causing it to act like an open. Consequently, nearly the entire V_{SS} voltage appears across the drain and source, resulting in nearly 0 V across R_D and at the output X.

4-11 Inverter Circuits

Often when a HIGH logic signal appears in one place in a digital system, a LOW must simultaneously appear elsewhere in the system. In such cases, inverter circuits, simply called inverters, are used. MOSFET inverters were

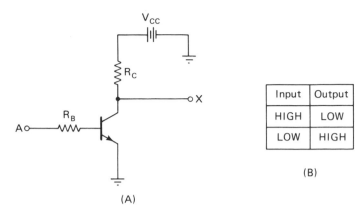

Figure 4-21. (A) Junction transistor inverter circuit; (B) functional (truth) table for the inverter.

shown in Figs. 4-19 and 4-20. A simple junction transistor inverter is shown in Fig. 4-21. Generally, a HIGH input on any one of these causes a LOW output and vice versa.

Symbols for the inverter are shown in Fig. 4-22. On diagrams of actual circuits, one or the other of these symbols is shown to represent each inverter used. If the inverter's output signal is active LOW, the symbol of Fig. 4-22(A) is usually used. If its output signal is active HIGH, the symbol of

Figure 4-22. Inverter symbols: (A) with ACTIVE LOW output; (B) with ACTIVE HIGH output.

Fig. 4-22(B) is usually used. If a digital signal causes succeeding circuitry to act (perform its function) when it goes HIGH, it is called an active HIGH signal. On the other hand, if a digital signal causes action in the circuits it is driving, when it goes LOW, it is called an active LOW signal. Signal names are usually shown with capital or bold letters. Overbars over signal names imply that the named signals are active LOW.

The circuits of Fig. 4-23 show how signal names are often identified. In (A) of this figure, the signal $\overline{\text{DISPLAY}}$, out of the inverter, being overbarred, implies that the LED will light when this signal is LOW. Similarly, in Fig. 4-23(B), the signal ON, out of the inverter, lacking an overbar, implies that it will light the LED when it is HIGH.

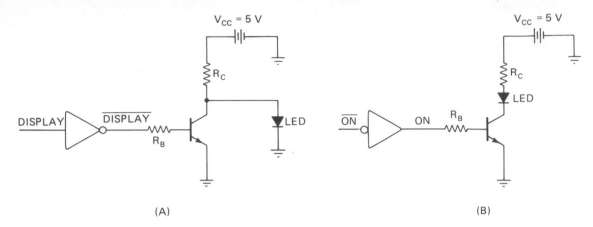

Figure 4-23. (A) LED lights when signal $\overline{\text{DISPLAY}}$ is LOW; (B) LED lights when signal ON is HIGH.

4-12 The TTL Family and Its Inverters

Transistor-transistor logic (TTL), also called T²L, is one of the most popular of digital logic families. TTL ICs are known for their high switching speed and good *noise immunity*. For the present, we should know that good noise immunity means reliable operation of a digital system even though heavy electrical equipment (motors, high-current relays, etc.) is nearby. The TTL family of ICs requires dc supply voltages in the range of 4.5–5.5 V. Typically regulated 5-V supplies are used. TTL ICs will not work reliably with dc supply voltages outside of this recommended range and will likely be destroyed if the recommended maximum of 5.5 V is exceeded.

A typical TTL package is shown in Fig. 4-24. This package is called a 7404 hex inverter. It contains six inverters; the circuitry of each is shown in Fig. 4-24(C). The output transistors are connected in what is commonly called a totem-pole arrangement. In logic applications, one of these transistors is turned on while the other is simultaneously turned off. The logic level of the signal on input A determines which of the two is on or off. When a HIGH is applied to input A, Q_4 turns off and Q_3 turns on. The conducting Q_3 pulls the output X down to about ground (O-V) potential. Because of its job in this circuit, Q_3 is called a *pull-down* transistor or an *active pull-down*.* A LOW on input A turns Q_3 off and Q_4 on. A turned on Q_4 pulls the output X up toward the V_{CC} voltage via resistor R_4. Therefore, Q_4 is called a *pull-up* transistor or an *active pull-up*. Typically, the output X is used to drive one or more inputs of other logic circuits or some other useful load(s). When Q_3 is on and conducting, it is said to be *sinking* current. When Q_4 is on and conducting, it is said to be *sourcing* current. A standard

---

* Transistors, and any components capable of amplification, are called active devices, whereas resistors, capacitors, etc., are called passive devices.

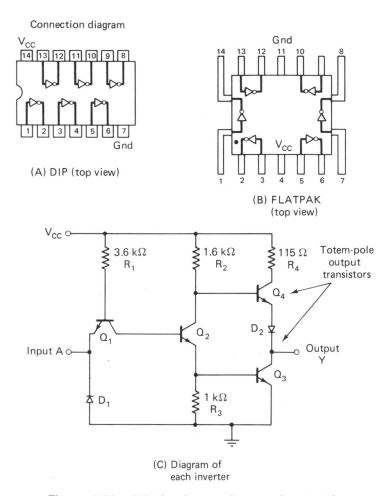

Connection diagram

(A) DIP (top view)

(B) FLATPAK
(top view)

(C) Diagram of
each inverter

Figure 4-24. 7404 hex inverter (totem-pole outputs).

TTL IC is able to sink about 16 mA and to source about 400μA. This source
and sink capability is about 10 times larger than the current requirements
of each input of standard TTL ICs. In other words, we can determine the
output drive capability of a logic circuit or IC from its fan-out or output
unit load (U.L.) specification, which is provided by the manufacturer. For
example, the 7404 IC is specified as having an output unit load (fan out)
of 10. This means that each inverter is able to drive up to 10 standard
TTL inputs. The diode D_1 in Fig. 4-24(C) is called a *clamping diode*. It
prevents input signal oscillations and thus helps prevent unreliable operation.

Most TTL ICs have totem-pole output transistors, and we should become familiar with the output levels of such ICs. A HIGH output signal
of a TTL totem-pole device might be as low as 2.4 V even though the V_{CC}
voltage is 5 V. On the other hand, its LOW output might be as high as

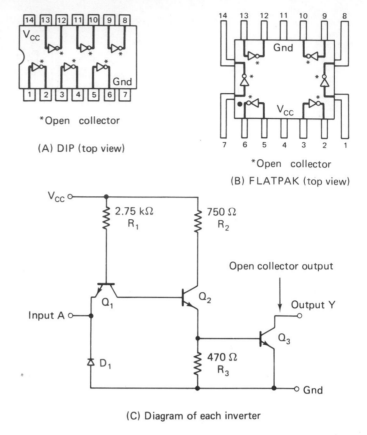

*Open collector

(A) DIP (top view)

*Open collector

(B) FLATPAK (top view)

(C) Diagram of each inverter

Figure 4-25. 7405 hex inverter (open collector outputs).

0.5 V. Although we should be aware of these HIGH and LOW output levels, they cause no difficulty in circuits built entirely of TTL ICs. That is, although a HIGH output of a TTL IC might be as low as 2.4 V, the next TTL IC will definitely interpret it as a HIGH input. On the other hand, a LOW output of 0.5 V or less will definitely be interpreted as a LOW by the TTL device being driven by this output signal. Typically, a TTL IC recognizes 2 V or more as a HIGH logic input and 0.8 V or less as a LOW input.

Some TTL ICs have *open collector* outputs instead of totem-pole arrangements as shown in Fig. 4-25. Open collector TTL outputs require externally wired *pull-up resistors,* such as R_x in Fig. 4-26. Such resistors are also called *passive pull-ups.* When a HIGH is applied to input A on the circuit of Fig. 4-26, the transistor Q_3 turns on and pulls the output X to ground potential. When a LOW is applied to input A, Q_3 turns off and the output X is pulled HIGH through the passive pull-up R_x. Open collector TTL devices are able to provide HIGH output signals that are higher than HIGHs out of totem-pole arrangements. In fact, the top of R_x can be connected to a dc source that is significantly larger than the 4.5–5.5-V required supply for TTL ICs.

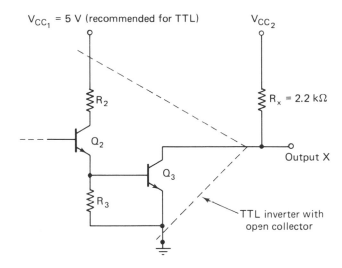

Figure 4-26. ICs with open cell collector outputs require pull-up resistors R_x connected externally.

This allows TTL ICs to work into (be compatible or interface with) other digital IC families. For example, if $V_{CC_2} = 12$ V in Fig. 4-26, the output X goes high to almost 12 V when the output transistor Q_3 turns off. This 12-V output could be a suitable HIGH input to a CMOS or DTL family IC—but more about this later.

Another advantage of open collector ICs is that their outputs can be directly connected to the same point or line, as shown in Fig. 4-27. This is an advantage that will be better appreciated later when we see how digital systems communicate with each other. For now we should note that the outputs of inverters 1, 3, and 5 are directly connected to the data line $\overline{D_2}$, while the outputs of inverters 4 and 6 are connected to line $\overline{D_1}$, etc. With these inverters, the *peripherals** are able to identify themselves to the computer or microprocessor. For example, when peripheral 5 is ready to communicate with the computer, its switch Sw_5† is closed. This causes lines $\overline{D_2}$, $\overline{D_1}$, and $\overline{D_0}$ to become L, H, and L, respectively, which is the inverse of binary 101_2 or decimal 5_{10}. Thus the computer reads the data bus and determines which peripheral is ready to communicate.

We should note in Fig. 4-27 that the inputs to the inverters are LOW, via the pull-down resistors R_y, when the switches are open. These pull-down resistors (passive pull-downs) are necessary because, generally, an open input on a TTL IC is interpreted by the IC as a HIGH input. Thus if the passive pull-downs (the R_ys) were removed, the inverter outputs would permanently

---

* Typical peripherals are teletypewriter terminals, tape drives, analog-to-digital converters, and digital-to-analog converters. Peripherals are to the microprocessor as arms, legs, hands, etc., are to the human brain.

† This kind of switching is typically performed electronically instead of mechanically.

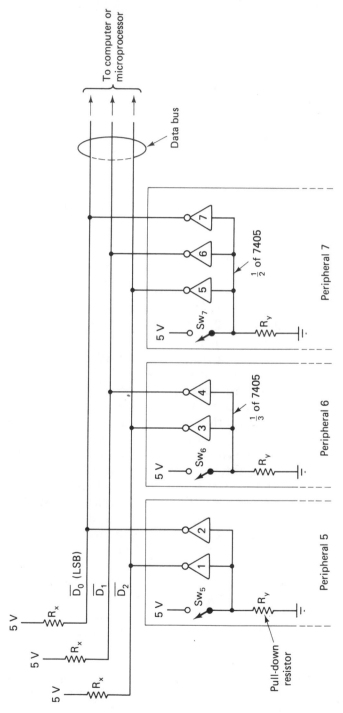

Figure 4-27. Open collector inverter outputs tied to data lines.

76

stay LOW even with the switches open. TTL inputs are not to be left hanging open in permanently wired circuits.*

Example 4-1

Referring to the circuit of Fig. 4-27, what are the logic levels on lines $\overline{D_2} - \overline{D_0}$ when Sw_6 is closed while Sw_5 and Sw_7 are open?

Answer

$\overline{D_2}$, $\overline{D_1}$, and $\overline{D_0}$ are LOW, LOW, and HIGH, respectively. When Sw_6 is closed, a HIGH logic level is applied to the inputs of inverters 3 and 4. Their output transistors are thus turned on and pull lines $\overline{D_2}$ and $\overline{D_1}$ LOW. With Sw_5 and Sw_7 open, the output transistors of inverters 2 and 7 remain off, and line $\overline{D_0}$ stays HIGH through the passive pull-up R_x.

4-13 Inverters in Other Logic Families

As shown in Figs. 4-19 and 4-20, an inverter can be made with a MOSFET and series resistor. To reduce power consumption and increase switching speed, however, MOSFET inverters are commonly constructed without resistors, as shown in Fig. 4-28. Note that this inverter uses two MOSFETs: one *N*-channel and one *P*-channel. This arrangement of MOSFETs is called a *complementary pair*. ICs using such pairs are called complementary metal oxide semiconductor (CMOS) ICs.

A LOW on input *A* of the circuit in Fig. 4-28 turns Q_1 on and turns Q_2 off. The conducting Q_1 pulls output *X* to a HIGH logic level. On the

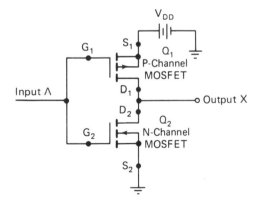

Figure 4-28. Practical complementary-pair metal oxide semiconductor (CMOS) inverter.

---

* When unused inputs of a standard TTL chip are tied to V_{CC}, it is usually done through a resistor of a few kilohms. This reduces current drain from the supply and heating of the chip.

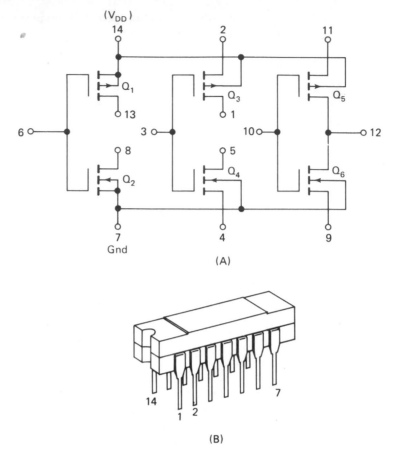

Figure 4-29. (A) Contents of the 4007 CMOS IC: (B) a 14-pin
dual in-line package (DIP) typically used to house
a 4007.

other hand, a **HIGH** on input A turns Q_2 on and Q_1 off. In this case, the
conducting Q_2 pulls the output X down to a **LOW** logic level. A typical
CMOS IC is shown in Fig. 4-29. The numbered and circled terminals represent
pins that are accessible outside of the package which can be used in a variety
of connections.

The 4007 CMOS IC, as do most other CMOS devices, requires a dc
supply in the range of 3–15 V. CMOS devices are particularly useful in applications where low power consumption is important. Battery-operated equipment, for example, works much longer between battery charges or replace-
ments with CMOS than with any other functionally equivalent logic circuit.
This is true partly because of the full-on or full-off operation of each complementary transistor. That is, as mentioned previously, one of the complementary MOSFETs is on while the other is off. This keeps current drain from
the V_{DD} supply down to insignificance. The extremely high input resistance
of each MOSFET draws virtually no power, which also contributes to its
high efficiency.

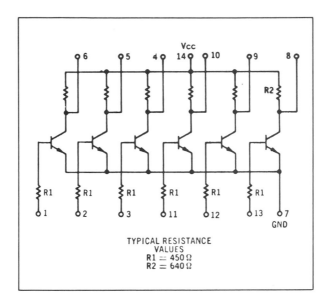

(A)

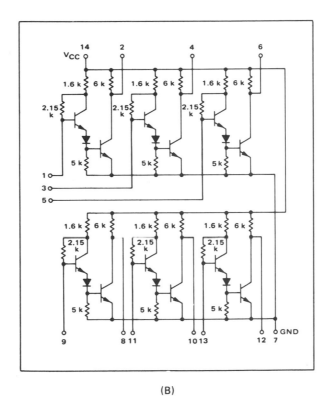

(B)

Figure 4-30. (A) RTL hex inverter (MC889 package);
(B) DTL hex inverter (MC834 package).

79

Hex inverter IC packages of other logic families are shown in Fig. 4-30. An RTL (resistor-transistor logic) diagram is shown in (A) of Fig. 4-30, and a DTL (diode-transistor logic) diagram is shown in (B).

4-14 Buffers/Drivers

A logic signal buffer/driver is used when the output of a TTL device is to drive loads, or other logic inputs, that draw current greater than the device's output current capability. For example, if a standard TTL gate, having an

Figure 4-31. Hex buffer/driver 7407 with open collectors.

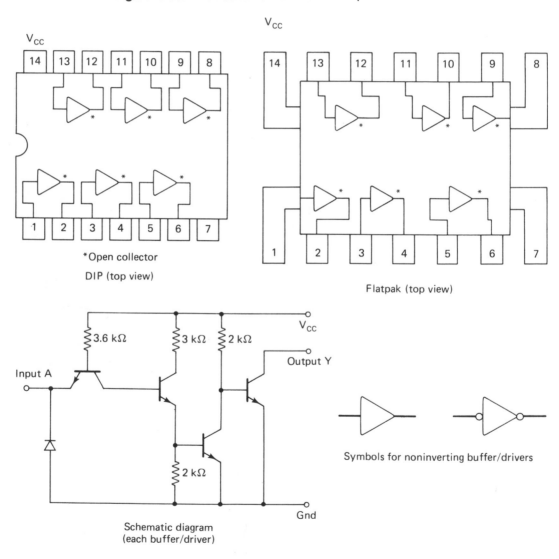

*Open collector

DIP (top view)

Flatpak (top view)

Schematic diagram
(each buffer/driver)

Symbols for noninverting buffer/drivers

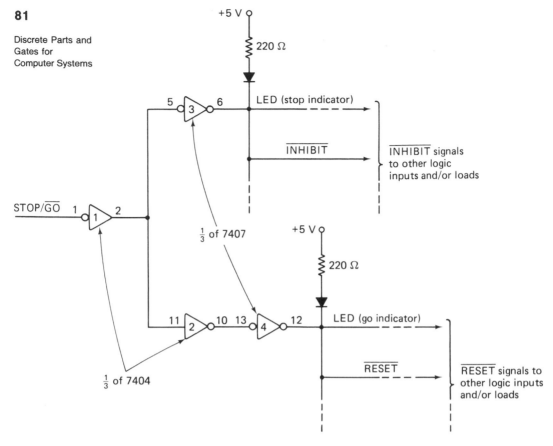

Figure 4-32. Application of buffer/driver.

output unit load of 10, must drive more than 10 standard TTL inputs, one or more buffers/drivers at the gate's output should be used. A TTL 7407 hex buffer/driver (noninverting) is shown in Fig. 4-31. Each buffer/driver output has about 2.5 times greater current sink capability than does each inverter of the 7404. Figure 4-32 shows how buffers/drivers can expand TTL devices' output drive capability. In this circuit, the inverter 1 cannot sink enough current to drive a number of $\overline{\text{INHIBIT}}$ inputs and light the LED too. Therefore the buffer/driver 3 expands this inverter's output drive capability. Similarly, the buffer/driver 4 increases the drive capacity of the output of inverter 2.

4-15 AND Gates; Their Function and Symbols

As mentioned previously, an AND gate's output is HIGH only if all its inputs are HIGH. In other words, its output is LOW if any one or more of its inputs are LOW. Generally, every type of logic gate can be represented

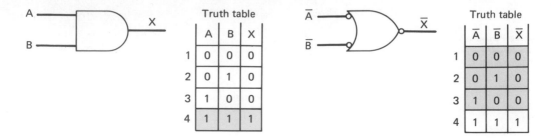

		Truth table	
	A	B	X
1	0	0	0
2	0	1	0
3	1	0	0
4	1	1	1

		Truth table	
	$\overline{A}$	$\overline{B}$	$\overline{X}$
1	0	0	0
2	0	1	0
3	1	0	0
4	1	1	1

(A) AND gate symbol used when the fact that two HIGH inputs cause a HIGH output (shaded area on truth table) is being used or emphasized.

(B) AND gate symbol used when the fact that either or both inputs being LOW cause a LOW output (shaded area on truth table) is being used or emphasized

Figure 4-33. Symbols and truth tables for the two-input AND gate.

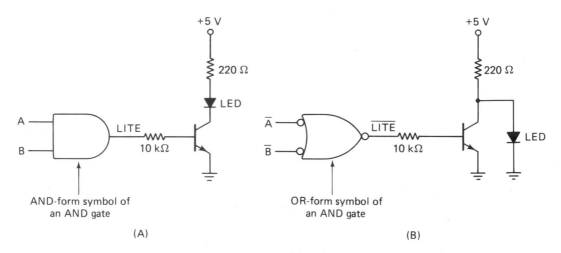

(A) AND-form symbol of an AND gate

(B) OR-form symbol of an AND gate

Figure 4-34. (A) The LED lights when input A and input B go HIGH, causing signal LITE to go HIGH; (B) the LED lights when input $\overline{A}$ or input $\overline{B}$ or both go LOW, causing signal $\overline{\text{LITE}}$ to go LOW.

by either of two symbols. In the case of a two-input AND gate, the symbols are shown in Fig. 4-33. Usually, depending on how the gate is being used, one or the other symbol is preferred. If a two-input AND gate is being used with an active HIGH output, the symbol (A) of Fig. 4-33 is recommended. On the other hand, if an AND gate is being used to output an active LOW signal, the symbol (B)* of Fig. 4-33 is better. Figure 4-34 shows

* This symbol is sometimes called a negated input NOR.

proper use of each AND gate symbol. In (A) of Fig. 4-34, the AND-form symbol of the AND gate emphasizes the fact that input *A and* input *B* must be HIGH to cause the signal LITE to go HIGH and light the LED. In the case of circuit (B) of Fig. 4-34, the OR-form symbol of the AND gate emphasizes that a LOW input $\overline{A}$ *or* a LOW input $\overline{B}$, or both, causes signal $\overline{\text{LITE}}$ to go LOW, which in turn lights the LED.

4-16 OR Gates; Their Function and Symbols

As described in a previous section, an OR gate's output is HIGH if any one or more of its inputs are HIGH. This means that an OR's output is LOW only if all its inputs are LOW. A two-input OR gate can be represented by either of the symbols in Fig. 4-35. If the OR gate is being used to provide an active HIGH output signal, the symbol (A) of Fig. 4-35 best illustrates

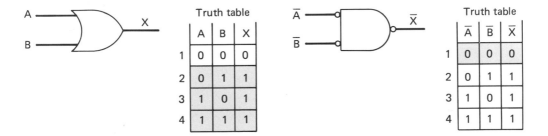

Truth table (A)

	A	B	X
1	0	0	0
2	0	1	1
3	1	0	1
4	1	1	1

Truth table (B)

	$\overline{A}$	$\overline{B}$	$\overline{X}$
1	0	0	0
2	0	1	1
3	1	0	1
4	1	1	1

(A) OR gate symbol used when the fact that either or both inputs being HIGH cause a HIGH output (shaded area on truth table) is being used or emphasized

(B) OR gate symbol used when the fact that both inputs have to be LOW to cause a LOW output (shaded area) is being used or emphasized

Figure 4-35. Symbols and truth tables for the two-input OR gate.

this application. If, on the other hand, the OR gate is used to output an active LOW signal, the symbol of Fig. 4-35(B)* is better. Figure 4-36 shows proper use of each OR gate symbol. In (A) of this figure, a HIGH input *A* or a HIGH input *B* or both inputs HIGH will cause a HIGH output DISPLAY signal, causing the LED to light. In the circuit of Fig. 4-36(B), the LED lights when the gate's output signal $\overline{\text{DISPLAY}}$ is LOW, which occurs only when both inputs, $\overline{A}$ and $\overline{B}$, are LOW.

* This symbol is sometimes called a negated input NAND.

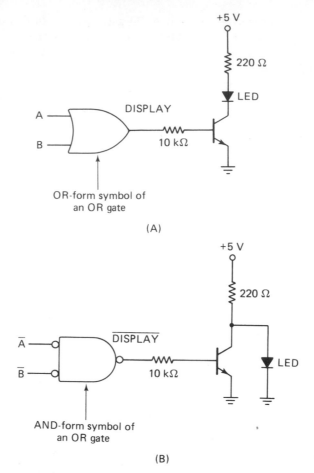

(A)

(B)

Figure 4-36. (A) The LED lights when input *A* or input *B* or both are HIGH, causing signal DISPLAY to go HIGH; (B) the LED lights when input $\overline{A}$ and input $\overline{B}$ are LOW, causing signal $\overline{\text{DISPLAY}}$ to go LOW.

4-17 NAND Gates; Their Function and Symbols

Symbols and truth tables for a two-input NAND gate are shown in Fig. 4-37. Usually, as with other gates, one or the other symbol better describes the NAND's action in any given application. Logically, a NAND gate performs the same function as does an AND gate followed by an inverter. This means that a NAND gate's output is LOW only if all its input are HIGH. The symbol (A) of Fig. 4-37 best illustrates this action. From another point of view, we can say that a NAND's output is HIGH if any one or more of its inputs are LOW. Symbol (B)* of Fig. 4-37 better illustrates this action.

Figure 4-38 shows how the NANDs' symbols can be used to describe each circuit's behavior. In (A) of Fig. 4-38, the AND-form symbol illustrates

---

* This symbol is sometimes referred to as a negated input OR.

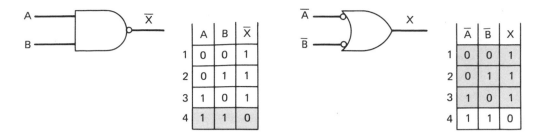

(A) NAND gate symbol used when the fact that two HIGH inputs cause a LOW output (shaded area) is being used or emphasized

	A	B	$\overline{X}$
1	0	0	1
2	0	1	1
3	1	0	1
4	1	1	0

(B) NAND gate symbol used when the fact that either or both inputs being LOW cause a HIGH output (shaded area) is being used or emphasized

	$\overline{A}$	$\overline{B}$	X
1	0	0	1
2	0	1	1
3	1	0	1
4	1	1	0

Figure 4-37. Symbols and truth tables for the two-input NAND gate.

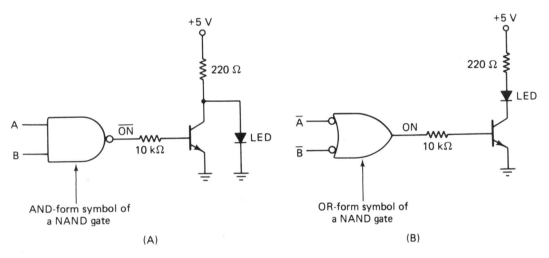

AND-form symbol of a NAND gate

(A)

OR-form symbol of a NAND gate

(B)

Figure 4-38. (A) The LED lights when input A and input B are HIGH, which causes signal $\overline{ON}$ to go LOW; (B) the LED lights when input $\overline{A}$ or input $\overline{B}$ or both inputs are LOW, which causes signal ON to go HIGH.

that input A and input B must be HIGH in order to drive signal $\overline{ON}$ LOW, which in turn turns off the transistor and causes the LED to light. In (B) of Fig. 4-38, the OR-form symbol better illustrates the fact that a LOW input $\overline{A}$ or input $\overline{B}$, or both, drives the signal ON to a HIGH logic level, which causes the transistor to saturate and the LED to light.

4-18 NOR Gates; Their Function and Symbols

The NOR gate performs the same logic function as does an OR gate with an inverter at its output. Therefore, as shown in the tables of Fig. 4-39, a NOR's output is LOW if any one or more of its inputs are HIGH. The

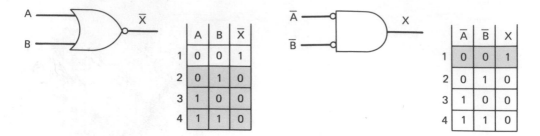

	A	B	$\overline{X}$
1	0	0	1
2	0	1	0
3	1	0	0
4	1	1	0

	$\overline{A}$	$\overline{B}$	X
1	0	0	1
2	0	1	0
3	1	0	0
4	1	1	0

(A) NOR gate symbol used when the fact that a HIGH on either or both inputs causes a LOW output (shaded area) is being used or emphasized

(B) NOR gate symbol used when the fact that both inputs have to be LOW to cause a HIGH output (shaded area) is being used or emphasized

Figure 4-39. Symbols and truth tables for the two-input NOR gate.

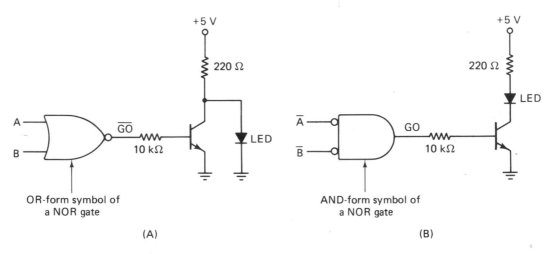

Figure 4-40. (A) The LED lights when input A or input B or both inputs are HIGH, which causes signal $\overline{GO}$ to go LOW; (B) the LED lights if input $\overline{A}$ and input $\overline{B}$ are LOW, causing signal GO to go HIGH.

symbol (A) of Fig. 4-39 better illustrates this function. The NOR can also be viewed as an AND-performing gate if we are working with active LOW inputs. That is, the NOR's output is HIGH only if all its inputs are LOW. The symbol (B)† of Fig. 4-39 better illustrates this AND-performing quality of the NOR gate.

The circuits of Fig. 4-40 show how each of the NOR gate's symbols can be used to emphasize the important features of their respective circuits.

† This symbol is sometimes referred to as a negated input AND.

In the circuit (A) of Fig. 4-40, the OR-form symbol of the NOR gate emphasizes the fact that if either input A or input B or both are HIGH, the output
signal $\overline{GO}$ is LOW, which in turn causes the LED to light. In (B) of Fig.
4-40, the AND-form symbol more clearly shows that only when input $\overline{A}$
and input $\overline{B}$ are LOW will signal GO go HIGH, which causes the LED to
light.

4-19 Data Transfer Techniques

Gates, as their name implies, are often used to control the flow of digital
information from one part of a system to another, much as gates are used,
say, on a cattle ranch to control the movement of livestock from one corral
to another. Figure 4-41 shows how ANDs and ORs can be used to control
the flow (transfer) of digital information (data). This circuit has nine terminals
for input signals and four for output signals. The 4-bit input A_3–A_0, call it

Figure 4-41. Data transfer circuit using two quad two-input ANDs (7408 dual
in-line packages) and one quad two-input OR (7432 DIP).

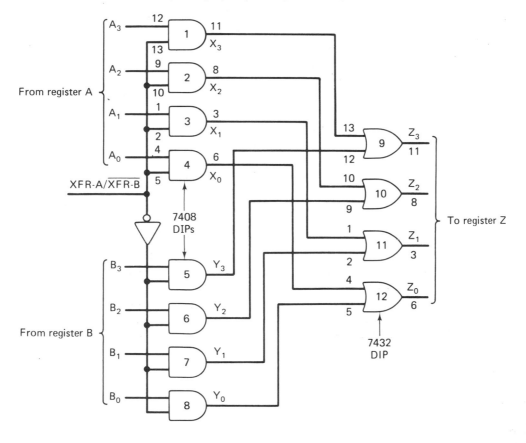

the A-word, is applied by register A.* The 4-bit input B_3–B_0, call it the B-word, is applied by register B. The input XFR-$A/\overline{XFR$-$B}$ is a *control input.* The output Z-word, bits Z_3–Z_0, is applied to the Z register. The control input controls data flow, 4 bits at a time, from register A *or* register B to register Z. In other words, when signal XFR-$A/\overline{XFR$-$B}$ is HIGH, this HIGH is applied to one input of each gate 1–4. These gates are thus *enabled,* which means that the A-word is able to pass from register A to register Z. Simultaneously, via the inverter, a LOW is on one input of each gate 5–8. These gates are thus *disabled* and block the transfer of the B-word. Of course, then, when XFR-$A/\overline{XFR$-$B}$ is LOW, gates 1–4 are disabled, while gates 5–8 are enabled. In this case, the B-word transfers to register Z. Note that the OR gates are well named because they serve to pass the A-word *or* the B-word to register Z.

The specific names on signals, as in Fig. 4-41, are not important. Signal names will differ in different circuits and systems. However, it is important that we understand how the gates and components work, individually and as parts of a system. It is also important that we understand how overbars, or a lack of them, are used on signal names. For example, the signal name XFR-$A/\overline{XFR$-$B}$ implies, from the absence of an overbar on the "XFR-A" part, that when it is HIGH, data transfer from the *source* register A to the *destination* register Z. It also implies, from the overbar on the "$\overline{XFR$-$B}$" part, that when it is LOW, data transfer from register B to register Z. Usually, circuit designers select names for signals that are contractions, abbreviations, or acronyms of the functions they perform or are related to.

As mentioned before, computers often must communicate with peripherals. As was shown in Fig. 4-27, each peripheral can identify itself to the computer via the data lines. After the peripheral is identified, some sort of transaction typically occurs between it and the computer. Some types of peripherals must send information (data) to the computer, others receive data, and still others must send and receive. Data lines, in the data bus, serve to carry this information. Figure 4-42 shows how peripherals can send data to the computer via the data bus.

The gates 1–8 are open collector types. Note that each data line has its own pull-up resistor. Therefore, when the gates 1–8 are disabled, that is, the ENBL-A and the ENBL-B signals are LOW, all the data lines are inactive HIGH. Only when a peripheral is sending data can one or more of these lines be LOW. When peripheral A sends data (its A-word), first its ENBL-A signal goes HIGH. This enables gates 1–4, and the A-word passes onto the data bus, each bit being inverted in the process. After the complement of the A-word *settles* on the bus (bits $\overline{D}_3$–$\overline{D}_0$), the LOAD signal goes HIGH and enables gates 9–12. These gates, in turn, pass the bus's data to C_3–C_0 outputs—again each bit being inverted along the way. The original (true) form of the A-word appears at the C outputs as a result. Similarly, then,

---

* Registers, generally, serve to temporarily store digital information and are discussed in detail later.

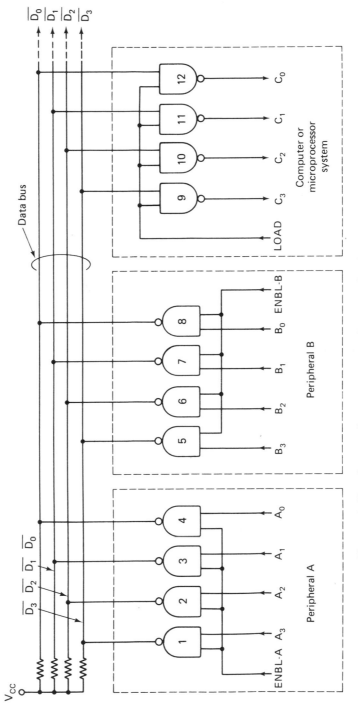

Figure 4-42. Open collector gates used to transfer data onto a data bus.

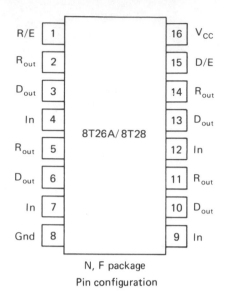

N, F package
Pin configuration

8T26A
Inverting output (3-state)

8T28
Noninverting output (3-state)

Logic diagram

(A)

Figure 4-43. Typical tri-state bidirectional buffers: (A) 8T26 inverting buffer and 8T28 noninverting buffer/driver; (B) 8226 inverting buffer and 8216 noninverting buffer/driver.

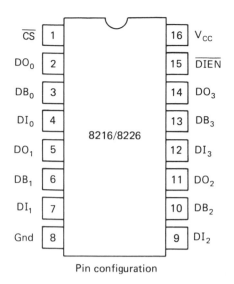

Pin configuration

DB$_0$–DB$_3$	Data bus bidirectional
DI$_0$–DI$_3$	Data input
DO$_0$–DO$_3$	Data output
$\overline{DIEN}$	Data in enable direction control
$\overline{CS}$	Chip select

Pin names

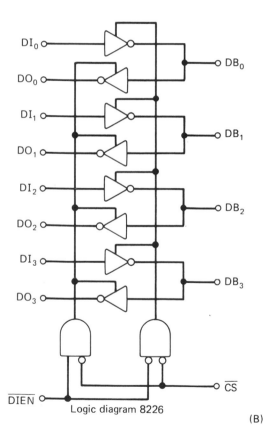

Logic diagram 8226

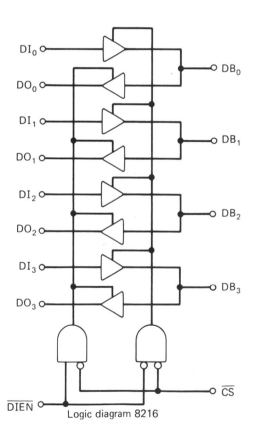

Logic diagram 8216

(B)

Figure 4.43. (Cont.)

91

the *B*-word of peripheral *B* can be transferred to the computer if first the ENBL-*B* and then the LOAD signals go HIGH.

The outputs of gates 1–4 in Fig. 4-42 are called the data *output port* of peripheral *A*. Similarly, the outputs of gates 5–8 are the data output port of peripheral *B*. On the other hand, the inputs to gates 9–12 are the data *input port* of the computer. As we shall see later, quite commonly the same port serves to output and also input data. In such cases it can be called a *bidirectional port*.

4-20 Tri-state Devices

When many peripherals and/or computers must work on a common bus, tri-state devices are usually used. Tri-state devices are made specifically for gating digital information onto or off of a data, address, or control bus. A tri-state device has three output states: the HIGH and LOW logic states, with which we are already familiar, and a third *high-impedance* (high-Z) state. Tri-state devices have totem-pole outputs of bipolar or FET transistors as in Figs. 4-24 and 4-28. When the device is in its high-impedance (third) state, both of its output transistors are simultaneously cut off, causing each output to have high resistance to ground and to the dc supply. Thus when a tri-state device is in its third state, it is virtually disconnected from the bus. This feature allows many peripherals' outputs to be connected to a common bus.

Figure 4-43 shows some typical tri-state bidirectional buffers/drivers. Each of the buffers/drivers of Fig. 4-43(A) has two control inputs, identified as R/E and D/E. When R/E is HIGH, the buffers 1, 3, 5, and 7 are in a high-Z state. When R/E is LOW, these buffers are enabled, which means that they pass logic signals. When input D/E is LOW, buffers 2, 4, 6, and 8 are in a high-Z state, whereas if D/E is HIGH, they are enabled and can pass signals. The circuit of Fig. 4-44 shows a typical application of these buffers/drivers. In this case, the computer or microprocessor unit (MPU) and the peripheral each have a bidirectional data port. That is, data can be sent or received via the same terminals. When, say, the MPU is receiving data, the $\overline{\text{RECV}}$ signal must be LOW to enable buffers 1, 3, 5, and 7 and thus allows data to flow from the bus to the data port of the MPU. Simultaneously, buffers 2, 4, 6, and 8 are in the high-Z state and therefore do not affect the bus. On the other hand, when $\overline{\text{RECV}}$ is HIGH, buffers 2, 4, 6, and 8 are enabled and can pass signals from the MPU's data port to the data bus. Of course, the bus can thus serve to transport the MPU's signals to peripherals or other devices on the bus. Simultaneously, buffers 1, 3, 5, and 7 are in the high-Z state and therefore do not affect the signals on the MPU's data port. The peripheral's buffers/drivers can be similarly analyzed. When the $\overline{\text{COPY}}$ signal is HIGH, buffers 2, 4, 6, and 8 are enabled, allowing data flow from peripheral to bus; buffers 1, 3, 5, and 7 are simultaneously in the high-Z state. When signal $\overline{\text{COPY}}$ is LOW, buffers 1, 3, 5, and 7 are

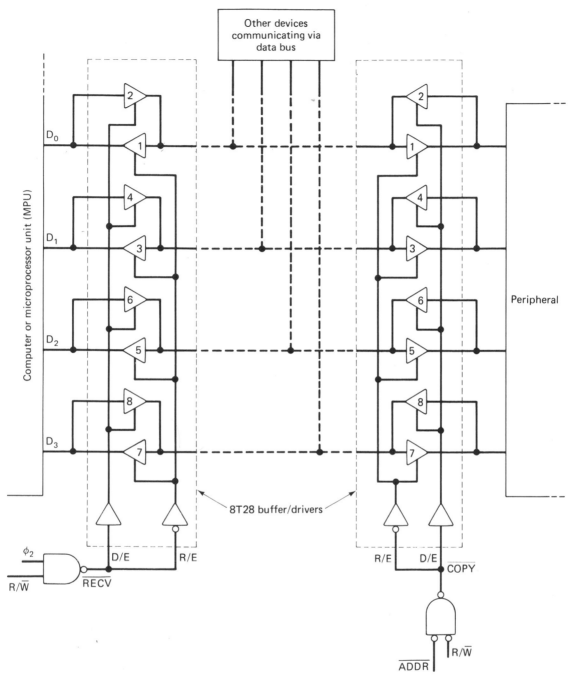

Figure 4-44. Typical application of tri-state bidirectional buffer/drivers.

enabled, and the MPU is able to write data into the peripheral. Simultaneously, buffers 2, 4, 6, and 8 are in the high-Z state.

4-21 Optically Coupled Isolators (OCIs)

In previous sections, we learned that in modern digital systems devices often must communicate with each other. Sometimes devices that must communicate have grounds or commons that are at different potentials. An equivalent circuit of this is shown in Fig. 4-45. Although the commons of such devices

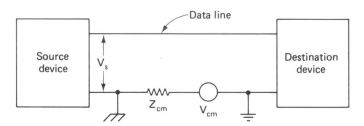

Figure 4-45. Equivalent circuit of digital transmission system.

are usually connected, there can be a finite impedance Z_{cm} between them, perhaps caused by resistance and reactance in the connecting wire. Or Z_{cm} can represent the very high resistance between commons of completely isolated devices. In either case, Z_{cm} can be a cause of potential differences across the devices' commons, which are called *common mode voltages* V_{cm}s. V_{cm} can be induced noise, via time-varying electric and magnetic fields, from nearby heavy equipment: motors, relays, etc. Since V_{cm} is in the ground loop with the source device's signal V_s, both signal V_s and noise V_{cm}, superimposed, appear at the input of the destination device. Needless to say, if V_{cm} represents noise or transients and V_s is a digital signal, errors or worse can occur in the destination device. In such cases, optically coupled isolators (OCIs), shown in Fig. 4-46, can be used.

Figure 4-46. (A) Photosensitive inverter; (B) photosensitive NAND gate; (C) typical package of an optically coupled isolator (OCI).

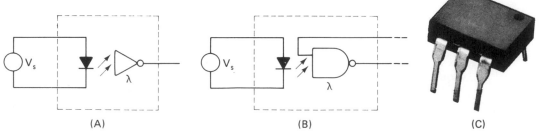

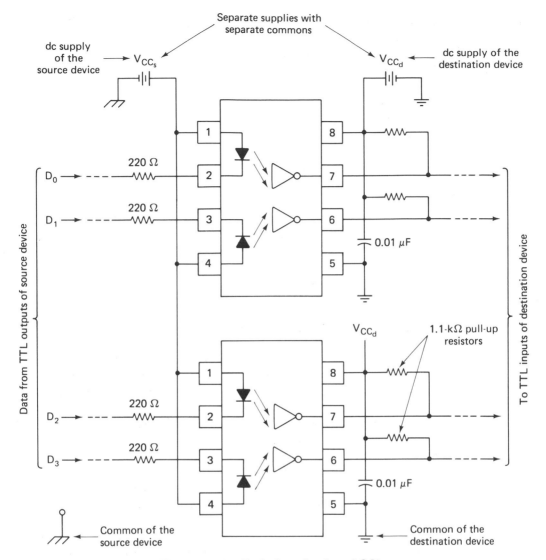

Figure 4-47. Typical application of OCIs.

A typical digital application of OCIs is shown in Fig. 4-47. The outputs of the photosensitive inverters are HIGH in the absence of *photons* (light). Thus if a logic HIGH is applied, say to the D_0 input, the LED does not emit light, and the inverter's output (pin 7) is HIGH. If the D_0 input is pulled LOW, the LED emits light, causing the inverter's output to go LOW. Thus logic signals can pass through the OCI even though its input and output terminals are electrically isolated; note the separate dc supplies and commons. Voltages V_{cm} across the separate commons can appear across the OCI's input and output terminals but will not easily pass through to the

95

inputs of the destination device. In other words, the OCI acts like an open in the ground loop as V_{cm} sees it. Actually, some small internal capacitance exists between the input and output terminals of an OCI, but only high-frequency V_{cm} could possibly couple through the OCI via its capacitance.

4-22 Combinational Logic

Logic gates are often used in decoder circuits of peripherals. For example, when an MPU is about to send or receive data to or from a peripheral, the MPU will place the peripheral's address on the address bus. Thus, of possibly many devices on the bus, only the addressed peripheral can respond. The addressed peripheral responds because it has decoding logic monitoring the bus. The decoding logic is designed to generate a signal when its device's address is on the bus. Examples of address decoding logic circuits are shown in Fig. 4-48.

By examining the decoder of peripheral A in Fig. 4-48, we can see that its $\overline{\text{SEL-}A}$ output is active LOW only when inputs $\overline{A_3}$–$\overline{A_0}$ are LHLH, respectively. The overbars on $\overline{A_3}$, $\overline{A_2}$, etc., imply that the 4-bit address, out of the MPU, was inverted, possibly by an inverting buffer between the MPU and the bus. Therefore, the actual address, A_3–A_0, is HLHL, which is equivalent to decimal 10 or hexadecimal A. Thus the peripheral A "knows" it is being called on to perform its function (send or receive data) when signal $\overline{\text{SEL-}A}$ is LOW, and this occurs when the MPU outputs an address A_{16}. We can similarly analyze peripheral B's decoder and see that its address is C_{16}. In other words, when $\overline{A_3}$–$\overline{A_0}$ are LLHH (A_3–A_0 are HHLL), signal SEL-B goes active HIGH. A HIGH SEL-B signal causes peripheral B to begin performing its function.

While peripherals A and B in Fig. 4-48 have unique addresses, peripheral C does not. Its $\overline{\text{SEL-}C}$ signal goes active LOW when lines $\overline{A_2}$–$\overline{A_0}$ are H, H, and L or when $\overline{A_3}$ is HIGH. This decoder's functional table is shown in Fig. 4-49. Note in this table that $\overline{\text{SEL-}C}$ goes active LOW when logic combinations of row 6 and of rows 8–15 are applied. These are equivalent to 9_{16} and to 7_{16}–0_{16} as shown in the hex column. That is, each $\overline{A_3}$–$\overline{A_0}$ bit is simply inverted, and the resulting 4-bit binary word can be rewritten in its decimal and hexadecimal equivalents as shown.

The combinations of binary inputs $\overline{A_3}$–$\overline{A_0}$ that cause $\overline{\text{SEL-}C}$ to become active can be more concisely shown as in the table of Fig. 4-50. In the first row, the X in the A_3 column means that this line can be either HIGH or LOW while the other lines are as shown. In other words, $\overline{\text{SEL-}C}$ goes active LOW when $\overline{A_2}$–$\overline{A_0}$ are HHL, and it doesn't matter what logic level is on the $\overline{A_3}$ line. Thus an X input is called a *don't care* input or an *irrelevant* input. In the second row of this table, when $\overline{A_3}$ is HIGH, the signal $\overline{\text{SEL-}C}$ is active regardless of the $\overline{A_2}$–$\overline{A_0}$ signals; that is, $\overline{A_2}$, $\overline{A_1}$, and $\overline{A_0}$ are don't care inputs.

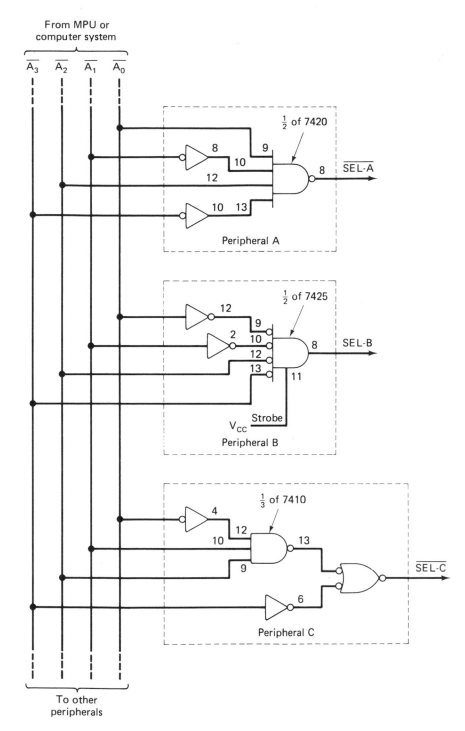

Figure 4-48. Logic gates used in decoding circuits.

Functional table

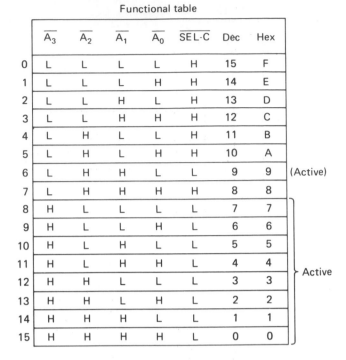

	$\overline{A_3}$	$\overline{A_2}$	$\overline{A_1}$	$\overline{A_0}$	SEL-C	Dec	Hex	
0	L	L	L	L	H	15	F	
1	L	L	L	H	H	14	E	
2	L	L	H	L	H	13	D	
3	L	L	H	H	H	12	C	
4	L	H	L	L	H	11	B	
5	L	H	L	H	H	10	A	
6	L	H	H	L	L	9	9	(Active)
7	L	H	H	H	H	8	8	
8	H	L	L	L	L	7	7	
9	H	L	L	H	L	6	6	
10	H	L	H	L	L	5	5	
11	H	L	H	H	L	4	4	Active
12	H	H	L	L	L	3	3	
13	H	H	L	H	L	2	2	
14	H	H	H	L	L	1	1	
15	H	H	H	H	L	0	0	

Figure 4-49. Table for the decoder of peripheral C.

Figure 4-50. Input combinations that cause signal $\overline{\text{SEL-}C}$ to become active LOW in Fig. 4-48; X denotes don't care or irrelevant input.

Inputs				Outputs
$\overline{A_3}$	$\overline{A_2}$	$\overline{A_1}$	$\overline{A_0}$	$\overline{\text{SEL-C}}$
X	H	H	L	L
H	X	X	X	L

Review Questions

1. Describe conventional current and electron flow directions in terms of charge flow.

2. What input logic conditions are required to cause a **HIGH** output of a (a) four-input **AND** gate, (b) four-input **OR** gate, (c) four-input **NAND** gate, and (d) four-input **NOR** gate?

3. What input logic conditions are required to cause a **LOW** output of a (a) four-input **AND** gate, (b) four-input **OR** gate, (c) four-input **NAND** gate, and (d) four-input **NOR** gate?

4. Using terms like *active pull-ups, passive pull-ups, active pull-downs,* or *passive pull-downs,* describe how HIGH and LOW logic signals appear at the outputs of the ICs in Fig. 4-30.

5. What logic function does the circuit of Fig. 4-51 perform?

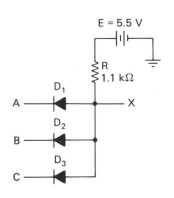

Functional table

	C	B	A	X	V_{D_1}	V_{D_2}	V_{D_3}	V_R
1	0 V	0 V	0 V					
2	0 V	0 V	5 V					
3	0 V	4 V	0 V					
4	0 V	4.5 V	5.2 V					
5	4.4 V	0 V	0.2 V					
6	5 V	0 V	5 V					
7	4 V	3.8 V	0.1 V					
8	3.8 V	4 V	5.3 V					

Figure 4-51.

6. What logic function does the circuit of Fig. 4-52 perform?

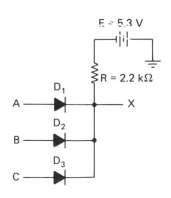

Functional table

	C	B	A	X	V_{D_1}	V_{D_2}	V_{D_3}	V_R
1	0.1 V	0 V	0.2 V					
2	0 V	0 V	4 V					
3	0.1 V	4.5 V	0.2 V					
4	0 V	5 V	4.5 V					
5	5 V	0.2 V	0 V					
6	3.5 V	0 V	5 V					
7	4 V	5 V	0 V					
8	3.8 V	4.1 V	5 V					

Figure 4-52.

7. Name three advantages that a transistor has over a vacuum tube.

8. What symbols are used to represent a transistor's forward current transfer ratio (I_C/I_B)?

9. In general terms, what is the collector-to-emitter voltage of a transistor when it is (a) saturated and (b) cut off?

10. What words do the letters in the term MOSFET represent?

11. How much current can a standard TTL output (a) sink and (b) source?

12. What does an overbar on a signal name mean?

13. In what way are the 7404 and the 7405 ICs alike, and in what way are they different?

14. What maximum output voltage might a standard TTL gate have and still be a logic LOW?

15. What minimum output voltage might a standard TTL gate have and still be a logic HIGH?

16. How large a voltage can we apply to a standard TTL input and still have it be interpreted as a logic LOW?

17. How small a voltage can we apply to an input of a standard TTL gate and still have the gate interpret it as a HIGH?

18. If we suspect a faulty totem-pole chip, such as a 7404, can we replace it with an open collector type, such as a 7405? Note that the 7404 and 7405 are pin compatible.

19. Describe the third state of a tri-state device.

20. For what purpose are tri-state devices used?

21. What do the letters in the term FET mean?

22. What do the letters in the term OCI mean?

23. Referring to the circuits of Fig. 4-48, why are the circles on the inputs of some inverters and on the outputs of other inverters?

Problems

4-1 If $E = 24$ V and $R = 2.2$ kΩ in the circuit of Fig. 4-2(A), what are (a) the circuit current, (b) the voltage across R, and (c) the voltage across the diode? Assume that the diode is ideal.

4-2 If $E = 24$ V in the circuit of Fig. 4-2(A) and the diode's maximum current rating is 1 A, what is the smallest resistor R that can be used?

4-3 If $E = 24$ V and $R = 2.2$ kΩ in the circuit of Fig. 4-2(B), what are (a) the circuit current, (b) the voltage across R, and (c) the voltage across the diode?

4-4 If the diode in the circuit of Fig. 4-3(A) has a PIV rating of 200 V, what maximum rms voltage can we apply? The PIV rating is the peak inverse (reverse bias) voltage rating.

4-5 Referring to the circuit and table of Fig. 4-51, fill in the table working one row at a time. The voltage values in rows A, B, and C represent voltages to ground at inputs A, B, and C. Show the resulting voltages at X to ground in the X column. Also show the resulting voltages across the diodes D_1, D_2, D_3 and across resistor R in columns V_{D_1}, V_{D_2}, etc. Assume that the diodes are ideal.

4-6 Referring to the circuit and table of Fig. 4-52, fill in columns X–V_R working one row at a time. Columns A, B, and C show voltage values that are at inputs A, B, and C of the circuit. Assume that the diodes are ideal.

4-7 If in the circuit of Fig. 4-12(C) $R_B = 10$ kΩ and $R_C = 2$ kΩ, what are the collector current I_C and the voltage at the collector C to ground if (a) $V_{in} = 0$ V and (b) $V_{in} = 5$ V?

4-8 If the lamp in the circuit of Fig. 4-14(A) is rated at 5 V and 3 W, what are the voltage at point C to ground and the collector current when (a) $V_{in} = 0$ V and (b) $V_{in} = 5$ V?

4-9 Select an R_C value for the circuit of Fig. 4-16 so that the LED's current is about 20 mA. Assume that a conducting LED drops about 1 V.

4-10 Select an R_C value for the circuit of Fig. 4-15(B) so that the LED's current is about 15 mA. Assume that a conducting LED drops 1 V.

4-11 Referring to the circuit of Fig. 4-15(A), when $V_{in} = 0$ V (point X is grounded), how much current does the source of V_{in} have to sink? In other words, what is the current in D_1 when point X is grounded? Assume that each diode, when conducting, drops 0.6 V.

4-12 If $V_{in} = 5$ V in the circuit of Fig. 4-15(A), how much current will the source of the signal V_{in} have to source?

4-13 Referring to your results of the previous two problems, is this lamp driver (Fig. 4-15) TTL compatible? In other words, can a standard TTL gate be used to drive this circuit?

4-14 What are the logic levels on the lines $\overline{D_0}$–$\overline{D_2}$ in the circuit of Fig. 4-27 if switch Sw_5 is closed while Sw_6 and Sw_7 are open?

4-15 What are the logic levels on the lines $\overline{D_0}$–$\overline{D_2}$ in the circuit of Fig. 4-27 if switch Sw_7 is closed while Sw_5 and Sw_6 are open?

4-16 What will happen to the logic levels $\overline{D_0}$–$\overline{D_2}$ in the circuit of Fig. 4-27 if the pull-down resistor R_v in peripheral 7 becomes open?

4-17 If only Sw_5 is closed in the circuit of Fig. 4-27, what are the logic levels at the outputs of inverters 5, 6, and 7?

4-18 Figure 4-53 shows a *transfer function* for a typical CMOS gate working on a 5-V power supply. Does it show that a standard totem-pole TTL gate can be used to drive a CMOS? Why?

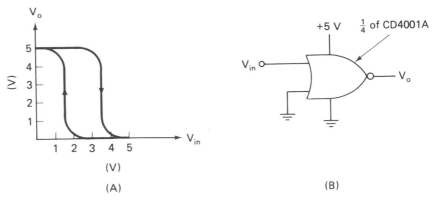

Figure 4-53. (A) Transfer function (output V_o vs. input V_{in}) characteristics of a typical CMOS as shown in (B) working on a 5-V dc supply.

4-19 If a CMOS gate is rated with sink and source current capabilities of 0.5 mA, can such a gate be used to drive one standard TTL input? Why?

4-20 If each gate in the 4007 CMOS IC of Fig. 4-29 is able to sink and source about 0.5 mA, show how it can be wired so that the entire 4007 will work as one inverter with sink and source capabilities of about 1.5 mA. Indicate all pin numbers.

4-21 Referring to Problem 4-20, will the circuit requested be able to drive one standard TTL input? Why?

4-22 Referring to the typical CMOS *transfer function* of Fig. 4-53, what is V_o with each of the following values of V_{in}: (a) 1 V, (b) 3 V, (c) 5 V.

4-23 Referring to the typical CMOS *transfer function* of Fig. 4-53, (a) what range of V_{in} is interpreted as a HIGH logic input if the CMOS gate is working off a 5-V dc supply? (b) What range of V_{in} is interpreted as a LOW logic input?

4-24 The Schmitt NAND gate of Fig. 4-54 behaves like any four-input NAND except for the precision of its noise margin. Referring to its transfer function, what range of input voltage V_{in} is (a) interpreted as a LOW logic input and (b) as a HIGH logic input?

4-25 Figure 4-55 shows some example inputs to the Schmitt NAND of Fig. 4-54(A). Directly below input waveform (A), sketch the

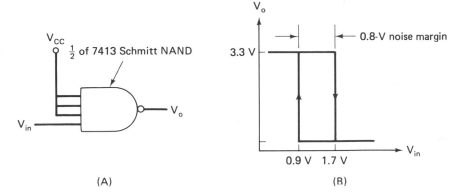

Figure 4-54. (A) Schmitt NAND gate; (B) its transfer function, which shows its precise noise margin.

resulting output. Directly below input waveform (B), sketch the resulting output.

4-26 Figure 4-55 shows some example inputs to the Schmitt NAND of Fig. 4-54(A). Directly below input waveform (C), sketch the resulting output. Directly below input waveform (D), sketch the resulting output.

4-27 If the noise voltage riding on the signal applied to the input of the circuit in Fig. 4-54 exceeds a peak of 0.8 V, what can we expect at the output?

4-28 If we connect three inputs to ground instead of to V_{CC} on the Schmitt NAND of Fig. 4-54(A), sketch the output waveform for each input waveform shown in Fig. 4-55.

4-29 How many standard TTL inputs can each buffer/driver of the 7407 drive?

4-30 If a type of LED we are to use requires about 15 mA, how many such LEDs can we drive simultaneously with each inverter of (a) a 7405 and (b) a 7407?

4-31 Referring to Fig. 4-28, if each FET has $10^{3}\text{-}\Omega$ resistance when it is on and $10^{10}\text{-}\Omega$ resistance when it is off, what are the HIGH and LOW voltage values at output X if $V_{DD} = 5$ V and output X drives another CMOS input?

4-32 Answer Problem 4-31 assuming that, instead of a CMOS input, a 1-kΩ load is connected to the output X and ground.

4-33 Referring to the circuit of Fig. 4-32, which output is active and which indicator is lit when the input signal STOP/$\overline{\text{GO}}$ is HIGH?

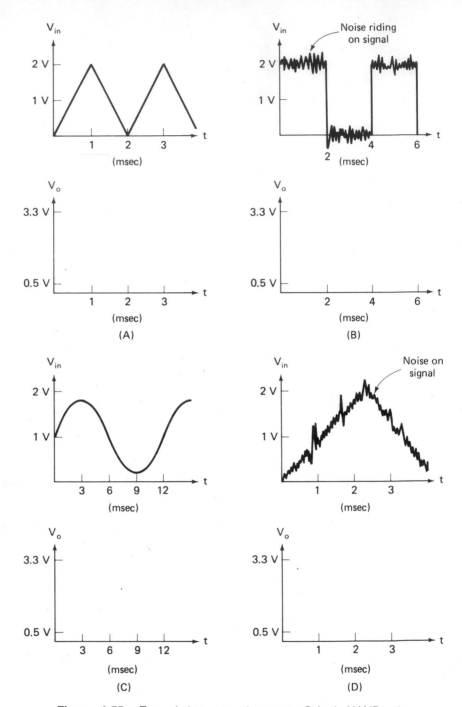

Figure 4-55. Example input waveforms on a Schmitt NAND gate.

4-34 Referring to the circuit of Fig. 4-32, which output is active and which indicator is lit when the input signal STOP/$\overline{GO}$ is LOW?

4-35 Sketch a symbol for each of the following gates that best illustrates an active HIGH output: (a) a four-input AND, (b) a four-input OR, (c) a four-input NAND, (d) a four-input NOR.

4-36 Sketch a symbol for each of the following gates that best illustrates an active LOW output: (a) a four-input AND, (b) a four-input OR, (c) a four-input NAND, (d) a four-input NOR.

4-37 Referring to the circuit of Fig. 4-41, if the A_3–A_0 inputs are 0111, the B_3–B_0 inputs are 1010, and the $XFR\text{-}A/\overline{XFR\text{-}B}$ input is LOW, what are the resulting X_3–X_0, Y_3–Y_0, and Z_3–Z_0 outputs?

4-38 Answer Problem 4-37 but make the $XFR\text{-}A/\overline{XFR\text{-}B}$ input HIGH.

4-39 How many and what types of TTL chips are needed for the circuit of Fig. 4-56?

Figure 4-56. Data transfer circuit using three quad two-input NANDs; 7400 DIPs.

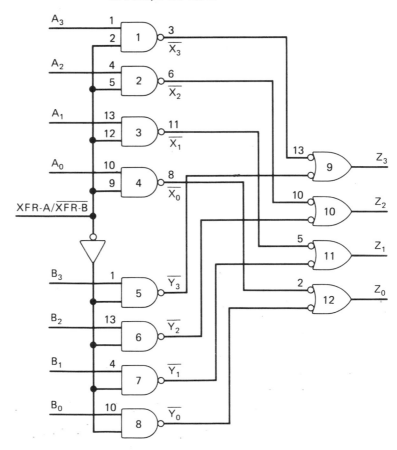

4-40 Referring to the circuit of Fig. 4-56, if the A_3–A_0 inputs are 0111 and the B_3–B_0 inputs are 1010, show the resulting $\overline{X_3}$–$\overline{X_0}$, $\overline{Y_3}$–$\overline{Y_0}$, and Z_3–Z_0 outputs when (a) the $XFR\text{-}A/\overline{XFR\text{-}B}$ input is HIGH and (b) when the $XFR\text{-}A/\overline{XFR\text{-}B}$ input is LOW.

4-41 How do the overall functions of the circuits in Figs. 4-41 and 4-56 compare?

4-42 Show how the same overall function of the circuit in Fig. 4-56 can be performed with 12 two-input NOR gates and 1 inverter.

For Problems 4-43–4-46, assume that the waveforms of Fig. 4-57 are applied to the inputs of the circuit in Fig. 4-42.

4-43 Between what times is the A-word (A_3–A_0 data) being placed on the bus?

4-44 Between what times is the B-word (B_3–B_0 data) being placed on the bus?

4-45 When both signals ENBL-A and ENBL-B are LOW, what logic level is on each line of the data bus?

4-46 On the scales of Fig. 4-57, sketch timing diagrams (waveforms) of the signals $\overline{D_3}$–$\overline{D_0}$ and of the signals C_3–C_0 that occur with the input signals shown.

4-47 Show all the missing pin numbers on the tri-state buffers/drivers of Fig. 4-44.

4-48 Redraw the circuit of Fig. 4-44 but replace the 8T28 tri-state buffers with 8216s. Indicate all pin numbers and properly account for the $\overline{CS}$ input. When the $\overline{CS}$ input is HIGH, the 8216 chip is disabled and cannot transfer data in either direction, and *all* buffers are in a high-Z state.

4-49 When the signals ϕ_2, $R/\overline{W}$, and $\overline{ADDR}$ are LOW in the circuit of Fig. 4-44, what is the direction of data flow?

4-50 When the signals ϕ_2, $R/\overline{W}$, and $\overline{ADDR}$ are HIGH in the circuit of Fig. 4-44, what is the direction of data flow?

4-51 If in the circuit of Fig. 4-47 $V_{CC_s} = 5$ V and each of the conducting LEDs drops about 1 V, how much current will each of the source device's outputs have to sink? Assume that each source device's output has a LOW of 0 V.

4-52 If in the circuit of Fig. 4-47 $V_{CC_s} = 6$ V and each of the conducting LEDs drops about 1.2 V, how much current will each of the source device's outputs have to sink? Assume that the source device's LOW output is 0.5 V.

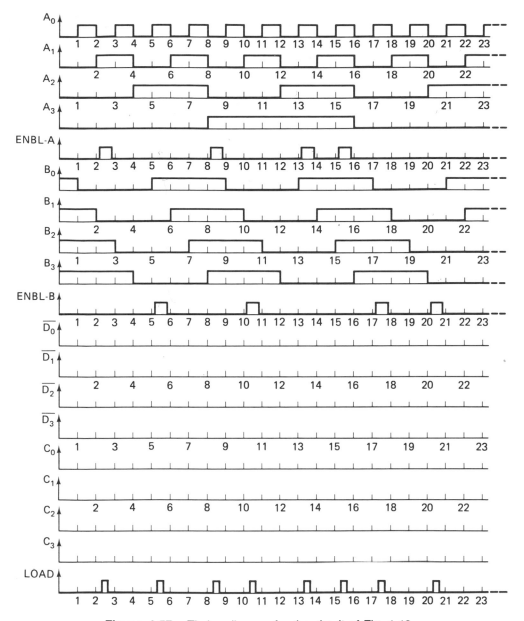

Figure 4-57. Timing diagram for the circuit of Fig. 4-42.

4-53 If the OCIs of Fig. 4-47 have 2 pF of internal capacitance C_i across each input and output and a V_{cm} of 60 Hz is across the separate commons, what is the reactance of C_i to V_{cm}? Should we expect significant 60 Hz to couple through this OCI's reactance? Why?

4-54 If the OCIs of Fig. 4-47 have 2 pF of internal capacitance C_i across each input and output and a 50-kHz square wave is across the separate commons, what is the reactance of C_i to this square wave's (a) fundamental frequency and (b) fifth harmonic? If a 20-mV peak-to-peak 50-kHz square wave can be measured across pins 2 and 7, what is the leakage current through C_i at (c) the fundamental, and (d) the fifth harmonic? *Note:* The peak-to-peak amplitudes of the fundamental and fifth harmonic are equal to one-half and one-tenth of the square wave's peak-to-peak value, respectively.

4-55 What kind of gate is used in peripheral A of Fig. 4-48?

4-56 What kind of gate is used in peripheral B of Fig. 4-48?

4-57 Referring to Fig. 4-48, what kind of gate is providing the $\overline{\text{SEL-}C}$ signal?

4-58 Referring to peripheral A of Fig. 4-48, if the inverter driving pin 10 of the gate is removed and replaced with a straight-through connection, what binary, octal, and hex addresses will cause signal $\overline{\text{SEL-}A}$ to become active?

4-59 Referring to peripheral B of Fig. 4-48, if two more inverters are placed in the circuit, one connecting the $\overline{A_2}$ line to pin 12 and the other connecting the $\overline{A_3}$ line to pin 13, what binary, octal, and hex addresses will cause signal SEL-B to become active?

4-60 If an inverter is used to connect the $\overline{A_2}$ line to pin 9 of the gate in peripheral C of Fig. 4-48, what binary, octal, and hex addresses will cause signal $\overline{\text{SEL-}C}$ to become active?

Figure 4-58. Start-up circuit used to clear system at instant the power switch is closed.

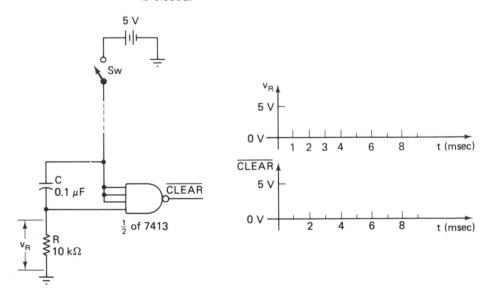

4-61 Referring to the circuit of Fig. 4-58, sketch its v_R and $\overline{\text{CLEAR}}$ signals assuming that the switch Sw is closed at $t = 0$. Assume also that the input resistance of the gate is much larger than 10 kΩ.

4-62 Referring to the circuit of Fig. 4-59, what are the binary, octal, and hex versions of the address that cause signal $\overline{\text{A/D CONV}}$ to become active?

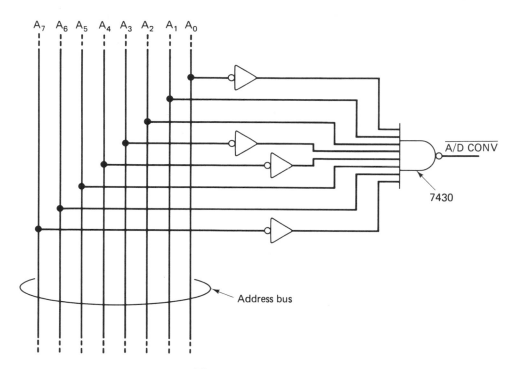

Figure 4-59. Decoder.

4-63 Referring to the 8 bits of the address bus shown in Fig. 4-59, show how to connect a 7430 and inverters to decode the address $8F_{16}$.

CHAPTER 5

Flip-flops, Counters, Registers, and Other MSI Devices

A number of very important digital devices are discussed in this chapter; most fall into the MSI category. They are important because they are commonly found in the interface and peripheral circuitry of computer- and MPU-based systems. By gaining an understanding of them, we shall be able to understand how computers and MPUs work internally and how they communicate, that is, exchange information, with the outside world. Comparatively, if the MPU is like the brain and if arms, legs, eyes, ears, etc., are like peripherals, we shall now be looking at the muscle tissue, heart, and other essential organs of an MPU-based system.

5-1 Flip-flops

The term flip-flop (FF) generally applies to a number of similar but different devices. This term somewhat describes how such devices work. Their outputs can be made to *flip* from one logic state to the other and also to *flop* back to their original states. Flip-flops serve to debounce mechanical switches, store data bits, provide voltage pulses, and actively participate in dynamic movement of data within and between processor systems and their peripherals.

5-1-1 *RS* Flip-flops

The *RS* FF is more specifically called the set/reset flip-flop. In TTL circuits, an *RS* FF is often constructed with NAND gates as shown in (A) of Fig. 5-1. The outputs Q and $\overline{Q}$ are *complementary,* that is, opposite logic

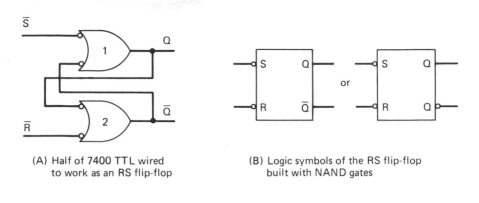

(A) Half of 7400 TTL wired to work as an RS flip-flop

(B) Logic symbols of the RS flip-flop built with NAND gates

Function table

	$\overline{S}$	$\overline{R}$	Q	$\overline{Q}$	
1	LOW	LOW	HIGH	HIGH	← Normally not used
2	HIGH (inactive)	LOW (ACTIVE)	LOW	HIGH	
3	LOW (ACTIVE)	HIGH (inactive)	HIGH	LOW	
4	HIGH (inactive)	HIGH (inactive)	No change		

(C)

Fig. 5-1 *RS* flip-flop with active LOW inputs.

levels. When the output Q is HIGH, $\overline{Q}$ is LOW, and the *RS* FF is said to be *set*. When output Q is LOW, $\overline{Q}$ is HIGH, and the *RS* FF is said to be *reset*. In this case, the set $(\overline{S})$ and reset $(\overline{R})$ inputs are active LOW. This means that this *RS* FF becomes set if its $\overline{S}$ input is pulled LOW. On the other hand, when its $\overline{R}$ input is pulled LOW, this *RS* FF becomes reset. A functional table of the active LOW input *RS* FF is shown in (C) of Fig. 5-1. Note that normally both inputs are not driven LOW at the same time.

The *RS* FF is frequently used in the bounceless switch circuit shown in Fig. 5-2. A mechanical switch tends to bounce after it is thrown. This means that the switch arm will first strike but then bounce off contact *s* after the arm is thrown in the up position; see (B) of Fig. 5-2. Typically, the arm will bounce many times before it finally settles to a good contact with *s*. Of course, then, the arm of the switch will bounce many times off contact *r* after Sw is thrown down; see Fig. 5-2(C). All mechanical switches tend to bounce and therefore are impractical as sources of logic pulses, especially where the number of pulses is critical. An electronic calculator keyboard is an example of mechanical push-button switches that are debounced. If they were not debounced, a single push of a keyboard button would usually cause more than one character to be displayed.

The waveforms in Fig. 5-2(D) show how the output voltages of the

111

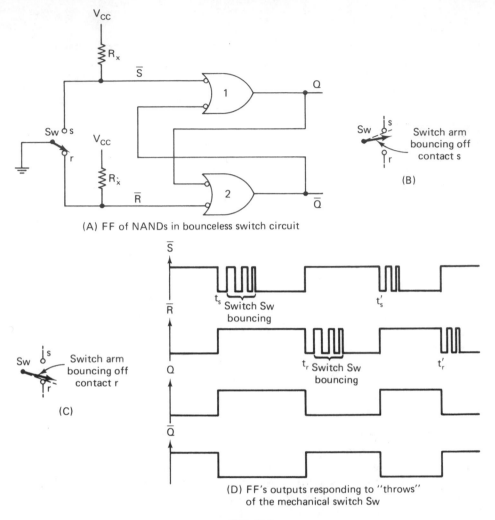

(A) FF of NANDs in bounceless switch circuit

Sw ⊸ s Switch arm
bouncing off
contact s

(B)

Sw ⊸ s Switch arm
bouncing off
contact r

(C)

(D) FF's outputs responding to "throws"
of the mechanical switch Sw

Fig. 5-2

circuit (A) respond to throws of the switch Sw. Since Sw is initially in the down position, it puts an active LOW signal on the $\overline{R}$ (reset) input, causing the FF to reset. At the same time, the $\overline{S}$ input is HIGH (inactive), being pulled HIGH to the V_{CC} voltage through the pull-up resistor R_x. At time t_s, Sw is thrown into the up position. This places an active LOW signal on the $\overline{S}$ (set) input at the instant the switch arm strikes contact s. At the same instant, $\overline{R}$ is pulled HIGH (inactive) through R_x. The FF is thus forced to become set at time t_s. As shown on the waveform of $\overline{S}$, Sw bounces after t_s, causing $\overline{S}$ to change from LOW to HIGH and back to LOW several times before settling to a steady LOW. On each HIGH to LOW swing of input $\overline{S}$, the RS FF is instructed to set, but because it was already set at t_s, it simply remains set.

At time t_r, Sw is thrown down. This puts an active LOW on input $\overline{R}$, causing the FF to reset. After t_r, the switch is shown bouncing, but the bounces are ignored, and the FF remains reset.

At t_s', the switch Sw is thrown to its up position, causing the FF to set again. Then after a short time, at t_r', Sw is thrown to its down position, causing the FF to reset again. The point to note here is that the switch can set or reset the FF, but the switch bounces have no effect on the FF's outputs.

A pair of two-input NOR gates can be wired to work as an *RS* FF as shown in Fig. 5-3. In this case, the set *(S)* and reset *(R)* inputs are active HIGH. Therefore, these inputs are shown without circles; see (B) of Fig. 5-3. The functional table (C) of Fig. 5-3 shows how this FF reacts to each possible combination of inputs. Row 1 shows that if both inputs are LOW, the outputs do not change. This means that the FF will remain in either its set or reset state. Row 2 shows that if the *S* input is momentarily pulled HIGH, while input *R* is LOW, the FF becomes set. If it is already set when a HIGH *S* input is applied, the FF simply stays set. As indicated in row 3, a momentary HIGH on input *R,* while *S* is LOW, causes the FF to

Fig. 5-3 *RS* flip-flop with active HIGH inputs.

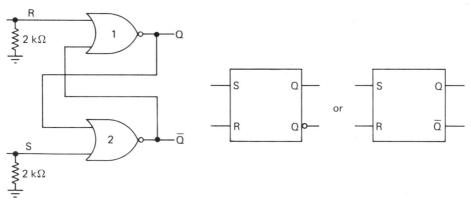

(A) Half of 7402 TTL wired
to work as an RS flip-flop

(B) Logic symbols of the RS flip-
flop built with NOR gates

Functional table

	S	R	Q	$\overline{Q}$
1	LOW (inactive)	LOW (inactive)	No change	
2	HIGH (ACTIVE)	LOW (inactive)	HIGH	LOW
3	LOW (inactive)	HIGH (ACTIVE)	LOW	HIGH
4	HIGH	HIGH	LOW	LOW	←—Normally not used

(C)

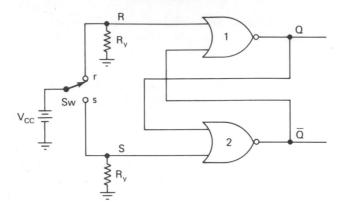

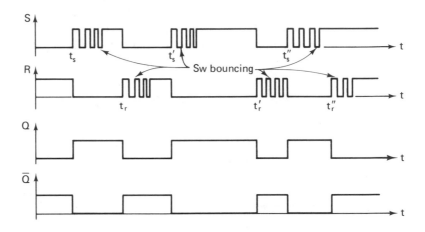

(A) FF of NORs in bounceless switch circuit (use pull-down resistors R_y of about 2 KΩ with TTL NORs)

(B) FF's outputs responding to "throws" of mechanical switch Sw

Fig. 5-4

become reset. If the FF is in the reset state when the HIGH is applied to its R input, it simply remains reset. In usual applications of the RS flip-flop, both inputs are not driven with active HIGH signals at the same time. Thus, as shown in row 4, two HIGH inputs are normally not used on this FF.

The RS FF, constructed with two-input NORs, can be used to debounce a mechanical switch, as shown in Fig. 5-4. In this case, when the switch Sw is thrown to the up position, a HIGH is placed on the R input, and the S input is pulled LOW through the passive pull-down R_y. When Sw is thrown down, the HIGH in the S input sets the FF; the R input is pulled LOW through R_y. As with the previous debouncing circuit (Fig. 5-2), contact bounces are ignored.

In Chapter 4 we learned of logic circuits that respond with an active output signal when a certain combination of inputs is applied. For example, in the circuit of Fig. 4-48, the output signal $\overline{\text{SEL-}A}$ is active LOW when inputs $\overline{A_3}$, $\overline{A_2}$, $\overline{A_1}$, and $\overline{A_0}$ are L, H, L, and H, respectively. The decoder (gate and inverters) that produce the $\overline{\text{SEL-}A}$ signal is called a *combinational logic* circuit. Use of flip-flops (1-bit memories) makes possible the construction of *sequential logic* circuits. A sequential logic circuit's output becomes active only when a certain sequence of inputs is applied.

The simplified digital combination lock of Fig. 5-5 is a sequential logic circuit. Its output signal $\overline{\text{OPEN}}$ is active (LED lighted) only after the input push-button switches *A, B,* and *C* are pushed in that order. Each capacitor, followed by a passive pull-up or pull-down, serves to differentiate the signal from its switch. Thus, though a step input signal can appear at the left of each capacitor, only a short spike can appear at its right. Note that if Sw *A* is pushed, FF *A* becomes set (signal OK-*A* becomes HIGH), and gate 1 becomes enabled. Now if Sw *B* is pushed, FF *B* becomes set, and the resulting HIGH OK-*B* signal enables gate 2. Finally, then, a push on Sw *C* sets FF *C,* causing its output $\overline{\text{OPEN}}$ to go LOW, which in turn admits current through the LED. The LED can optically turn on a phototransistor or silicon controlled rectifier (SCR) which in turn can energize a solenoid that pulls the bolt of the lock. Of course, an OCI (optically coupled isolator) can be used at an output of the FF *C* in place of the LED.

The switches in Fig. 5-5 can be on a standard calculator keyboard. The designer can select the keyboard numbers for his or her desired combination and wire them as the *A, B,* and *C* switches shown in Fig. 5-5. The unused switches should then be connected to the reset *(R)* inputs as shown. Thus the unauthorized button pusher, trying to guess his or her way past the lock, will reset the FFs every time he or she pushes a numbered or lettered switch that is not in the combination.

5-1-3   *D*-Type Flip-flops

Digital circuits fall in two general classifications, synchronous and asynchronous (not synchronous). All circuits that we have studied so far were asynchronous. We shall start looking at some synchronous components and circuits in this chapter. Synchronous circuits require one or more clocks (square-wave generators) to pulse life and action within them. In synchronous circuits, nothing happens if the clock or clocks are not running. Clock circuits are discussed later (Sec. 5–10) in this chapter.

Like the *RS* FF, the *D*-type FF has two outputs and two *stable states:* the set and reset states. When in either of its stable states, the *D*-type FF's outputs are complementary. This means that when its *Q* output is HIGH, its $\overline{Q}$ output is LOW, and the FF is said to be set. On the other hand,

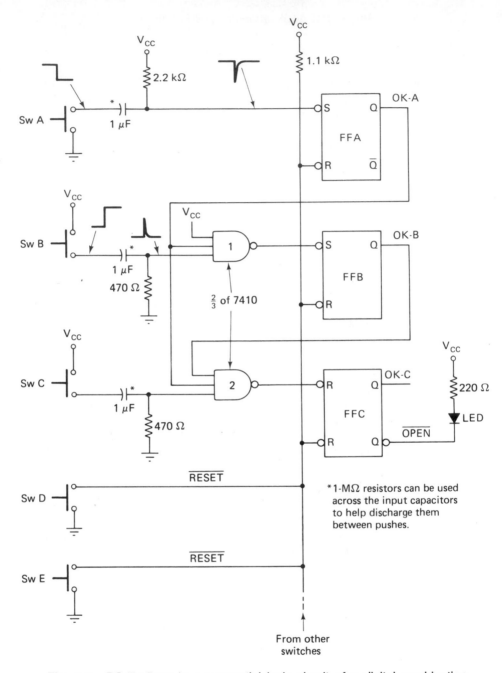

Fig. 5-5 *RS* flip-flops in a sequential logic circuit of a digital combination lock.

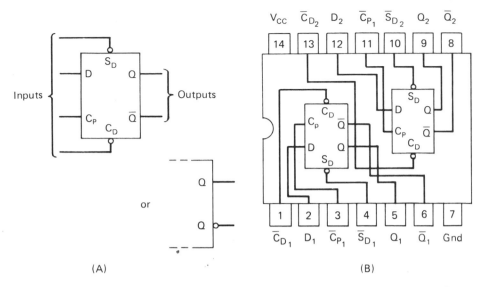

Fig. 5-6 (A) Symbol for the D-type flip-flop; (B) IC package containing D-type flip-flops (TTL/SSI: 5474/7474).

when its Q output is LOW, its $\overline{Q}$ output is HIGH, and the FF is said to be reset.

The logic symbol and typical IC package for the D-type FF are shown in Fig. 5-6. Note that each FF has four inputs:

1. The $\overline{S_D}$ input (also called the direct set, the set, or the preset input)

2. The $\overline{C_D}$ input (also called the clear or reset input)

3. The D data input

4. The C_p input (also called the clock *CK,* trigger *T,* or strobe *S* input)

The $\overline{S_D}$ and $\overline{C_D}$ inputs on the D-type FF work like the $\overline{S}$ and $\overline{R}$ inputs on the *RS* FF. That is, the D-type FF responds to LOW or LOW-going signals on its $\overline{S_D}$ and $\overline{C_D}$ inputs. These inputs provide us with the capability to set or reset the FF asynchronously—without a clock input.

The table in Fig. 5-7 shows how the outputs of the D-type FF respond to the four possible combinations on its $\overline{S_D}$ and $\overline{C_D}$ inputs. Row 1 shows that if both inputs are pulled LOW, both outputs go HIGH. The FF is not normally used in this way because it is not in one of its stable states (set or reset) when both outputs are HIGH. This means that both outputs remain HIGH only as long as both inputs ($\overline{S_D}$ and $\overline{C_D}$) are held LOW. If we allow one or both inputs to become inactive HIGH, the D-type FF will immediately switch to one of its two stable states.

As shown in row 2 of the table in Fig. 5-7, a LOW signal on the $\overline{S_D}$ input, while the $\overline{C_D}$ input is HIGH or open, causes the Q output to go

117

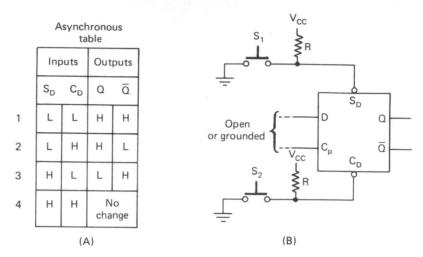

Asynchronous table

Inputs		Outputs	
S_D	C_D	Q	$\bar{Q}$
1			
L	L	H	H
2			
L	H	H	L
3			
H	L	L	H
4			
H	H	No change	

(A)

(B)

Fig. 5-7 (A) Asynchronous functional table for the *D*-type flip-flop; (B) *D*-type flip-flop wired for asynchronous operation.

HIGH; that is, it sets the FF. If additional LOW-going signals or pulses are applied to the $\bar{S_D}$ input, after it becomes set, the FF remains stable in the set state. Row 3 shows that when $\bar{C_D}$ is pulled LOW, while the $\bar{S_D}$ input is HIGH (inactive), this FF resets. If additional LOW-going signals or pulses are applied to the $\bar{C_D}$ input, after it resets, this FF remains reset. Finally, row 4 in the table of Fig. 5-7 shows that if both $\bar{S_D}$ and $\bar{C_D}$ are HIGH or open, the FF's outputs do not change. This means that the *D*-type FF will stay in one of its stable states, set or reset, when both inputs are inactive HIGH.

Example 5-1

Show how a two-pole mechanical switch can be debounced using a *D*-type FF.

Answer

See Fig. 5-8.

During synchronous operation, the *D*-type FF requires a clock (square-wave) signal applied to its input. The leading edge (LOW to HIGH-transition) of the clock signal can cause the *D*-type FF to change states. Whether or not the FF does change depends on the logic level on the *D* (data) input at the instant the leading edge on C_p arrives.

In the following discussion of how the *D*-type FF behaves during synchronous operation, we can assume that the $\bar{S_D}$ and $\bar{C_D}$ inputs are wired to HIGHs (+5 V) or simply left open. A HIGH on the *D* input of the *D*-type FF puts it in the *set mode*. This means that this FF is instructed to,

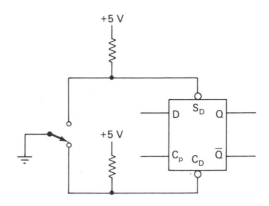

Fig. 5-8 *D*-type FF used to debounce a mechanical switch. If unused, the *D* and C_p inputs should be tied to ground in a permanent circuit.

and will, set on the next leading edge of the clock. If the FF is already set when the HIGH *D* input is applied, it simply stays set regardless of the number of incoming clock pulses.

When a LOW logic level is applied to the *D* input, the *D*-type FF is in the *reset mode*. This means that it is instructed to, and will, reset on the next leading edge of the clock input. After the *D*-type FF resets, it stays reset as long as the *D* input is LOW regardless of the number of incoming clock pulses.

A *D*-type FF working synchronously is shown in Fig. 5-9. In this case, the *Q* and $\overline{Q}$ outputs are shown to be initially LOW and HIGH, respectively; that is, the FF is initially in the reset state. With the switch *S* in the down position as shown, the *D* input is LOW, putting the FF in the reset mode. Since it is already reset, the FF remains reset, and the clock pulses 1, 2, and 3 have no effect.

If we throw the switch *S* in the up position, the *D* input is HIGH, and the FF is in the set mode. This does *not* mean that this FF sets at the instant its *D* input goes HIGH. A HIGH on the *D* input instructs the FF to set on the next HIGH-going C_p input. Therefore, as shown, the leading edge 4 of the clock pulse causes the FF to become set. The next clock pulse 5 is then ignored because the HIGH on the *D* input holds the FF in the set mode but it is already set.

Just before the clock pulse 6, the *D* input is pulled LOW again (switch *S* is thrown down). Thus, the FF is again in the reset mode, but it does not reset until the next HIGH-going C_p input. Note that the *Q* output goes LOW and $\overline{Q}$ goes HIGH at the instant of the sixth C_p input. After being reset on the sixth pulse, this FF ignores clock pulses 7, 8, and 9 because the LOW *D* input holds the FF in the reset mode.

Studying Fig. 5-9 further, we can see that the *D* input is pulled HIGH

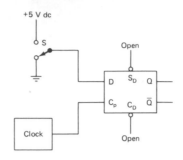

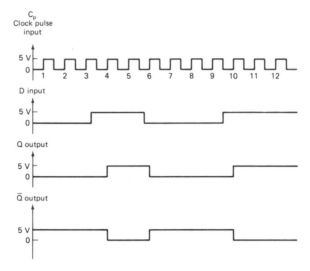

Fig. 5-9 *D*-type flip-flop wired to work synchronously with example input and output sig-
nal waveforms.

again after clock pulse 9. This puts the FF back into the set mode of operation,
causing it to become set on the tenth leading edge on the C_p input. The
subsequent pulses 11 and 12 are ignored because the continuous HIGH on
the *D* input holds the FF in the set mode.

The synchronous action of the *D*-type FF is often summarized as in
the table of Fig. 5-10. The notation t_n refers to the time before the leading

Synchronous table

	t_n	t_{n+1}	
	Input D	Output Q	$\overline{Q}$
1	L	L	H
2	H	H	L

Fig. 5-10 *D*-type flip-flop's synchronous table.

t_n is the time before the positive clock pulse.

t_{n+1} is the time after the positive clock pulse.

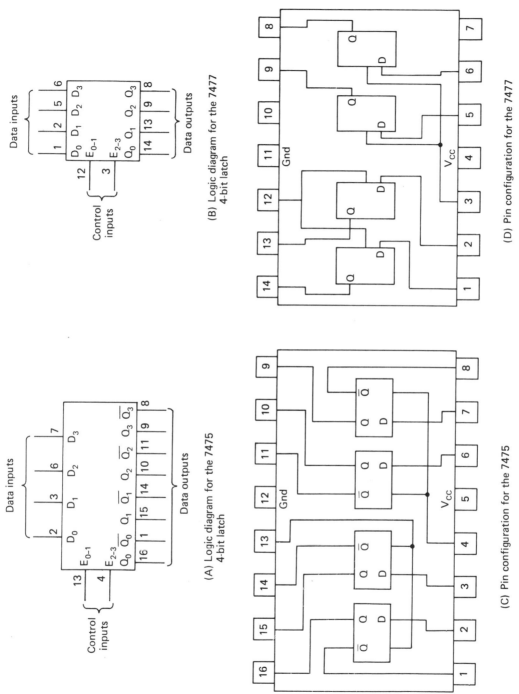

(A) Logic diagram for the 7475 4-bit latch

(B) Logic diagram for the 7477 4-bit latch

(C) Pin configuration for the 7475

(D) Pin configuration for the 7477

Fig. 5-11 Four-bit transparent latches.

121

edge of the applied clock pulse. The notation $t_n + 1$ refers to the time after the clock's leading edge. Therefore, row 1 shows that if the D input is LOW before the clock pulse (time t_n), the outputs Q and $\overline{Q}$ are LOW and HIGH, respectively, after the clock pulse ($t_n + 1$). Row 2 shows that if the D input is HIGH before the clock pulse C_p, the outputs Q and $\overline{Q}$ are HIGH and LOW, respectively, after C_p.

5-1-4   The Four-Bit Latch

The 4-bit latch, also called a transparent latch, contains four flip-flops that are similar to D-type FFs. Logic diagrams and pin configurations for two types of 4-bit latches are shown in Fig. 5-11. Note that the 7475 differs

Fig. 5-12   Transparent latches used for temporary storage of data from the MPU.

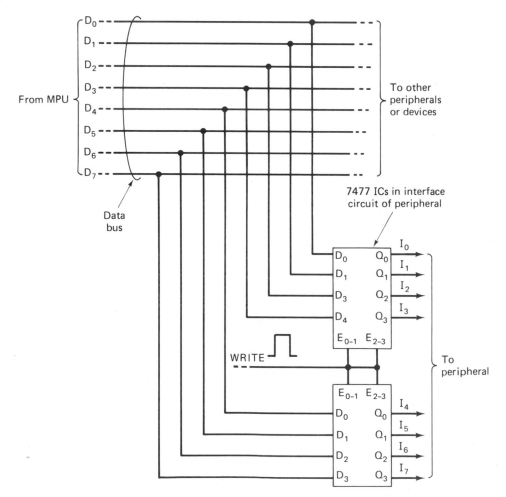

in that it has Q and $\overline{Q}$ outputs, whereas the 7477 has Q outputs only. The E_{0-1} control input, when HIGH, enables the latch, causing the data on the D_0 and D_1 inputs to appear at the Q_0 and Q_1 outputs, respectively. Similarly, a HIGH E_{2-3} signal enables D_2 and D_3 data to appear at the Q_2 and Q_3 outputs.

Commonly, the E_{0-1} and E_{2-3} control inputs of the 4-bit latch are tied together as shown in Fig. 5-12. When the enabling inputs E_{0-1} and E_{2-3} are pulled LOW, the latch locks in (latches) the input data onto the Q outputs, and the D inputs become disabled. When the latch is disabled, changes in the data on the D inputs are ignored. The circuit of Fig. 5-12 shows how an MPU can *write* 8-bit words (bytes) into a latch. A latch might be necessary in the interface circuitry of a peripheral if the peripheral is slow compared to the MPU. In this circuit, the MPU can write the data into the latch and then go on to service other peripherals or devices. This peripheral can then process the data stored in its latch when it is ready.

5-1-5 JK Flip-flops

Because of its flexibility, the *JK* FF is the most common type used in digital equipment. It is available in several TTL packages: the 7476, 7478, 74103, and the 74107 to name a few. Its logic symbol and typical package are shown in Fig. 5-13. Note in this figure that the typical *JK* FF has five inputs and two outputs. For asynchronous operation, it has a

$\overline{S_D}$ (direct set, set, or preset) input*
$\overline{C_D}$ (direct clear, clear, or reset) input

For synchronous operation, the *JK* FF has the

J input
K input
$\overline{C_p}$ (clock pulse, clock CK, or trigger T) input

As with the previously discussed FFs, the outputs are Q and $\overline{Q}$.

The $\overline{S_D}$ and $\overline{C_D}$ inputs of the *JK* flip-flop work exactly as do the $\overline{S_D}$ and $\overline{C_D}$ inputs of the *D*-type FF discussed previously. A table for asynchronous operation of the *JK* FF is shown in Fig. 5-14.

The *JK* FF shown in Fig. 5-15 is wired to work synchronously. When working synchronously, the $\overline{S_D}$ and $\overline{C_D}$ inputs are open† or held HIGH and a square-wave source (clock) drives the $\overline{C_p}$ input. The J and K inputs are controlling inputs. They tell the FF what to do on the next LOW-going clock pulse. Since the synchronously operated *JK* FF can act (respond) only

---

* Some IC packages, such as the 74103 and the 74107, do not have an $\overline{S_D}$ input and therefore cannot be set asynchronously.
† TTL inputs are not to be left open on a permanent basis.

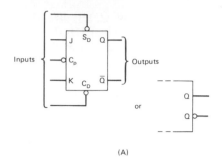

(A)

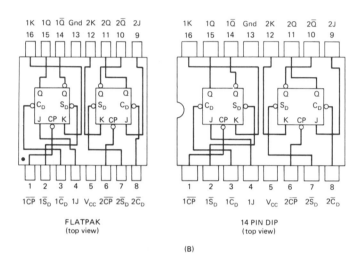

FLATPAK
(top view)

14 PIN DIP
(top view)

(B)

Fig. 5-13 (A) Logic symbol for the *JK* flip-flop; (B) IC packages containing *JK* flip-flops (TTL/SSI: 5476/7476 manufacturers' types).

Fig. 5-14 (A) Table for asynchronous operation of the JK flip-flop; (B) *JK* flip-flop wired for asynchronous operation.

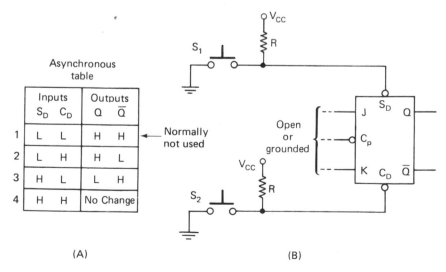

Asynchronous table

	Inputs		Outputs	
	S_D	C_D	Q	$\bar{Q}$
1	L	L	H	H
2	L	H	H	L
3	H	L	L	H
4	H	H	No Change	

Normally not used

(A)   (B)

124

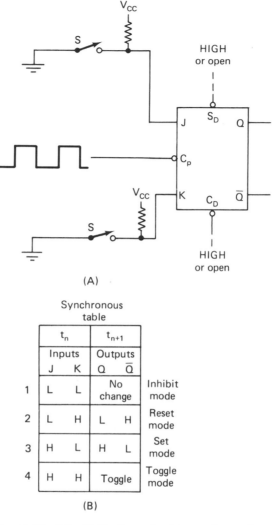

(A)

Synchronous
table

t_n		t_{n+1}		
Inputs		Outputs		
J	K	Q	$\overline{Q}$	
1 L	L	No change		Inhibit mode
2 L	H	L	H	Reset mode
3 H	L	H	L	Set mode
4 H	H	Toggle		Toggle mode

(B)

Fig. 5-15 (A) *JK* flip-flop wired to work synchronously; (B) functional table for the *JK* flip-
flop that is working synchronously.

to LOW-going clock pulses, the $\overline{C_p}$ input is circled. The table of Fig. 5-15 shows how the *JK* FF works synchronously. The term t_n refers to the time before a LOW-going clock pulse is applied. The term $t_n + 1$ refers to the time after the LOW-going clock pulse.

Row 1 of the table in Fig. 5-15 shows that if both the *J* and *K* inputs are LOW, the *Q* outputs of the *JK* FF will not change. This is the *inhibit mode* of operation. When in the inhibit mode, the *JK* FF ignores all incoming clock pulses. Thus if it is in the set state before the *J* and *K* inputs are pulled LOW, it will remain set regardless of the number of clock pulses applied. On the other hand, if this FF is initially in a reset state, it will remain reset no matter how many clock pulses are applied.

When the J input is LOW and the K input is HIGH, as shown in row 2 of the table in Fig. 5-15, the JK FF is in a *reset mode*. This means that if $J = 0$ and $K = 1$ at t_n (time before the LOW-going clock pulse), the JK FF will be reset at $t_n + 1$ (time after the LOW-going clock pulse). If it initially is in a reset state, when the J and K inputs are made LOW and HIGH, respectively, the JK FF stays reset regardless of the number of LOW-going clock pulses applied.

When the J input is HIGH and the K input is LOW, as shown in row 3 of the table in Fig. 5-15, the JK FF is in the *set mode*. When working in the set mode, the JK FF becomes set on the next LOW-going clock pulse. If the JK FF is already in the set state when placed in the set mode, it will remain set regardless of the number of clock pulses applied.

Row 4 of the table in Fig. 5-15 shows that if both the J and K inputs are HIGH (or open), the FF is in the *toggle mode*. When in the toggle mode, the JK FF's outputs change states on each and every LOW-going pulse applied to the $\overline{C_p}$ input.

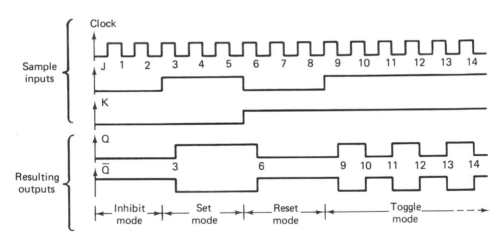

Fig. 5-16 Sample inputs and resulting outputs on the JK flip-flop.

Sample input and resulting output voltage waveforms for the JK FF are shown in Fig. 5-16. Note that though the FF is placed in the set mode, between clock pulses 2 and 3, it does not set until the third LOW-going clock pulse arrives. Similarly, this FF is placed in a reset mode, between pulses 5 and 6, but it becomes reset only after the sixth pulse arrives. Also note that the output frequency, on the Q and $\overline{Q}$ output, is half the clock frequency when the JK FF is working in the toggle mode.

5-2 Counters

JK flip-flops have many uses. Here we shall see how they work in serial counters. Serial counters, also called ripple or binary counters, are used to reduce the frequency of a clock or to keep track of the number of incoming pulses and then initiate action when the appropriate number of pulses arrives. A serial counter can also serve as the program counter in a computer or MPU. As we shall see later, the program counter enables the computer or

Fig. 5-17 (A) *JK* flip-flops wired to work as a 2-bit serial counter; (B) functional table of the 2-bit serial counter; (C) timing diagram for the 2-bit serial counter.

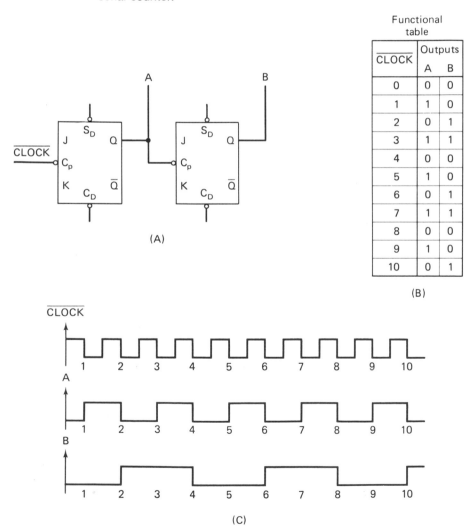

Functional table

$\overline{CLOCK}$	Outputs	
	A	B
0	0	0
1	1	0
2	0	1
3	1	1
4	0	0
5	1	0
6	0	1
7	1	1
8	0	0
9	1	0
10	0	1

(A)

(B)

(C)

MPU system to read instructions and data, out of its memory or a peripheral, in sequential order.

The simplest serial counter is one of two *JK* FFs, as shown in Fig. 5-17(A). The set and reset inputs and the *J* and *K* inputs are tied HIGH or left open temporarily, causing each FF to work in the toggle mode. When toggling, each FF's *Q* output changes state when driven by a LOW-going $\overline{C_p}$ input. Note that the $\overline{\text{CLOCK}}$ signal drives the $\overline{C_p}$ input of the first FF and that the *Q* output of this first FF drives the $\overline{C_p}$ input of the second FF. When the clock is running and the FFs are initially in the reset state, this counter's action is as shown in Figs. 5-17(B) and (C). The numbers in the $\overline{\text{CLOCK}}$ input column of the functional table represent the numbers of LOW-going $\overline{\text{CLOCK}}$ pulses applied to the $\overline{C_p}$ input of the first (left) FF. The *A* and *B* columns show the *Q* outputs of the first and second FFs, respectively.

In both Figs. 5-17(B) and (C), note that both *A* and *B* outputs are initially LOW; that is, both FFs are in the reset state. After the LOW-going $\overline{\text{CLOCK}}$ pulse 1, output *A* goes HIGH (first FF becomes set). This HIGH-going *A* output does not affect the second FF because only LOW-going $\overline{C_p}$ inputs cause toggling. After $\overline{\text{CLOCK}}$ pulse 2, output *A* goes back to LOW. This LOW-going *A* signal causes the second FF toggle, that is, to become set and cause signal *B* to go HIGH. After the next $\overline{\text{CLOCK}}$ input 3, output *A* goes HIGH again, and output *B* remains HIGH. Then $\overline{\text{CLOCK}}$ pulse 4 toggles the first FF, which in turn toggles the second, and thus both FFs return to a reset state. Therefore, two FFs, wired to work as a serial (2-bit) counter and driven by a clock, will *naturally* progress through 2^2 or 4 distinct states. We should especially note in the functional table that this 2-bit serial counter counts in binary, output *A* being the least significant bit (LSB).

If we add another FF to the 2-bit counter, we have a 3-bit counter, as shown in Fig. 5-18(A). With a $\overline{\text{CLOCK}}$ signal driving the first (far-left) FF, this counter will naturally count through 2^3 or 8 states before starting over again (overflowing). Note in Fig. 5-18(B) that this 3-bit serial counter also progresses in binary, output *A* being the LSB. Also note in Fig. 5-18(C) that output *A* changes logic levels every time the $\overline{\text{CLOCK}}$ input goes LOW. Output *B,* in turn, changes states every time signal *A* goes LOW. Likewise, output *C* changes every time signal *B* goes LOW.

As we would expect, four *JK* FFs in a 4-bit ripple counter will naturally count through 2^4 or 16 states. Each additional FF simply doubles the number of possible states.

5-2-1 Altering the Natural Count Sequence

The natural counting sequence of a serial counter can be changed. For example, the 3-bit counter of Fig. 5-18 counts through eight states. If some application demands a counter, say, with seven states, one of the natural

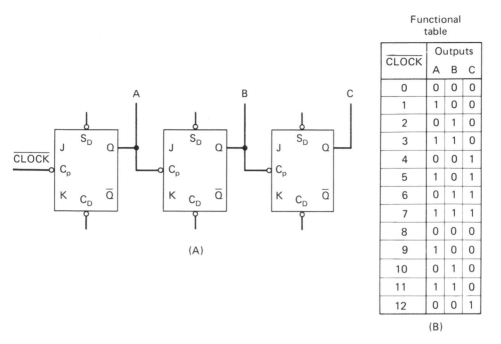

$\overline{CLOCK}$	Outputs		
	A	B	C
0	0	0	0
1	1	0	0
2	0	1	0
3	1	1	0
4	0	0	1
5	1	0	1
6	0	1	1
7	1	1	1
8	0	0	0
9	1	0	0
10	0	1	0
11	1	1	0
12	0	0	1

(B)

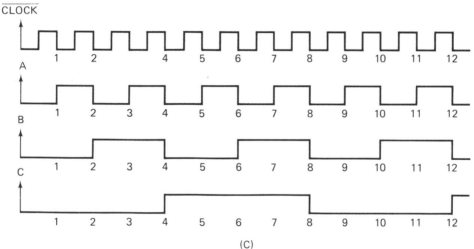

(C)

Fig. 5-18 (A) *JK* flip-flops wired to work as a 3-bit serial counter; (B) functional table of the 3-bit serial counter; (C) timing diagram for the 3-bit serial counter.

states can be skipped. The circuit of Fig. 5-19 shows how this can be done. The circuit of Fig. 5-19 is wired to skip one state, the state with outputs *A, B,* and *C* all HIGH (equivalent to decimal 7). That is, the use of the NAND gate does not permit all outputs to stay HIGH between $\overline{CLOCK}$ pulses. Therefore, as this modified 3-bit counter arrives to the state equivalent

129

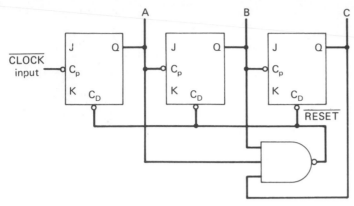

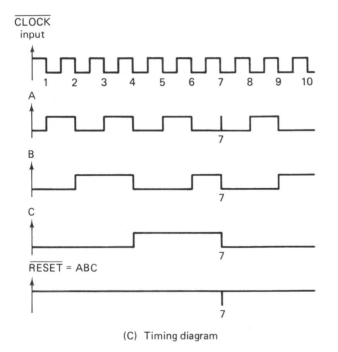

(A) A 3-bit serial counter modified to reset when the state equivalent to decimal 7 arrives

CLOCK input	A B C	Decimal equivalents	
0	L L L	0	⎫
1	H L L	1	⎪
2	L H L	2	⎪
3	H H L	3	Seven states
4	L L H	4	⎪
5	H L H	5	⎪
6	L H H	6	⎭
7	L L L	0	← Counter is reset here.
8	H L L	1	
9	L H L	2	
10	H H L	3	

(B) Functional table

(C) Timing diagram

Fig. 5-19 Mod-7 counter.

to decimal 7, outputs *A, B,* and *C* go HIGH but for only an instant. At this instant, three HIGHs are applied to the input of the NAND gate, causing its output, the $\overline{\text{RESET}}$ signal, to go LOW. The momentary active LOW $\overline{\text{RESET}}$ signal asynchronously resets all FFs. Thus, as shown in the timing diagram of Fig. 5-19, the outputs *A, B,* and *C* are all HIGH for only an instant, long enough to cause a LOW-going $\overline{\text{RESET}}$ pulse to be applied to each FF's $\overline{C_D}$ (direct clear) input. Therefore, immediately after the seventh pulse but before the eighth, outputs *A*, *B*, and *C* are all LOW.

The circuit of Fig. 5-20 is similar to the circuit of Fig. 5-19 except that the former skips states 0 and 7 when driven by a series of $\overline{\text{CLOCK}}$ pulses. In this case, instead of being reset to zero, the counter in Fig. 5-20

Fig. 5-20 Mod-6 counter.

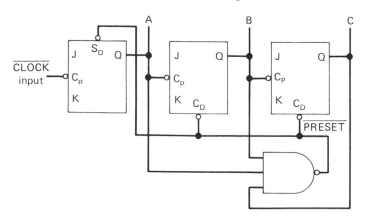

(A) A 3-bit serial counter modified
to preset to a state equivalent
to decimal 1 after state 6

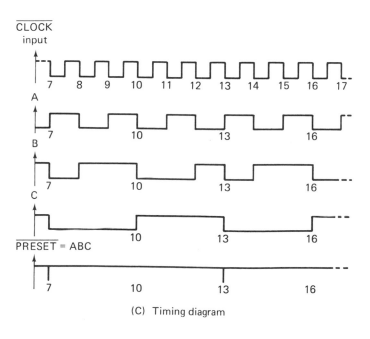

(C) Timing diagram

$\overline{\text{CLOCK}}$ inputs	A B C	Decimal equivalents	
0	L L L	0	
1	H L L	1	
2	L H L	2	
.			
.			
.			
6	L H H	6	
7	H L L	1	Counter is preset here
8	L H L	2	
9	H H L	3	Six states
10	L L H	4	
11	H L H	5	
12	L H H	6	
13	H L L	1	Preset here
14	L H L	2	
15	H H L	3	
16	L L H	4	

(B) Functional table

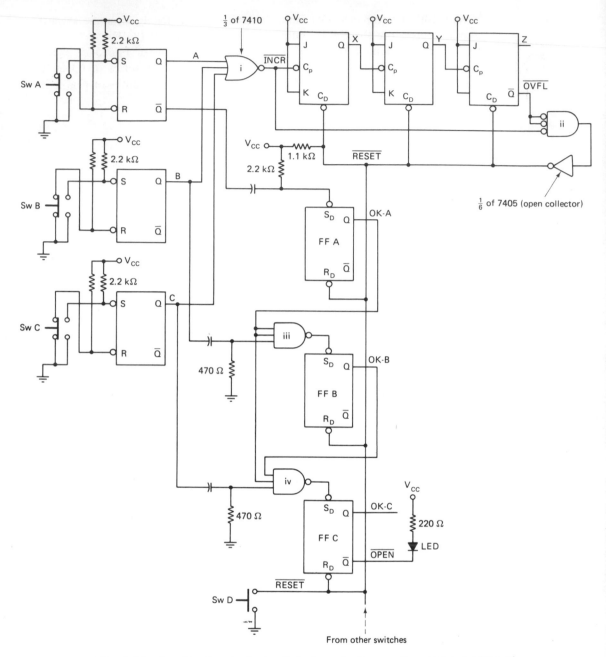

Fig. 5-21 Combination lock circuit that resets if more than three pushes of Sw *A*, Sw *B*, or Sw *C* are tried.

is *preset* to state 1 once every six $\overline{\text{CLOCK}}$ pulses. The natural state 7, with outputs *A, B,* and *C* being HIGH, exists only for an instant, long enough to preset the counter. At the instant state 7 occurs, the *Q* outputs of the FFs are all HIGH, causing a momentary active LOW $\overline{\text{PRESET}}$ signal out of the NAND gate. This momentary $\overline{\text{PRESET}}$ pulse sets the first FF and keeps the other two FFs reset, thus presetting the counter to state 1.

The circuits of Figs. 5-19 and 5-20 will repetitively progress through seven and six states respectively when a series of $\overline{\text{CLOCK}}$ pulses is applied. Counters that count through seven states are often called modulus-7 counters. Similarly, counters that have, say, five or nine states are called mod-5 or mod-9 counters, respectively.

The frequency of the output square wave from the last FF in a serial counter is much lower than the frequency of the $\overline{\text{CLOCK}}$ driving the first FF. If a 3-bit counter is counting through its eight natural states, the output frequency of the last FF is one-eighth of the $\overline{\text{CLOCK}}$ input frequency. Similarly, then, the output signal *C* of the mod-7 counter is one-seventh the $\overline{\text{CLOCK}}$ input frequency. Counters, therefore, are frequently used as square-wave frequency dividers in digital systems.

5-2-2 Counter Applications

We can improve the security of the digital combination lock circuit (Fig. 5-5) by adding a counter and other components, as shown in Fig. 5-21. The counter portion of the circuit consists of the *JK* FFs shown with outputs *X, Y,* and *Z.* After being reset, this counter counts the number of pushes of any one of the switches Sw *A,* Sw *B,* or Sw *C.* If more than three pushes are tried, this counter generates a $\overline{\text{RESET}}$ signal that clears the counter and FF *A,* FF *B,* and FF *C.* Since the number of pushes is important, the switches are debounced with the *RS* FFs. Of course, these *RS* FFs can be constructed with 7400s (quad NANDs), or *JK* FFs or *D*-type FFs can be used instead.

The serial counter, as mentioned before, can be used as a frequency divider. For example, a divide by 60 counter is shown in Fig. 5-22. With a

Fig. 5-22 Mod-6 and mod-10 counters combined to work as a divide by 60 counter.

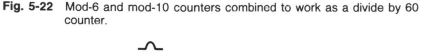

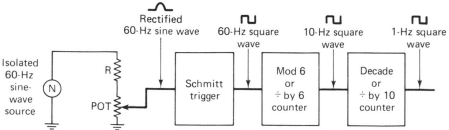

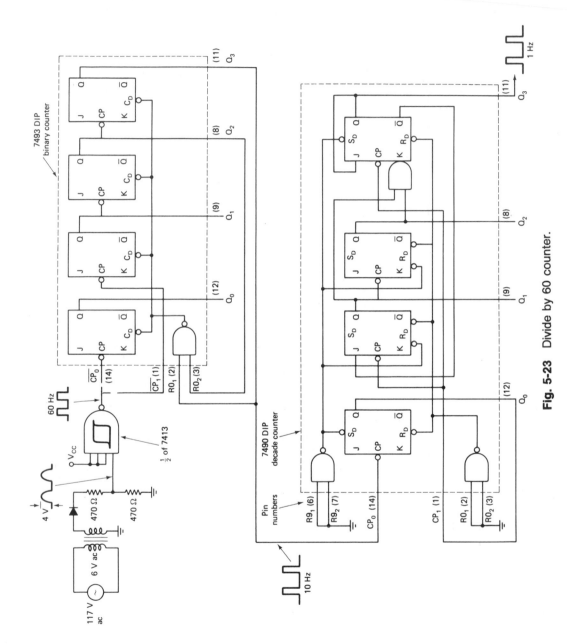

Fig. 5-23 Divide by 60 counter.

60-Hz input, this circuit has a 1-Hz output. Its details can be shown as in Fig. 5-23. In this case, the mod-6 and mod-10 counters are constructed with MSI ICs. The transformer serves to reduce the line voltage to about 6 V ac. The diode rectifies the secondary and via the voltage divider applies about 4 V peak to peak on the input of the Schmitt NAND ($\frac{1}{2}$ of 7413). The 7413 converts the halfwave-rectified waveform, off the divider, to a 60-Hz square wave. The 60-Hz square wave then drives the 7493 binary counter, which is wired to work as a mod-6 counter. Note that this 7493 has an internal NAND gate with two active HIGH inputs: the $R0_1$ and the $R0_2$ (reset to zero inputs). When $R0_1$ and $R0_2$ are HIGH, they asynchronously reset all flip-flops. In this application, $R0_1$ and $R0_2$ are wired so that the 7493 counter resets to zero on every sixth LOW-going pulse applied to its $\overline{CP_1}$ input. Only the three more significant FFs are used; that is, the far left (LSB) FF is not used in this case.

The Q_3 output of the 7493 has a 10-Hz signal that drives the $\overline{CP_0}$ input of the 7490 decade (by tens) counter. The 7490 has two sets of asynchronous inputs. When $R0_1$ *and* $R0_2$ are HIGH, the counter resets, asynchronously, to zero (all FFs reset). When asynchronous inputs $R9_1$ *and* $R9_2$ are HIGH, the counter presets to state 9 (first and fourth FFs set, second and third FFs reset). These asynchronous inputs override the clock. This means that the *JK* FFs cannot respond to clock pulses if any pair of the asynchronous inputs is active. In this application of the 7490, both sets of asynchronous inputs are disabled, causing it to count through 10 states repetitively. Thus every tenth LOW-going signal on the $\overline{CP_1}$ input of the 7490 causes it to overflow, resulting in a 1-Hz output on Q_3 when the input is 10 Hz.

5-3 Shift Counters and Registers

So far we have studied *JK* FFs in serial counters. In serial counters *JK* FFs work in toggle mode. Now we shall see how *JK* FFs work in shift counters and registers. In these applications, the *JK* FFs work in set and reset modes (rows 2 and 3 of the table in Fig. 5-5). As we shall see, shift counters and registers are used in timing generators, serial-to-parallel converters, parallel-to-serial converters, and arithmetic circuits.

A basic 4-bit shift counter is shown in Fig. 5-24. If all FFs are initially reset (cleared), this circuit will respond to a series of $\overline{CLOCK}$ pulses as shown in the table (B) and timing diagram (C) of Fig. 5-24. Note that with all FFs initially reset, the first $\overline{CLOCK}$ pulse places a HIGH into the A position (output). The second $\overline{CLOCK}$ pulse shifts the H from A to B, and another H moves into the A position. Generally, HIGHs shift into and through the counter from left to right. After the counter becomes filled with HIGHs, the LOWs proceed to shift in from the left and eventually replace the Hs with Ls. Note that a shift counter does not count in binary and that this 4-bit shift counter has eight states. Generally, a shift counter has twice as

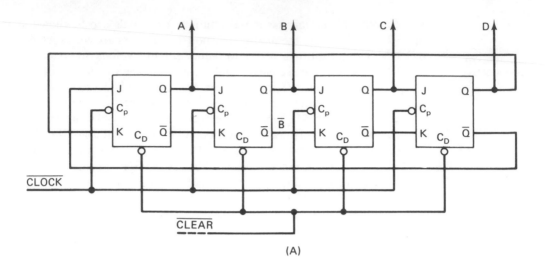

(A)

CLOCK	A	B	C	D
0	L	L	L	L
1	H	L	L	L
2	H	H	L	L
3	H	H	H	L
4	H	H	H	H
5	L	H	H	H
6	L	L	H	H
7	L	L	L	H
8	L	L	L	L
9	H	L	L	L
10	H	H	L	L
11	H	H	H	L
12	H	H	H	H
13	L	H	H	H

(B)

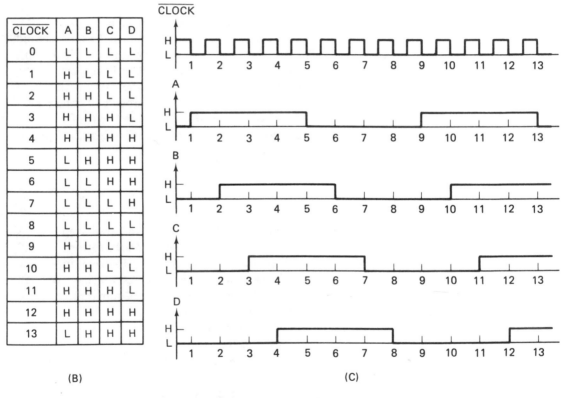

(C)

Fig. 5-24 Four-bit shift counter.

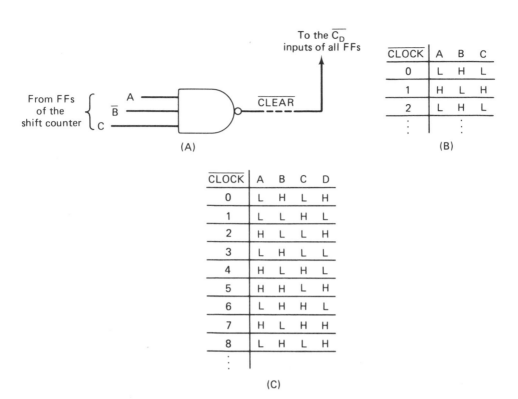

CLOCK	A	B	C
0	L	H	L
1	H	L	H
2	L	H	L
⋮		⋮	

(B)

CLOCK	A	B	C	D
0	L	H	L	H
1	L	L	H	L
2	H	L	L	H
3	L	H	L	L
4	H	L	H	L
5	H	H	L	H
6	L	H	H	L
7	H	L	H	H
8	L	H	L	H
⋮				

(C)

Fig. 5-25 (A) NAND gate used to prevent the shift counter from counting illegally; (B) table of illegal states in a 3-bit counter; (C) table of illegal states in a 4-bit counter.

many states as it has flip-flops. Therefore, a 2-bit shift counter has four states, a 3-bit shift counter has six states, etc.

It is important to know that a shift counter will not work reliably or consistently without the NAND gate of Fig. 5-25. Without this gate, or its equivalent, a shift counter might count through illegal states. Illegal states are those not following the normal shift counter's sequence, shown in Fig. 5-24(B), but instead might be as shown in (B) or (C) of Fig. 5-25. Should the counter start an illegal mode of operation, the NAND gate generates an active $\overline{\text{CLEAR}}$ signal at the instant illegal state 1010 appears at outputs A–D. When $\overline{\text{CLEAR}}$ goes LOW, all FFs become reset, and this forces the counter into its legal mode of operation.

A shift register constructed with *JK* FFs is shown in Fig. 5-26. Its name somewhat describes what it does. It is able to accept serial digital data* and shift it to the right, from FF to FF. The term *serial data* refers to information that can be processed or transferred one bit with each CLOCK

---

* The terms *data* or *data words*, used in this chapter, refer to digital information in general. Later, they will more specifically represent quantities or numbers as compared to instruction words that are used to tell the computer what to do.

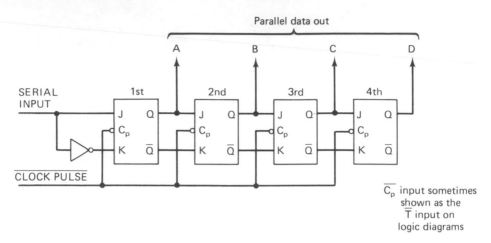

Parallel data out

A   B   C   D

$\overline{C_p}$ input sometimes
shown as the
$\overline{T}$ input on
logic diagrams

Fig. 5-26   Shift register.

pulse. In the case of the 4-bit shift register of Fig. 5-26, a 4-bit word can be serially shifted into it, and therefore be available at its A–D outputs, after four $\overline{\text{CLOCK}}$ pulses.

Serial data can be processed or transferred via a single pair of conductors. Telephone lines, for example, are commonly used to carry serial data between digital systems. Parallel data, on the other hand, require more conductors but can be processed or transferred much faster. The circuit of Fig. 5-26 is a simple serial-to-parallel converter.

Four-bit words enter the register of Fig. 5-26 by shifting in from the left by way of the SERIAL INPUT. The logic level on the SERIAL INPUT determines the logic level out of the first FF after the next LOW-going $\overline{\text{CLOCK}}$ pulse. A HIGH on the SERIAL INPUT causes a 1 to shift into the first FF and appear at output A on the next active $\overline{\text{CLOCK}}$ pulse. A LOW on the SERIAL INPUT causes a 0 at output A on the next LOW-going $\overline{\text{CLOCK}}$ pulse. With each $\overline{\text{CLOCK}}$ pulse, the logic level that was at output A moves over to B, and what was on output B moves over to C, and what was on C moves over to D, and what was on D simply disappears. The tables and timing diagrams in Fig. 5-27 show how 0101 (equivalent of decimal 5) and 0111 (equivalent of decimal 7) are shifted into the 4-bit register.

Shift registers are also used to convert parallel data to their serial equivalent. An 8-bit parallel-to-serial converter is shown in Fig. 5-28. This circuit is able to accept 8-bit data words applied to its D_7–D_0 inputs and then shift them out, serially, via the Q_H and $\overline{Q_H}$ outputs. It can also accept serial data, for temporary storage, and when needed, shift the data out. A LOW parallel load $(\overline{PL})$ input enables the 74165's NAND gates, and the 8-bit word on

	t_n	t_{n+1}			
	SERIAL INPUT	A	B	C	D
1	1	1	0	0	0
2	0	0	1	0	0
3	1	1	0	1	0
4	0	0	1	0	1

t_n is time before the LOW-going CLOCK PULSE

t_{n+1} is time after the LOW-going CLOCK PULSE

	t_n	t_{n+1}			
	SERIAL INPUT	A	B	C	D
1	1	1	0	0	0
2	1	1	1	0	0
3	1	1	1	1	0
4	0	0	1	1	1

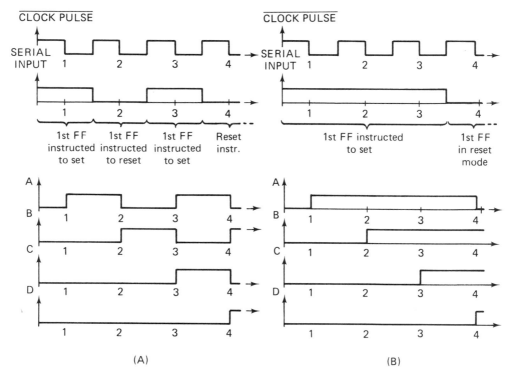

Fig. 5-27 Two examples of CLOCK PULSE and SERIAL INPUT signals and the resulting outputs on the shift register; (A) serial 0101 (decimal 5) shifted in; (B) serial 0111 (decimal 7) shifted in by four pulses of the clock.

the D_7–D_0 inputs is loaded (written) into the register. When the $\overline{PL}$ input is HIGH (inactive), the data on the D_7–D_0 inputs are ignored. While $\overline{PL}$ is HIGH, a series of clock pulse *(CP)* inputs will shift the register's data to the right, provided the chip enable $\overline{(CE)}$ input is LOW. New data can simultaneously be shifted in via the *DS* input. Since this 74165 is an 8-bit register, it takes eight clock pulses (HIGH-going) to shift an entire 8-bit word in and/or out.

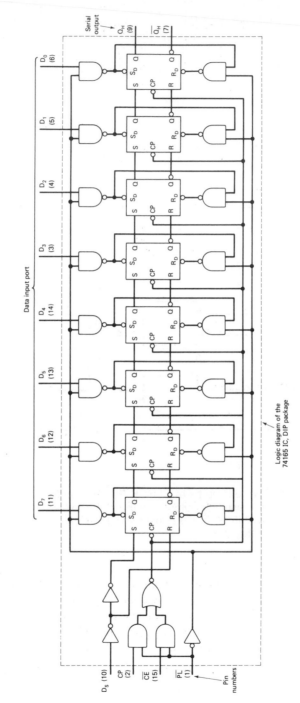

Fig. 5-28 Eight-bit serial/parallel-in, serial-out shift register.

5-4 Decoders

As mentioned in Sec. 4-20, decoders are commonly used in computer- and processor-based digital systems—so commonly in fact, that the IC manufacturers provide several MSI devices made specifically to decode combinational logic. Figure 5-29 shows a 1 of 16 decoder, sometimes called a demultiplexer.

Fig. 5-29 Four-bit binary decoder, also known as the 9311 1 of 16 decoder and the 74154 4-line to 16-line decoder.

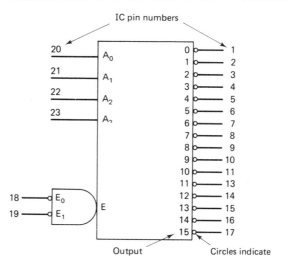

(A) Logic symbol; ACTIVE LOW output names are identified without overbars when shown inside the symbol and with overbars when shown outside the symbols

Binary numbers	Equivalent 4-bit binary input words	Output names
0	LLLL	$\overline{0}$
1	LLLH	$\overline{1}$
10	LLHL	$\overline{2}$
11	LLHH	$\overline{3}$
100	LHLL	$\overline{4}$
101	LHLH	$\overline{5}$
110	LHHL	$\overline{6}$
111	LHHH	$\overline{7}$
1000	HLLL	$\overline{8}$
1001	HLLH	$\overline{9}$
1010	HLHL	$\overline{10}$
1011	HLHH	$\overline{11}$
1100	HHLL	$\overline{12}$
1101	HHLH	$\overline{13}$
1110	HHHL	$\overline{14}$
1111	HHHH	$\overline{15}$

Outputs that go LOW only when the 4-bit input word to its left is applied while $\overline{E}_0$ and $\overline{E}_1$ are LOW

(B) Functional table

(C) DIP package (top view)

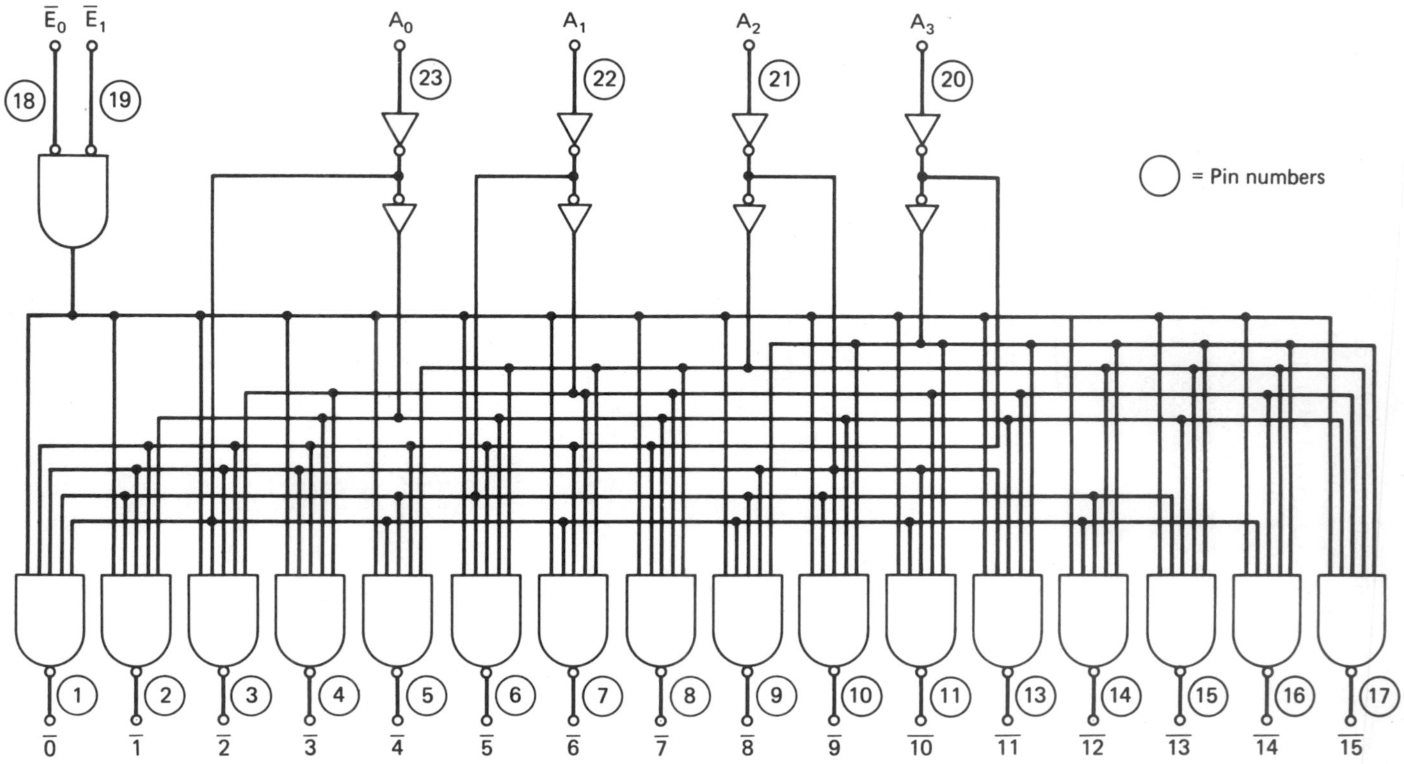

(D) Logic diagram showing equivalent gate arrangement in IC package

Fig. 5-29 (Cont.)

142

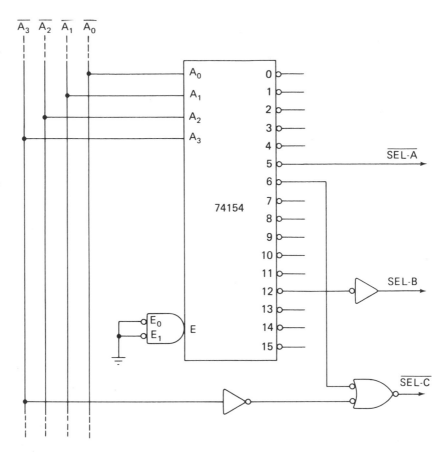

Fig. 5-30 Typical application of a 1 of 16 decoder.

It has four inputs that accept binary numbers, A_0, A_1, A_2, and A_3, and two enabling (controlling) inputs, $\overline{E_0}$ and $\overline{E_1}$. Its outputs are $\overline{0}$–$\overline{15}$. Both of the enabling inputs have to be LOW before this IC can perform its decoding function. If both $\overline{E_0}$ and $\overline{E_1}$ are LOW, one of the numbered outputs will go LOW. As shown in the table of Fig. 5-29, the output whose number corresponds with the binary equivalent input goes LOW. For example, if the A_3, A_2, A_1, and A_0 inputs are L, L, L, and L, the output $\overline{0}$ goes LOW, while all other outputs remain HIGH. Likewise, then, if binary words LLHL or HLLL are applied to the A_3–A_0 inputs, output $\overline{2}$ or $\overline{8}$ will go LOW, respectively. If either or both of the $\overline{E_0}$ and $\overline{E_1}$ inputs are HIGH, this chip (IC) is disabled, and all outputs, $\overline{0}$–$\overline{15}$, remain inactive HIGH. The circuit of Fig. 5-30 shows how a single 74154 can be used to perform the function of all three decoding circuits in Fig. 4-48.

BCD numbers must often be converted to their decimal equivalents. For example, after an electronic calculator performs arithmetic in binary, BCD, or similar number system, the final answer must be converted to decimal

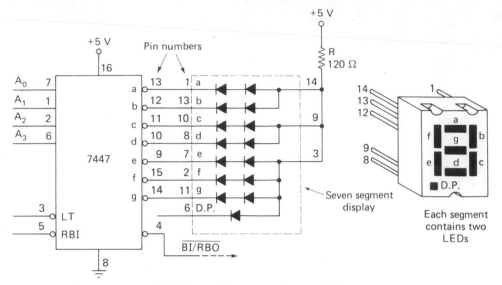

(A) BCD to seven segment decoder driving
seven segment display

	Decoder inputs				Decoder outputs							
	A_3	A_2	A_1	A_0	$\bar{a}$	$\bar{b}$	$\bar{c}$	$\bar{d}$	$\bar{e}$	$\bar{f}$	$\bar{g}$	
0	L	L	L	L	L	L	L	L	L	L	H	□
1	L	L	L	H	H	L	L	H	H	H	H	l
2	L	L	H	L	L	L	H	L	L	H	L	੨
3	L	L	H	H	L	L	L	L	H	H	L	੩
4	L	H	L	L	H	L	L	H	H	L	L	੫
5	L	H	L	H	L	H	L	L	H	L	L	S
6	L	H	H	L	H	H	L	L	L	L	L	੬
7	L	H	H	H	L	L	L	H	H	H	H	੭
8	H	L	L	L	L	L	L	L	L	L	L	੪
9	H	L	L	H	L	L	L	H	H	L	L	੧
10	H	L	H	L	H	H	H	L	L	H	L	⊏
11	H	L	H	H	L	L	H	H	L	L	H	⊐
12	H	H	L	L	L	H	L	L	L	H	H	⊔
13	H	H	L	H	L	H	H	L	H	L	L	⊏
14	H	H	H	L	L	H	H	L	H	L	L	⊑
15	H	H	H	H	H	H	H	H	H	H	H	

Active high inputs ↑

Active low outputs ↑

BCD characters

Non-BCD characters

(B) Functional table showing how the seven segment decoder's output
respond to all possible combinations of four bit inputs

Fig. 5-31 Decoder/driver.

144

so that the operator of the calculator can easily interpret it. Likewise, an electronic clock or watch runs (counts time) in binary, BCD, or related number system but must display the time in decimal. Hardware that can convert BCD numbers to their decimal equivalents is shown in Fig. 5-31. The circuit of this figure consists of two ICs: a BCD to seven-segment decoder (a 7447) and a seven-segment LED display.*

The lamp test $\overline{LT}$ input of the 7447 is used to check if all segments of the display are working. When $\overline{LT}$ is LOW, all outputs, $\bar{a}$–$\bar{g}$, of the 7447 are LOW. Thus the V_{CC} supply pushes current through each segment's LEDs via the resistor R and ground. If the ripple blanking input $\overline{RBI}$ is LOW, all outputs are HIGH, and all segments go out. If both $\overline{LT}$ and $\overline{RBI}$ are inactive HIGH, the 7447 and the seven-segment display can respond to BCD words on the A_3–A_0 inputs.

As shown in the table of Fig. 5-31, all decoder outputs except $\bar{g}$ must be LOW to illuminate a 0. LOW $\bar{b}$ and $\bar{c}$ signals display a 1, etc. The 7447 decoder is designed to provide the appropriate logic levels on the outputs $\bar{a}$–$\bar{g}$ that will display a decimal character equivalent to the 4-bit BCD word on its A_3–A_0 inputs. The resistor R in Fig. 5-31 serves to limit the current through the lighted segments. While this single resistor is convenient for experimental circuits, it does not give consistent brilliance of the various decimal characters. Individual resistors for each segment, as shown in Fig. 5-32, are better for such consistency. The $\overline{RBI}$ input and the $\overline{BI/RBO}$ output

Fig. 5-32 Decoder driving a seven-segment display with separate current-limiting resistors for each segment.

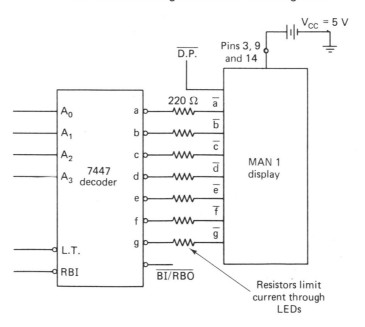

---

* This type of seven-segment display is available from several manufacturers, such as the MAN 1 by Monsanto and the TIL 302 by Texas Instruments.

are used in systems where decimal characters, that are not significant figures, are to be prevented from lighting. The $\overline{D.P.}$ input, when LOW, causes the decimal point to illuminate.

5-5 A BCD Encoder

A BCD encoder is a circuit that accepts signals from 1 of 10 push-button switches and then outputs 4-bit BCD equivalents. The keyboard of an electronic calculator requires an encoder. A simple encoder circuit is shown in Fig. 5-33. When one of its numbered push-button switches is depressed, an equivalent 4-bit BCD word appears at its outputs A_3–A_0. Typically, these 4-bit words are loaded into a register and/or a latch. In this case, for simplicity, the BCD outputs of the encoder are shown working into a decoder/driver.

When none of the push buttons in Fig. 5-33 is depressed, the $\overline{\text{INHIBIT}}$ signal is active LOW—held at ground potential by the passive pull-down R_5. This disables the decoder by holding its $\overline{RBI}$ input LOW, and all the display's segments remain dark. The term *active*, in this case, refers to the way the circuit acts to prevent a character from being displayed before any push button is depressed.

If we depress push button 0, the V_{CC} supply is applied to the $\overline{\text{INHIBIT}}$ line, causing it to go HIGH (inactive). This releases the decoder and allows it to respond to its A_3–A_0 inputs and to drive the seven-segment display. While 0 is depressed, the A_3–A_0 encoder outputs are held LOW by passive pull-downs R_1, R_2, R_3, and R_4. Four LOW outputs are equivalent to decimal 0, and all segments except g become lighted. When we depress, say, 5, diodes D_6 and D_7 become forward-biased, causing outputs A_0 and A_2 to go HIGH. Outputs A_1 and A_3 remain LOW. This set of outputs, of course, is equivalent to decimal 5, and the character 5 appears on the seven-segment display. The effects of pushing the other buttons can similarly be analyzed.

Fig. 5-33 Encoder.

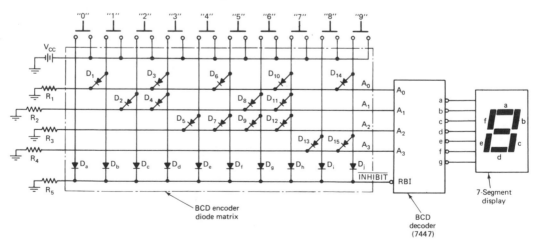

5-6 Multiplexers

Logic symbols and diagrams of two common IC multiplexers are shown in Fig. 5-34. As shown in Fig. 5-34(A), the four-input multiplexer (MUX) has four data inputs D_0–D_3. The logic signal on any one of these data inputs can be made to flow, internally through the IC, to output Y. Therefore, four separate signals can be inputs D_0–D_3 but only one of them can pass on to output Y, provided that the $\overline{\text{STROBE}}$ or $\bar{S}$ input* is active LOW. When the $\overline{\text{STROBE}}$ input is HIGH, this IC is disabled, which means that output Y remains LOW regardless of the logic signals on the other inputs. A 2-bit binary address in inputs A_1 and A_0† determines which of the four data inputs is passed through to output Y. For example, when inputs A_1 and A_0 are 0 and 0 (equivalent to decimal 0), the logic signal on input D_0 passes through to output Y. Similarly, when A_1 and A_0 are 0 and 1, respectively (equivalent to decimal 1), the signal on input D_1 passes through to output Y, etc. Generally, the decimal equivalent of each 2-bit address indicates the number of the data input that becomes internally connected (addressed) to output Y.

The eight-input multiplexer (MUX), shown in Fig. 5-34(B), works much like the four-input type. In this case, one of the eight data inputs D_0–D_7 is addressed by a 3-bit binary word on the A_3–A_0 inputs, provided that the $\overline{\text{STROBE}}$ input is active LOW. As before, the decimal equivalent of the input address indicates the number of the data input that becomes connected to output Y through the IC. The output $\overline{W}$ is always logically opposite to output Y. The output $\overline{W}$ is used if the logic signal flow through the IC is to be inverted.

The circuit of Fig. 5-35 shows a MUX application. In this example, a 2-bit binary counter drives the address inputs, A_1 and A_0, of the MUX. The strobe $\bar{S}$ input is grounded and therefore permanently enables the MUX. With each $\overline{\text{CLOCK}}$ pulse, the counter increments and thus addresses the next successive data input. The addressed data input is connected to the Y output through the MUX. As shown on the timing diagram in Fig. 5-35, four different signals, from four source devices, are applied to the data inputs. The counter's initial outputs $A_1 = 0$ and $A_0 = 0$ (between times 0 and 1) cause SIG 1 to appear at output Y. Similarly, when $A_1 = 0$ and $A_0 = 1$ (times 1 to 2), SIG 2 appears at output Y, etc. In this way multiplexers are used to transfer many different logic signals over a single pair of wires. Frequently, seven-segment displays are multiplexed to reduce the amount of hardware and the number of interconnections.

5-7 Parity Generators/Checkers

As discussed in Sec. 2-11, there is a probability of error, due to noise or device failure, when digital information is transmitted from one location to

---

* The $\overline{\text{STROBE}}$ input is also called the $\overline{\text{ENABLING}}$ or $\bar{E}$ input by some IC manufacturers.

† The address inputs A_1 and A_0 are also referred to as the select inputs S_1 and S_0.

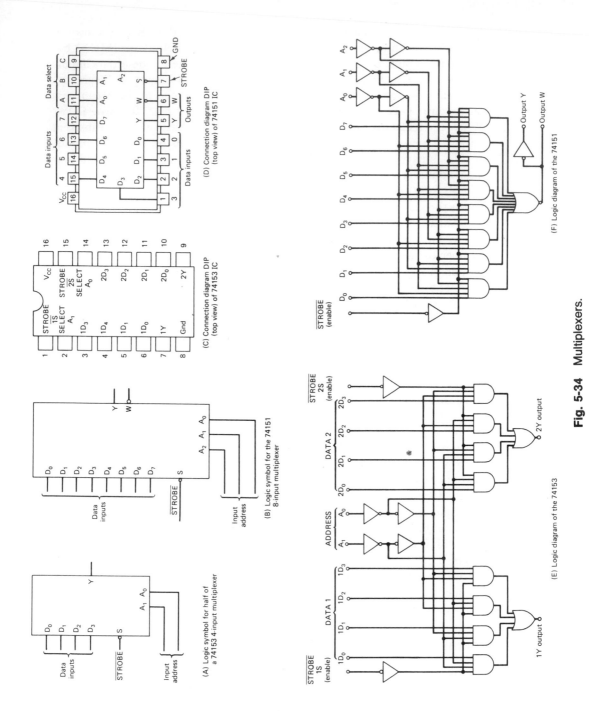

Fig. 5-34 Multiplexers.

148

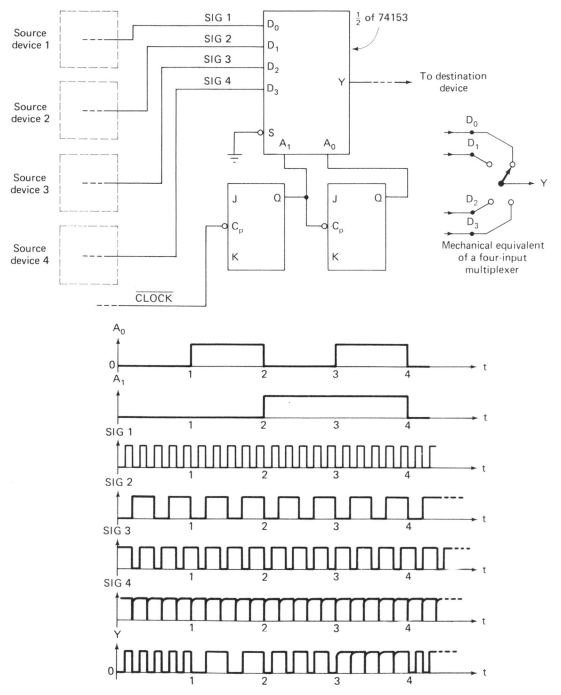

Fig. 5-35 Signals from four source devices being multiplexed to a single destination device.

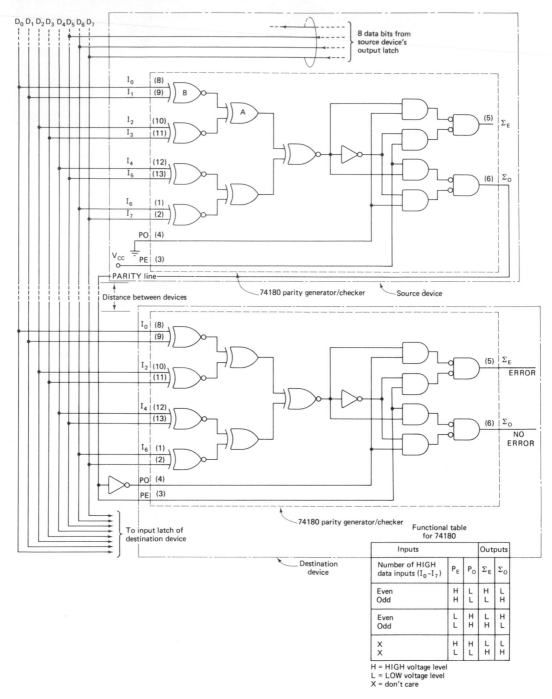

Functional table
for 74180

Inputs			Outputs	
Number of HIGH data inputs (I_0-I_7)	P_E	P_O	Σ_E	Σ_O
Even	H	L	H	L
Odd	H	L	L	H
Even	L	H	L	H
Odd	L	H	H	L
X	H	H	L	L
X	L	L	H	H

H = HIGH voltage level
L = LOW voltage level
X = don't care

Fig. 5-36 Application of parity generator/checker.

another. Use of a parity bit on each digital word transferred is a common method of detecting such errors. That is, the source device can add a parity bit such that the total number of HIGH bits in each word transmitted is even in an even parity system. Or the parity bit can make the total number of HIGHs odd in an odd parity system. The destination device then "looks at" the number of HIGHs in each word received. If an odd number of HIGHs arrives, at the destination, in an even parity system, the destination device can execute appropriate action, such as request retransmission, signal (flag) the operator, or simply stop transmission.

Parity generator/checker circuits are shown in Fig. 5-36. The 74180 in the source device generates even parity by applying the appropriate logic on the PARITY line. If an error occurs and an odd number of HIGHs arrives at the destination device, its 74180 generates an active HIGH ERROR signal which can be used to initiate a retransmission or halt routine.

A functional table for the 74180 is shown in Fig. 5-36. It shows that if the *PE* and *PO* inputs are tied HIGH and LOW, respectively, as they are in the source device of Fig. 5-36, and if the number of HIGHs on the data line is odd, the Σ_O output (PARITY bit) is HIGH. Thus the total number of HIGHs transmitted is even. On the other hand, if the number of HIGHs on the data bus is even, the Σ_O output pulls the PARITY line LOW, and the number of HIGHs in the 9-bit word applied to the bus is again even. Therefore, if the *PE* input is tied HIGH in the source device, it generates an even parity bit.

In the destination device, the 74180 is wired so that its output ERROR signal is inactive LOW and its signal NO ERROR is active HIGH when the number of HIGHs received is even, as would be the case if no error occurs during transfer of the 9-bit word. On the other hand, if an error occurs causing an odd number of HIGHs in the 9-bit word received, the signals ERROR and NO ERROR become HIGH (active) and LOW (inactive), respectively.

Gate *A* in the upper 74180 of Fig. 5-36 is an exclusive OR. Its output is HIGH only if one of its inputs is HIGH. In other words, the *exclusive OR* gate's output is LOW if both inputs are LOW or if both inputs are HIGH. Gate *B,* on the other hand, is an *exclusive NOR*. Its output is HIGH only if both inputs are HIGH or if both inputs are LOW; that is, its output is LOW if its two inputs have opposite logic levels applied.

When data are to be transferred serially, parity bits can be generated and checked with the use of flip-flops, as shown in Fig. 5-37. For even parity, the flip-flops are initially reset, and the parity time bit (PTB) is LOW. One bit of SERIAL DATA is then transferred with each $\overline{\text{CLOCK}}$ pulse. If the SERIAL DATA bit is HIGH, the source FF toggles on the next $\overline{\text{CLOCK}}$ pulse. If the SERIAL DATA bit is LOW, this FF's state is unchanged on the next $\overline{\text{CLOCK}}$ pulse. The source FF has a LOW Q output if an even number of HIGHs (SERIAL DATA pulses) passes through to the transmission line. Its Q output is HIGH if an odd number of HIGHs passes. Thus if there is an even number of HIGHs in an 8-bit serial word, the source

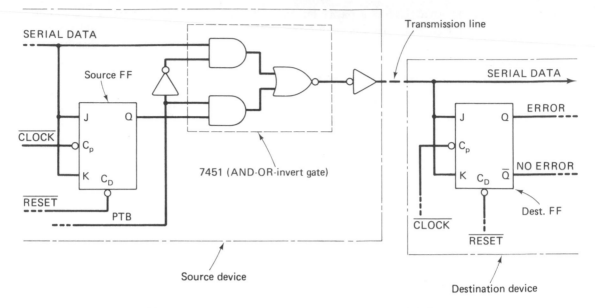

Fig. 5-37 Parity generator and checker for serial data.

FF is reset after the eighth $\overline{\text{CLOCK}}$ pulse. The PTB signal goes HIGH on the ninth $\overline{\text{CLOCK}}$ pulse and thus places a LOW on the transmission line as the ninth (parity) bit. Had an odd number of HIGHs passed in the first eight $\overline{\text{CLOCK}}$ pulses, the source FF's Q output would be HIGH on the ninth pulse, causing a HIGH parity bit to be placed on the transmission line. In a similar way, the dest. FF, in the destination device, is in the set or reset state after the number of HIGHs received is odd or even, respectively. Therefore, the ERROR and NO ERROR outputs of the dest. FF can be interrogated after each ninth $\overline{\text{CLOCK}}$ pulse to determine if an error occurred during the transfer.

5-8 Arithmetic Circuits

We shall often be confronted with arithmetic-performing circuits in digital systems. Sometimes the IC or circuit of ICs that specifically does (is dedicated to) arithmetic operations is called the arithmetic logic unit (ALU). Here we shall see how addition and subtraction of binary numbers can be performed.

Figure 5-38 shows a circuit that is capable of adding two 8-bit binary numbers. In microprocessor language, each such number is called a byte of data. Each 7483 IC is a 4-bit binary adder with carry-in (C_{in}) and carry-out (C_o) capability. This means that each 7483 accepts two 4-bit binary numbers, one on its A_4–A_1 inputs and the other on the B_4–B_1 inputs. It also has a C_{in} input that accepts *carries* from lesser significant bits being added.

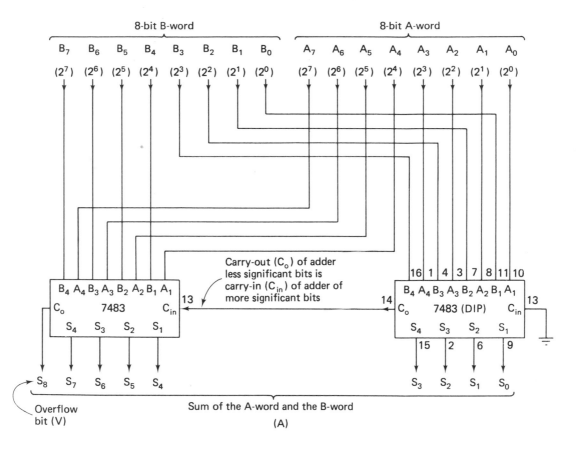

Fig. 5-38 (A) Two *r*-bit binary adder chips (7483s) wired to add two 8-bit binary numbers; (B) table of 8-bit binary numbers and their binary sums.

Each adder's outputs include a 4-bit sum, the S_4–S_1 output, and a C_o output that serves to carry overflows into more significant binary columns.

In the circuit of Fig. 5-38, the right-hand 7483 adds the 4 lower significant bits of the *A*-word to the 4 lower bits of the *B*-word. Its C_{in} pin is grounded because there are no bits of lesser significance that can produce a

The A-word		The B-word		The S-word or sum		Ninth-bit overflow
In binary	Hex	In binary	Hex	In binary	Hex	
0 1 1 0 1 1 0 1	6D	0 0 1 1 1 0 1 1	3B	1 0 1 0 1 0 0 0	A8	0
0 0 1 1 0 1 1 1	37	0 1 0 1 1 1 0 0	5C	1 0 0 1 0 0 1 1	93	0
0 0 0 1 1 1 1 1	1F	0 0 1 1 0 1 1 0	36	0 1 0 1 0 1 0 1	55	0
0 0 0 0 0 0 0 1	01	1 1 1 1 1 1 1 1	FF	0 0 0 0 0 0 0 0	00	1
1 0 1 0 1 0 1 0	AA	0 1 0 1 0 1 0 1	55	1 1 1 1 1 1 1 1	FF	0

(B)

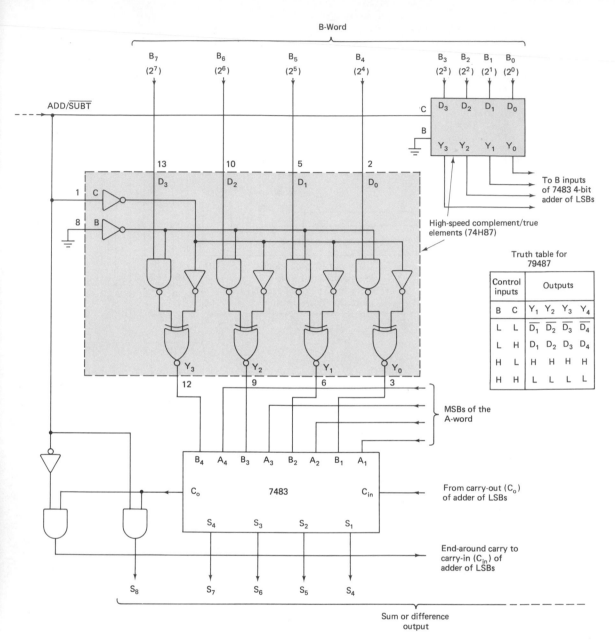

Fig. 5-39 A one's complementer chip (74H87) gives the adder chip (7483) capability to add or subtract binary numbers.

carry-in. A carry can result, however, from the addition of the $A_3–A_0$ bits with the $B_3–B_0$ bits. If such a carry occurs, sometimes called a half-carry in microprocessor language, the C_o output of the right-hand 7483 goes HIGH. This C_o becomes the carry-in of the left-hand (more significant bit) adder.

This left adder then adds the 4 higher significant bits of the A-word to the 4 higher bits of the B-word; the C_{in} bit (half-carry) is added to the 2^4 bits. Overall, the 9-bit output, bits S_8–S_0, is the binary sum of the 8-bit A-word and the 8-bit B-word. Some examples of inputs and resulting outputs are shown in the table of Fig. 5-38(B).

The basic 8-bit binary adder circuit of Fig. 5-38 can be modified, as shown in Fig. 5-39, to perform *either* addition or subtraction. The 74H87s in Fig. 5-39 can be instructed to pass the B-word in true form on to the B inputs of the 7483 adders. True form means that the logic levels of the individual bits are unchanged. Or the 74H87 can be instructed to complement each bit before applying it to the B inputs of the 4-bit adders. In this circuit, the B-word passes in true form when the control signal ADD/$\overline{SUBT}$ is HIGH. On the other hand, when the signal ADD/$\overline{SUBT}$ is LOW, the B-word is complemented. We can recall Sec. 2-7 to note that if a number B is to be subtracted from number A, we can add the one's complement of B to A to obtain their difference less 1. The 1 is then added, by an end-around-carry process, to obtain the correct difference. In this circuit of Fig. 5-39, the left-hand C_0 bit is the ninth or overflow bit during add operations, or C_0 provides the end-around-carry bit during subtract operations. Overall, the sum of the A-word and B-word appears at the S outputs when control signal ADD/$\overline{SUBT}$ is HIGH, or the difference in the A-word and the B-word appears at the S outputs when signal ADD/$\overline{SUBT}$ is LOW.

5-9 The Monostable Multivibrator/Timer

The TTL family's 74121 IC is called a *monostable multivibrator,* or a *one-shot* or a *single-shot.* It is similar to a single JK flip-flop in that it has two complementary outputs, the Q and the $\overline{Q}$ outputs. In the previous sections we learned that the JK FF has *two* stable output states, the set and the reset states, and is therefore called a bistable FF. The monostable multivibrator, as its name implies, has only one stable state. The 74121's stable state can be called the reset state because when stable, the one-shot's Q output is LOW and its $\overline{Q}$ output is HIGH. The one-shot (OS) stays in its stable state until the proper combination of input signals is applied. When this proper combination is applied, the OS switches (is triggered) to its unstable (set) state but typically stays that way for only a short time. After this short time, the OS switches back to its stable state.

The pin configuration and functional table of the 74121 are shown in Fig. 5-40. Its inputs are $\overline{A_1}$, $\overline{A_2}$, and B. If input B is hard-wired HIGH and a LOW-going signal is applied to either the $\overline{A_1}$ or the $\overline{A_2}$ input, the 74121 switches, momentarily, from its stable to its unstable state. Or if either or both $\overline{A_1}$ or $\overline{A_2}$ are LOW and a HIGH-going signal is applied to input B, this OS is triggered to go into its momentary unstable state.

The 74121's outputs vs. LOW-going $\overline{A_1}$ or $\overline{A_2}$ or HIGH-going B inputs

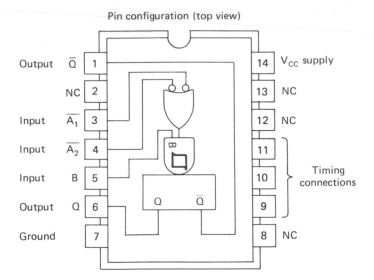

Pin configuration (top view)

Output	Q̅	1
	NC	2
Input	A̅₁	3
Input	A̅₂	4
Input	B	5
Output	Q	6
Ground		7

14 — V_{CC} supply
13 — NC
12 — NC
11 — } Timing connections
10 — }
9 — }
8 — NC

Function table

Inputs			Outputs	
A̅₁	A̅₂	B	Q	Q̅
L	X	H	L	H
X	L	H	L	H
X	X	L	L	H
H	H	X	L	H
H	↓	H	⊓	⊔
↓	H	H	⊓	⊔
↓	↓	H	⊓	⊔
L	X	↑	⊓	⊔
X	L	↑	⊓	⊔

H = HIGH voltage level
L = LOW voltage level
X = don't care
↑ = LOW to HIGH-transition
↓ = HIGH to LOW transition

Fig. 5-40   74121's (monostable multivibrator's) pin configuration and function table.

are shown in (A) and (B) of Fig. 5-41. The output pulse widths t_W can be varied from fractions of microseconds to several seconds by selecting proper timing components. The nomograph in Fig. 5-41 shows how the output pulse widths t_W vary vs. externally connected timing components C_{ext} and R_{ext}. For example, if $C_{ext} = 1$ μF and $R_{ext} = 3$ kΩ, the 74121 will output pulses with $t_W \cong 2$ msec.

An IC called the 555 timer is a very flexible device that is used to perform a variety of logic functions. This timer is available in 8-pin packages, shown in Fig. 5-42. With just two external timing components, R_{ext} and C_{ext}, shown in Fig. 5-43, the 555 timer works as a one-shot.

As shown in Fig. 5-43, a voltage divider of three equal resistors R is inside the 555 timer. This divider provides reference voltages, $\frac{2}{3}V_{CC}$ and $\frac{1}{3}V_{CC}$, for the *comparators* 1 and 2. When the 555 is used in TTL circuits, $V_{CC} = 5$ V typically, and $\frac{2}{3}V_{CC} \cong 3.3$ V and $\frac{1}{3}V_{CC} \cong 1.7$ V. Comparator 1's output $\overline{SET}$ is HIGH if the voltage on pin 6 is less than 3.3 V. Signal $\overline{SET}$ goes LOW if the voltage on pin 6 becomes larger than 3.3 V. Comparator 2's output $\overline{RESET}$ is HIGH if signal $\overline{IN}$ is larger than 1.7 V. Signal $\overline{RESET}$ goes LOW if input $\overline{IN}$ is pulled LOW.

Assuming that the input signal $\overline{IN}$ is inactive HIGH and that the flip-flop is initially set, the HIGH logic of the Q output saturates transistor Q_D, which is called the discharge transistor. This effectively places a short

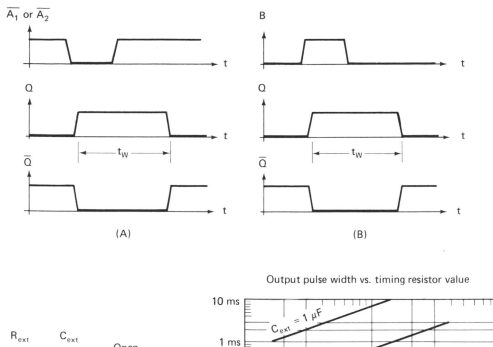

(A)

(B)

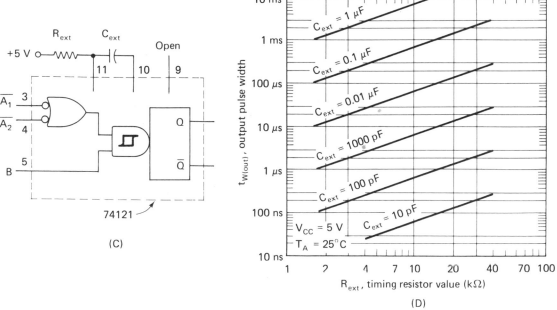

Output pulse width vs. timing resistor value

(C)

(D)

Fig. 5-41 (A) Outputs Q and $\overline{Q}$ vs. LOW-going A_1 and A_2 while input B is HIGH; (B) outputs Q and $\overline{Q}$ vs. HIGH-going input B while $\overline{A_1}$ and $\overline{A_2}$ are LOW; (C) typical connection of external timing components; (D) nomogram for selection timing components.

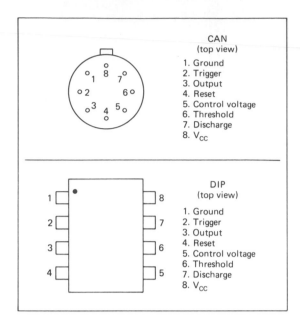

CAN
(top view)
1. Ground
2. Trigger
3. Output
4. Reset
5. Control voltage
6. Threshold
7. Discharge
8. V_{CC}

DIP
(top view)
1. Ground
2. Trigger
3. Output
4. Reset
5. Control voltage
6. Threshold
7. Discharge
8. V_{CC}

Fig. 5-42 Packages and pin configurations for the
555 timer.

across the external capacitor C_{ext}, preventing it from accepting a charge. The 555 is thus in its stable state, and its output signal OUT is LOW. Now if a LOW-going $\overline{IN}$ signal is applied, a LOW $\overline{RESET}$ signal is generated, within the 555, causing the FF to become reset. Its resulting LOW Q output causes transistor Q_D to cut off, and the signal OUT goes HIGH (into its unstable state). The capacitor C_{ext} starts to charge, through R_{ext}, and when its voltage V_c crosses 3.3 V, the $\overline{SET}$ signal goes LOW and sets the FF, causing signal OUT to go LOW again. The transistor then saturates again and discharges C_{ext}.

Generally, as shown in (B) of Fig. 4-43, a LOW-going $\overline{IN}$ signal causes a momentary HIGH OUT signal. The pulse width t_W of the OUT signal is determined by the time constant of the timing components. More specifically, $t_W = 1.1 R_{ext} C_{ext}$.

5-10 Clock Circuits

Microcomputers are complex systems that contain many circuits with specialized functions. Each of these circuits must perform its function at the proper instant of time. Clocks or clock circuits are used in such systems to provide the correct timing.

The 555 timer, discussed in Sec. 5-9, can also be used as a rectangular

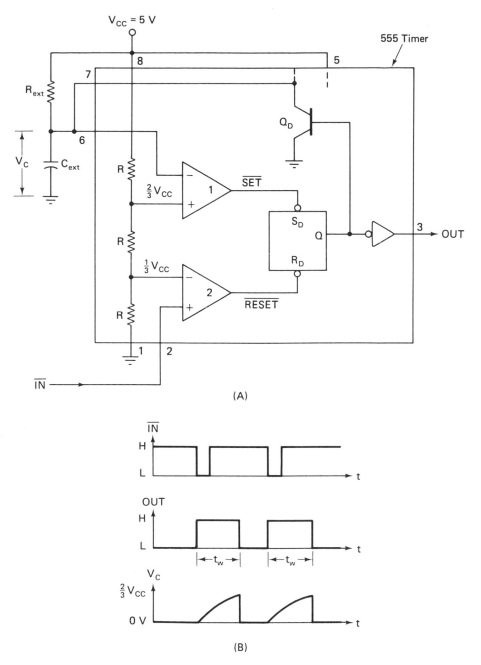

Fig. 5-43 (A) 555 timer wired to work as a monostable multivibrator (one-shot); (B) output vs. input, and C_{ext}'s voltage waveforms of the 555 one-shot.

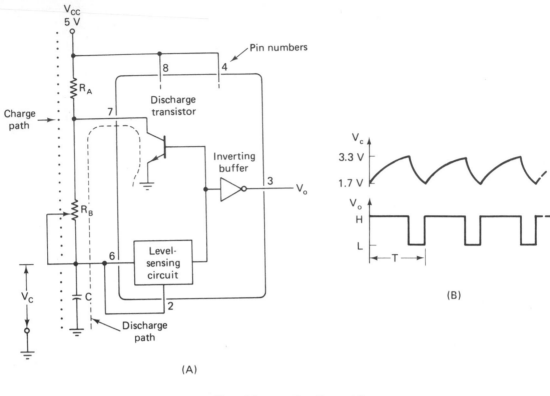

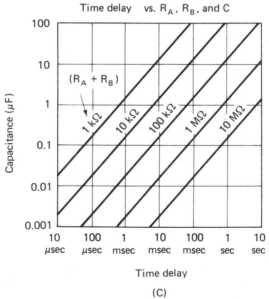

Fig. 5-44 (A) 555 timer wired to work as a variable square-wave generator; (B) its capacitor and output voltage waveforms; (C) nomogram for selection of timing components.

wave generator when wired as shown in Fig. 5-44(A). When the 5-V supply is applied, the capacitor C proceeds to charge through resistances R_A and R_B (dotted-line path). Initially, when the capacitor's voltage is small, the output of the level-sensing circuit is LOW. This LOW cuts off the transistor and, via the inverting buffer, causes a HIGH output V_o at pin 3. As the capacitor C charges and V_c reaches 3.3 V, the level-sensing circuit's output goes HIGH. This turns transistor Q_D on, which provides a discharge path to ground through R_B (dashed-line path). When C discharges to 1.7 V, the level-sensing circuit's output goes LOW again, which starts another cycle. See the capacitor's voltage V_c and the output voltage V_o waveforms in Fig. 5-44(B). Since R_B is variable, the time constant of the charge and discharge paths can be varied, and therefore the output frequency of V_o can be varied.

Fig. 5-45 *RC* clock circuits; (A) transistor astable multivibrator; (B) Schmitt NAND clock; (C) CMOS NOR gate clock; (D) Schmitt inverter clock.

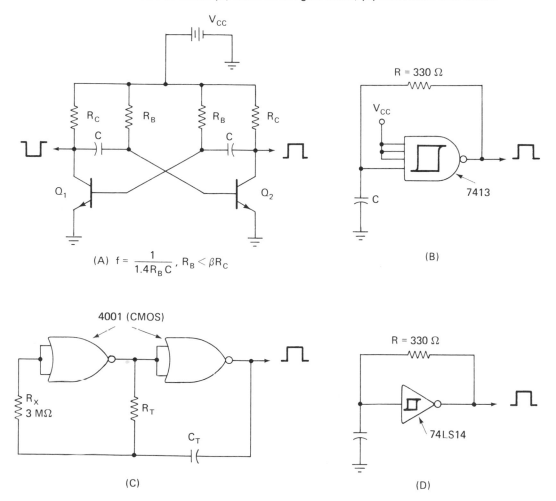

(A) $f = \dfrac{1}{1.4 R_B C}$, $R_B < \beta R_C$

(B)

(C)

(D)

The nomograph of Fig. 5-44(C) can be used to determine the output frequency for various values of R_A, R_B, and C.

The 555 rectangular wave generator is called an RC (resistor-capacitor) generator because its output frequency is determined by the values of the externally wired resistors and capacitor. Other commonly used RC clock circuits are shown in Fig. 5-45. All these clock circuits, including the 555 generator, are in the category called *astable* (not stable) *multivibrators*.

Most MPUs require clock sources that are more complex and accurate than are simple RC clock circuits. The 6800 MPU requires a two-phase clock. As shown in Fig. 5-46, crystal oscillator clocks are available for this

Fig. 5-46 Packaged crystal oscillator clock for the 6800 microprocessor; (A) package; (B) logic diagram; (C) output waveforms.

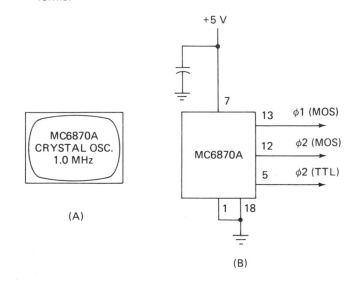

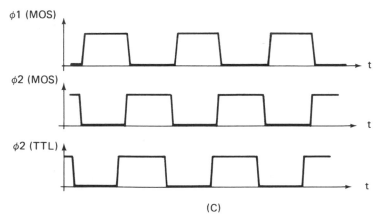

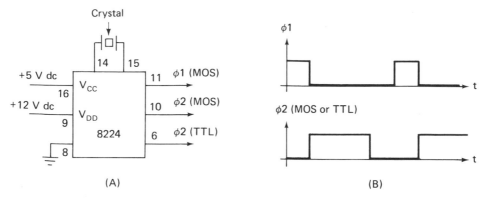

Fig. 5-47   8224 clock for the 8080 microprocessor; (A) partial logic diagram; (B) output waveforms.

purpose.* Its ϕ_1(MOS) and ϕ_2(MOS) output signals are used to drive the 6800 MPU, while the ϕ_2(TTL) output is available to synchronize peripherals with the MPU. The peripherals often contain TTL devices, and the ϕ_2(TTL) signal is able to drive, at least a few, TTL inputs. The ϕ_2(MOS) signal is intended to drive the MOS input of the MPU.

The 8080 MPU also requires a two-phase clock, and the 8224 package is available for this purpose. As shown in Fig. 5-47, its ϕ_1 and ϕ_2 signals differ from those of the 6800 MPU.

Problems

5-1   Referring to the circuit and signals $\bar{S}$ and $\bar{R}$ of Fig. 5-48, sketch the resulting outputs Q and $\bar{Q}$.

Fig. 5-48

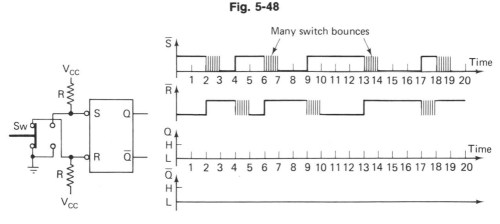

* A number of MPUs have a built-in clock. Such MPUs require an external capacitor or crystal for frequency selection.

5-2 Referring to the circuit and signals S and R of Fig. 5-49, sketch the resulting outputs Q and $\overline{Q}$.

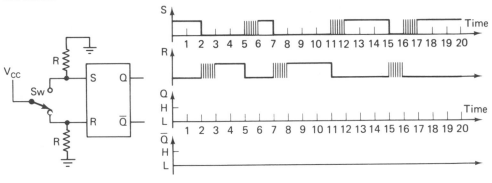

Fig. 5-49

5-3 Referring to the circuit of Fig. 5-50, and assuming that the A and B (left side) FFs are initially set while the C and D FFs are reset, sketch a functional table that shows how the A–D outputs respond to eight consecutive CLOCK pulses.

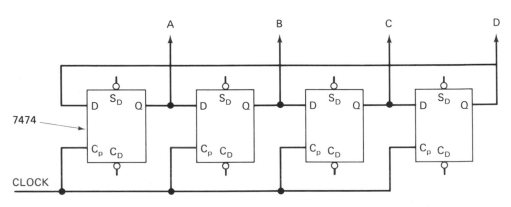

Fig. 5-50 Circuit consisting of two dual D-type flip-flops (7474s).

5-4 Referring to the circuit of Fig. 5-50, and assuming that the A (far-left) FF is initially set while the B, C, and D FFs are reset, sketch a functional table that shows how the A–D outputs respond to eight consecutive CLOCK pulses.

5-5 Show how to wire a $\overline{\text{PRESET}}$ input signal onto the circuit of Fig. 5-50 that will, when LOW, cause signals A, B, C, and D to asynchronously preset to 1, 1, 0, and 0, respectively.

5-6 Show how to wire a $\overline{\text{PRESET}}$ input signal onto the circuit of Fig. 5-50 that will, when LOW, cause signals *A, B, C,* and *D* to asynchronously preset to 1, 0, 0, and 0, respectively.

For Problems 5-7–5-10, assume that the signals of Fig. 5-51 are applied to the circuit of Fig. 5-12.

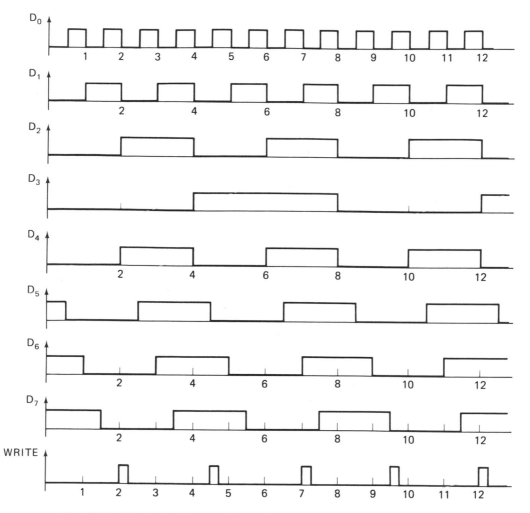

Fig. 5-51 Example of type of data that can be carried by an 8-bit bus.

5-7 What are the hexadecimal and octal equivalents of the binary information on the data bus immediately after times 1, 2, 3, 4, 5, and 6?

5-8 What are the hexadecimal and octal equivalents of the binary information on the data bus immediately after times 7, 8, 9, 10, 11, and 12?

5-9 What are the hexadecimal and octal equivalents of the binary information on the latches' outputs (I_7-I_0) immediately after times 1, 2, 3, 4, 5, and 6?

5-10 What are the hexadecimal and octal equivalents of the binary information on the latches' outputs (I_7-I_0) immediately after times 7, 8, 9, 10, 11, and 12?

5-11 A *JK* flip-flop has the inputs of Fig. 5-52 applied. Sketch the resulting Q and $\overline{Q}$ output signals on the scales provided.

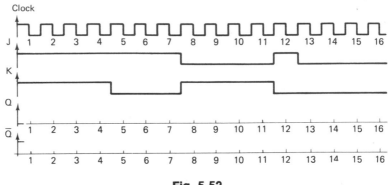

Fig. 5-52

5-12 Redraw the circuit of Fig. 5-5 using *JK* flip-flops instead of *RS* types. Use them asynchronously.

5-13 Referring to the circuit and $\overline{\text{CLOCK}}$ input signal of Fig. 5-53, (a) sketch the resulting *A–D* outputs onto the scales provided, and (b) fill in the functional table.

5-14 Referring to the circuit of Fig. 5-54, show how its outputs *A, B,* and *C* respond to a series of $\overline{\text{CLOCK}}$ pulses. Use the table provided, and note that this counter is initially cleared.

5-15 Referring to the circuit of Fig. 5-55, show how its outputs *A, B,* and *C* respond to a series of $\overline{\text{CLOCK}}$ pulses. Use the table provided, and note that this counter is initially in state 6.

5-16 If, in the circuit of Fig. 5-54, the $\overline{Q}$ output of the *B* flip-flop disconnects from the NAND gate's input, show a functional table of how the *A, B,* and *C* outputs will respond to a series of $\overline{\text{CLOCK}}$ pulses. The NAND gate is $\frac{1}{3}$ of 7410. Assume that the disconnected input lead is open.

5-17 If, in the circuit of Fig. 5-55, the $\overline{S_D}$ input of the *A* flip-flop disconnects, show a functional table of how the *A, B,* and *C* outputs

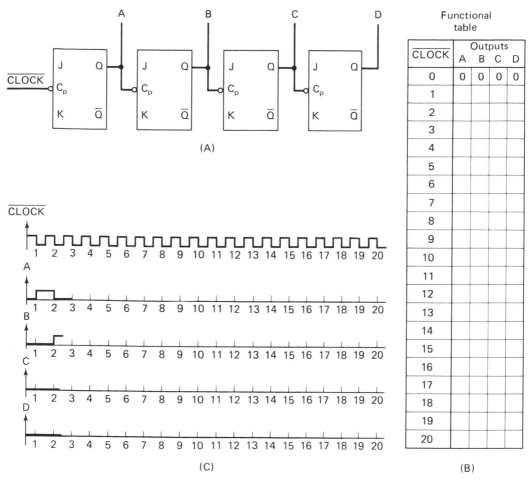

Fig. 5-53 (A) *JK* flip-flops wired to work as a 4-bit serial counter; (B) functional table of the 4-bit serial counter; (C) timing diagram for the 4-bit serial counter.

respond to a series of $\overline{\text{CLOCK}}$ pulses. Assume that this counter is initially in state 6.

5-18 Referring to the circuit of Fig. 5-21, what will cause the $\overline{\text{INCR}}$ (increment) signal to go active LOW?

5-19 If the Sw *D* switch is pushed in the circuit of Fig. 5-21, what happens?

5-20 Can gate i and gate ii be on the same chip (a 7410)? Why?

5-21 Referring to the circuit of Fig. 5-21, what will cause the $\overline{\text{OVFL}}$ (overflow) signal to go active LOW? Can it stay LOW for very long? Why?

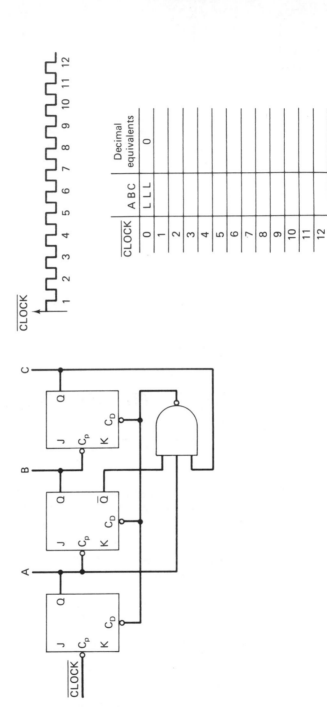

$\overline{\text{CLOCK}}$	A B C	Decimal equivalents
0	L L L	0
1		
2		
3		
4		
5		
6		
7		
8		
9		
10		
11		
12		

Fig. 5-54

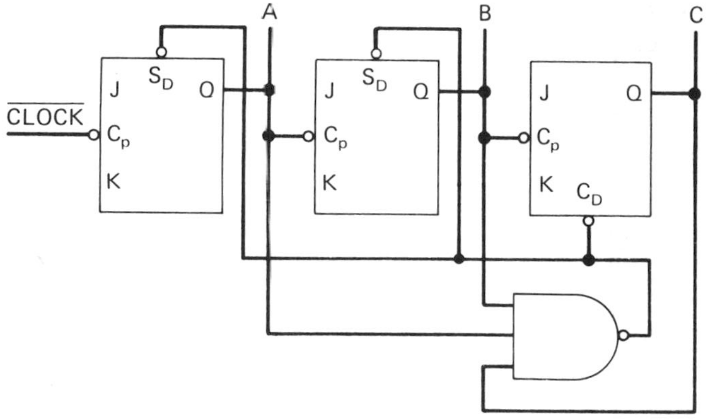

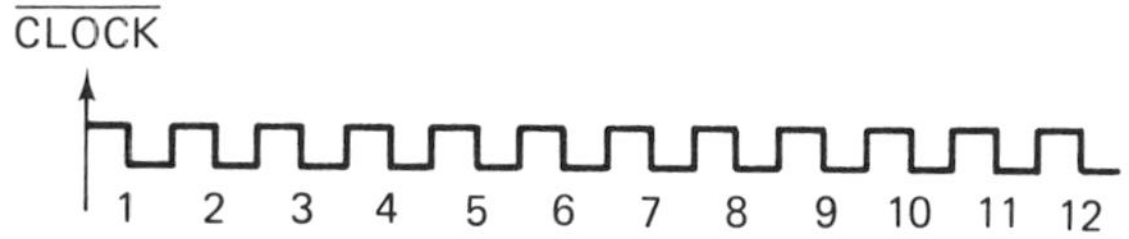

CLOCK

CLOCK	A B C	Decimal equivalents
0	L H H	6
1		
2		
3		
4		
5		
6		
7		
8		
9		
10		
11		
12		

Fig. 5-55

5-22 Referring to Fig. 5-21, if switches Sw *D*, Sw *C*, Sw *A*, and Sw *B* are pushed in that order, what are the resulting states of signals *X*, *Y*, OK-*A*, OK-*B*, and OK-*C*?

5-23 Referring to Fig. 5-21, if switches Sw *D*, Sw *A*, Sw *B*, and Sw *C* are pushed in that order, what are the resulting logic levels of signals *X*, *Y*, OK-*A*, OK-*B*, and OK-*C*?

5-24 Referring to Fig. 5-21, if switches Sw *A*, Sw *B*, and Sw *C* are pushed in that order, can we expect the LED to definitely light? Why?

5-25 Show a block diagram of a circuit, using mod-10 (decade) and lower-modulus counters, to generate a square wave that has about 33.3 sec between leading edges. Use 60 Hz as the reference frequency. See Fig. 5-22.

5-26 Show how to wire a 7493 binary counter IC to work as a mod-12 counter.

5-27 Show how to wire the 7493 so that it works as a binary counter, that is, counts through 16 states.

5-28 Show how to wire the 7490 so that it works as a mod-7 counter.

5-29 Using Fig. 5-24 as a guide, show how to wire a 5-bit shift counter with individual *JK* FFs. Sketch a timing diagram and functional table that shows how outputs *A–E* respond to a series of 14 $\overline{\text{CLOCK}}$ pulses. Start with all FFs initially in their reset states.

5-30 Why do the manufacturers of the 7496 IC (see Fig. 5-56) use two inverters on the SERIAL INPUT instead of just one as in the circuit of Fig. 5-26?

5-31 Which of the following describes applications in which the 7496 (see Fig. 5-56) can be used: (a) serial-to-serial conversion, (b) parallel-to-parallel conversion, (c) serial-to-parallel conversion, (d) parallel-to-serial conversion?

5-32 Referring to the circuit of Fig. 5-56, must a $\overline{\text{CLEAR}}$ pulse be applied before a 5-bit parallel word is loaded into this register? Why?

5-33 Which of the input signals in the circuit of Fig. 5-56 causes the register's data to shift?

5-34 Must the register of Fig. 5-28 be cleared before a new word is parallel-loaded? Why?

5-35 Referring to the circuit of Fig. 5-28, with a clock source applied to the *CP* input, what logic levels must be on the $\overline{CE}$ and the $\overline{PL}$ inputs to shift the register's data?

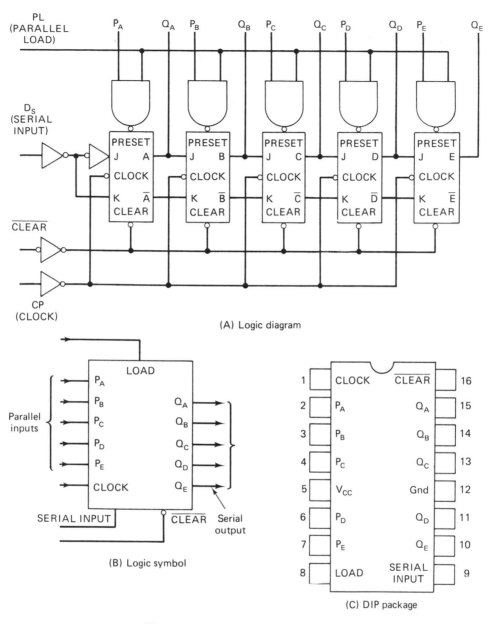

Fig. 5-56 7496 5-bit shift register.

5-36 Name two ways that each flip-flop in the shift register of Fig. 5-28 can be cleared (reset).

5-37 What logic levels on the address lines A_{12}, A_{11}, and A_{10} will cause the MPU's data to load into the shift register of Fig. 5-57?

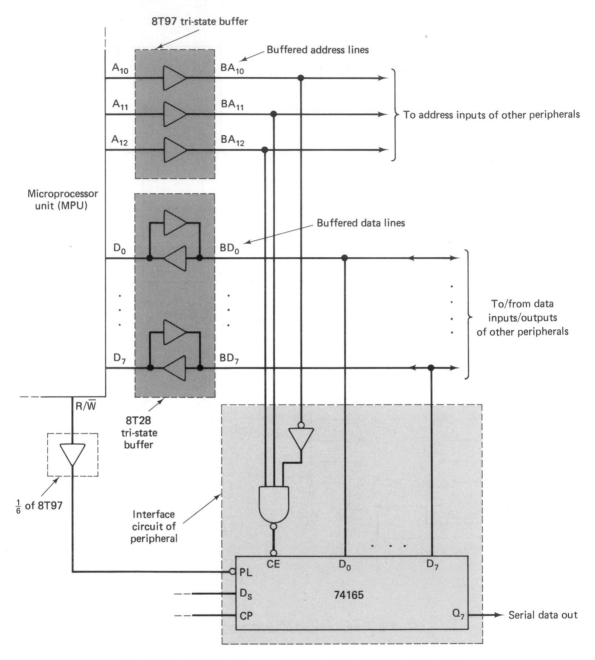

Fig. 5-57 MPU loading parallel data into a 74165 shift register.

5-38 Referring to the circuit of Fig. 5-57, if the total number of address lines is 16 $(A_{15}-A_0)$, with what range of addresses can the MPU load the 8-bit shift register? Give answers (a) in hexadecimal and (b) in octal.

5-39 Referring to the circuit of Fig. 5-57, show how to use two 7430s (eight-input NAND gates) and a two-input OR gate ($\frac{1}{4}$ of 7432) in the interface of the peripheral to decode the unique address 1800H. Use as many inverters as necessary.

5-40 Referring to the circuit of Fig. 5-57, show how to use one 1 of 16 decoder, one gate of any type, and as few inverters as possible in the interface of the peripheral so that it responds to any one of the addresses 0100H–01FFH.

5-41 Show how to wire a 74154 decoder onto a 6-bit active LOW address bus $(A_5–A_0)$ so that it will output active LOW signals $\overline{\text{START}}$, $\overline{\text{STOP}}$, or $\overline{\text{WAIT}}$ with octal addresses 77_8, 74_8, or 63_8, respectively.

5-42 Referring to the circuit of Fig. 5-58, determine the address that

Fig. 5-58 Typical address decoding circuit with simple I/O (input/output) hardware.

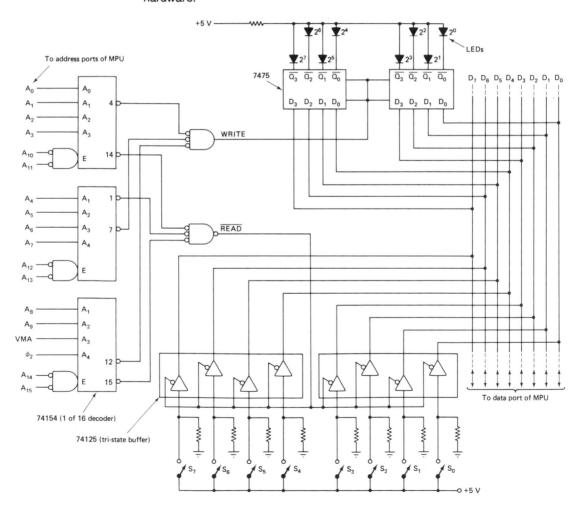

will cause the WRITE signal to go HIGH when signals VMA and φ2 are HIGH. Give your answer in hexadecimal and in octal.

5-43 Referring to the circuit of Fig. 5-58, determine the address that will cause the $\overline{\text{READ}}$ signal to go LOW when signals VMA and φ2 are HIGH. Give your answer in hexadecimal and in octal.

5-44 Referring to the circuit of Fig. 5-58, if S_5 and S_2 are closed while the remaining switches are left open, what data byte will appear on the data bus (D_7-D_0) at the time $\overline{\text{READ}}$ goes LOW? Give your answer in hex and in octal.

5-45 Referring to the circuit of Fig. 5-33, which diodes are forward-biased, which diodes are back-biased, and which of the decoder's outputs *(a–g)* are LOW with each of the following: (a) Switch 2 is closed; (b) switch 5 is closed; (c) switch 8 is closed?

5-46 What symptoms would we observe on the seven-segment display in the circuit of Fig. 5-33, if (a) the diode D_g becomes open, (b) the diode D_{15} becomes open, or (c) the diode D_{11} becomes open?

5-47 Show how to use an eight-input multiplexer to multiplex signals from eight source devices to a single destination device; see Figs. 5-34 and 5-35. Use a 7490 wired to work as a binary mod-8 counter to drive the A_2-A_0 inputs.

5-48 If the parity generator/checker of the source device in the circuit of Fig. 5-36 is working properly, what is the logic level of the PARITY bit with each of the following data bytes out of the latch of the source device: (a) $A6_H$, (b) $9F_H$, (c) 83_H, (d) 00_H, (e) CB_H?

5-49 What are the logic levels of the ERROR and NO ERROR signals in the circuit of Fig. 5-36 if the PARITY bit goes HIGH when the destination device receives each of the following data bytes: (a) FF_H, (b) DE_H, (c) 42_H, (d) $B4_H$, (e) $4A_H$?

5-50 What simple change(s) can we make in the source device in the circuit of Fig. 5-37 to cause it to transmit odd parity instead of even parity?

5-51 If the *A*-word, the *B*-word, and the ADD/$\overline{\text{SUBT}}$ inputs applied to the circuit of Fig. 5-39 are as shown in the table of Fig. 5-59, what are the resulting outputs? Work one row at a time, and give the answers in hex or octal to match the input words.

5-52 Show how to wire a 74121 to generate a 20-μsec $\overline{\text{CPU RESET}}$ pulse on a trailing edge input.

5-53 Show how to wire a 74121 to generate a 20-msec ENBL pulse on a leading edge input.

The A-word	The B-word	ADD/$\overline{\text{SUBT}}$	The S-word
7A (hex)	6F (hex)	1	
9C (hex)	7E (hex)	0	
DF (hex)	32 (hex)	0	
354 (octal)	077 (octal)	1	
277 (octal)	246 (octal)	0	
377 (octal)	200 (octal)	0	
300 (octal)	257 (octal)	0	

Fig. 5-59

5-54 Show how to wire a 555 timer to generate a 1-sec positive pulse when it receives a LOW-going input pulse.

5-55 If the $\phi2$ input in the circuit of Fig. 5-58 is from an MC6870A crystal oscillator, as shown in Fig. 5-46, which output pin of this MC6870A should we use? Why?

CHAPTER 6

Memories

We have seen that computers use memories to store instructions and data. Information is stored in memory in the form of binary *words*. A *word* is simply a group of bits representing either a coded instruction; or a piece of data, such as a number; or a character, like *A, B,* etc. The number of bits in a word varies with different computers. For example, most microprocessors today use 8-bit words, called *bytes*. But some systems use 1, 4, 12, or 16 or even more bits per word.

Although some large machines use magnetic memories, we shall first discuss solid-state memory chips, such as are commonly used with microprocessors.

In this chapter, you'll see how memory cells work and how large-scale memories are constructed. You'll get familiar with READ and WRITE operations and with commonly used memory chips. Last, you'll see how memories are used in systems.

6-1 Solid-State Memory Chips

Each memory chip can store many, often thousands of, bits. When referring to the number of bits stored in one chip, we use the symbol K to represent the total number of bits to the nearest 1000. Actually, the number of bits varies in a binary progression, so that a 1K memory contains 2^{10} or 1024

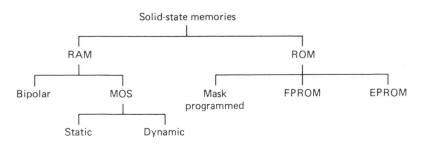

Fig. 6-1 Commonly used types of solid-state memories.

bits. Similarly, a 2K chip stores 2048 bits, a 4K chip stores 4096 bits, etc.

Figure 6-1 shows how commonly used solid-state memories are classified. Note that there are two major divisions according to use. These are RAMs and ROMs. Then each of these is further subdivided according to the hardware technology.

A device that is used for *temporary* storage is called a *RAM,* which stands for *random access memory.* The name implies that we can access any memory location, at any time, without sequentially going through a large number of locations, as we would have to do with magnetic disk or drum storage. RAMs are used to store program variable data or as *scratch pads* for arithmetic operations.

The ROM, or *read only memory,* is used for *permanent* storage. Unchangeable information, such as the computer's background, or *monitor,* program, is stored in ROM. The monitor program would include the system's initialization routine, input/output routines, and arithmetic algorithms. Programs and tasks stored in ROMs are referred to as the system's *firmware.* *

Actually, both RAM and ROM are random access memories, but the RAM is the READ/WRITE memory. That is, data can be written (stored) into the chip or read out of it at will, whereas once the ROM has been loaded, the data essentially cannot be changed. Another point to remember is that the ROM will retain the data stored in it, even after the power to the chip has been cut off. But the data in RAM is lost whenever power is removed. For this reason, the RAM is said to be *volatile.* Occasionally, if the data in a RAM must be saved in a power down condition, a battery backup is used. We shall examine RAMs first and then ROMs.

6-2 RAMs (Random Access or Read/Write Memories)

RAMs can be built with either bipolar or MOS transistors. Bipolar types are faster and are used in high-speed applications. The length of time it takes to read from, or write into, a memory location is called *access time.*

* Firmware is somewhat more permanent than software, which is usually stored in RAM or on disk or magnetic tape.

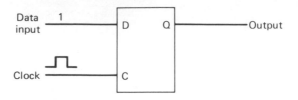

Fig. 6-2 Simple memory cell.

Some bipolar types have access times of about 20–50 nsec, as compared with 100–500 nsec or more for MOS RAMs.

A typical storage *cell* in a bipolar RAM is essentially a *D* flip-flop, as shown in Fig. 6-2. This could be either a TTL type, like the ones you studied in an earlier chapter, or ECL (emitter coupled logic) for even shorter access times.

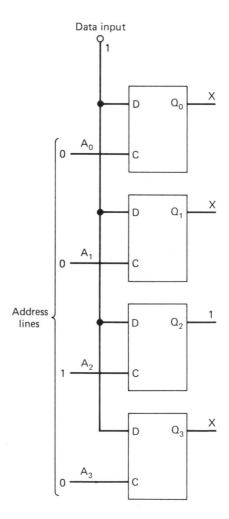

Fig. 6-3 Addressing a cell.

If we want to store a 1 bit in the cell, we simply place a 1 (HIGH) level on the data *(D)* input and clock the chip. The flip-flop will then retain (remember) the 1 bit until we either store in a 0 or remove power. Similarly, we can store a 0, and it will be remembered.

Now the memory chip contains a large number of bits, so how do we select *which* of the cells to write into or read out of? The answer is by *addressing* the appropriate cell. As shown in Fig. 6-3, four cells all have their data input lines tied together. Now suppose we wish to store a 1 in cell 2. We simply apply a 1 to the data input and clock *only cell 2*. The 1 bit will then appear at its output. The other cells will retain their previous data, since they were not clocked.

You will remember from the chapter on programming, that each memory location has its own address. Well, addressing is done by selectively clocking a particular cell, or group of cells. To select one of 1024 different cells, you clock only 1 of 1024 lines. This sounds like a cumbersome task at first, but it is greatly simplified by internal gating on the chip. These gates, called *address decoders,* will be discussed in detail later.

Although bipolar RAMs are faster than MOS RAMs, the bipolar cells consume many times more power and take up more space on a chip than do MOS cells. So in systems where speed is less important than space and power considerations, such as in most microprocessor applications, MOS RAMs are a better choice.

A typical MOS RAM cell is shown in Fig. 6-4. The cell consists of six *N*-channel enhancement mode MOSFETs. This type of FET is turned ON by applying a positive potential to its gate. With 0 V applied to its gate, the FET is OFF and acts like an open switch. Transistors Q_1 and Q_2 act as load resistors in the drain leads of FETs Q_3 and Q_4. Since Q_3 and Q_4 are cross-coupled, drain to gate, they form an *RS* flip-flop; that is, one FET is ON while the other is OFF.

Transistors Q_5 and Q_6 act like switches to connect the flip-flop outputs to the data INPUT and $\overline{\text{INPUT}}$ lines when the cell is addressed. To store a 1 bit in the cell, a 1 (HIGH) is applied to the data INPUT. Then the WORD SELECT line is made HIGH, turning ON Q_5 and Q_6. The HIGH level on the INPUT line is thus connected to the drain of Q_3, forcing it HIGH, while at the same time turning ON Q_4, pulling its drain LOW. Note also that level on the $\overline{\text{INPUT}}$ line is applied to the drain of Q_4, jamming it LOW and simultaneously turning Q_3 OFF. So Q_3 turns OFF and Q_4 turns ON. When the WORD SELECT line is returned LOW again, turning OFF Q_5 and Q_6, the flip-flop will remain in its present state. That is, Q_3 will remain OFF, and Q_4 will remain ON. With Q_3 OFF, its drain will be held HIGH. We then interpret a HIGH at the drain of Q_3 as being a 1 bit stored in the cell. Similarly, we can analyze that Q_3 is turned ON and Q_4 is turned OFF when INPUT is LOW and a select pulse is applied. That explains the WRITE operation; now let's consider the READ operation.

To READ a bit from a cell, the INPUT and $\overline{\text{INPUT}}$ lines are placed in their high-impedance states—exactly how will be shown later. Then the WORD SELECT line is made HIGH, thus addressing the cell. The HIGH

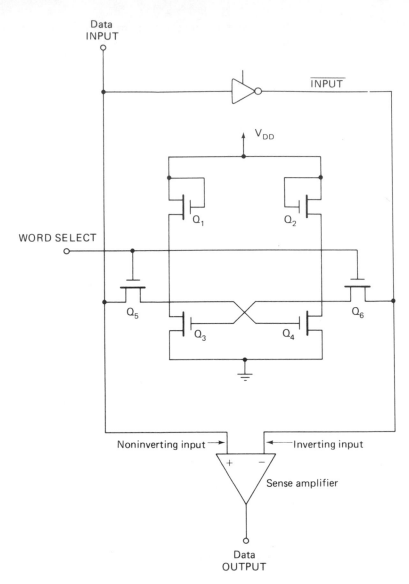

Fig. 6-4 MOS RAM cell.

level at the drain of Q_3 is thus connected to the **INPUT** line through Q_5, while the **LOW** level at the drain of Q_4 is connected to the $\overline{\text{INPUT}}$ line through Q_6. Note that these lines run down to the inputs of the sense amplifier, which is simply a buffer with two inputs, inverting (−) and noninverting (+). The **HIGH** level at the drain of Q_3 connected to the noninverting input of the sense amp causes the amplifier's output to go **HIGH**. Similarly, if a 0 had been stored in the cell, Q_3's drain would have been **LOW**. Then when

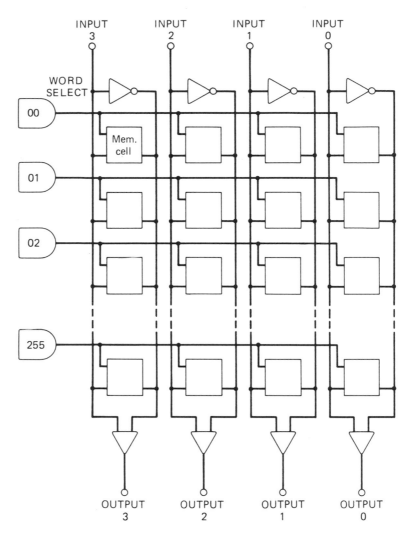

Fig. 6-5 256 × 4 bit memory array.

the cell was selected, the LOW level applied to the noninverting input of the sense amp would drive its output LOW.

Now let's see how MOS RAM cells are combined in a chip to make a multibit memory.

Figure 6-5 shows how a typical 256 × 4 bit RAM can be constructed. Note that INPUT 0, at the top, is connected to every cell in *column* 0, and similarly for the other inputs. Also note that each horizontal *row* is selected by *WORD SELECT* lines 00 through 255_{10}. These *WORD SELECT* lines come from address decoders, as shown in Fig. 6-6.

Depending on the combination of address inputs, only one row of four

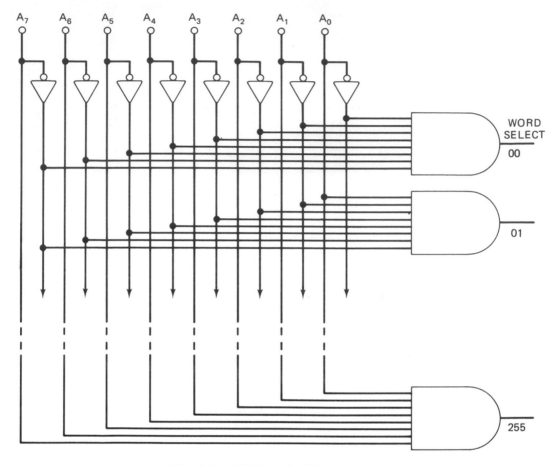

Fig. 6-6   A 256-word address decoder.

cells is selected, because only one gate's output will be HIGH at any time. Then data are written into or read from those four cells simultaneously.

The diagram of Fig. 6-5 shows separate input lines and output lines, but typical 256 × 4 bit RAMs use the same terminals for both input and output by incorporating two sets of tri-state buffers in a bidirectional arrangement like that of Fig. 6-7. Note that when chip enable $\overline{CE}$ is LOW and the READ/$\overline{\text{WRITE}}$ line $(R/\overline{W})$ is HIGH, gate 2's output is HIGH, so only the *output* buffers are enabled. This allows the addressed memory word to be *read* on the I/O lines. Likewise, when $\overline{CE}$ is LOW and $R/\overline{W}$ is LOW, the *input* buffers are enabled, causing the data on the input lines to be *written into* the addressed memory location. Also note that whenever $\overline{CE}$ is HIGH, *both* sets of buffers are disabled, thereby placing the I/O lines in their high-impedance state. In this manner, several chips can have their outputs tied

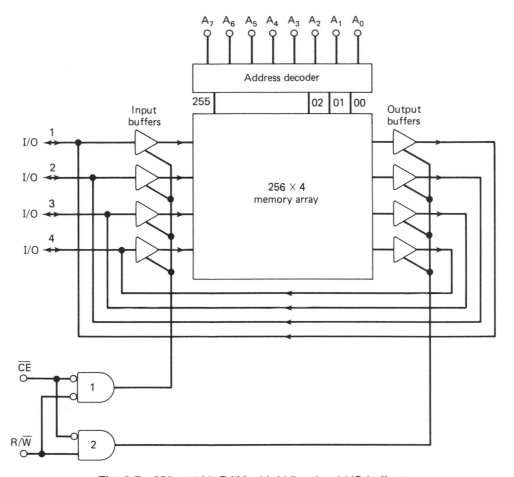

Fig. 6-7 256 × 4 bit RAM with bidirectional I/O buffers.

to the same data bus without interfering with one another, because only one chip will be using a given set of data lines at any one time.

Two commonly used static RAM chips having a similar arrangement are the 2112, which is a 256 × 4 bit RAM, and the 2114, a 1024 × 4 bit RAM. See Fig. 6-8.

Another chip that has been very popular is the 2102, which is 1024 × 1 bit RAM. As you can see in Fig. 6-9, the 2102 has only a single input and a single output line. Although it is considerably less expensive and smaller than the 2114 chip, eight of the 2102s in parallel are needed to store 1024 8-bit words, whereas only two of the 2114s are needed. We shall discuss this paralleling idea in more detail later.

Both the bipolar and MOS memory cells discussed thus far are called *static* cells because once written into, they will retain the data bit indefinitely

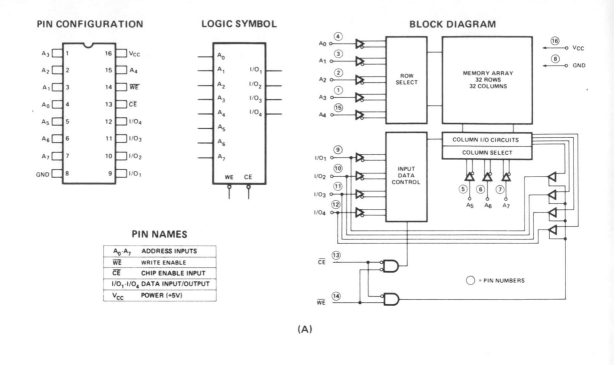

(A)

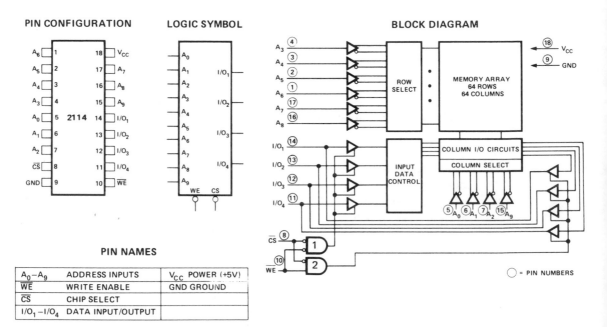

(B)

Fig. 6-8 Two popular static RAMs: (A) 2112, 256 × 4; (B) 2114, 1024 × 4. (Courtesy of Intel Corporation.)

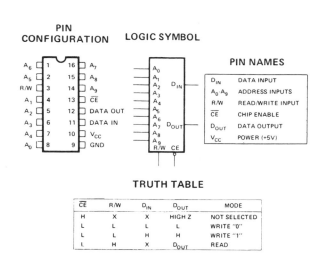

PIN CONFIGURATION   LOGIC SYMBOL

PIN NAMES

D_{IN}	DATA INPUT
$A_0 \cdot A_9$	ADDRESS INPUTS
R/W	READ/WRITE INPUT
$\overline{CE}$	CHIP ENABLE
D_{OUT}	DATA OUTPUT
V_{CC}	POWER (+5V)

TRUTH TABLE

$\overline{CE}$	R/W	D_{IN}	D_{OUT}	MODE
H	X	X	HIGH Z	NOT SELECTED
L	L	L	L	WRITE "0"
L	L	H	H	WRITE "1"
L	H	X	D_{OUT}	READ

Fig. 6-9 M2102, 1K × 1 bit static RAM. (Courtesy of Intel Corporation.)

until either new data are stored or the power is removed. There is another type of MOS cell called a *dynamic* memory cell which only retains its data for a short period of time, perhaps only a millisecond or so. It must then be *refreshed* periodically, that is, rewritten with the same data over and over again—hence the name dynamic.

A simplified diagram of the dynamic cell is shown in Fig. 6-10. Data are stored not in a flip-flop but rather as a charge on a capacitor. To write a 1 into the cell, line X is made HIGH, and line Y is also made HIGH,

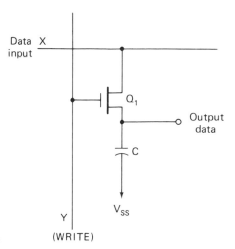

Fig. 6-10 Simple dynamic RAM cell.

turning ON transistor Q_1. The HIGH level on line X charges the cap. Similarly, to store a 0 in the cell, line X is made LOW, and line Y is made HIGH. The conducting transistor connects the cap to the LOW level, thereby discharging it.

To READ the data bit stored in the cell, we simply examine the charge on capacitor C.

Unfortunately, capacitor C is so small, usually just a few picofarads, that it cannot retain its charge very long. It must therefore be recharged or *refreshed* periodically, about every millisecond or so, to keep it from losing the stored information. Therefore, relatively extensive circuitry is needed to periodically examine each cell in memory and refresh it. Since the refresh circuitry is quite complex, it will not be discussed in this text.

The advantage of the dynamic cell over the static cell is that only three transistors (two not shown in Fig. 6-10) are needed in the dynamic cell, whereas the static cell requires six. So obviously the dynamic memory chip can be smaller and less expensive and consume less power than an equivalent static device. In addition, the access time of the dynamic cell is often shorter than that of a static cell, due to its smaller size and because it has fewer transistors to be switched on and off. The disadvantages of the dynamic memory chip are the extra refresh circuitry needed, making it more difficult to use. Another disadvantage is the fact that it usually requires three separate power supplies, as compared to a single +5-V dc supply for a static chip.

The general trend is that static RAMs are used much more often than dynamic, particularly in smaller systems. Dynamic RAMs occasionally offer some savings in systems requiring very large numbers of words in memory.

6-3 ROMs and PROMs (Read Only Memories and Programmable ROMs)

As stated earlier, in addition to RAMs, which are used to store program variable data and instructions, microprocessor systems almost always use read only memories (ROMs) to store the system's initialization and operating routines as well as codes for special control. Rather than containing flip-flops, ROMs are essentially combinations of AND gates and OR gates, arranged to output specific bit patterns when addressed. Let's see how this is done.

Figure 6-11(A) shows a simple two-diode OR gate whose output table is shown in Fig. 6-11(B). When either input A or input B is HIGH, output X is HIGH.

Now suppose, rather than single inputs A and B connected to the gate, we connect the outputs of decoder gates to the inputs of OR gates, as shown in Fig. 6-12(A).

Note that the line labeled b_0 is really the output of a two-input OR gate, whose inputs are the outputs of gate 00 and gate 10. So whenever the

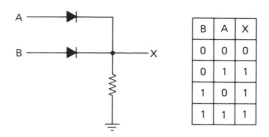

B	A	X
0	0	0
0	1	1
1	0	1
1	1	1

(A) Simple gate   (B) Truth table

Fig. 6-11 Simple diode OR gate.

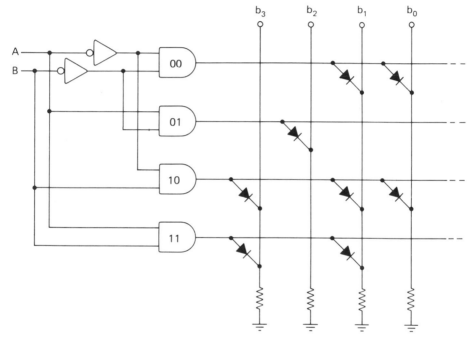

(A) Decoder feeding diode
     OR gates

B	A	b_3	b_2	b_1	b_0
0	0	0	0	1	1
0	1	0	1	0	0
1	0	1	0	1	1
1	1	1	0	1	0

(B) Truth table

Fig. 6-12 Simple 4 × 4 ROM.

187

output of either of the two AND gates is HIGH, output line b_0 will be pulled HIGH. Study this carefully to make sure you get the idea.

Similarly, output b_1 will be HIGH whenever gate 00, or 10, or 11 is HIGH, etc. The complete table for the circuit showing all outputs for every input combination is shown in Fig. 6-12(B).

Looking at the entire circuit, we can say that it has two inputs, A and B, and four outputs, b_3, b_2, b_1, and b_0. The four outputs, taken collectively, represent a 4-bit word. These words are effectively stored at locations which can be accessed by applying the appropriate combination of inputs, or *addresses.*

Whenever we apply the address 00 to the input, that is, $A = 0$ and $B = 0$, the word 0011 appears at the output, and similarly for the remainder of the words. These words can represent instructions to a computer, or codes for a combination lock, or whatever we choose.

So you see that a ROM is composed of two major sections: an address decoder (AND gates) to select a word and elements of OR gates whose outputs represent bits in each word. In an actual chip, the output bit lines are normally connected to tri-state buffers to increase the drive capability and improve bus compatibility.

The ROM of Fig. 6-12(A) stores four words, because of the four combinations of inputs A and B. It also has 4 bits per word, due to the four vertical lines to which diodes can be connected. This ROM is referred to as a 4×4 ROM, that is, 4 words $\times$ 4 bits per word. ROMs are available in a wide variety of sizes such as 128×8, 256×8, 512×4, $1K \times 8$, and $2K \times 8$, to mention a few. The first number indicates the number of *words* stored in the ROM, while the second number tells you the number of *bits* per word.

There are basically three types of ROMs in use today. They are the *mask-programmed,* or factory-programmed, ROM, simply abbreviated ROM; the *field-programmable* ROM, or FPROM; and the *ultraviolet-erasable* PROM, abbreviated UVPROM or EPROM.

First let's consider the mask-programmed ROM. These ROMs are programmed by the manufacturer to the customer's specifications. That is, the user tells the manufacturer what word is to be programmed at each address. One way to do this is for the user to supply a truth table showing the bit pattern wanted at the output for each combination of inputs. The address decoders for all ROMs are essentially the same, so, for example, if you wanted the manufacturer to program a 4×4 ROM for you, you simply fill in the blanks for the bit pattern. A blank ROM table for the circuit of Fig. 6-12 would look like Fig. 6-13.

By examining your table, the manufacturer would simply put a diode in at every junction corresponding to a 1 bit in your table. Refer again to the ROM and table of Fig. 6-12 to see the correspondence between the diode locations and a 1 bit in the table.

Of course, since this ROM is custom-made to the user's specifications, there is a set-up charge, possibly $500 to $1500 to make the mask. But

Address		Data			
A_1	A_0	b_3	b_2	b_1	b_0
0	0				
0	1				
1	0				
1	1				

Fig. 6-13 Typical blank ROM table.

each ROM made exactly the same would then cost just a few dollars. You can see that the mask-programmed ROM would only be used for mass production. Hundreds of units would have to be used to justify the cost.

A lower-cost item, used when just a few units are needed, is the FPROM. The FPROM is supplied by the manufacturer with all address decoders already in place but with diodes at *every* intersection of a decoder line and a bit line. See Fig. 6-14.

Fig. 6-14 Unprogrammed FPROM with diodes and fusable links at every intersection.

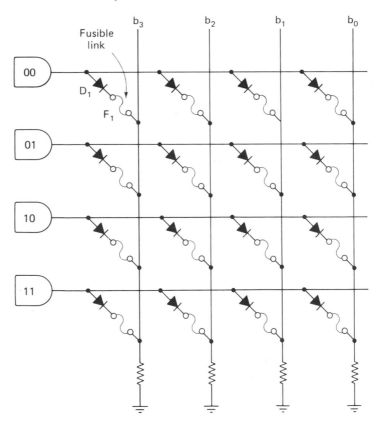

Since the FPROM has diodes at every intersection, the user removes the ones not wanted. This is done by burning open tiny fusible links which are in series with each diode. The manufacturer gives exact programming instructions, but you can see that if, for example, you apply address 00, causing gate 00 output to go HIGH, and then force bit line b_3 LOW, current will flow through fuse F_1 and diode D_1. If the current is high enough, F_1 will burn open. No damage is done to any other link, so you can selectively remove any diodes you choose. This process is referred to as *burning the PROM.* Obviously, if you accidentally open the wrong link, it can't be repaired, so care must be taken while burning. There are programmable devices on the market called *PROM burners,* which can program an entire PROM in a matter of a minute or so without making any errors. The PROM programmer of Fig. 6-15 can program FPROMs as well as EPROMs.

EPROMs are programmed by a PROM burner similarly to the FPROM. However, rather than opening a fusible link, the burning or programming process simply stores a charge in an essentially perfect insulator. The burning process takes only a few minutes, even for a 2K × 8 EPROM, and the EPROM will retain the stored data indefinitely. However, should the user decide to reprogram the chip, he or she can erase the previously stored data by shining a very strong ultraviolet light through a tiny window on

Fig. 6-15 PROM programmer. (Courtesy of Data I/O Corporation.)

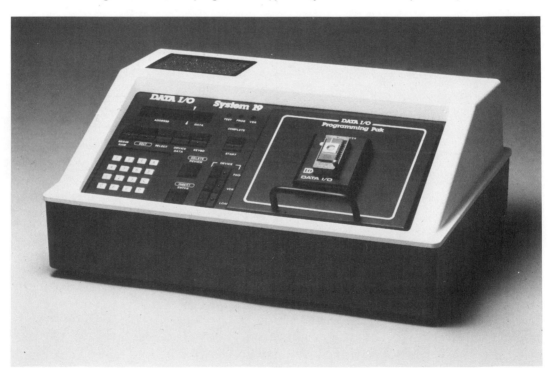

Fig. 6-16 Package of a 2K × 8
UVPROM.

top of the chip for about 20 min. Figure 6-16 shows a typical **EPROM** with a clear window on top. Previous data are thus erased, and new data can be programmed in. This process can be repeated 100 times or more. The EPROM is used primarily in development work, where the engineer might want to test a program and then alter it later as changes are made in the system. Of course, the EPROM is more expensive than the FPROM, and usually has a longer access time, but nevertheless is a valuable firmware device.

Three very popular EPROMs in use today are the 1702A, 256 × 8; the 2708, 1K × 8; and the 2716, 2K × 8. See Fig. 6-17 for pinouts.

6-4 Core Memories

Thus far we have looked only at solid-state memories. But another type of memory device that has been used for many years is the magnetic core memory. The basic core memory cell is a tiny toroid, or doughnut-shaped ring, often about 0.05 in. or so in diameter. The core is made of ferrite material, which can be easily saturated (completely magnetized) by sending a pulse of current through a winding on the core.

Figure 6-18 shows a toroid being saturated in a clockwise direction by a pulse of current flowing into the top of the coil. Once the core becomes saturated, the current can be cut off, but the core remains magnetized in the clockwise direction. If sufficient current is caused to flow through the coil in the *opposite* direction, the core will switch into saturation in the counterclockwise direction. It will then remain saturated in the counterclockwise direction even after the current stops flowing.

So you see that the magnetic core can "remember" which way the current flowed last. We can interpret the direction of flux in the core to represent either a logic 1 or a logic 0. Note that no power is needed to

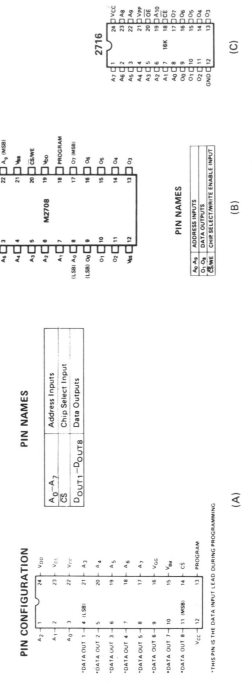

Fig. 6-17 UV-erasable PROMs: (A) 1702A, 256 × 8; (B) M2708, 1K × 8; (C) 2716, 2K × 8.

WRITE pulse switches flux ϕ to clockwise direction

Fig. 6-18 Basic toroid.

maintain the flux in the core. Once the core is saturated in one direction, it remains in that state until switched again. Therefore the magnetic core memory is considered a permanent memory, as opposed to a volatile memory like the solid-state types.

The physical size of the core determines how much magnetizing force is needed to switch a core. The magnetizing force is measured in *ampere turns* (AT). For example, if 1 AT is needed to switch the core and two turns of wire are wrapped around the core, then a current of 0.5 A is all that is needed to cause switching.

Typically, the access time of a magnetic core memory is less than 0.5 μsec, or about equal to that of solid-state memory. The question that now arises is, How do we determine the direction of core saturation? Well we can't measure the direction of this static magnetic field, because it is totally contained inside the core. But if we can cause the core to switch, we can sense the switching.

Refer to Fig. 6-19(A). Assume the flux in the core is originally clockwise, representing a stored 1. When a READ pulse is applied to the READ winding, the flux in the core is switched to the counterclockwise direction. While the flux is changing, a short-duration pulse occurs in the *sense* winding. But in Fig. 6-19(B), assuming the flux was originally in the counterclockwise direction, representing a logic 0, a READ pulse does *not* change the flux direction. Therefore no pulse occurs in the sense winding. So we can determine whether a 1 or 0 was stored in the core by whether a sense pulse appears or not.

Fig. 6-19 Reading a core.

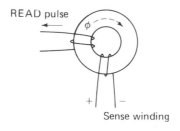

Sense winding

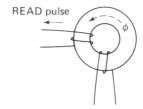

(A) CW flux switches to CCW direction, causing pulse on sense winding

(B) CCW flux does not change directions when READ pulse is applied—no SENSE pulse

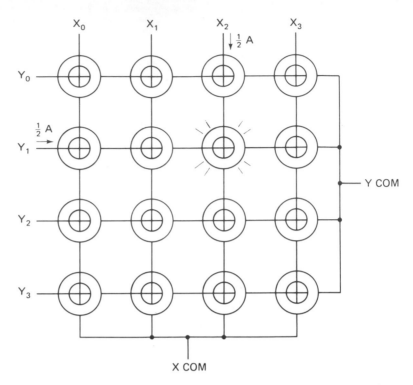

Fig. 6-20 Selecting core $X_2 Y_1$ with the coincidence of two half-select pulses.

Now let's look at a typical core *plane* construction. Refer to Fig. 6-20. Since there are 16 cores in the plane, 16 bits of information can be stored. The particular core which is to be written into or read from is selected by its X-Y coordinate position in the plane.

Suppose we want to write a 1 bit into core $X_2 Y_1$. We simply send current pulses down lines X_2 and Y_1 simultaneously. Now remember that the total magnetizing force required to cause switching depends on the core size. Let's suppose that 1 AT is required to cause switching.

If we send a current of 0.5 A into lines X_2 and Y_1, cores $X_0 Y_1$, $X_1 Y_1$, and $X_3 Y_1$ only received *half* the required magnetizing force, so no switching occurs (a single wire woven through a core acts like a single turn), and similarly for cores $X_2 Y_0$, $X_2 Y_2$, and $X_2 Y_3$. But the core at the intersection of lines X_2 and Y_1 receives a *half-select* pulse from each line threading it. The effect of the two half-select pulses are additive, so the core switches. Since only the core at the coincidence of the two pulses switches, this type of memory is called a *coincident current* memory.

Although the core plane shown contains only 16 cores, a typical plane might contain 1024 (32 × 32) or 4096 (64 × 64) cores.

Besides the X and Y select lines, the plane also contains a sense winding,

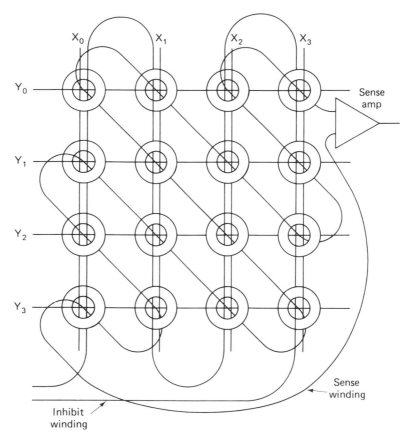

Fig. 6-21 Sixteen-bit core memory with X and Y core select lines, sense winding, and inhibit winding.

whose purpose, as you already know, is to sense a change in flux when a core switches. Note in Fig. 6-21 that a single wire, woven through each core on the plane, is all that is needed for the sense winding, because only one core, the selected one, can switch at any one time. Since we know which core we addressed when we sent half-select pulses down the two lines, we know which core switches.

In addition to the sense winding, there is another wire, called an *inhibit* winding, whose purpose will be seen shortly.

You will recall that in order to read a 1 bit from a core, the core had to be switched, thus clearing it to 0. That is, the original information stored in the core was destroyed. So to make a nondestructive readout, some method must be used to rewrite the 1 bit back into the core. Therefore, following each READ pulse, the line drivers always turn around and send WRITE pulses into the same lines. This writes a 1 back into the core that was just read. But suppose the core had a 0 in it instead of a 1. We would then want to *inhibit* a 1 from being written back into that core. This is

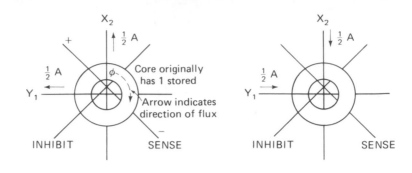

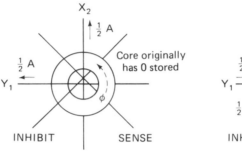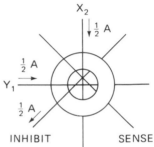

(A) READ pulses cause
core to switch.

(B) WRITE pulses store 1 back
into core. No INHIBIT
pulse is sent.

(C) READ pulses do not switch
core. No SENSE pulse is sent.

(D) WRITE pulses do not store
1 due to canceling effect of
INHIBIT pulse.

Fig. 6-22 READ/WRITE cycle.

done by sending a half-select pulse through the inhibit winding in a direction
opposite to one of the WRITE pulses. The magnetizing force of the INHIBIT
pulse cancels the effect of the magnetizing force of one of the WRITE wind-
ings, thus preventing the core from switching to the 1 state. The actual
direction of weaving the inhibit line through the cores may differ from that
shown in Fig. 6-21, but the general idea remains the same. Figure 6-22 summarizes the operation for reading a 1 or 0. Note that the READ operation is
always immediately followed by a WRITE.

The actual circuitry required for the line drivers, sense amplifiers, inhibit
drivers, address decoders, and other necessary logic is rather complex and
will not be covered here. Magnetic core memory systems are quite expensive
and are normally used only in larger computer systems requiring permanent

storage. Most MPU-based systems use solid-state memories and rely on battery backup, floppy disk, or cassette tape if permanent storage is necessary.

6-5 Applications of Solid-State Memories

One of the most common applications of solid-state memories is to provide program and data storage for a microprocessor. Figure 6-23 shows a 2708, $1K \times 8$ EPROM and two 2114 $1K \times 4$ RAMs tied to a microprocessor. Typical microprocessors, such as the Motorola MC6800 and the Intel 8080A, have 16-bit address buses and 8-bit data buses as shown. Note that only 10 address lines are needed to select 1 of 1024 words stored in memory; hence address lines A_0–A_9 are tied to each chip.

Note also that the EPROM has 8 output bits, 1 bit connected to each line on the data bus. But the RAM chips, having only 4 bits each, are connected to different sets of four data lines. Chip 7 feeds lines D_0–D_3, while chip 6 feeds lines D_4–D_7.

Also note that the READ/$\overline{\text{WRITE}}$ control line from the MPU connects to the $\overline{\text{WRITE ENABLE}}$ input on the RAMs but is not connected to the EPROM. The reason is that the EPROM can't be written into anyway, so it is always in the READ mode whenever the chip is enabled.

This brings us to the address decoder chips 2 and 3. The MPU must select either the EPROM or the RAM when talking to memory—never both. So we must devise some way to enable one or the other.

Typically, in the Motorola system, the EPROM, which contains the MPU's *monitor* or operating system programs, is placed at the high end of memory. That is, memory responding to the highest addresses will be in ROM. Likewise, RAM, which is used for scratch-pad or variable data, is usually located at the lower end of memory.

Examination of Fig. 6-23 shows that the EPROM chip is selected whenever address lines A_{15}–A_{10} are all HIGH along with VMA and $\phi 2$. At that time only will $\overline{\text{ROMSEL}}$ be LOW. Similarly, the RAM chips are both enabled only when lines A_{15}–A_{10} are all LOW; that is, $\overline{\text{RAMSEL}}$ will then be LOW. ROM and RAM are *never* both enabled at the same time. VMA and $\phi 2$ are used to ensure that the address lines have stabilized before enabling a chip.

If we make a short table showing all possible addresses to which the EPROM can respond, we see that it looks like Fig. 6-24. Note that lines A_{15}–A_{10} *must* be HIGH but that lines A_9–A_0 can be either HIGH or LOW, depending on the particular *word* being addressed. So we list those as dashes. We see then that the EPROM will be enabled for all addresses from $FC00_{16}$ to $FFFF_{16}$.

Similarly, the RAM will be selected for all addresses from 0000_{16} to $03FF_{16}$.

The table of Fig. 6-24 is called a *memory map* and is very useful in

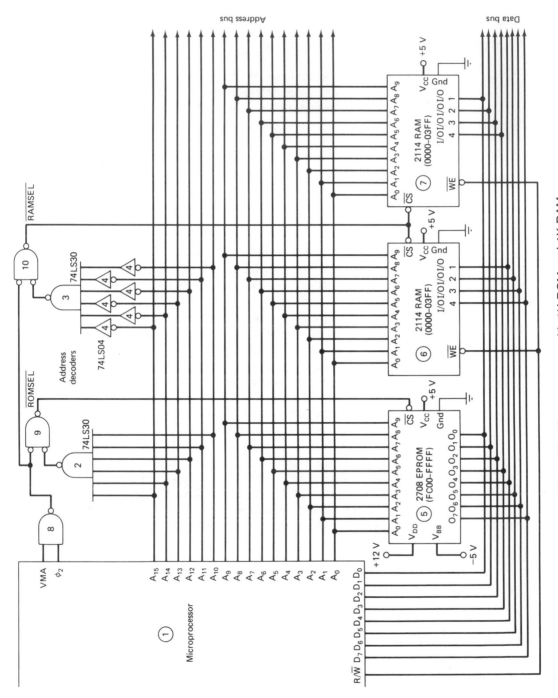

Fig. 6-23 Microprocessor with 1K ROM and 1K RAM.

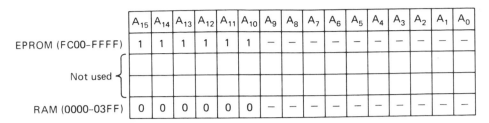

	A$_{15}$	A$_{14}$	A$_{13}$	A$_{12}$	A$_{11}$	A$_{10}$	A$_9$	A$_8$	A$_7$	A$_6$	A$_5$	A$_4$	A$_3$	A$_2$	A$_1$	A$_0$
EPROM (FC00–FFFF)	1	1	1	1	1	1	–	–	–	–	–	–	–	–	–	–
Not used																
RAM (0000–03FF)	0	0	0	0	0	0	–	–	–	–	–	–	–	–	–	–

Fig. 6-24 Memory map for circuit of Fig. 6-23.

keeping track of, and assigning, address space to various devices. The memory space between 03FF and FC00 is unused in this example, so any part of it can be assigned to other devices, such as additional memory, or peripheral devices like printers, keyboards, etc.

Figure 6-25 shows another use for a ROM. The diagram is that of a simple digital combination lock, such as might be used to allow only authorized employees to gain access to certain locked rooms. Code numbers of the combination are stored in the ROM, and the person wishing to open the lock must match 16 digits in exactly the correct sequence.

Here's how it works. The person operating the circuit has access only to the switches to the left of the dashed line. To start the sequence, the operator first presses the RESET button to ensure that the counter is reset to 0. Let's assume the code digits stored in the ROM are as shown in Fig. 6-26. With the counter reset, the outputs of the ROM are 0101 as shown for word 00000. These code digits were randomly chosen here, but they could represent someone's employee number or whatever is desired.

After pressing the RESET button, the operator then sets the toggle switches to the first code digit. Then he or she presses the ENTER push button, which enables AND gates 1–4, applying the signals from the toggles to the comparator. The digit he or she is entering via the toggle switches is compared to the outputs of the ROM by the 7485 4-bit comparator. If they match exactly, the "=" output goes HIGH.

At the same time, gates 8 and 9 are enabled. With the "=" output HIGH, the output of gate 8 goes LOW. Nothing happens at this time, but as soon as the operator releases the ENTER push button, the output of gate 8 goes HIGH again. This HIGH-going signal clocks the 74193 up counter, advancing its outputs to 0001 and thus causing the next word in memory to appear at the ROM outputs.

The operator then sets the toggle switches to the next code digit and presses the ENTER button again. He or she continues in this manner until all 16 digits have been entered in the correct sequence.

If all 16 digits have been entered correctly, the counter overflows, producing a CARRY output signal, which triggers the "unlock" circuitry.

Note, however, that if at any time an incorrect digit is entered, the "=" output will remain LOW and either the ">" or "<" outputs of the

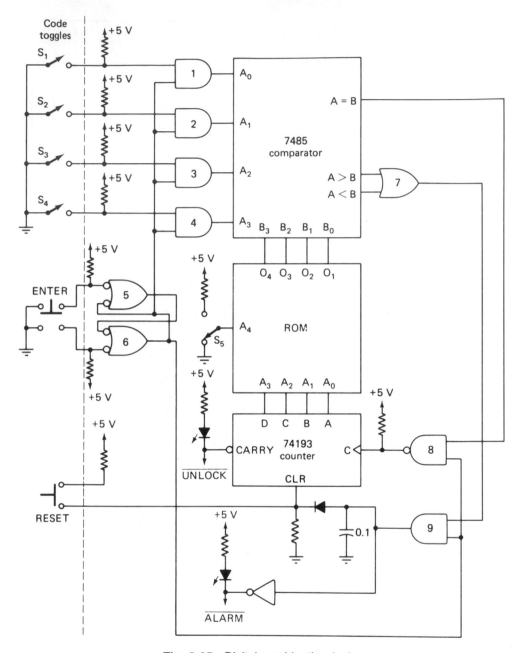

Fig. 6-25 Digital combination lock.

comparator will go HIGH. This HIGH signal will be fed through gate 9, clearing the counter. So the operator must begin again from word 0. Of course the HIGH signal appearing at the 9 could be used to trigger an alarm if desired. Or some additional circuitry could be added to count the

Addresses					Code digits				Decimal
A_4	A_3	A_2	A_1	A_0	O_4	O_3	O_2	O_1	equivalent
0	0	0	0	0	0	1	0	1	5
0	0	0	0	1	0	0	0	1	1
0	0	0	1	0	0	0	1	1	3
0	0	0	1	1	1	0	0	0	8
0	0	1	0	0	1	0	0	1	9
0	0	1	0	1	0	0	1	0	2
0	0	1	1	0	1	0	0	0	8
0	0	1	1	1	0	1	1	0	6
0	1	0	0	0	0	1	0	0	4
0	1	0	0	1	0	0	1	1	3
0	1	0	1	0	0	1	1	0	6
0	1	0	1	1	0	0	0	1	1
0	1	1	0	0	0	0	1	0	2
0	1	1	0	1	0	1	0	1	5
0	1	1	1	0	0	1	1	1	7
0	1	1	1	1	0	1	1	1	7
1	0	0	0	0	–	–	–	–	
–	–	–	–	–	–	–	–	–	

Fig. 6-26   Code digits stored in ROM.

number of incorrect entries. Then, perhaps after three tries, an alarm could sound, or some "lock-out" circuit might be switched in to prevent someone from eventually getting the correct sequence by trial and error.

Note that the ROM stores 32 4-bit words but that the counter only has four outputs. The fifth address input bit is set by toggle switch S_5. So depending on the position of S_5, either of two entirely different sets of code digits can be chosen. Similarly, if a larger ROM is used, several different sets of code digits can be switched in, making it virtually impossible for anyone to guess the correct sequence.

A refinement of the system would be to use a decimal- or hexadecimal-encoded keyboard, rather than toggle switches, to enter the code digits. Similarly, the number of code digits to be entered could be reduced by presetting the counter to some number, say, for example, 10. Then only a six-digit sequence of numbers would be needed to open the lock.

Review Questions

1. RAMs are used for (temporary, permanent) storage of data, whereas ROMs are used for (temporary, permanent) storage.

2. What is a monitor?

3. How can RAM chips be used to store data after power is shut down?

4. What characteristic of a memory chip indicates whether it is suitable for high-speed operations?

5. What type of RAM is the most power efficient, bipolar or MOS? Which is usually faster?

6. What type of RAM must be refreshed periodically? What are its advantages?

7. Describe the differences between a ROM, FPROM, and EPROM.

8. Magnetic core memories are used for both temporary and permanent storage. Explain.

9. In reference to magnetic core memories, what is meant by a destructive readout?

10. What is the purpose of an inhibit winding in a core memory?

Problems

6-1 How many bits can be stored in a 1K × 4 memory chip?

6-2 How many bits can be stored in a 2K × 8 memory chip?

6-3 How many 2102 chips do you need to build a 16K × 8 memory?

6-4 How many 2114 chips do you need to build a 16K × 8 memory?

6-5 To store a 0 in FF 1 of Fig. 6-3, you place a (0, 1) on the data input line and pulse the clock line of (FF 1, all FFs) with a (0, 1).

6-6 If the WRITE operation described in Problem 6-5 were done correctly, FF 2 would (be cleared, retain its previous data).

Refer to Fig. 6-4 for Problems 6-7–6-10.

6-7 To store a 0 into the cell, you place a (0, 1) on the data INPUT and a (0, 1) on the WORD SELECT line.

6-8 This causes Q_3 to turn (ON, OFF) and Q_4 to turn (ON, OFF).

6-9 When writing data into the cell, (a) Q_5 is turned ON, Q_6 OFF; (b) Q_5 is turned OFF, Q_6 ON; (c) Both Q_5 and Q_6 are turned ON whenever WORD SELECT is HIGH; (d) Q_5 or Q_6 is turned ON, depending on whether a 1 or 0 is stored.

6-10 When reading data from the cell, (Choose your answer from Problem 6-9).

6-11 Figure 6-5 shows the arrangement of a 256 × 4 bit memory. In a 128 × 8 bit array, how many memory cells would there be? How many rows? How many columns? How many WORD SELECT decoders? How many sense amps?

6-12 Refer to Fig. 6-8(B). [*Note:* Intel Corporation chose to use the labels $\overline{CS}$ (chip select) rather than $\overline{CE}$ (chip enable) and $\overline{WE}$ (write enable) rather than $R/\overline{W}$.] To store a 4-bit nibble in the RAM, you place the nibble on the I/O lines and then make $\overline{CS}$ (LOW, HIGH) and $\overline{WE}$ (LOW, HIGH). This action (enables, disables) the input buffers and (enables, disables) the output buffers by making the output of gate 1 (HIGH, LOW) and the output of gate 2 (HIGH, LOW).

6-13 Again referring to Fig. 6-8(B), to read a 4-bit nibble stored in the RAM, you make $\overline{CS}$ (LOW, HIGH) and $\overline{WE}$ (LOW, HIGH). This action (enables, disables) the input buffers and (enables, disables) the output buffers, making the output of gate 1 (HIGH, LOW) and the output of gate 2 (HIGH, LOW).

6-14 Referring to Fig. 6-12(A), when $A = 0$ and $B = 1$, which gate(s) will have a HIGH output? How many diodes will be conducting? What will be the output word?

6-15 Draw a diagram, like that of Fig. 6-12(A), showing the placement of all necessary diodes to satisfy the truth table of Fig. 6-27.

B	A	b_3	b_2	b_1	b_0
0	0	1	0	1	0
0	1	1	1	0	0
1	0	0	0	1	0
1	1	0	1	1	1

Fig. 6-27 Truth table for Problem 6-15.

6-16 How many decoder gates would be needed for a 512×8 bit ROM constructed like the one in Fig. 6-12(A)? How many address inputs? How many data output lines?

6-17 How many 1702A EPROMs would be needed to store a monitor program consisting of 1750, 8-bit bytes? How many 2708 EPROMs? How many 2716 EPROMs?

6-18 A pulse is present on the sense winding of a magnetic core memory (whenever a READ pulse is applied, whenever a READ pulse causes the flux in the core to switch).

6-19 If a half-select READ pulse is sent simultaneously down lines X_1 and Y_2, how many cores could possibly switch? Explain.

6-20 An INHIBIT pulse is used (to clear a core, to prevent a 1 from being written into a core, to inhibit reading a core).

Problems 6-21–6-27 refer to Figs. 6-23 and 6-24.

6-21 To read from the EPROM, A_{15}–A_{10} must all be (HIGH, LOW).

6-22   If the circuit is working normally and the MPU outputs an address EFFF, will RAM be selected? Will PROM be selected?

6-23   Suppose the printed circuit foil connecting A_{12} to the input of gate 2 breaks open. When the MPU outputs address EFFF, will RAM be selected? Will PROM be selected? Explain.

6-24   If inverter 4 becomes defective so that one of its outputs is always LOW, would RAM ever be selected?

6-25   If inverter 4 becomes defective so that one of its outputs is always HIGH, would RAM ever be selected? If so, what other problems could this cause?

6-26   What would happen if the MPU tried to WRITE into location FC00?

6-27   Suppose you are troubleshooting the system of Fig. 6-23 and find that erroneous data are being read from the PROM. You measure the $\overline{CS}$ pins and find that both the PROM and RAM chips have a LOW $\overline{CS}$ input level. Which of the following could possibly be the problem (check all possibilities): (a) defective MPU, (b) defective gate 2, (c) defective gate 3, (d) defective inverter 4?

Problems 6-28–6-35 refer to Fig. 6-25. Assume that the ROM contains the codes shown in Fig. 6-26.

6-28   To start the operation, the operator presses the RESET button. Then he or she closes toggle switches to match the ROM outputs. Which switches should he or she close?

6-29   Next the operator presses the ENTER button, causing the output of gate 6 to go (HIGH, LOW). While the ENTER button is depressed, the output of gate 8 should be (LOW, HIGH) if he or she had entered the correct code. At the same time, the output of gate 9 should be (LOW, HIGH).

6-30   When the operator releases the ENTER button, the 74193 gets clocked. He or she then sets the toggle switches for the next digit. Which switches should he or she close this time?

6-31   When the operator presses the ENTER button again, the output of gate 8 goes (LOW, HIGH), and the output of gate 9 (goes HIGH, remains LOW).

6-32   Suppose the operator next closes toggle switches S_1 and S_4 and then presses ENTER. $A = B$ output will be (LOW, HIGH), $A >$ B output will be (LOW, HIGH), and $A < B$ output will be (LOW, HIGH). (A_3 is the MSB.)

6-33   This will cause gate 8's output to be (HIGH, LOW), and gate 9's output to be (HIGH, LOW). What else will happen?

6-34 Before the ENTER button is pressed, what code appears on 7485 inputs A_0–A_3? Explain which comparator output will be HIGH.

6-35 Even when the correct code is set on the toggles, a slight timing problem could cause an undesired reset of the counter. Due to the propagation time of the comparator, it could take 30 to 40 nsec for the $A = B$ output to go HIGH after the ENTER button is pressed. Whenever the $A = B$ output is LOW, gate 7's output is HIGH. As soon as the operator presses ENTER and gate 6's output goes HIGH, both inputs to gate 9 are HIGH until the $A = B$ output of the comparator finally goes HIGH and gate 7's output goes LOW. Thus a glitch (short positive spike) could occur at gate 9's output for several nanoseconds. What component in the circuit is used to suppress the glitch?

CHAPTER 7

Computer Architecture

Although some differences exist in instruction sets for various computers and in how different manufacturers design the hardware to execute programs, the basic structure, or architecture, of computers hasn't changed significantly since the first electronic computers were built in the 1940s. Our purpose in this chapter is to familiarize you with the basic operation and sequence of events common to all computers, large or small.

To make these general concepts more concrete, however, we shall study the operation of an actual small computer, the J-100. This simple computer has an instruction set of only seven instructions and a memory of only 32 words, but it can be programmed, and it can execute a wide variety of programs to demonstrate computer operation. After examining its operation using block diagrams, we shall look at the actual hardware construction of the J-100 to take the mystery out of how the control signals are generated at the proper time.

Once you understand how the J-100 works, you should have no difficulty adapting to more sophisticated systems, even those in which practically the entire computer is on a single chip. Even if all the hardware is on a single chip, you still must understand the sequence of events taking place in order to be able to work effectively with the computer.

7-1 CPU Registers

As you learned in Chapter 3, a computer program is stored in *memory* with instructions in consecutive locations in the order in which the instructions are to be executed. We shall now see how the computer gets each instruction from memory and how it decides what to do next.

Figure 7-1 shows the block diagram of a simple computer system, the J-100. It is an actual computer designed and built by the authors to teach computer architecture. We believe that a real concrete example is more meaningful than a lot of vague general statements. A great deal of care was taken in this design to be consistent with current industry techniques and terminology.

Fig. 7-1 J-100 computer system block diagram.

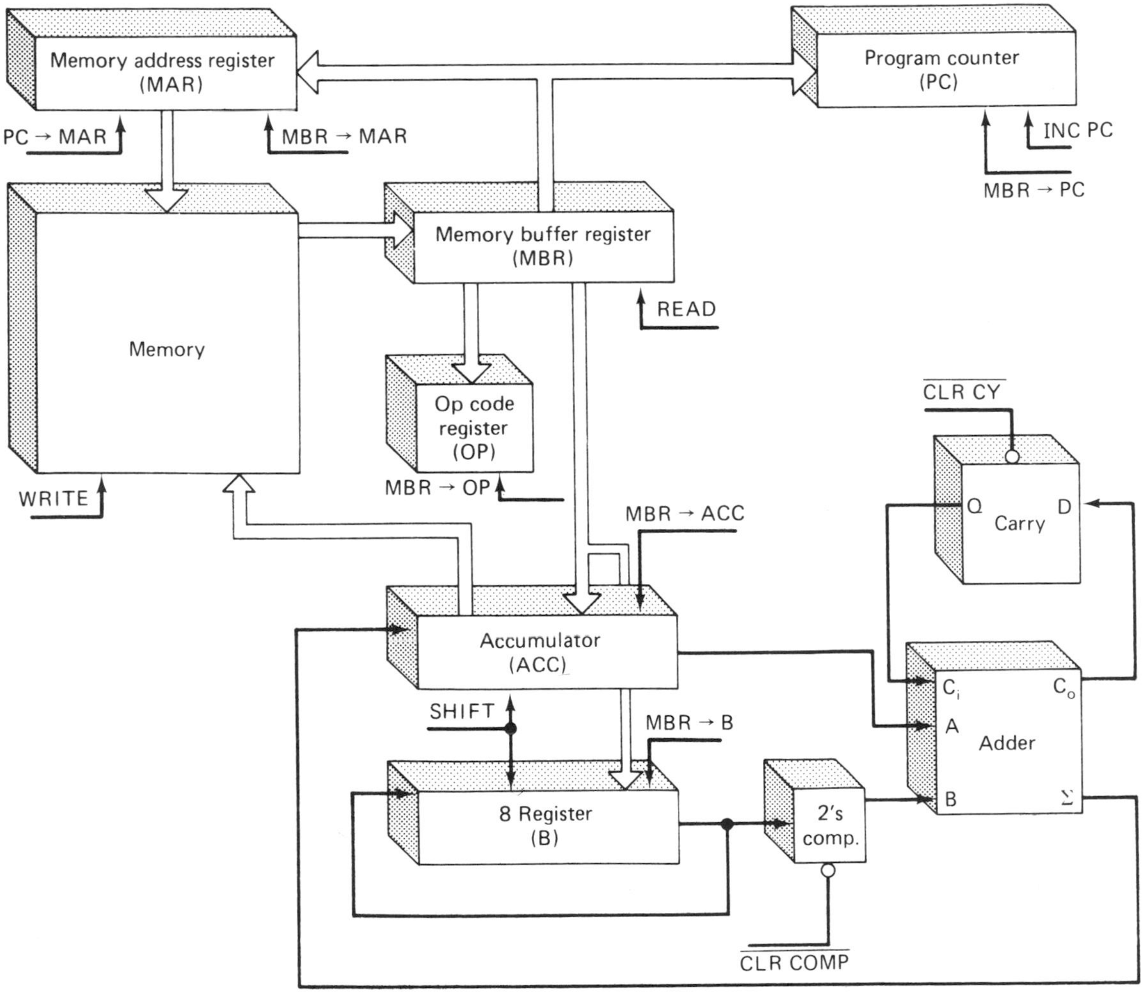

Note that the memory is fed by a *memory address register* (MAR). The MAR selects the location in memory to be read from or written into. The memory outputs drive the *memory buffer register* (MBR), which latches the byte read from memory for later use.

The MBR, in turn, can output information to the MAR, to the *program counter* (PC), or to the *accumulator* (ACC) or *B register* in the arithmetic unit. The particular register that the MBR loads is determined by control signals such as MBR → PC (read as "memory buffer register into program counter"), or MBR → MAR, etc. These control signals are generated by logic circuits and usually depend on the specific instruction being executed. These signals are shown on the diagram by little right-angle arrows pointing to the register that each signal controls. The wide arrows in the diagram represent address and data buses over which either 3, 5, or 8 bits of information are transferred simultaneously.

The arithmetic unit is a serial adder-subtracter in this case, but parallel arithmetic circuits can also be used.

The program counter (PC) is a presettable binary up counter whose job it is to keep track of where in memory to get the next instruction. You'll see its operation when we step through a program later.

One other register fed by the MBR is the *op code register* (OP). The job of the op code register is to latch the op code of the instruction currently being executed and present it to the op code decoder. The op code decoder, in turn, feeds a variety of control logic gates which generate the control signals, such as MBR → MAR, which were mentioned earlier.

The combination of circuits in the block diagram shown in Fig. 7-1 (excluding the memory) is often called the *central processing unit* (CPU). To make a complete computer, we also need to add some form of *input/ output* (I/O) devices to the CPU. The I/O devices could be as simple as switches and LEDs or as complex as a tape reader and video display. We'll look at I/O devices and schemes in a later chapter. For now, let's concentrate on the CPU operation.

You will remember that instructions and data are both stored in the same memory. To keep track of whether an instruction or data byte is being read from memory, a timing distributor (TD) is used. The TD generates two timing cycles called the *FETCH* cycle and the *EXECUTE* cycle. Each of these cycles is further subdivided into four time periods, or T states, T_0, T_1, T_2, T_3. During the FETCH cycle, the control circuitry fetches, or reads, an instruction from memory. Then during the EXECUTE cycle, the instruction is carried out.

Figure 7-2 shows the sequence of events governed by the TD. After a system RESET, the computer is placed in the RUN mode. Thereafter, the TD generates a FETCH signal and T_0, T_1, T_2, T_3 in that order followed by EXECUTE and T_0, T_1, T_2, T_3. The TD continues this operation over and over, FETCH, EXECUTE, FETCH, EXECUTE, etc., until it is told to HALT.

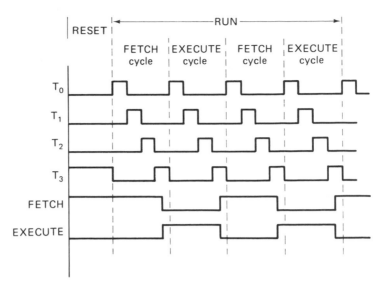

Fig. 7-2 Timing distributor waveforms.

It is during the various T states that control signals, such as READ, INC PC, etc., are generated.

Table 7-1 lists the sequence of operations for all possible instructions for our small computer. Note that for the LDA instruction, for example, at F (fetch) and T_0, signals READ and INC PC are generated. Then at F and T_1, MBR $\rightarrow$ OP is generated, etc. Immediately after completing F and T_3, the EXECUTE mode is set by the signal SET E. At E (execute) and T_0, a READ occurs. At E and T_1, MBR $\rightarrow$ ACC is generated, etc.

Although some of the signals differ for various instructions, the first two T states during the FETCH cycle are identical for all, because each instruction must be fetched and decoded before any execution can take place. The computer cannot anticipate what is should do next; it must be told what to do each step of the way.

We shall study the operation of this typical CPU thoroughly as we follow its actions step by step through a simple program. Later we shall look at actual SSI and MSI circuitry used to build the entire system.

7-2 Step-by-Step Program Execution

We shall now examine the contents of each of the CPU registers for each T state while executing a program to add two numbers and store the sum. The program of Fig. 7-3 adds the number 12_{10} stored in location 14H to the number 7_{10} stored in location 15H and stores the sum in location 16H.

Before the computer can begin execution, the operator must load the

Table 7-1 Sequence of Operation[a]

Instruction (op code)	T State	FETCH Cycle	EXECUTE Cycle
NOP (100)	T_0	READ, INC PC	None
	T_1	MBR → OP	None
	T_2	PC → MAR	None
	T_3	—	None
LDA (101)	T_0	READ, INC PC	READ
	T_1	MBR → OP	MBR → ACC
	T_2	MBR → MAR	PC → MAR
	T_3	SET E	SET F
ADD (110)	T_0	READ, INC PC	READ
	T_1	MBR → OP	MBR → B, start SHIFT ctr, CLR COMP
	T_2	MBR → MAR	PC → MAR
	T_3	SET E	SET F
CAD (111)	T_0	READ, INC PC	READ
	T_1	MBR → OP	MBR → B, start SHIFT ctr
	T_2	MBR → MAR	PC → MAR
	T_3	SET E	SET F
STO (000)	T_0	READ, INC PC	WRITE
	T_1	MBR → OP	—
	T_2	MBR → MAR	PC → MAR
	T_3	SET E	SET F
BMI (001)	T_0	READ, INC PC	None
	T_1	MBR → OP	None
	T_2	MBR → PC → MAR	None
	T_3	—	None
HLT (011)	T_0	READ, INC PC	None
	T_1	MBR → OP	None

[a] See Table 3-1 for a description of op codes.

program into memory. Let's assume that the memory already contains all information as shown in Fig. 7-3, and the operator RESETs the computer. As shown in Fig. 7-4, after RESET, the MAR, PC, and op code register are all cleared. The MBR, ACC, and B register may or may not be cleared, depending on the CPU design. Whether they are or not is unimportant now.

Also, upon RESET, the FETCH flip-flop is SET, and the timing distributor is ready to generate a T_0 pulse. The operator then throws a switch that puts the computer in the RUN mode. From here on, the computer runs the program automatically, all the way to the end. The operator doesn't do any more.

As soon as the computer is placed in the RUN mode, timing pulse

Memory location	Op code	Operand address	Mnemonic
0 0 0 0 0	1 0 1	1 0 1 0 0	LDA
0 0 0 0 1	1 1 0	1 0 1 0 1	ADD
0 0 0 1 0	0 0 0	1 0 1 1 0	STO
0 0 0 1 1	0 1 1	X X X X X	HLT
0 0 1 0 0	X X X	X X X X X	
1 0 1 0 0	0 0 0	0 1 1 0 0	12_{10}
1 0 1 0 1	0 0 0	0 0 1 1 1	7_{10}
1 0 1 1 0	X X X	X X X X X	

Fig. 7-3 Simple machine language program to add two numbers and store sum.

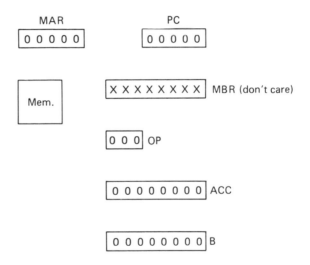

Fig. 7-4 CPU after RESET.

T_0 is generated, causing a READ from the memory location pointed to by the MAR, that is, from location 00000.

Let's examine the sequence of events through the entire program for each cycle and T state.

FETCH CYCLE

F and T_0 . . . READ, INC PC   (See Fig. 7-5)

The byte in location 00000 is transferred to the MBR. Note in this case that the 8-bit byte now in the MBR contains both the op code 101 and the operand address 10100. The op code and address are

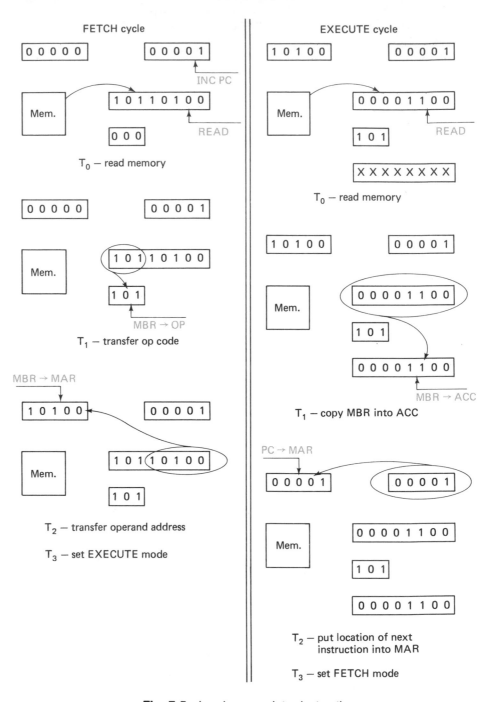

Fig. 7-5 Load accumulator instruction.

transferred together as a single byte, but they will be separated later. Simultaneously, the PC gets INCremented (clocked) so that it points to where the next instruction will come from.

F and T_1 . . . MBR → OP (memory buffer register into op code register)

MBR → OP causes the op code (101) portion of the byte in the MBR to be transferred into the op code register for decoding.

As mentioned previously, these first two T states are exactly the same for *any* instruction FETCH. We are simply following it through for the LDA instruction as a specific example.

Once the op code decoder has determined that this is an LDA instruction, it sets up appropriate gates so that the next pulse, T_2, generates a load pulse called MBR → MAR.

F and T_2 . . . MBR → MAR (memory buffer register into memory address register)

The operand address portion of the byte in the MBR is transferred into the MAR, as shown at T_2 in Fig. 7-5. With the operand address in the MAR, the computer will be able to locate the data to be loaded into the ACC.

F and T_3 . . . SET E

The final pulse, T_3, of the FETCH cycle is used to toggle the FETCH/EXECUTE flip-flop, thus setting the computer to the EXECUTE mode. Now we begin the EXECUTE cycle of the LDA instruction as shown in Table 7-1 and Fig. 7-5.

EXECUTE CYCLE

E and T_0 . . . READ

The CPU does a memory READ again, this time placing the contents of location 14H into the MBR.

E and T_1 . . . MBR → ACC

Pulse T_1 activates gates to generate a load pulse called MBR → ACC (memory buffer register into accumulator). This copies the data into the ACC, thus completing the instruction.

E and T_2 . . . PC → MAR

At T_2 a pulse is generated to transfer the contents of the program counter into the MAR, so that the MAR will point to the location where the next instruction will come from.

E and T_3 . . . SET *F*

Finally, at T_3, the FETCH mode is set again and the CPU is ready to go to work on the next instruction. This completes the LDA instruction.

Unless told to HALT, the timing distributor will continue generating pulses. So, after completing the EXECUTE cycle, T_0 is once again generated, beginning the next FETCH cycle.

FETCH CYCLE

F and T_0 . . . READ, INC PC

A READ is done from the location pointed to by the MAR. This is shown in Fig. 7-6. Note once again that the PC gets incremented to point to the next instruction.

F and T_1 . . . MBR → OP

At T_1, the op code (110) is transferred into the op code register and decoded as before.

F and T_2 . . . MBR → MAR

Since the instruction is an ADD, the operand address is transferred to the MAR at T_2, so that the computer will know where to get the data to be added.

F and T_3 . . . SET *E*

The EXECUTE mode is set.

EXECUTE CYCLE

E and T_0 . . . READ

Going to the EXECUTE cycle in Fig. 7-6, we see that at T_0 a memory READ brings the data byte into the MBR.

E and T_1 . . . MBR → B

At T_1 the data to be added to the ACC is transferred to the B register, which is simply one of the registers in the arithmetic unit. At this time, the addition takes place, either by means of serial or parallel adder circuits. In the J-100, addition is accomplished by clocking the shift registers eight times. The sum of the two numbers appears in the ACC after addition, while the number being added stays in the B register. The 2's complementer circuit is used only for subtraction, so it is cleared during addition.

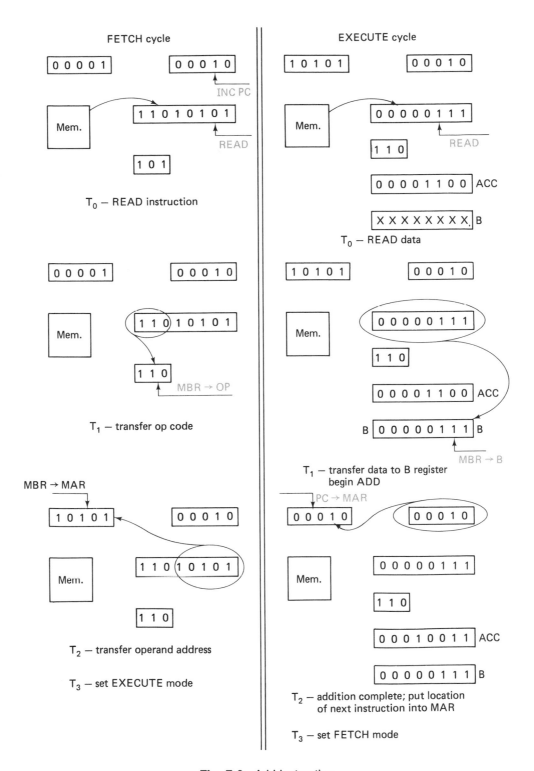

Fig. 7-6 Add instruction.

E and T_2 . . . PC → MAR

The contents of the PC are transferred to the MAR to get ready for the next instruction FETCH. Note that the sum of the two numbers, 19_{10}, now appears in the ACC.

E and T_3 . . . Set F

Finally, at T_3, the FETCH mode is set again. The ADD instruction is now completed.

FETCH CYCLE

F and T_0 . . . READ, INC PC

Once again the computer READS another instruction, this time from location 00010, as shown in Fig. 7-7.

F and T_1 . . . MBR → OP

The op code 000, transferred at T_1, tells the CPU to STORE the ACC contents.

F and T_2 . . . MBR → MAR

At T_2, the location where the byte is to be stored is given to the MAR.

F and T_3 . . . SET E

EXECUTE CYCLE

E and T_0 . . . WRITE

Since the instruction is a STORE, rather than generating a memory READ at E and T_0, the control circuitry generates a memory WRITE. This pulse copies the ACC into memory at location 10110, the address in the MAR. The STORE operation does not destroy the ACC contents.

E and T_1 . . . no action for this instruction

E and T_2 . . . PC → MAR

As always, at E and T_2, the PC must be transferred into the MAR to point to the next instruction.

E and T_3 . . . SET F

This completes the store instruction.

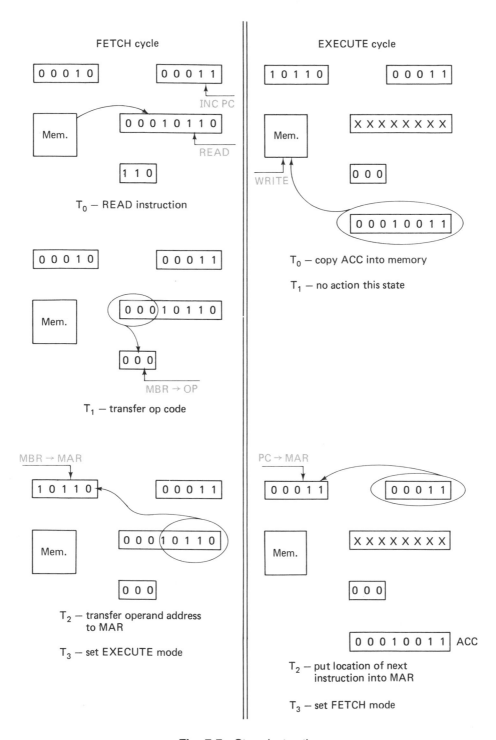

Fig. 7-7 Store instruction.

FETCH CYCLE

F and T_0 . . . READ, INC PC

The instruction in location 00011 is transferred into the MBR, as shown in Fig. 7-8.

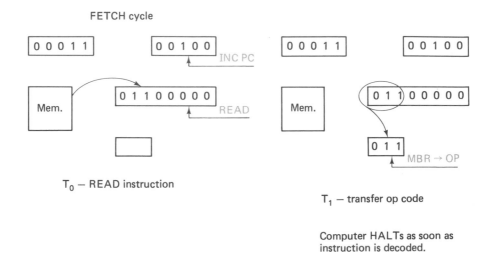

FETCH cycle

T_0 – READ instruction

T_1 – transfer op code

Computer HALTs as soon as instruction is decoded.

Fig. 7-8 Halt instruction.

F and T_1 . . . MBR → OP

Last, the op code for the HALT instruction is transferred to op code register and decoded. As soon as it is decoded, the computer stops. The program has now been completely executed.

Regardless of the program being executed, the sequence of events is almost identical to those of the previous example. Although some variation exists in signal names and in how different computers handle the operand addresses, basically all computers operate in the same manner. We recommend that you study the previous example thoroughly to become familiar with the sequence.

One type of instruction that differs somewhat from the previous example is the BRANCH instruction. Our small computer has a single conditional branch instruction called BRANCH IF MINUS (BMI). Let's see how it works.

Suppose our computer has been executing the program shown in part in Fig. 7-9. Let's also suppose that after executing the instruction at location 08 which is COMPLEMENT AND ADD (CAD), the contents of the ACC are as shown in the figure at T_0. (CAD is used to subtract a number from

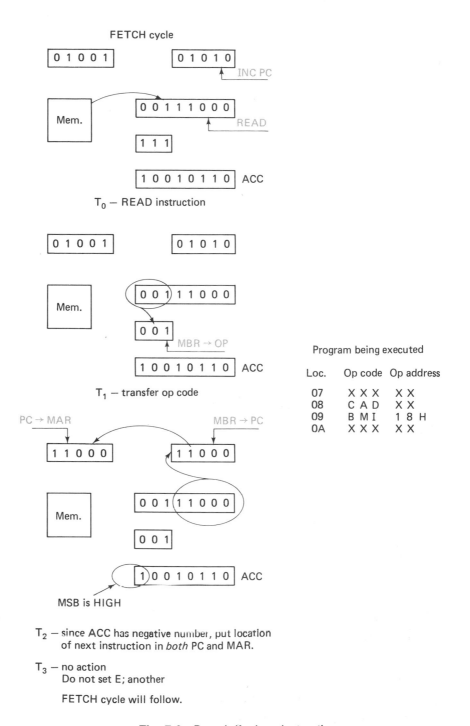

Fig. 7-9 Branch if minus instruction.

the accumulator.) Note that the most significant bit of the ACC is a 1. Whenever this occurs, the number in the ACC is considered *negative*. The instruction at 09 tells the computer to branch to location 18H for its next instruction if the number in the ACC is minus. Let's go through it.

Starting at F and T_0, the instruction is READ from memory and PC incremented as usual. Then at T_1, the op code portion of the instruction is transferred to the op code register and decoded.

The control circuitry then examines the MSB of the ACC and sees that it is a 1. So at time T_2, the address portion of the instruction word, the five LSBs, are transferred into the PC and also into the MAR. This way, rather than taking its next instruction from location 01010, the CPU will get it from 11000. Finally, there is no EXECUTE cycle for this instruction. The computer simply goes into another FETCH cycle. That is, at T_3, the EXECUTE mode is *not* set.

More powerful computers have many branch instructions, but generally the idea is similar to that presented here.

The NOP instruction simply increments the program counter. It does not affect the accumulator. It is often used to increase the length of a timing loop. This will be covered in a later chapter.

Fig. 7-10. J-100 computer. (Courtesy of Electronic Technology Institute.)

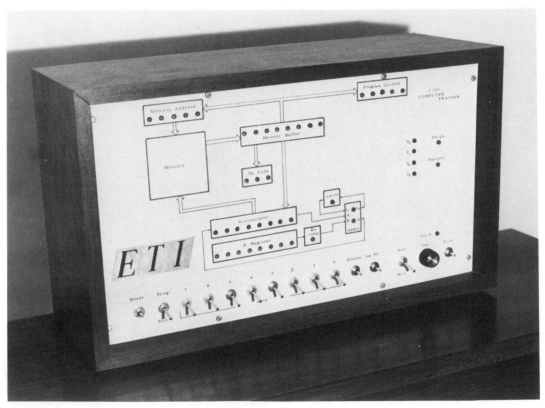

7-3 A Small SSI/MSI Computer

If it is desired, this section could be skipped in the interest of making a shorter course. However, we believe that by presenting an example of a complete computer system, constructed with all relatively simple devices, we can "tie together" a lot of loose ends often left dangling in other computer texts. Since most of the circuitry has already been covered in isolated topics thus far, the descriptions will be brief. What we shall emphasize is how clocks, counters, gates, registers, latches, decoders, etc., are put together to form a complete working system.

Figure 7-10 shows the front panel of the J-100 computer. Note that the system block diagram is shown with LED indicators representing each bit in each register. In addition, there are LED status lamps which indicate the timing distributor's mode and T states.

Also note the bank of switches along the bottom. These are used for programming and for memory examination. Reference will be made to these switches as we discuss the operation of the unit.

Clock The CLOCK circuitry, shown in Fig. 7-11, initiates all timing pulses. When the MAN/AUTO switch is in the AUTO position, a 555 timer,

Fig. 7-11 Clock for J-100.

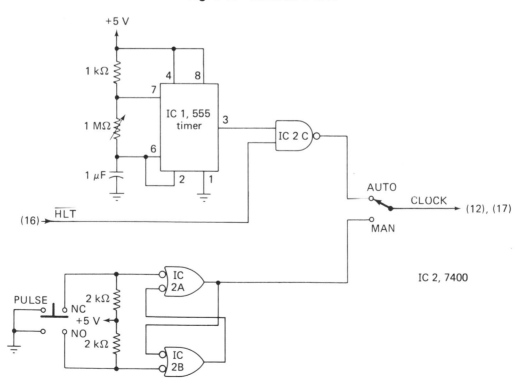

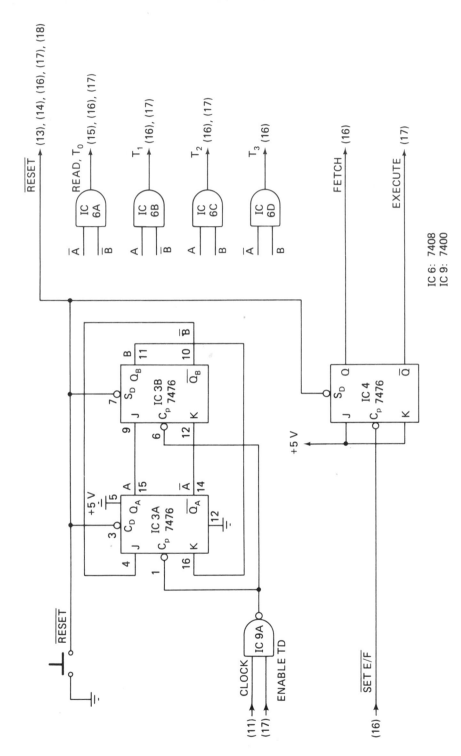

Fig. 7-12 Timing distributor.

IC 1, is used as the automatic clock. The clock period is adjustable by means of the 1-MΩ pot from about 1 Hz to 1 kHz. Note that the $\overline{\text{HLT}}$ signal must be inactive HIGH to enable gate IC 2C. When the MAN/AUTO switch is in the MANUAL position, clocking is done by means of a push-button switch (PULSE) which drives an *RS* flip-flop, IC 2A, and IC 2B. The option of a MANUAL pulse generator is useful in *single-stepping* through a program for *debugging*. Debugging a program refers to executing the program one step at a time to find errors.

Generally speaking, input signals are shown on the drawings coming in from the left, and outputs are shown on the right. Signal names are shown in capital letters, and the number in parentheses refers to the figure number where the signal line connects. For example, the $\overline{\text{HLT}}$ signal comes from Fig. 7-16, and the CLOCK signal goes to Figs. 7-12 and 7-17.

Timing distributor Moving on to the timing distributor of Fig. 7-12, note that two signals are gated by IC 9A. The CLOCK signal passes through the gate if ENABLE TD is HIGH. The signal ENABLE TD is controlled by the arithmetic control circuitry of Fig. 7-17 which will be studied later.

The output of IC 9A clocks IC 3A and IC 3B, which form a shift counter. The outputs of the shift counter drive the gates of IC 6 to generate the timing pulses T_0–T_3. A shifter counter is used here rather than a ripple counter to avoid glitches from appearing at the gate outputs. It is left as an exercise for the student to verify that the gates of IC 6 generate the waveforms of Fig. 7-2.

Note also that IC 4 generates the mode control signals, FETCH and EXECUTE. The toggling signal, $\overline{\text{SET } E/F}$, comes from the control circuitry of Fig. 7-16, to be discussed later.

Program counter A 5-bit binary counter is needed for the program counter, since there are 32 locations in memory to access. IC 7B of Fig. 7-13 outputs the LSB of the counter, and IC 8 contains the upper 4-bit circuitry. (Of course a single 5-bit counter could have been used if one was available.) The C_p input of IC 7B is driven by the output of gate IC 9B. One input for the gate is INC PC, generated by the control circuitry of Fig. 7-16, and the other is the output of IC 7A. IC 7A is used here simply as a switch debouncer for the MANUAL INC PC push button. Cross-coupled NAND gates could also have been used, but only one flip-flop of IC 7 was needed for the counter, so the other was used as an *RS* flip-flop.

A system RESET clears IC 7B and IC 8. Thereafter, with the MANUAL INC PC switch in the position shown, the control INC PC signal clocks the 5-bit counter on each rising edge, causing it to count up. (You will recall that this occurs at F and T_0.) Note that the RESET signal is fed to IC 7B via gates IC 9C and IC 2D. The other input to IC 9C will be explained shortly.

Remember that the PC must be loaded with the address bits from the MBR on a BRANCH IF MINUS instruction. At that time, providing

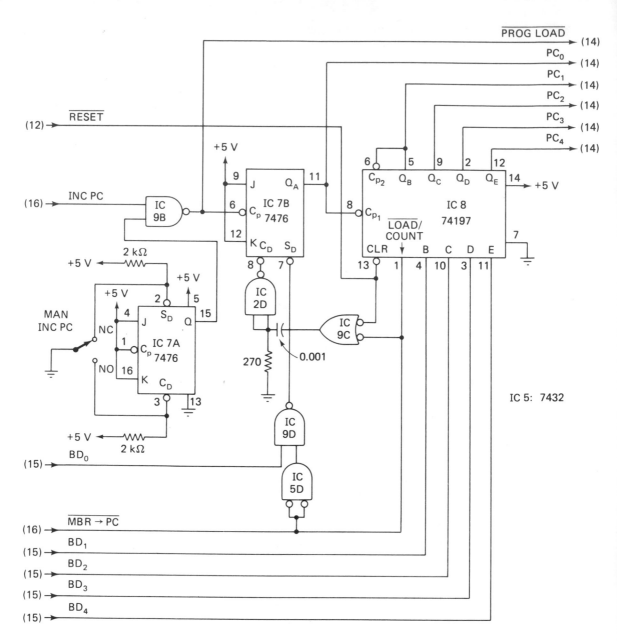

Fig. 7-13 Program counter.

that the ACC most significant bit is HIGH, the signal $\overline{MBR \rightarrow PC}$, fed to the COUNT/$\overline{LOAD}$ input of the 74197, loads the four MSBs of the address into the upper 4-bit positions of the PC. Simultaneously, the LOW-going $\overline{MBR \rightarrow PC}$ signal is fed to gates IC 9C and IC 5D. The signal at IC 9C output goes HIGH, causing a HIGH-going spike to appear at the input of IC 2D. This spike gets inverted by IC 2D, causing a short-duration CLEAR pulse to appear at the C_D input of IC 7B. Then, immediately after being cleared, IC 7B is loaded with the A_0 bit of the address bus through IC 9D. Note that IC 5D has enabled IC 9D because of the $\overline{MBR \rightarrow PC}$ signal at its own input.

It was not necessary to clear the 74197 before loading it because the LOW COUNT/$\overline{LOAD}$ signal forces the chips outputs to follow its inputs.

Memory address register Now let's go on to the memory address register circuitry of Fig. 7-14. Remember that the MAR can be loaded either from the MBR or the PC, depending on the instruction. To select one or the other set of inputs, 74157 multiplexers are used. With the RUN/$\overline{PROG}$

Fig. 7-14 Memory address register control circuitry.

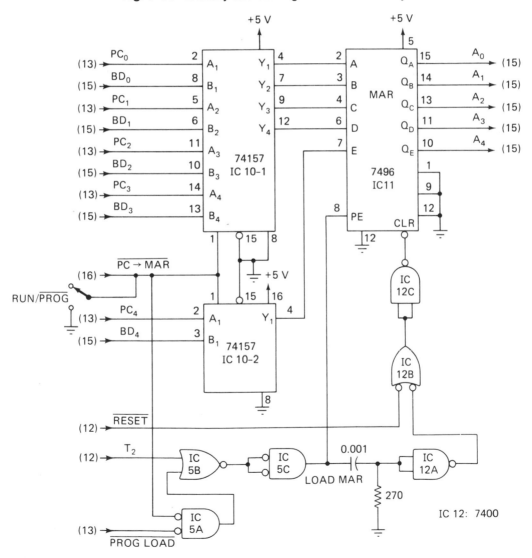

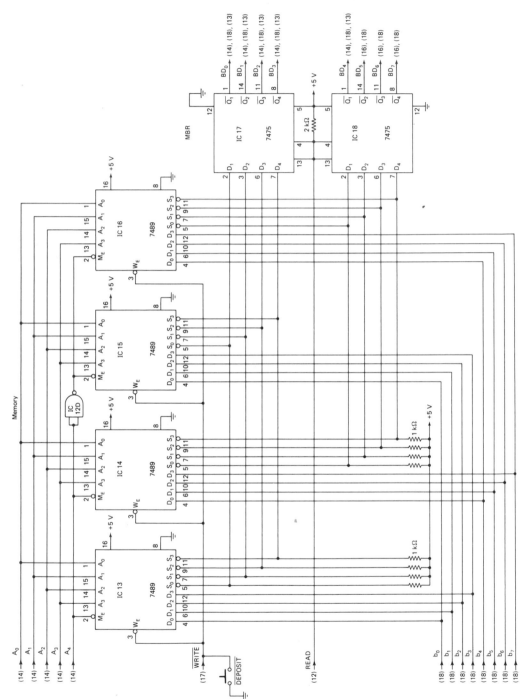

Fig. 7-15 Memory and memory buffer register.

226

toggle switch in the RUN mode, the signal $\overline{PC \rightarrow MAR}$, which comes from Fig. 7-16, determines which inputs are fed to IC 11. If $\overline{PC \rightarrow MAR}$ is LOW or if the RUN/$\overline{PROG}$ switch input is LOW, the PC inputs are fed to IC 11. Otherwise the MBR inputs (BD_0–BD_4) are selected. Once either set of inputs is selected, a LOAD MAR signal is developed at the output gate of IC 5C. When this HIGH signal is fed to the input of IC 12A, through the differentiator, a short-duration clear pulse is fed through IC 12B and IC 12C to the CLR input of the 7496. The 7496 is a 5-bit shift register, used here as a 5-bit latch.

Once the 7496 has been cleared, the HIGH LOAD MAR signal causes the address bits from the multiplexers to be latched in. The outputs Q_A–Q_E now contain the address of the location in memory to be accessed.

Memory and memory buffer register The memory circuitry of Fig. 7-15 is very easy to follow. Note that address lines A_0–A_3 are connected to all four memory chips. Address line A_4 connects directly to the memory enable input of IC 13 and IC 14. But A_4 is fed to chips IC 15 and IC 16 after being inverted by IC 12D. In this manner, chips 13 and 14 are enabled for the first 16 words in memory, while chips 15 and 16 hold the upper 16 words.

The open collector outputs (S_0–S_3) of the 7489 memory chips are pulled up through 1-kΩ resistors. Note that chips 13 and 15 store bits 0–3, while chips 14 and 16 store bits 4–7.

The outputs of the memory chips are connected to the memory buffer register, consisting of two 7475 4-bit latches. The $\overline{Q}$ outputs of the latches are used because the 7489 chips output the complement of the data bits stored.

To store words in memory, an address is first applied to the address lines. This enables the appropriate chips and points to a particular location. Then the write enable is driven LOW, either by a $\overline{WRITE}$ signal from the control circuitry or by the manual $\overline{DEPOSIT}$ switch used in programming. When $\overline{WRITE}$ is inactive HIGH, data present at the addressed location appear on the S_0–S_3 outputs if the 7489 is enabled.

A READ signal to the inputs of the 7475s latches the memory byte into the MBR.

Op code decoder and control Going to Fig. 7-16, we see the op code latch and decoder as well as the control circuitry for the FETCH cycle signals. To understand the use of each of the gates, it is helpful to go through the sequence of operation of Table 7-1.

Let's start with gate IC 21A. At F and T_0, the signal INC PC is generated. This signal is fed to the PC of Fig. 7-13. Although not shown in this figure, a READ signal is always generated at T_0. This signal is shown at the output of IC 6A of Fig. 7-12.

Next, at F and T_1, the output of IC 21B goes HIGH, thus generating MBR $\rightarrow$ OP. This HIGH signal is fed to the clock input of the 74175, thus

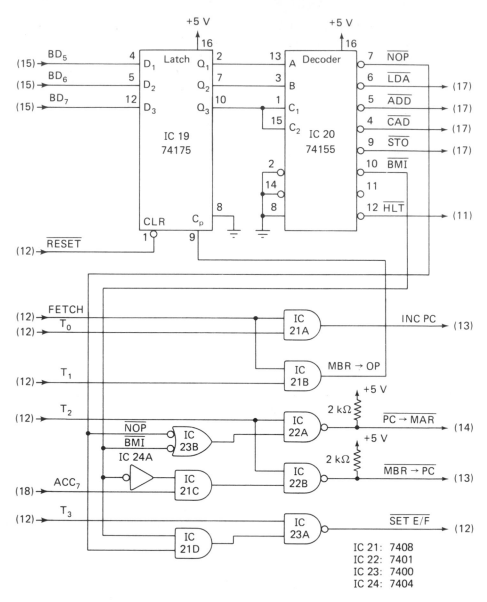

Fig. 7-16 Op code decoder and FETCH logic.

latching in the op code. The latched op code is fed to the inputs of the decoder IC 20, causing one of its outputs to go LOW, depending on the code.

It is left to the student to follow through the remaining gates of the control circuitry of Figs. 7-16 and 7-17.

EXECUTE and arithmetic control   Figure 7-17 shows the EXECUTE control circuitry and the arithmetic control.

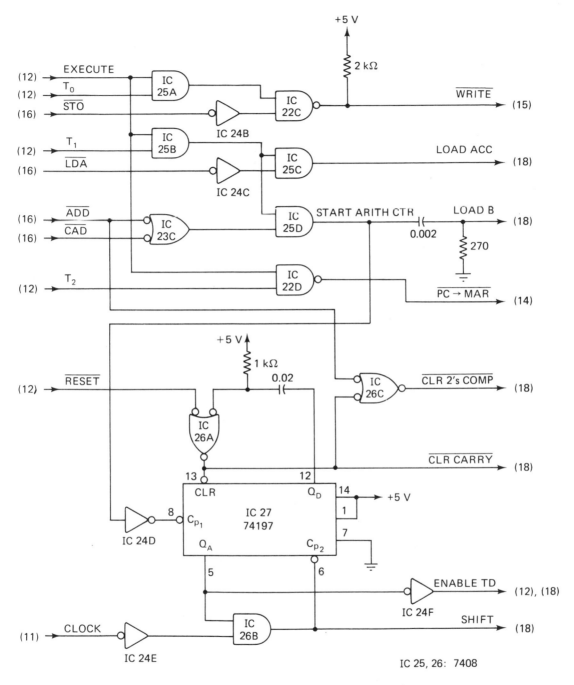

Fig. 7-17 EXECUTE and arith control logic.

The purpose of the arithmetic control circuit is to generate exactly *eight* SHIFT CLOCK pulses for the serial arithmetic circuit. Here's how it works.

Assuming the instruction is an ADD, the output of gate IC 25D goes HIGH at E and T_1. The HIGH signal, called START ARITH CTR, is fed to IC 24D, causing its output to go LOW. This LOW signal clocks the 74197 counter, which had been initially RESET.

The 74197 has two built-in counters: a single flip-flop, whose output is Q_A, and $\div$ 8 counter, whose MSB is Q_D. When the C_{p_1} input to the chip goes LOW, Q_A goes HIGH, enabling IC 26B and simultaneously *disabling* the TD (timing distributor) through IC 24F.

As long as the TD is disabled, the control circuitry will remain in E and T_1, even though the CLOCK continues to run.

Note that the CLOCK is also fed to IC 26B through inverter IC 24E. So each time the CLOCK goes LOW, the $\div$ 8 counter is incremented by the signal at C_{p_2}, and a SHIFT pulse is sent to the arithmetic circuits. After the eighth CLOCK pulse, however, Q_D output goes from HIGH to LOW. The LOW-going signal is fed through a differentiator circuit and through IC 26A, clearing the counter to zero. Output Q_A also gets cleared by this pulse, disabling IC 26B and thus preventing any more SHIFT pulses from being generated. Simultaneously, when Q_A goes LOW, the TD is once again enabled, and the computer goes on to state T_2 to continue its operations.

The $\overline{\text{ADD}}$ signal also keeps the 2's complementer cleared during the entire ADD operation.

Arithmetic circuit Figure 7-18 shows the accumulator and B register, each consisting of two 4-bit shift registers. To load the accumulator, the ENABLE TD line must be HIGH. It is connected to the S_1 (mode control) input of this register. When S_1 is pulled LOW, the accumulator register is placed in the *shift* mode. In addition to the mode control, a LOAD ACC signal, coming from IC 25C of Fig. 7-17, is fed through OR gate IC 32A. When in the shift mode, the SHIFT clock is fed through the same gate.

Register B is loaded and shifted in the same manner.

Finally, we see the remainder of the ADDER circuitry and the 2's complementer. The LSB of the B register simply passes through the complementer unchanged if the instruction is an ADD. However, for a CAD instruction, the 2's complementer is *not* cleared all the time, so the 2's complement of the number in the B register is fed to the adder input. Every bit after but not including the first 1 bit is complemented.

Programming the J-100 To program the computer, we throw the MAN/AUTO switch to MAN and the RUN/$\overline{\text{PROG}}$ switch to PROG. Then we RESET the system by pressing the RESET button.

Next we press the manual PULSE once, which puts the computer in F and T_0, thus making the READ line HIGH, so that we can READ each location in memory immediately after loading it for verification.

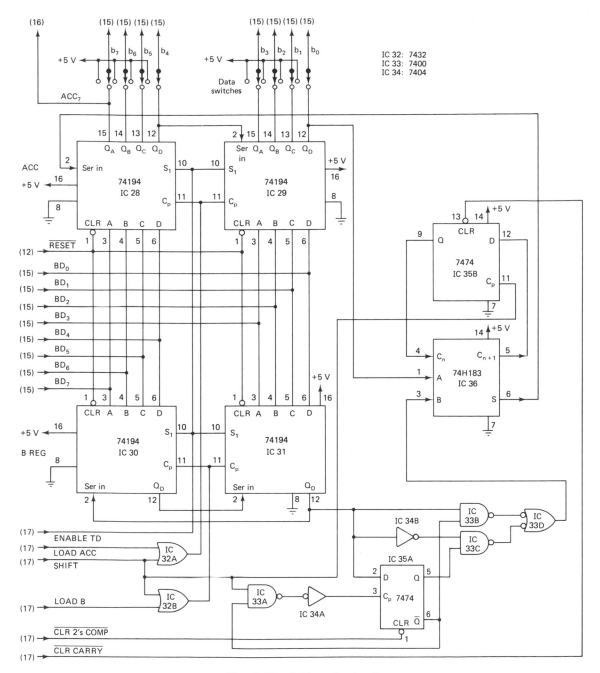

Fig. 7-18 Arithmetic circuit.

We next set the data switches to 1 or 0, as desired, depending on the byte to be stored. Note that the data switches are connected to the ACC outputs of Fig. 7-18. In the RUN mode, the ACC outputs are connected to memory, but in the PROG mode, the toggles are switched either to VCC for a 1 bit or to ACC for a 0 bit. (Remember, the ACC was cleared on RESET.)

After setting the data word on the switches, the DEPOSIT switch is pressed. This, as shown in Fig. 7-15, acts the same as a $\overline{\text{WRITE}}$ signal, so the data are loaded into memory at location 00000.

Next we press INC PC, which advances the PC and MAR to 00001.

We now set the toggles to data to be entered at this location and press DEPOSIT.

We continue in this manner—set data, DEPOSIT, INC PC—over and over, until all locations have been loaded with either instructions or data.

Finally, after the program is loaded, we RESET again to put the PC at the starting location in the program. Then we throw the RUN/$\overline{\text{PROG}}$ switch to RUN. If we leave the MAN/AUTO switch on MAN, we can step through the program one CLOCK pulse at a time. Or we can throw the switch to AUTO, and the computer will execute the program until it reaches a HALT instruction.

Not shown in any of the figures are the LEDs and drivers to show the state of each bit. The drivers can be any of the active HIGH drivers covered previously.

Review Questions

1. What register points to where the next instruction will come from?

2. What register points to the location in memory that will be read?

3. In all memory-referenced instructions (not including HLT and NOP), the instruction word contains two parts. What are they?

4. Each memory-referenced instruction has how many T states?

5. Which register holds the results of arithmetic operations?

6. What does the J-100 computer always do immediately after completing the execution of an instruction (after E and T_3)?

7. Why doesn't the NOP instruction word contain an operand address?

8. In a BMI instruction, what signals the computer whether or not to branch?

9. In a BMI instruction, why does the PC get loaded from the MBR?

10. In the BMI instruction, why doesn't the FETCH/EXECUTE flip-flop get toggled at F and T_3?

Problems

7-1 If the computer had 100 possible instructions, rather than just 8, how many bits would be required in the op code register?

7-2 If the computer was capable of accessing 16K bytes of memory, rather than just 32, how many bits would be required in the MAR?

7-3 Referring to Problem 7-2, how many bits would be required for the program counter?

7-4 If the computer had just fetched a CAD instruction, what would be the contents of the op code register after F and T_1?

7-5 Referring to Problem 7-4, what would be the contents of the op code register after E and T_1?

7-6 Referring to Fig. 7-5, from which memory location were the data read at E and T_0?

7-7 During the ADD instruction shown in Fig. 7-6, the operand (number to be added to ACC) is transferred into the _____ register at E and T_1.

7-8 Refer to the program of Fig. 7-3. Suppose the contents of memory location 10100 were changed to 00101100 and the contents of 10101 were changed to 00010110 and then the program was run as before. List the contents of the various registers after E and T_2 of the ADD instruction. (*Hint:* See Fig. 7-6.)

PC   _____
MAR _____
MBR _____
OP   _____
ACC _____
B   _____

7-9 Again refer to Fig. 7-3. Suppose the program is as shown but the contents of memory location 00001 are changed to 11110101. Show the contents of all registers after E and T_2 of the STORE instruction.

PC   _____
MAR _____
MBR _____
OP   _____
ACC _____
B   _____

7-10 Suppose you erroneously loaded memory location 00001 with 11010100 while loading the program of Fig. 7-3 into the computer's memory. What value would be stored into location 10110 after execution?

The remaining problems refer to the J-100 computer.

7-11 What kinds of gates are ICs 2A and 2B in the clock circuit of Fig. 7-11: (a) ANDs, (b) ORs, (c) NANDs, (d) NORs, (e) exclusive ORs?

7-12 What is the main purpose of the 1-MΩ POT in the clock circuit: (a) vary the CLOCK pulse width, (b) vary the CLOCK signal amplitude, (c) vary the CLOCK signal frequency, (d) vary the amount of dc component in the CLOCK signal?

7-13 In the timing distributor of Fig. 7-12, the counter is (a) a shift register, (b) a serial type, (c) a decade type, (d) MOD-2 type, (e) used to temporarily store the address of the next instruction.

7-14 The output pulses T_0–T_3 are (a) active LOW one at a time, (b) active LOW one or more at a time, (c) active HIGH one at a time, (d) active HIGH one or more at a time.

7-15 When RESET goes LOW, IC 3's outputs Q_A and Q_B are (a) 0, 0; (b) 1, 1; (c) 1, 0; (d) 0, 1.

7-16 What is the word size of the program counter of Fig. 7-13: (a) 4 bits, (b) 5 bits, (c) 16 bits, (d) 32 bits?

7-17 If the $\overline{\text{SET } E/F}$ signal goes LOW, (a) signal FETCH goes HIGH, (b) signal EXECUTE goes HIGH, (c) neither FETCH nor EXECUTE goes HIGH, (d) either FETCH or EXECUTE goes HIGH depending on the FF's state before the signal was applied.

7-18 What is the purpose of IC 7A in the program counter: (a) debounce the INC PC (manual) switch, (b) keep IC 9B disabled and block the INC PC signal until the INC PC (manual) switch is depressed?

7-19 The PC is a (a) shift counter, (b) binary counter, (c) decade counter, (d) ring counter.

7-20 What is the purpose of the IC 7B of the program counter: (a) it debounces the INC PC switch, (b) it is a 1-bit time delay for signal INC PC, (c) it temporarily holds the MSB of the PC, (d) it temporarily holds the LSB of the PC?

7-21 In Fig. 7-14, IC 5B and IC 5C were used to generate the required signals. Although it seems like a waste of parts, it was more economical to make use of these spare gates rather than using an additional chip. What single gate could replace the combination of these two gates: (a) AND, (b) OR, (c) NAND, (d) NOR?

7-22 IC 9 and IC 10 in Fig. 7-14 are capable of (a) multiplexing two 4-bit words, (b) multiplexing two 5-bit words, (c) decoding 8-bit inputs, (d) decoding address inputs.

7-23 When $\overline{PC \rightarrow MAR}$ is LOW while LOAD MAR is HIGH, the memory address register (a) receives and holds a 4-bit word from the program counter, (b) receives and holds a 4-bit word from the memory buffer register, (c) transfers a 5-bit word to the memory, (d) receives a 5-bit word from the memory buffer register, (e) receives and holds a 5-bit word from the program counter.

7-24 ICs 13 and 14 in Fig. 7-15 are able to store (a) 16 of 32 8-bit words in the upper part of memory, (b) 16 of 32 8-bit words in the lower part of memory, (c) up to 32 8-bit words, (d) up to 8 16-bit words.

7-25 ICs 15 and 16 are able to store (Choose from the selections of Problem 7-24).

7-26 The D_0–D_3 inputs on the memory chips are (a) ports through which data enter, (b) ports out of which data are read out, (c) address inputs that determine where the data are to be written or read, (d) control inputs that admit or block data flow.

7-27 The S_0–S_3 ports are (a) used to sense the status of the data bus, (b) used to transfer data in a given memory location to the data bus, (c) used to directly transfer data from one memory location to another via the data lines, (d) used to sense the data bus and load into memory during READ operations.

7-28 The S_0 and S_3 ports are (a) open collector outputs, (b) totem-pole outputs, (c) active LOW inputs, (d) active HIGH inputs.

7-29 Why are the outputs of the memory buffer register taken off the $\overline{Q}$s instead of the Q terminals: (a) each data word out of the MBR is to be the complement of the data word stored in memory, (b) each data word placed on the data lines is the complement of the word actually stored in memory, (c) each word stored in memory must be complemented for the arithmetic unit, (d) the $\overline{Q}$ outputs have a higher source and sink capability?

7-30 Referring to the decoder IC 20 in Fig. 7-16, (a) only one output can be LOW at any time, (b) only one output can be HIGH at any time, (c) more than one output can be active at any time, (d) all outputs are LOW until a 3-bit op code is applied to its *A, B,* and *C* inputs.

7-31 The latch IC 19 is (a) strobed when $\overline{RESET}$ is LOW, (b) cleared when MBR → OP is HIGH, (c) disabled when MBR → OP is HIGH, (d) strobed when FETCH and T_1 are HIGH.

7-32 The signal $\overline{WRITE}$ in Fig. 7-17 is (a) LOW when EXECUTE, T_0, and $\overline{STO}$ are HIGH, (b) HIGH when EXECUTE, T_0, and $\overline{STO}$ are HIGH, (c) HIGH when EXECUTE and T_0 are HIGH but $\overline{STO}$ is LOW, (d) LOW when EXECUTE and T_0 are HIGH but $\overline{STO}$ is LOW.

7-33 Referring to the decoder of Fig. 7-16, $\overline{\text{NOP}}$ is LOW with which of the following inputs on the C, B, and A terminals: (a) 100, (b) 101, (c) 110, (d) 111, (e) 000?

7-34 Referring to the decoder, what inputs on terminals C, B, and A will cause output $\overline{\text{STO}}$ to become active LOW? (Choose from the selections of Problem 7-33.)

7-35 Under what conditions will the signal LOAD B in Fig. 7-17 become active: (a) when EXECUTE and T_0 are HIGH and either $\overline{\text{ADD}}$ or $\overline{\text{CAD}}$ are LOW, (b) when both $\overline{\text{ADD}}$ and $\overline{\text{CAD}}$ are LOW, (c) when FETCH and T_0 are HIGH, (d) when signals EXECUTE, T_0, $\overline{\text{ADD}}$, and $\overline{\text{CAD}}$ are HIGH, (e) when EXECUTE and T_1 are HIGH and either $\overline{\text{ADD}}$ or $\overline{\text{CAD}}$ is LOW?

7-36 Referring to Fig. 7-18, what are the 74194 chips: (a) binary counters, (b) shift counters, (c) shift registers, (d) latches, (e) up/down counters?

7-37 What kind of chip is IC 36: (a) part of a D-type flip-flop, (b) part of a latch, (c) a full adder, (d) a subtracter?

7-38 When the Q output of IC 35A is HIGH, the 2's complementer (a) complements each bit passing through it, (b) does not complement each bit passing through it, (c) does or does not complement each bit depending on the state of the other 7474 flip-flop, (d) clears the contents of the accumulator.

7-39 When signal LOAD ACC is HIGH, (a) an 8-bit word from the op code register loads into the accumulator, (b) an 8-bit word from the memory buffer register loads into the accumulator, (c) the accumulator is cleared, (d) the contents of the accumulator shift right, (e) the contents of the accumulator increment.

7-40 When the SHIFT signal goes HIGH, (a) the contents of ACC shift right, (b) the contents of register B shift right, (c) an 8-bit word shifts into the accumulator, (d) an 8-bit word shifts into register B, (e) the contents of ACC and register B shift right 1 bit.

CHAPTER 8

The Microprocessor

We are now ready to study the microprocessor. We shall see what it needs to make it operate, how to program it, and how to read and interpret the instruction set.

We shall study the Motorola MC6800 MPU thoroughly. The MC6800 is one of the leading MPUs in use today. Due to its straightforward hardware design and readily understandable instruction set, it provides an excellent example of microprocessors in general. You'll also find that once you understand the MC6800, you'll also be able to understand practically any other MPU as well, should the need arise.

You'll find that although the op codes may differ for different MPUs, most of the programming techniques are very similar.

In addition, as newer devices evolve, manufacturers try to make the newer units *software compatible* with the older ones. That is, any programs written for a device, such as the MC6800, will also run on some newer devices currently under development by Motorola. So your efforts to learn the MC6800 will be time well spent.

8-1 MC6800 Architecture

The Motorola M6800 chip set is a family of LSI devices designed to work together as a microcomputer system. Although the MC6800 MPU can be used with other chips not of the M6800 family, the use of family members

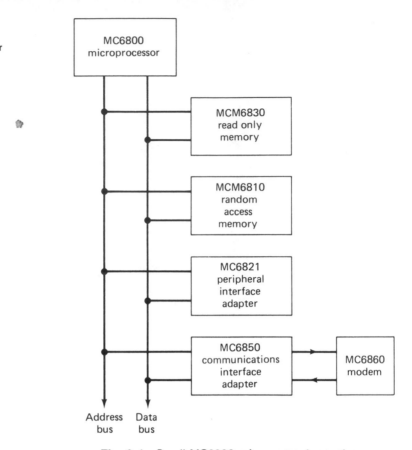

Fig. 8-1 Small MC6800 microcomputer system.

usually results in a system which is simpler to put together, because address decoding and control signal gating can often be done by the LSI chips themselves, without the need for additional gating. This will become apparent when we look at a small system.

A typical small system might look like that of Fig. 8-1. Note that the MC6800 MPU connects to a ROM (6830), a RAM (one or more 6810s), and one or more interface adapters (6821 or 6850). We shall see more of the other family members later, but for now let's concentrate on the MC6800 MPU.

Figure 8-2(A) shows the pin assignments of the MC6800 MPU, whose package is depicted in Fig. 8-2(B). Refer to Fig. 8-2(A) and to Fig. 8-3, the symbolic diagram, for the discussion that follows. Arrows pointing into the diagram represent externally generated signals, and arrows pointing out represent signals originating inside the MPU.

Note that there are several registers inside the MPU chip. You are already familiar with the program counter and accumulator registers from

PIN ASSIGNMENT

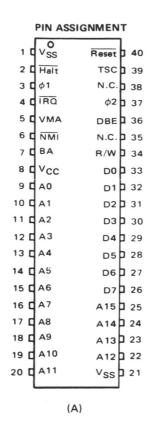

1	V$_{SS}$	Reset	40
2	Halt	TSC	39
3	ϕ1	N.C.	38
4	IRQ	ϕ2	37
5	VMA	DBE	36
6	NMI	N.C.	35
7	BA	R/W	34
8	V$_{CC}$	D0	33
9	A0	D1	32
10	A1	D2	31
11	A2	D3	30
12	A3	D4	29
13	A4	D5	28
14	A5	D6	27
15	A6	D7	26
16	A7	A15	25
17	A8	A14	24
18	A9	A13	23
19	A10	A12	22
20	A11	V$_{SS}$	21

(A)

P SUFFIX
PLASTIC PACKAGE
CASE 711

Fig. 8-2 MC6800.　　　　　　　(B)

the chapter on computer architecture. The MC6800 actually has two accumulators, making it more flexible. The index register and stack pointer will be discussed later, when we study programming of the MC6800. The other register, shown as separate blocks *H, I, N, Z, V, C,* is called the condition code or flag register. The little squares represent individual flip-flops which act as *flag* or *status* bits, which are examined by the MPU during program execution.

Also within the MPU, but not shown here, are the memory address

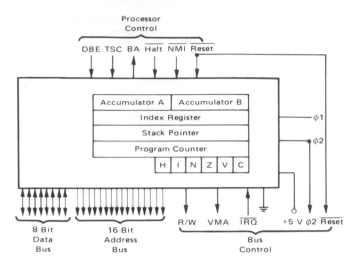

Fig. 8-3 Symbolic diagram of MC6800.

register, which connects to the address bus; the memory buffer register, which connects to the data bus; and all op code decoding and control circuitry. Part of the timing distributor circuitry is contained within the MPU, but the clock signals must be generated externally and fed to the chip.

Now let's look at the lines connected to the chip. Figures 8-3 and 8-2(A) show that there are 8 bidirectional data lines and 16 address lines. The MPU can address up to 2^{16} or 65,536 memory locations. Most applications surely would not require that much memory, but the capability is there if it is needed.

Both the address bus and data bus have three-state output drivers capable of driving one standard TTL load each. However, care must be taken not to exceed a capacitance of 130 pF on any line.

The READ/$\overline{\text{WRITE}}$ $(R/\overline{W})$ control line, pin 34, is fed to memory and to other chips to signal whether the MPU is doing a memory read or write operation.

Whenever pin 39, the THREE-STATE CONTROL (TSC) pin, is driven HIGH, the address bus and the $R/\overline{W}$ control lines are placed in their high-impedance states. This is sometimes done to allow an external device to gain access to the system's memory. The technique is referred to as *direct memory access* (DMA).

In a similar manner, driving pin 36, DATA BUS ENABLE (DBE), HIGH places the data bus in its high-impedance state.

A control line called VALID MEMORY ADDRESS (VMA, pin 5) goes active HIGH when a valid address appears on the address bus. This signal is useful as a chip enable so that a device is not accidentally enabled by an erroneous address temporarily appearing on the address bus.

When the $\overline{\text{HALT}}$ line (pin 2) is driven low, the MPU halts operation after completing its present instruction. When the MPU is halted, all three-state* outputs go to their high-impedance (OFF) state.

Whenever the MPU is halted, the BUS AVAILABLE (BA) signal (pin 7) goes active HIGH, indicating that the address bus is in its high-impedance state and is available for use by an external device.

The $\overline{\text{INTERRUPT}}$ $\overline{\text{REQUEST}}$ ($\overline{\text{IRQ}}$, pin 4) and the $\overline{\text{NONMASKABLE}}$ $\overline{\text{INTERRUPT}}$ ($\overline{\text{NMI}}$, pin 6) are inputs by which external devices signal the MPU whenever they want to interrupt the current program. We shall see how these interrupts work in Chapter 9.

The two pins 1 and 21, labeled V_{SS}, connect to system ground, and pin 8, labeled V_{CC}, connects to a +5–V power supply.

When the $\overline{\text{RESET}}$ input (pin 40) is driven LOW, the MPU begins its restart sequence. Appropriate registers are initialized internally, and the program counter is loaded with the address of the first instruction to be decoded. Unlike the J-100, which you studied earlier, and some other types of MPUs which reset the PC to zero to begin the program, the MC6800 uses what is called a *vectored restart*. When the MC6800 is reset, the *contents* of memory locations FFFE and FFFF are loaded into the program counter. Then the MPU effectively does a jump to the location now loaded in the PC and begins execution of the program.

Normally, in the MC6800 system, the designer connects a ROM in the highest memory locations and a RAM in the lowest. The programmer must place the *address* of the starting location of his or her program in locations FFFE and FFFF, with the most significant byte in FFFE. In this way, the programmer can direct the MPU to begin the program wherever he or she wishes it to start—not necessarily at location 0000.

Finally, we come to the CLOCK inputs, pins 3 and 37, labeled $\phi 1$ and $\phi 2$. These signals, which must be generated externally by a CLOCK circuit, correspond to the T-state signals of the J-100.

Signals $\phi 1$ and $\phi 2$ are two nonoverlapping phases of a two-phase clock, whose output waveforms are shown in Fig. 8-4. To obtain higher speeds, rather than generating four separate pulses for each cycle, the leading and trailing edges are used to generate the desired control signals. That is, the rising edge of $\phi 1$ corresponds to T_1 of the J-100, and the falling edge of $\phi 1$ corresponds to T_2, etc. The total time required to complete one MPU cycle depends on the clock frequency and is typically 1 μsec.

Due to the wide variety of instructions that can be executed by the MC6800, some instructions take several MPU cycles. The waveforms shown in Fig. 8-4 represent clock signals needed to perform a relatively simple instruction, such as *load accumulator*. For that instruction, the timing of events is almost identical to that of the J-100. We shall not examine the waveforms for every instruction of the MC6800, but keep in mind that one MPU cycle extends from a rising edge of $\phi 1$ until the next rising edge of $\phi 1$.

---

* Three-state is the same as tri-state, described in Chapter 4.

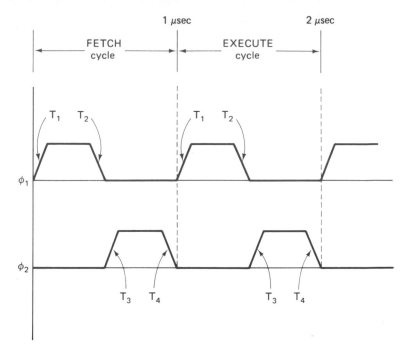

Fig. 8-4 Clock timing waveform.

The circuitry required to generate the two-phase clock signals can be built with SSI components, but clock chips with internal crystals are manufactured by Motorola for this purpose.

8-2 MC6800 Instruction Set

The instruction set of the J-100 was very simple. It contained just seven instructions. Generally speaking, the larger the instruction set, the more powerful the computer. The MC6800 has an instruction set of 72 instructions, but by using various *addressing modes,* these 72 instructions are expanded to almost 200 different possible operations. The addressing mode refers to how the MPU obtains the operand.

You will remember that the J-100 had a 3-bit op code. Three bits are sufficient to decode eight possible instructions. But to decode almost 200 instructions, the MC6800, like many other MPUs today, uses an 8-bit op code. Rather than giving the op code in binary, the instruction set lists the op code in hexadecimal form.

Refer to the MC6800 instruction set listed in Table 8-1. Note that the leftmost column lists the instructions, such as add, etc., in alphabetical order. Next to the instructions is listed the assembly language mnemonic for each. ADDA means add the operand to accumulator *A,* etc.

Table 8-1 Accumulator and memory instructions[a]

OPERATIONS	MNEMONIC	IMMED OP	~	#	DIRECT OP	~	#	INDEX OP	~	#	EXTND OP	~	#	IMPLIED OP	~	#	BOOLEAN/ARITHMETIC OPERATION (All register labels refer to contents)	H	I	N	Z	V	C
Add	ADDA	8B	2	2	9B	3	2	AB	5	2	BB	4	3				A + M → A	↕	●	↕	↕	↕	↕
	ADDB	CB	2	2	DB	3	2	EB	5	2	FB	4	3				B + M → B	↕	●	↕	↕	↕	↕
Add Acmltrs	ABA													1B	2	1	A + B → A	↕	●	↕	↕	↕	↕
Add with Carry	ADCA	89	2	2	99	3	2	A9	5	2	B9	4	3				A + M + C → A	↕	●	↕	↕	↕	↕
	ADCB	C9	2	2	D9	3	2	E9	5	2	F9	4	3				B + M + C → B	↕	●	↕	↕	↕	↕
And	ANDA	84	2	2	94	3	2	A4	5	2	B4	4	3				A · M → A	●	●	↕	↕	R	●
	ANDB	C4	2	2	D4	3	2	E4	5	2	F4	4	3				B · M → B	●	●	↕	↕	R	●
Bit Test	BITA	85	2	2	95	3	2	A5	5	2	B5	4	3				A · M	●	●	↕	↕	R	●
	BITB	C5	2	2	D5	3	2	E5	5	2	F5	4	3				B · M	●	●	↕	↕	R	●
Clear	CLR							6F	7	2	7F	6	3				00 → M	●	●	R	S	R	R
	CLRA													4F	2	1	00 → A	●	●	R	S	R	R
	CLRB													5F	2	1	00 → B	●	●	R	S	R	R
Compare	CMPA	81	2	2	91	3	2	A1	5	2	B1	4	3				A − M	●	●	↕	↕	↕	↕
	CMPB	C1	2	2	D1	3	2	E1	5	2	F1	4	3				B − M	●	●	↕	↕	↕	↕
Compare Acmltrs	CBA													11	2	1	A − B	●	●	↕	↕	↕	↕
Complement, 1's	COM							63	7	2	73	6	3				M̄ → M	●	●	↕	↕	R	S
	COMA													43	2	1	Ā → A	●	●	↕	↕	R	S
	COMB													53	2	1	B̄ → B	●	●	↕	↕	R	S
Complement, 2's	NEG							60	7	2	70	6	3				00 − M → M	●	●	↕	↕	①	②
(Negate)	NEGA													40	2	1	00 − A → A	●	●	↕	↕	①	②
	NEGB													50	2	1	00 − B → B	●	●	↕	↕	①	②
Decimal Adjust, A	DAA													19	2	1	Converts Binary Add. of BCD Characters into BCD Format	●	●	↕	↕	↕	③
Decrement	DEC							6A	7	2	7A	6	3				M − 1 → M	●	●	↕	↕	④	●
	DECA													4A	2	1	A − 1 → A	●	●	↕	↕	④	●
	DECB													5A	2	1	B − 1 → B	●	●	↕	↕	④	●
Exclusive OR	EORA	88	2	2	98	3	2	A8	5	2	B8	4	3				A ⊕ M → A	●	●	↕	↕	R	●
	EORB	C8	2	2	D8	3	2	E8	5	2	F8	4	3				B ⊕ M → B	●	●	↕	↕	R	●
Increment	INC							6C	7	2	7C	6	3				M + 1 → M	●	●	↕	↕	⑤	●
	INCA													4C	2	1	A + 1 → A	●	●	↕	↕	⑤	●
	INCB													5C	2	1	B + 1 → B	●	●	↕	↕	⑤	●
Load Acmltr	LDAA	86	2	2	96	3	2	A6	5	2	B6	4	3				M → A	●	●	↕	↕	R	●
	LDAB	C6	2	2	D6	3	2	E6	5	2	F6	4	3				M → B	●	●	↕	↕	R	●
Or, Inclusive	ORAA	8A	2	2	9A	3	2	AA	5	2	BA	4	3				A + M → A	●	●	↕	↕	R	●
	ORAB	CA	2	2	DA	3	2	EA	5	2	FA	4	3				B + M → B	●	●	↕	↕	R	●
Push Data	PSHA													36	4	1	A → M$_{SP}$, SP − 1 → SP	●	●	●	●	●	●
	PSHB													37	4	1	B → M$_{SP}$, SP − 1 → SP	●	●	●	●	●	●
Pull Data	PULA													32	4	1	SP + 1 → SP, M$_{SP}$ → A	●	●	●	●	●	●
	PULB													33	4	1	SP + 1 → SP, M$_{SP}$ → B	●	●	●	●	●	●
Rotate Left	ROL							69	7	2	79	6	3				M	●	●	↕	↕	⑥	↕
	ROLA													49	2	1	A	●	●	↕	↕	⑥	↕
	ROLB													59	2	1	B	●	●	↕	↕	⑥	↕
Rotate Right	ROR							66	7	2	76	6	3				M	●	●	↕	↕	⑥	↕
	RORA													46	2	1	A	●	●	↕	↕	⑥	↕
	RORB													56	2	1	B	●	●	↕	↕	⑥	↕
Shift Left, Arithmetic	ASL							68	7	2	78	6	3				M	●	●	↕	↕	⑥	↕
	ASLA													48	2	1	A	●	●	↕	↕	⑥	↕
	ASLB													58	2	1	B	●	●	↕	↕	⑥	↕
Shift Right, Arithmetic	ASR							67	7	2	77	6	3				M	●	●	↕	↕	⑥	↕
	ASRA													47	2	1	A	●	●	↕	↕	⑥	↕
	ASRB													57	2	1	B	●	●	↕	↕	⑥	↕
Shift Right, Logic	LSR							64	7	2	74	6	3				M	●	●	R	↕	⑥	↕
	LSRA													44	2	1	A	●	●	R	↕	⑥	↕
	LSRB													54	2	1	B	●	●	R	↕	⑥	↕
Store Acmltr.	STAA				97	4	2	A7	6	2	B7	5	3				A → M	●	●	↕	↕	R	●
	STAB				D7	4	2	E7	6	2	F7	5	3				B → M	●	●	↕	↕	R	●
Subtract	SUBA	80	2	2	90	3	2	A0	5	2	B0	4	3				A − M → A	●	●	↕	↕	↕	↕
	SUBB	C0	2	2	D0	3	2	E0	5	2	F0	4	3				B − M → B	●	●	↕	↕	↕	↕
Subtract Acmltrs.	SBA													10	2	1	A − B → A	●	●	↕	↕	↕	↕
Subtr. with Carry	SBCA	82	2	2	92	3	2	A2	5	2	B2	4	3				A − M − C → A	●	●	↕	↕	↕	↕
	SBCB	C2	2	2	D2	3	2	E2	5	2	F2	4	3				B − M − C → B	●	●	↕	↕	↕	↕
Transfer Acmltrs	TAB													16	2	1	A → B	●	●	↕	↕	R	●
	TBA													17	2	1	B → A	●	●	↕	↕	R	●
Test, Zero or Minus	TST							6D	7	2	7D	6	3				M − 00	●	●	↕	↕	R	R
	TSTA													4D	2	1	A − 00	●	●	↕	↕	R	R
	TSTB													5D	2	1	B − 00	●	●	↕	↕	R	R

CONDITION CODE REGISTER bit positions: 5 = H, 4 = I, 3 = N, 2 = Z, 1 = V, 0 = C

LEGEND:

- OP   Operation Code (Hexadecimal);
- ~   Number of MPU Cycles;
- #   Number of Program Bytes;
- +   Arithmetic Plus;
- −   Arithmetic Minus;
- ·   Boolean AND;
- M$_{SP}$ Contents of memory location pointed to be Stack Pointer;

- +   Boolean Inclusive OR;
- ⊕   Boolean Exclusive OR;
- M̄   Complement of M;
- →   Transfer Into;
- 0   Bit = Zero;
- 00   Byte = Zero;

Note − Accumulator addressing mode instructions are included in the column for IMPLIED addressing

CONDITION CODE SYMBOLS:

- H   Half-carry from bit 3;
- I   Interrupt mask
- N   Negative (sign bit)
- Z   Zero (byte)
- V   Overflow, 2's complement
- C   Carry from bit 7
- R   Reset Always
- S   Set Always
- ↕   Test and set if true, cleared otherwise
- ●   Not Affected

[a] Courtesy of Motorola.

243

Next you will note five columns under the heading of addressing modes. These are IMMED (immediate), DIRECT, INDEX, EXTEND (extended), and IMPLIED. We shall discuss the meanings of the various modes as we study how to program. For now, let's look at the column labeled DIRECT. DIRECT addressing means that the address of the operand is given directly following the op code. This is similar to the addressing of the J-100.

For example, using the J-100, if we wanted to add the contents of memory location 10100 to the accumulator, the instruction would be 11010100, the first 3 bits representing the op code and the last 5 bits representing the operand address.

But since the MC6800 requires an 8-bit op code, we must use a *second* byte to represent the operand address. In other words, to instruct the MC6800 to add the contents of memory location 14 to the accumulator, we would list the instruction in 2 bytes, the first byte being 9B, the op code in hexadecimal, and the second byte being 14, which is the operand address. You'll find this op code listed under the heading DIRECT.

Note also that under each heading there are the symbols $\sim$ and #. The symbol $\sim$ stands for the number of MPU cycles (clock cycles) required to perform the operation. For the add instruction, three MPU cycles are needed. So it would take 3 μsec to complete if a 1-MHz clock were being used.

The symbol # indicates the number of program bytes necessary for that mode, which we know to be 2.

Let's skip over to the column labeled Boolean/arithmetic operation. The notation $A + M \rightarrow A$ signifies that when the operation is carried out, the present contents of the accumulator *plus* the contents of the indicated memory location will be placed in the accumulator.

The column on the far right of Table 8-1 shows how the various flag

Table 8-2 Index Register and Stack Pointer Instructions[a]

POINTER OPERATIONS	MNEMONIC	IMMED OP	~	#	DIRECT OP	~	#	INDEX OP	~	=	EXTND OP	~	=	IMPLIED OP	~	=	BOOLEAN/ARITHMETIC OPERATION	H	I	N	Z	V	C
Compare Index Reg	CPX	8C	3	3	9C	4	2	AC	6	2	BC	5	3				$X_H - M, X_L - (M+1)$	•	•	①	:	②	•
Decrement Index Reg	DEX													09	4	1	$X - 1 \rightarrow X$	•	•	•	:	•	•
Decrement Stack Pntr	DES													34	4	1	$SP - 1 \rightarrow SP$	•	•	•	•	•	•
Increment Index Reg	INX													08	4	1	$X + 1 \rightarrow X$	•	•	•	:	•	•
Increment Stack Pntr	INS													31	4	1	$SP + 1 \rightarrow SP$	•	•	•	•	•	•
Load Index Reg	LDX	CE	3	3	DE	4	2	EE	6	2	FE	5	3				$M \rightarrow X_H, (M+1) \rightarrow X_L$	•	•	③	:	R	•
Load Stack Pntr	LDS	8E	3	3	9E	4	2	AE	6	2	BE	5	3				$M \rightarrow SP_H, (M+1) \rightarrow SP_L$	•	•	③	:	R	•
Store Index Reg	STX				DF	5	2	EF	7	2	FF	6	3				$X_H \rightarrow M, X_L \rightarrow (M+1)$	•	•	③	:	R	•
Store Stack Pntr	STS				9F	5	2	AF	7	2	BF	6	3				$SP_H \rightarrow M, SP_L \rightarrow (M+1)$	•	•	③	:	R	•
Indx Reg → Stack Pntr	TXS													35	4	1	$X - 1 \rightarrow SP$	•	•	•	•	•	•
Stack Pntr → Indx Reg	TSX													30	4	1	$SP + 1 \rightarrow X$	•	•	•	•	•	•

COND. CODE REG. 5 4 3 2 1 0 = H I N Z V C

① (Bit N) Test: Sign bit of most significant (MS) byte of result = 1?
② (Bit V) Test: 2's complement overflow from subtraction of ms bytes?
③ (Bit N) Test: Result less than zero? (Bit 15 = 1)

[a] Courtesy of Motorola.

Table 8-3 Jump and Branch Instructions[a]

OPERATIONS	MNEMONIC	RELATIVE			INDEX			EXTND			IMPLIED			BRANCH TEST	COND. CODE REG.					
															5	4	3	2	1	0
		OP	~	#	OP	~	#	OP	~	#	OP	~	#		H	I	N	Z	V	C
Branch Always	BRA	20	4	2										None	•	•	•	•	•	•
Branch If Carry Clear	BCC	24	4	2										C = 0	•	•	•	•	•	•
Branch If Carry Set	BCS	25	4	2										C = 1	•	•	•	•	•	•
Branch If = Zero	BEQ	27	4	2										Z = 1	•	•	•	•	•	•
Branch If ≥ Zero	BGE	2C	4	2										N ⊕ V = 0	•	•	•	•	•	•
Branch If > Zero	BGT	2E	4	2										Z + (N ⊕ V) = 0	•	•	•	•	•	•
Branch If Higher	BHI	22	4	2										C + Z = 0	•	•	•	•	•	•
Branch If ≤ Zero	BLE	2F	4	2										Z + (N ⊕ V) = 1	•	•	•	•	•	•
Branch If Lower Or Same	BLS	23	4	2										C + Z = 1	•	•	•	*	•	•
Branch If < Zero	BLT	2D	4	2										N ⊕ V = 1	•	•	*	*	•	•
Branch If Minus	BMI	2B	4	2										N = 1	•	•	•	•	•	•
Branch If Not Equal Zero	BNE	26	4	2										Z = 0	•	•	•	•	•	•
Branch If Overflow Clear	BVC	28	4	2										V = 0	•	•	•	•	•	•
Branch If Overflow Set	BVS	29	4	2										V = 1	•	•	•	•	•	•
Branch If Plus	BPL	2A	4	2										N = 0	•	•	•	•	•	•
Branch To Subroutine	BSR	8D	8	2											•	•	•	•	•	•
Jump	JMP				6E	4	2	7E	3	3					•	•	•	•	•	•
Jump To Subroutine	JSR				AD	8	2	BD	9	3					•	•	•	•	•	•
No Operation	NOP										01	2	1	Advances Prog. Cntr. Only	•	•	•	•	•	•
Return From Interrupt	RTI										3B	10	1		——————① ——————					
Return From Subroutine	RTS										39	5	1		•	•	•	•	•	•
Software Interrupt	SWI										3F	12	1		•	•	•	•	•	•
Wait for Interrupt *	WAI										3E	9	1		•	②	•	•	•	•

*WAI puts Address Bus, R/W, and Data Bus in the three state mode while VMA is held low.

① (All)   Load Condition Code Register from Stack.
② (Bit 1). Set when interrupt occurs. If previously set, a Non-Maskable Interrupt
is required to exit the wait state.

[a] Courtesy of Motorola.

---

bits are affected by a particular instruction. For the ADDA instruction, we see that there is a dot (·) listed for the *I* flag. This means that the *I* flag is not affected by that instruction. All other flags show double-headed arrows. These mean that each flag may change according to the result of the operation. For example, if the addition causes a *carry* to occur, the *C* flag will set (↑). If no carry occurs, the *C* flag will reset (↓).

Similarly, if the result of the addition causes the number in the accumulator to be negative, the *N* flag will set (↑); otherwise it will reset (↓)—and likewise for other flags. Tables 8-2, 8-3, and 8-4 will be discussed later.

8-3 Straight-Line Programs

Now we are ready to examine a simple program written in MC6800 machine language. Figure 8-5 shows a program to add two numbers and store the sum using DIRECT addressing. Refer to the instruction set of Table 8-1 to see where the op codes came from. The numbers shown in locations 0050 and 0051 are the values that will be added together. After addition, of course, the accumulator and location 0052 will both contain the value 0EH.

Note that the instruction WAI is used at the end of the program. Since the Motorola instruction set does not contain a halt instruction, we simply tell the MPU to *wait* until we tell it to do something else.

Table 8-4 Condition Code Register Instructions[a]

OPERATIONS	MNEMONIC	IMPLIED			BOOLEAN OPERATION	COND. CODE REG.					
						5	4	3	2	1	0
		OP	~	#		H	I	N	Z	V	C
Clear Carry	CLC	0C	2	1	$0 \rightarrow C$	•	•	•	•	•	R
Clear Interrupt Mask	CLI	0E	2	1	$0 \rightarrow I$	•	R	•	•	•	•
Clear Overflow	CLV	0A	2	1	$0 \rightarrow V$	•	•	•	•	R	•
Set Carry	SEC	0D	2	1	$1 \rightarrow C$	•	•	•	•	•	S
Set Interrupt Mask	SEI	0F	2	1	$1 \rightarrow I$	•	S	•	•	•	•
Set Overflow	SEV	0B	2	1	$1 \rightarrow V$	•	•	•	•	S	•
Acmltr A → CCR	TAP	06	2	1	$A \rightarrow CCR$	———①———					
CCR → Acmltr A	TPA	07	2	1	$CCR \rightarrow A$	•	•	•	•	•	•

R = Reset
S = Set
• = Not affected
① (ALL) Set according to the contents of Accumulator A.

CONDITION CODE REGISTER BIT DEFINITION

b_5 b_4 b_3 b_2 b_1 b_0

H	I	N	Z	V	C

H = Half-carry; set whenever a carry from b_3 to b_4 of the result is generated by ADD, ABA, ADC; cleared if no b_3 to b_4 carry; not affected by other instructions.

I = Interrupt Mask; set by hardware or software interrupt or SEI instruction; cleared by CLI instruction. (Normally not used in arithmetic operations.) Restored to a zero as a result of an RT1 instruction if I_m stored on the stacked is low.

N = Negative; set if high order bit (b_7) of result is set; cleared otherwise

Z = Zero; set if result = 0; cleared otherwise.

V = Overlow; set if there was arithmetic overflow as a result of the operation; cleared otherwise.

C = Carry; set if there was a carry from the most significant bit (b_7) of the result; cleared otherwise.

[a] Courtesy of Motorola.

Thus far, we have used only DIRECT addressing. Using DIRECT addressing, we specified the operand address with a single byte following the op code. However, with a single-byte address, we can only specify 1 of 256 memory locations. For this reason, DIRECT addressing can only be used for operands in memory locations 0000–00FF. For all these addresses, the left two digits are 00, which is what DIRECT addressing assumes. However, when we want to specify operands at higher memory addresses, we simply use a different op code, listed under the EXTENDed mode column. Then we follow the op code with 2 *bytes* of address. Figure 8-6 lists a program

Mem. loc.	Op code/address	Mnemonic	Comments
0000	96*	LDAA	Load ACCA with contents of loc 50H
0001	50		
0002	9B	ADDA	Add to ACCA contents of loc 51H
0003	51		
0004	97	STAA	Store ACCA into loc 52H
0005	52		
0006	3E	WAI	Wait for interrupt (halt)
0050	08		
0051	06		
0052	XX		

*All values shown in hexadecimal

Fig. 8-5 Program to add two numbers and store result.

Fig. 8-6 Addition program using extended addressing.

Mem. loc.	Op code/address	Mnemonic	Comments
0000	B6	LDAA	Load ACCA, extended mode*, with contents of 015A
0001	01	(MSB)	
0002	5A	(LSB)	
0003	BB	ADDA	Add to ACCA, extended, the contents of 0147
0004	01	(MSB)	
0005	47	(LSB)	
0006	B7	STAA	Store ACCA, extended into 0130
0007	01	(MSB)	
0008	30	(LSB)	
0009	3E	WAI	Wait for interrupt

*If using MEK-D2 kit, additional memory is available in 2000H-5FFFH.

to add a number in memory location 015A to a number in 0147 and store the sum in 0130. This program uses the EXTEND addressing mode by which the MPU can access any of its possible 2^{16} memory locations.

Occasionally we would like to add or load a particular numerical *value* into the accumulator. We can do this without placing the value in memory by using the IMMED mode. For example, in a program, the op code 8B followed by the digits 05 would instruct the MPU to add 05 to the present accumulator contents—not the contents of memory location 05 but the numerical value 05. We shall see more applications of this mode later.

The IMPLIED addressing mode means that no address byte is necessary. For example, the instruction to add accumulators (1B) simply places the sum of A plus B accumulators into accumulator A. The operand (accumulator B) is implied in this instruction.

We shall study some additional programming examples before going into the INDEX mode. For now, you should be able to determine the op

Fig. 8-7 Flowchart for program to compare two numbers and store the larger.

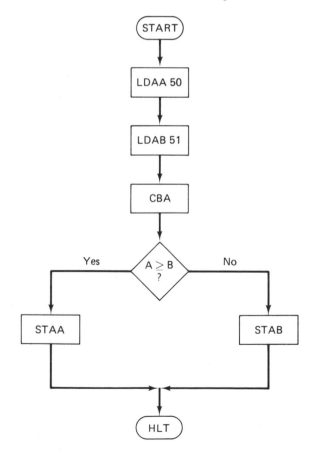

code for any instruction in the **IMMED, DIRECT, EXTEND**, and **IMPLIED** modes. You should also know how to find the number of MPU cycles, program bytes, and flag conditions for any instruction.

8-4 Branches and Jumps

You are already familiar with the concept of branching from previous chapters. The Motorola MC6800 MPU has several branch and jump instructions, as shown in Table 8-3. Having a variety of branching conditions makes the computer very powerful.

Let's study a program to compare two numbers and store the larger. Figure 8-7 shows the flowchart for a program to compare a number stored in location 50 to a number stored in location 51 and store the larger number in location 52. The program is shown in machine code in Fig. 8-8.

Fig. 8-8 Program to compare two numbers and store the larger.

Mem. loc.	Op code/address	Mnemonic	Comments
0000	96	LDAA	LD ACCA with contents of 50*
0001	50		
0002	D6	LDAB	LD ACCB with contents of 51
0003	51		
0004	11	CBA	Compare accumulators
0005	2B	BMI	If A < B, branch to 000A
0006	03		
0007	97	STAA	A ≥ B; store A in 52
0008	52		
0009	3E	HLT	
000A	D7	STAB	B is larger; store B in 52
000B	52		
000C	3E	HLT	

*Numbers to be compared must be stored in 0050 and 0051. Location 0052 will hold larger number after run.

First, the contents of locations 50 and 51 are loaded into accumulators *A* and *B,* respectively. Then the accumulators are compared. Note in Table 8-1 that the CBA (IMPLIED mode) instruction will set the *N* flag if $B > A$ and clear it otherwise. The *N* flag is then tested by the BMI instruction. If $A \geq B$, *A* is stored in 52, as directed by the instruction in location 0007. But if the *N* flag is set, the MPU branches to location 000A for its next instruction.

Note that the branch instructions of Table 8-2 are listed under still another addressing mode called RELATIVE addressing. The RELATIVE mode tells the MPU to take its next instruction from a location specified *relative* to the *program counter.* The byte 03H at location 0006 is added to the program counter to obtain the address of the next instruction.

Remember that the program counter gets incremented immediately after the MPU reads a byte from memory. So after decoding the BMI instruction, the MPU reads the byte 03 from location 0006 and immediately gets incre-

Fig. 8-9 Program to multiply two numbers by successive additions.

Mem. loc.	Op code/address	Mnemonic
0000	D6	LDAB 40
0001	40	
0002	4F	CLRA
0003	99	ADDA 41
0004	41	
0005	5A	DECB
0006	26	BNE
0007	FB	(−5)
0008	3E	HLT
0009		
0040	6	
0041	5	

Table 8-5

Binary	Hex	Decimal
00000101	05	+5
00000100	04	+4
00000011	03	+3
00000010	02	+2
00000001	01	+1
00000000	00	0
11111111	FF	−1
11111110	FE	−2
11111101	FD	−3
11111100	FC	−4
11111011	FB	−5
11111010	FA	−6
	etc.	

mented, so that the PC holds the number 0007. Then, if the N flag is set, the byte 03 (called the *offset* or *displacement*) is added to the PC, thus making the PC contents 000A. Finally, the MPU takes its next instruction from location 000A.

Now let's take a look at a program that branches backward. The program shown in Fig. 8-9 can be used to multiply two binary numbers. The multiplicand is first stored in 0041. The program simply adds the multiplicand to itself the number of times specified by the multiplier.* Note that the instruction stored in 0005 decrements the multiplier stored in accumulator B. If accumulator B does not equal zero after being decremented, the PC branches back to location 0003 for its next instruction.

To branch backward, we add a negative number (−5) to the PC. The negative number is given in its 2's complement form, which in this case is FBH. Table 8-5 shows how negative numbers can be given in 2's complement form. Note that if you had an 8-bit binary up/down counter, its outputs would correspond to the table. For example, if you started at 02 and decremented the counter three times, all bits would go from 0 to 1 as you passed through the count of 00. Thus, the number FFH represents −1, FEH represents −2, etc.

The RELATIVE mode of addressing uses only a single-byte offset to be added to the program counter. For this reason, RELATIVE addressing can only access locations $+127_{10}$ (01111111) to -128_{10} (10000000) from the current PC location.

If it is necessary to go out to some location far from the present PC contents, the *jump* (JMP) instruction is used. The JMP instruction uses either the EXTENDed or INDEX mode.

* This method of multiplication is rather time-consuming. More efficient algorithims can be found in texts on software development. This method is used here to demonstrate the concept of branching.

Mem. loc.	Op code/address	Mnemonic	Comments
0000	CE	LDX	Load index reg. immediately with starting address of lookup table
0001	01		
0002	00		
0003	B6	LDAA	Load ACCA with code word from mem.
0004	00		
0005	50		
0006	A1	CMPA	Compare ACCA with byte from table
0007	00		
0008	27	BEQ	If match occurs, store code in 0062
0009	0A		
000A	08	INX	Increment index reg. to point to next byte
000B	8C	CPX	Compare index reg. to final table location
000C	01		
000D	64		
000E	26	BNE	If not final byte, go back and repeat
000F	F6		
0010	B7	STAA	If no match occurs in table, store code word in 0060
0011	00		
0012	60		
0013	3E	HLT	
0014	B7	STAA	
0015	00		
0016	62		
0017	3E	HLT	

Fig. 8-10 Program to find a match for a code work in lookup table.

Now let's take a look at the INDEX mode. The index register is a 16-bit register which is used as a pointer to point to a memory location. It can be incremented, decremented, and compared to a number, thus making it a valuable programming aid. Index register instructions are shown in Table 8-2.

The program of Fig. 8-10 uses the INDEX mode. The program is used to see if a given code word matches a code stored in a table.

The code word, initially stored in location 0050, is compared to each byte stored in a table, which starts at memory location 0100 and ends at 0164, until a match is found. If a match is found, the word is stored in location 0062. If no match is found, it is stored in 0060.

Read through the program carefully to see that you understand it. The instruction at 0006 tells the MPU to compare the contents of ACCA to the contents of the memory location pointed to by the index register plus the offset (00 in this case). In other words, the index register points directly to the location whose contents are to be compared. It is also possible to use some other offset byte, in which case a comparison would be made of the location pointed to by the index register *plus* the offset.

This type of program demonstrates how a relatively short program can be used to find a match for a code in a large table. The lookup table in this case has 100_{10} (64H) entries, and therefore up to 100 comparisons can be made. The lookup table, extending from 0100 to 0164, is not shown in the program listing. The program keeps looping back, incrementing the index register to point to the next location, and comparing until a match is found.

A program like this one can be used to check identification codes, say to open a combination lock. A card, coded with some number, is read by the computer, simulated here by loading the byte from 0050. Then the code is compared to a table of codes which open the lock. In this example, opening the lock is simulated by storing the byte into 0062. In a later chapter on input/output techniques, you'll see how a peripheral device, such as a lock, can be accessed like a memory location. So storing a byte into 0062 is equivalent to unlatching the lock.

8-5 Stack Operations

The *stack* is a section of RAM set aside by the programmer as a temporary storage area. The *stack pointer* (SP) is a 16-bit register, similar to the index register. It simply points to a location in memory where information can be stored or retrieved. However, it differs from the index register in that the stack pointer is automatically decremented when a byte is stored, or "pushed" onto the stack, and it is automatically incremented when a byte is retrieved, or "popped" off of the stack. This type of stack is therefore known as a *push-down/pop-up* stack.

The programmer must initialize the stack pointer before he or she can use it. The programmer initializes it by loading the stack pointer with the address of the *highest* location he or she wishes to use for the stack. Thereafter, he or she doesn't have to keep track of the contents of the stack pointer but simply remembers that the last byte pushed onto the stack will be the first byte pulled off. Stack instructions are listed in Table 8-2.

The program of Fig. 8-11 shows how to swap the contents of one memory location with those of another location.

The first instruction initializes the stack pointer at 00FF. Then the MPU loads a byte from location 0050 and pushes it onto the stack. This operation temporarily stores the contents of the accumulator into location 00FF, and decrements the stack pointer to 00FE, to wait for the next byte. The contents of 0060 are then loaded into ACCA and stored into 0050. The instruction PULA at location 000A pulls the byte off the stack. When this instruction is executed, the stack pointer is automatically incremented to 00FF, and the byte at that location is loaded into ACCA. Finally, the accumulator contents are stored into 0060, completing the program.

Fig. 8-11 Program to swap contents of one memory location with another; RAM locations 50, 60, and FF are not shown but must exist.

Mem. loc.	Op code/address	Mnemonic	Comments
0000	8E	LDS	Load stack pointer with 00FF
0001	00		
0002	FF		
0003	96	LDAA	Load ACCA with the contents of loc. 50
0004	50		
0005	36	PSHA	Push A onto stack
0006	96	LDAA	Load ACCA with the contents of loc. 60
0007	60		
0008	97	STAA	Store A into 50
0009	50		
000A	32	PULA	Pull byte from stack
000B	97	STAA	Store it into 60
000C	60		
000D	3E	HLT	

The point to note is that the programmer does not have to specify an address in which to temporarily store the byte from 0050. The push/pull instructions handle the temporary storage for him or her. Of course consecutive PSHA instructions can be used to store several bytes, but keep in mind that the stack is a last-in/first-out type of memory.

The real power of the stack becomes evident when using *subroutines.* Subroutines are short *miniprograms* that may be used over and over several times during execution of a larger program. Rather than rewriting the routine each time it is used, the programmer sets it up as a subroutine to be called on each time it is needed.

Whenever the MPU decodes an instruction to jump to subroutine (JSR), the present contents of the program counter are automatically pushed onto the stack. Then, upon completion of the subroutine, when the MPU decodes a return from subroutine (RTS) instruction, the program counter is automatically loaded with the 2 bytes from the top of the stack. These 2 bytes, of course, tell the MPU where to return to continue the main program. In this manner, the subroutine may be used over and over at different points in the main program without the programmer having to worry about how to tell the MPU where to resume its previous operations.

An example of when to use such a subroutine is in the use of a time delay. Let's suppose we want to build a flasher circuit to light a lamp *A* for 1 sec, then turn off *A* and light lamp *B* for 1 sec, then light *A* again, and so on, over and over. In a later chapter you'll learn how to interface the lamp drivers to the MPU. For now, just assume that if you can set bit 0 in memory location 1000, lamp *A* will light. Likewise, if you set bit 1 in the same location, lamp *B* will light.

What our program should do, then, is to load the accumulator with 01 and store it into location 1000; after 1 sec, load the accumulator with 02 and store it into location 1000 for 1 sec; and then repeat the operation over and over.

The main program is shown in Fig. 8-12(A) and the subroutine in Fig. 8-12(B). Note that the program starts out by initializing the stack pointer and then loads the accumulator with the byte 01 and stores it into location 1000 (thus lighting lamp *A*). The instruction at 0008 tells the MPU to jump to the subroutine starting at 0020.

Here's where the stack comes in. As soon as the JSR instruction is decoded, the program counter contents (000B) are pushed onto the stack for temporary storage, low byte first, then high byte. Then the program counter automatically gets loaded with the starting location of the subroutine (0020).

The time delay subroutine is then executed. Then, when the subroutine is finished, the instruction at 002A tells the MPU to return from subroutine.

This causes 2 bytes to be automatically pulled off of the stack and loaded into the program counter. These 2 bytes, of course, are 00 and 0B, the address of the next instruction in the main program.

Then the program continues at 000B by loading the accumulator with

Mem. loc.	Op code/address	Mnemonic	Comments
0000	8E	LDS	Load stack pointer immediately with 00FF
0001	00		
0002	FF		
0003	86	LDAA	Load IMMED with 01
0004	01		
0005	B7	STAA	Store into 1000
0006	10		
0007	00		
0008	BD	JSR	Jump to time delay subroutine
0009	00		
000A	20		
000B	86	LDAA	Load IMMED with 02
000C	02		
000D	B7	STAA	Store into 1000
000E	10		
000F	00		
0010	BD	JSR	Jump to time delay subroutine
0011	00		
0012	20		
0013	20	BRA	Branch back to start of loop
0014	EE		

(A)

Fig. 8-12 (A) Program to alternately store bytes for 1 sec each; (B) time delay subroutine.

Mem. loc.	Op code/address	Mnemonic	~	Comments
0020	CE	LDX		Load index reg. IMMED with delay byte
1	FF			
2	FF			
3	01	NOP	2	
4	01	NOP	2	
5	01	NOP	2	
6	01	NOP	2	
7	09	DEX	4	Decrement index reg.
8	26	BNE	4	Done yet?
9	F9			No; loop again
A	39	RTS		Yes; return to main program

(B)

Fig. 8-12 (Cont.)

02 and storing it into 1000 (causing lamp *A* to go out and lamp *B* to light).

When the MPU decodes the instruction at 0010, the subroutine is called again. This time the program counter contents of 0013 are pushed onto the stack, and the MPU executes the subroutine again.

The subroutine can thus be called as many times as desired during the execution of a larger program. The programmer never has to specify a return address at the end of the subroutine. It is automatically taken care of by the stack.

Before we leave this example, let's take a look at the time delay subroutine to see how we get a total delay of 1 sec.

First, the index register is loaded with FFFFH (65,536). Then, after a few NOPs, the index register gets decremented. Since the contents of the index register have not yet gone to zero, the MPU is directed to branch back to 0023 and repeat the loop. This loop is repeated over and over until finally the index register goes to zero.

If we count up the machine cycles for every instruction in the loop, we get a total of 16 cycles. Assuming 1 μsec per machine cycle, we get 16 μsec per loop. Since the loop is repeated 65,536 times, the total time is approximately 1.048 sec.

From this you can see that the time delay can be adjusted accurately to almost any desired value by adding or subtracting NOPs and also by slightly changing the value loaded into the index register. Engineers often prefer to "tweak up" these delays to an exact value by observing the output (bit 0 of location 1000) with a scope while trying different values for the index register.

Review Questions

1. How many standard TTL loads can each output line of the MC6800 drive?

2. Which pin on the MC6800 goes HIGH after all address lines have stabilized?

3. When the CPU is doing a WRITE to memory, pin 34 goes (HIGH, LOW).

4. How many bytes of memory can the MC6800 access?

5. What is the purpose of the condition code register?

6. What is the state of the address and data bus lines (HIGH, LOW, high-Z) when the HALT line is made active?

7. Explain what gets loaded into the program counter when $\overline{\text{RESET}}$ is made active.

8. Should the monitor program (in ROM) normally be stored in the highest or lowest memory space? Explain.

9. Where can you find out how many clock cycles are required for each instruction?

10. A common error, often made by novice programmers, is failure to initialize the stack pointer. That is, the programmer forgets to load the stack pointer with the address of the RAM space he or she intends to use for the stack. Describe what problems could result from this oversight.

Problems

8-1 What would be the contents of accumulator A after executing the following 2 bytes of program: 86, 57? (*Hint:* 86 is the op code.)

8-2 Write 2 bytes of program to add the value 14H to the present contents of accumulator B.

8-3 How long would it take to execute the 2 bytes of Problem 8-1 if the clock frequency were 1 MHz?

8-4 How long would it take to execute the 2 bytes of Problem 8-2 if the clock frequency were 500 kHz?

8-5 Show the state of the N and Z flags after executing the 2 bytes of Problem 8-1.

8-6 Show the state of the N and Z flags and the contents of B after executing the 2 bytes of Problem 8-2. Assume the previous contents of B were 95H.

Refer to the program of Fig. 8-5 for the next four problems.

8-7 What will be the contents of accumulator A after executing the instruction at 0000?

8-8 What will be the contents of the program counter after executing the instruction at 0000?

8-9 What will be the contents of accumulator A after executing the instruction at 0006?

8-10 What will be the contents of memory location 0052 after executing the instruction at 0006?

8-11 Write a short program in MC6800 machine language to subtract a number in location 0125 from a number in 0120 and store the result in location 01A0.

8-12 How long will it take to execute the program of Problem 8-11, assuming a 1-MHz clock?

8-13 Refer to the program of Fig. 8-8. Suppose that location 50 contained the value 27H and that location 51 contained the value 18H. Also suppose that the program byte at location 0006 was erroneously loaded with the value 02H. After running the program, what would be stored into location 52?

8-14 Suppose in the program of Fig. 8-8 that the value 23H was loaded into location 50 and that the value 37H was loaded into location 51. Also suppose that location 0006 was erroneously loaded with the value 02H. What would be loaded into location 52 when the program was executed? Explain.

8-15 You are writing a program in which you are using a BEQ instruction in location 0025. If the Z flag of the condition code register is set, you want the program to jump forward to location 0032; otherwise it should continue sequentially. What value of offset should you put in location 0026? (Remember that the PC will be pointing to the next *instruction* before executing the BEQ.)

8-16 Refer to Problem 8-15. If you want the program to jump back to location 001B if the Z flag is set, what offset should you put in location 0026?

Problems 8-17–8-25 refer to the program of Fig. 8-10.

8-17 What are the contents of the index register after executing the instruction at 0000?

8-18 What is the purpose of the instruction at 0003?

8-19 What is the address of the word being compared to the accumulator in the instruction at 0006 the first time it is executed?

8-20 What is the address of the word being compared to the accumulator in the instruction at 0006 assuming no match was found during the first seven comparisons?

8-21 What will be the contents of the index register the first time the instruction at 000A is executed?

8-22 What will be the state of the Z flag the first time the instruction at 000B is executed?

8-23 How many possible codes are stored in the lookup table?

8-24 What will be the final value of the index register if a match is never found?

8-25 Suppose you wanted to sound an alarm if no match was found for the code word. You could start an alarm by writing into some specific memory location. Which location could signify an alarm condition when written into?

The remaining problems refer to the program of Fig. 8-12.

8-26 For this program to run, there must be (RAM, ROM) at locations 00FF and lower. Why?

8-27 What is the result of executing instructions 0003 and 0005?

8-28 When the instruction at 0008 is executed, what will be the contents of memory location 00FF? What will be the contents of 00FE?

8-29 What will be the contents of the program counter after executing the instruction at 0008?

8-30 What will be the contents of the index register after executing the instruction at 0020?

8-31 What will be the contents of the index register after executing the instruction at 0026 the first time?

8-32 What will be the contents of the index register after executing the instruction at 0027 the first time?

8-33 What flag is examined by the instruction at 0028? What will be its state the first time this instruction is executed?

8-34 What will be the contents of the index register when the subroutine is finished?

8-35 What will be the contents of the program counter after the instruction at 002A is executed the first time? What will be the contents of the stack pointer?

8-36 What will be the result of executing the instructions at 000B and 000D?

8-37 What will be the contents of the program counter after executing the instruction at 0013?

8-38 What would be the program counter contents after executing the instruction at 0013 if the byte at 0014 were erroneously loaded as F0H?

8-39 Explain what would happen if location 0014 were loaded with F0H. Would the computer continue to run? What would you see on lamps *A* and *B?*

8-40 Modify the subroutine so as to light each lamp for approximately 0.5 sec.

CHAPTER 9

Interface Devices

By now you know how to program a microprocessor and how to connect it to memory chips where its programs are stored. But the real value of the microprocessor lies in its ability to control real-world devices, such as motors, solenoids, lamps, and cathode ray tubes (CRTs).

To be able to drive those loads and to allow the user to input data by means of switches, keyboards, or phone lines some additional hardware is needed. The technique of connecting the MPU to input and output devices is called *interfacing*.

In this chapter we shall deal with common interface devices, beginning with very simple SSI devices, such as latches and buffers, up through some very interesting programmable LSI devices. The LSI devices can be configured, by means of a program, to operate in a variety of different ways, thereby minimizing the amount of hardware needed to do the job.

9-1 Parallel I/O (Input/Output)

The simplest way to output a byte from an MPU is to use a latch, or pair of latches, such as the 74LS75. Latches are required for two reasons. First, the output data are available on the data bus for only an instant, so therefore it must be latched for later use. In addition, the data lines from the MPU can only drive one TTL load. So in the event you must drive more loads, buffering of the data lines is also necessary. Both of these jobs are handled by the output latch.

In Fig. 9-1, we see two 74LS75 quad latches whose data *(D)* inputs

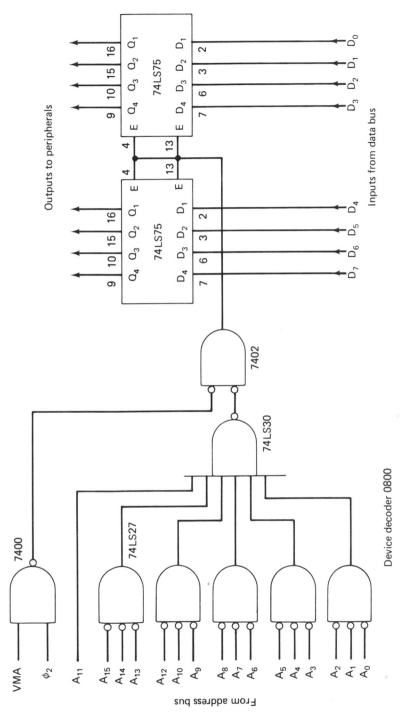

Fig. 9-1. Output latch and decoder.

263

are connected to data bus lines. To output a byte, we place the desired data on the D inputs and then strobe it into the latches by driving the enable inputs HIGH. On the 74LS75 chips, when the enable inputs go HIGH, the data present at each D input are transferred to its corresponding Q output. Then, when the enable inputs go LOW, data that were present at the inputs at the time the transition occurred are retained at the Q outputs. Thereafter, the information on the data bus can change, but the Q outputs will retain the latched-in data.

Examination of Fig. 9-1 shows that the enable input is driven active HIGH only when the address lines are in the following condition:

A_{15}	A_{14}	A_{13}	A_{12}	A_{11}	A_{10}	A_9	A_8	A_7	A_6	A_5	A_4	A_3	A_2	A_1	A_0
0	0	0	0	1	0	0	0	0	0	0	0	0	0	0	0

which corresponds to address 0800H.

The gates form the *device decoder* and are generally referred to as *device select logic.*

To output a byte to the latch, the MC6800 simply must execute the following instructions:

```
86      LDAA          (IMMED)
--                    (byte to be output)
87      STAA 0800
08                    (address of output port)
00
```

where the two dashes (--) represent the byte to be output. The address 0800 is the address of the output device (the latch).

This type of I/O structure is called *memory-mapped I/O.* In other words, writing to an output port is done in exactly the same manner as storing a byte in memory. All MC6800 I/O is handled in this manner.

Note that all 16 address lines are decoded in Fig. 9-1. Usually, it is not necessary to completely decode *all* address lines. Figure 9-2 shows a much simpler decoder that will enable the latch when the address lines stabilize at 0800. Here, only address lines A_{11} and A_{12} are used along with VMA

Fig. 9-2. Simplified decoder for device at 0800 using partial address decoding.

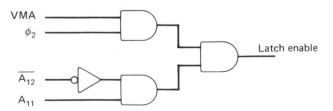

and ϕ_2. This scheme will work fine in a small system in which no other device (including memory) uses address line A_{11} HIGH and A_{12} LOW. Keep in mind that the latch will also be enabled on any read or write to any memory location in which A_{11} is HIGH and A_{12} is LOW. The active LOW input, A_{12}, is used to prevent the latch from being enabled when all address and control lines are in their high-impedance states, such as during RESET. (High-impedance or disconnected inputs to TTL circuits act like HIGH's.) The programmer must therefore be careful, when using partial address decoding, to prevent overlapping of address space.

Now let's see how we can input data to the MPU.

The circuit of Fig. 9-3 shows a simple circuit used to input data from a bank of switches. The switches feed inputs of three-state buffers whose outputs connect to the data bus. To read in data from the switches, the MPU simply executes the following instruction:

$$\text{LDAA} \qquad 0400$$

This causes the switch data to be loaded into accumulator A, just as if the accumulator were being loaded from memory.

The three-state buffers are necessary here so that the switch data appear on the data bus *only* when device 0400 is enabled. When device 0400 is not being addressed, the buffer outputs are in their high-impedance state.

Although individual toggle switches are shown in Fig. 9-3, the inputs to the buffers could be outputs from a keyboard, paper tape reader, or any similar parallel data device.

As an example of using both input and output devices, suppose we want to read data in from the bank of switches and output the same data to be displayed on LEDs. We simply connect LED drivers to the output latches and then execute the following instructions:

B6	LDAA 0400	(extended)
04		
00		
B7	STAA 0800	(extended)
08		
00		

9-2 Peripheral Interface Adapter (PIA)

Although all parallel data interfacing could be accomplished with latches, gates, and three-state buffers as described, much greater flexibility is gained by using programmable interface chips. Programmable LSI devices, such as the peripheral interface adapter (PIA), allow the system designer to use standard parts whose operating modes are controlled by the program.

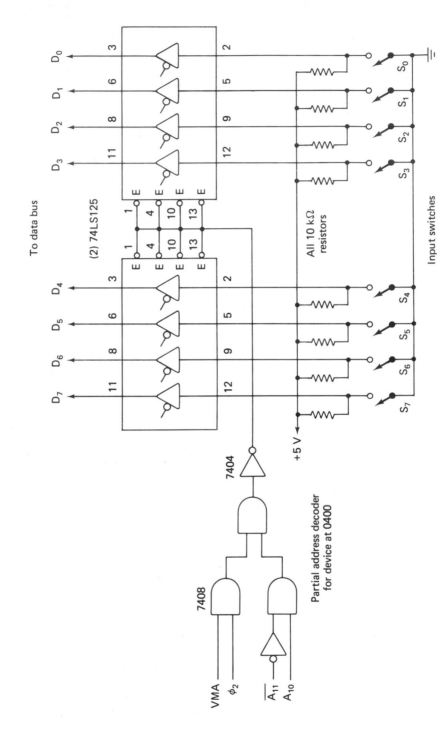

Fig. 9-3. Parallel input circuit using three-state buffers.

266

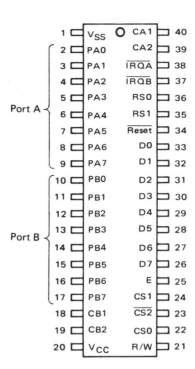

Fig. 9-4. MC6821 PIA pin assignments.

The MC6821 PIA, shown in Fig. 9-4, has two 8-bit I/O ports, called port *A* and port *B*. Each bit line in each port is individually programmable as either an input or an output. Usually the ports are programmed on power up by part of the initialization routine stored in ROM. Any system reset should also reinitialize the PIA. However, the PIA can be reprogrammed to perform a different function at any time during the execution of the main program.

Figure 9-5 shows how the PIA can connect peripherals to the MPU. Each port has its own eight data lines as well as two control lines (*CA*1, *CA*2 and *CB*1, *CB*2) which connect to its corresponding peripheral. But on the MPU side, note that the two ports share a common data bus and common lines to the address bus and control bus.

The chip select pins, *CS*0, *CS*1, and $\overline{CS2}$ connect to address lines and are used, of course, to select the PIA. That is, the chip select pins connect to internal gating and often eliminate the need for external device select logic. Examination of the address lines connected to these three pins will show that the lowest address that will select the PIA is 2004.* Study Fig. 9-5 to see why. Of course, different address lines could have been used, at the discretion of the designer.

As shown in Fig. 9-6, there are six registers inside the PIA. The *output*

* *Note:* On the Motorola MEK D2 kit, the PIA is wired to respond to addresses 8004–8007.

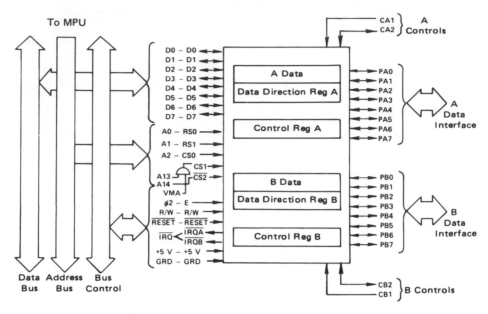

Fig. 9-5. MC6821 PIA bus interface.

Fig. 9-6. PIA registers.

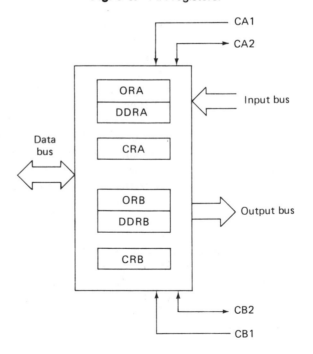

registers, OR*A* (*A* data) and OR*B* (*B* data), are the registers which connect to pins PA0–PA7 and PB0–PB7, respectively, which in turn connect to the output and input devices. For example, if side *B* is configured as an output port, output register *B* takes the place of the 74LS75 latches we studied earlier. Similarly, if we configure side *A* as an input port, OR*A* takes the place of the 74LS125 three-state buffers.

The question now arises as to how do we configure a port as an input or output. The answer is simple. All we have to do is to write a word into each *data direction register* (DDR). If we store all 1s into DDR*B*, side *B* will act as an output port. Similarly, if we store all 0s into DDR*A*, OR*A* will act as an input port. We also have the option of storing a few 1s and a few 0s into either DDR to make some lines act as inputs and the rest as outputs. For example, storing the byte 00101100 into DDR*A* would configure PA5, PA3, and PA2 as output lines and the remainder as inputs.

The third pair of registers in the PIA are the two *control registers,* CR*A* and CR*B*. These registers handle the interrupt and handshaking capabilities of the two ports. In addition, bit 2 of each control register helps to select which register is actually being addressed by the MPU. This will be made clear shortly.

As pointed out earlier, the PIA in Fig. 9-5 will respond to address 2004. But note also that register select pins RS0 and RS1 connect to address lines *A*0 and *A*1, respectively. So actually, the PIA has four addresses that it will respond to. These are 2004, 2005, 2006, and 2007. Thus we have six registers to write into or read from but only four addresses with which to

Fig. 9-7. PIA addressing scheme.

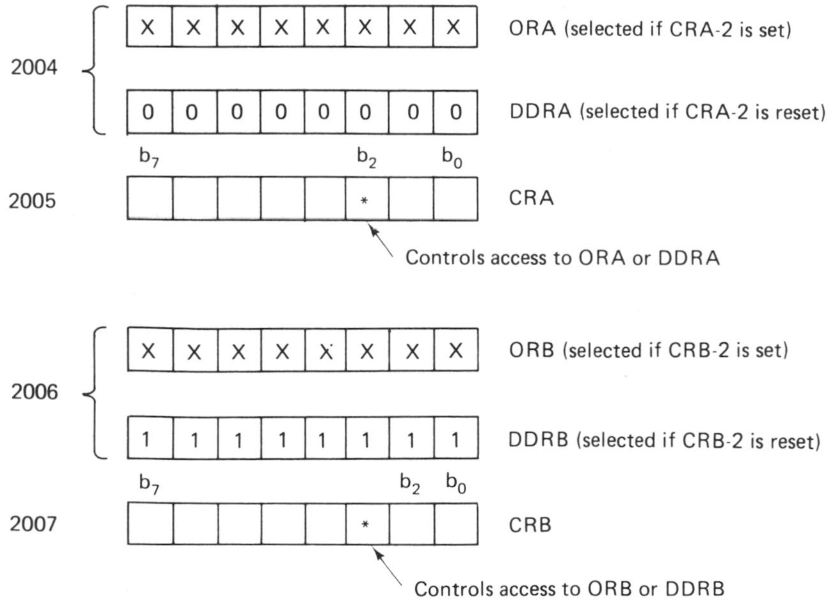

do it. Rather than add more pins to the chip to allow for more addresses, which would be costly, Motorola chose to use bit 2 of each control register to control MPU access to either the data direction register or the output register.

Here's how it works. If bit 2 of CRA is LOW, DDRA responds to 2004. But if bit 2 of CRA is HIGH, ORA responds to 2004. Figure 9-7 shows the addressing scheme in detail.

Fig. 9-8. PIA with side *A* wired as input port and side *B* as output port.

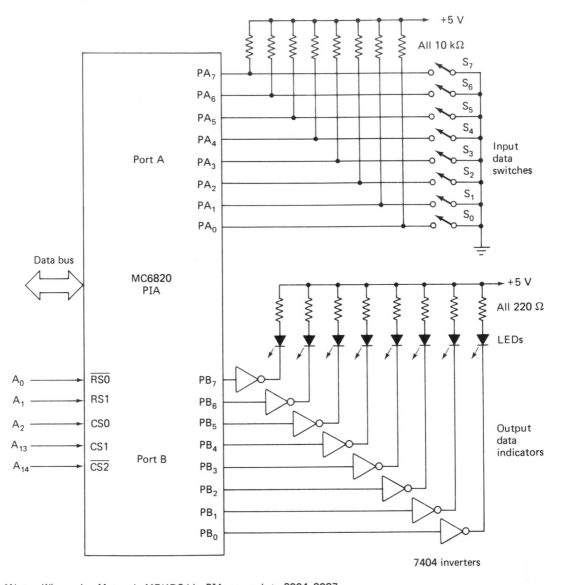

*Note: When using Motorola MEKD2 kit, PIA responds to 8004–8007.

To initialize the PIA, on power up, for example, we first store a word in each data direction register to configure the ports as inputs or outputs. We then store a control word into each control register, setting bit 2 and thus gaining access to each output register. Thereafter, we can write into or read from an output peripheral just as though it were a memory location.

A simple program to set up port A as an input and port B as an output could be as follows:

```
RESET (clears all PIA registers)
86      LDAA            (IMMED)
FF
B7      STAA 2006       (sets up port B as output)
20
06
86      LDAA            (IMMED)
04
B7      STAA 2005       (sets bit 2 of CRA)
20
05
B7      STAA 2007       (sets bit 2 of CRB)
20
07
```

Figure 9-8 shows how a PIA could be wired to input data to port A from switches and output data to LED drivers on side B. After initialization, data can be read from the switches and output to the LEDs as follows:

```
LDAA    2004    (input data from switches)
STAA    2006    (output data to port B)
```

The data output to port B is latched in until the program stores a different byte into 2006.

Of course in the simple I/O sequence shown, the same data that are read in from the switches are output to the LEDs. But in most cases the input data will be operated upon by the program; then various outputs are set or reset accordingly. For example, suppose you want to multiply the input data by 4 and then output it. The sequence could be written as follows:

```
B6      LDAA 2004
20
04
48      ASLA            shift left
48      ASLA            shift left
B7      STAA 2006
20
06
```

The two shift left instructions effectively multiply the contents of ACCA by 4.

Other arithmetic or logical operations can be performed on the input data, and then a byte can be output to port *B* based on the results of the operation. This is where the flexibility of programmable logic really has its value. We shall see more of this in the chapter on applications of microprocessors.

9-3 Interrupt Handling

There are basically two ways of handling I/O routines. The first method is called *polling*. The MPU continually polls, or looks at, the input, then does an output, looks at the input again, does an output, etc. It continues in this manner indefinitely. Of course the MPU could scan more than one input and perform more than one output, but the idea is that the operation of the MPU is *dedicated* to this scanning operation. In a large system, where the MPU might be tied to several peripherals or where it might have some rather lengthy tasks to do beside scanning the I/O devices, the polling method is very inefficient.

A much more time-efficient way of handling I/O is by the use of *interrupts.** We shall now see how the M6800 system handles interrupts.

First we shall outline the steps involved in servicing the interrupt and then see how to use interrupts with the PIA.

STEPS IN SERVICING AN INTERRUPT

1. The interrupting device requests interrupt by pulling $\overline{IRQ}$ (pin 4 of MPU) LOW.

2. The MPU finishes its current instruction and then tests the interrupt mask bit (the *I* bit) in the condition code register. If the *I* bit is set, MPU ignores the request and continues its present task. (The *I* bit can be set or cleared by software control by instructions SEI and CLI.)

3. If the interrupt mask is not set, the MPU pushes the present contents of the PC, index register, ACC*A*, ACC*B*, and CC registers onto the stack. It then sets the *I* bit to prevent further interrupts.

4. Next, the MPU loads the program counter with the contents of memory locations FFF8 and FFF9. The contents of these two locations, called the *interrupt vector,* are the *starting address* of the interrupt service routine. The locations FFF8 and FFF9 reside in ROM and, of course, must have been previously loaded by the programmer. That is, the programmer decided, when the program for the ROM was

---

* An interrupt is a technique by which the MPU is forced to suspend its present operation in order to do a more important task.

written, where the interrupt service routine was to start. He or she then loaded the starting address of the routine into FFF8 and FFF9.

5. With the starting address of the interrupt service routine in the PC, the MPU effectively makes a jump to that location and begins the service routine.

6. The last instruction of the service routine must be a return from interrupt (RTI).

7. As soon as the MPU decodes the RTI instruction, it pulls bytes off of the stack in the reverse order of how they were pushed on. This process restores the contents of the PC, IX, ACCA, ACCB, and CC registers to what they were prior to the interrupt. It then clears the interrupt mask bit.

8. Finally, the MPU resumes the task it was doing prior to the interrupt.

So far we have only seen how bit 2 of the control register in the PIA is used to select either the DDR or the output register. The remainder of the bits in the control register are used for interrupt control and handshaking.* If the user wants to use the PIA in the interrupt mode, he or she sets bit 0. With b_0 set, $CA1$ acts as an interrupt request line for the peripheral on side A. The programmer also has the option of choosing whether the interrupt request responds to an active HIGH or active LOW input by setting or clearing bit 1.

Bit 7 of control register A gets set when an external device on port A requests an interrupt and gets cleared by an MPU read of that port and similarly for port B. Table 9-1 summarizes the actions of bits 0, 1, and 7 of the control registers.

As shown in Fig. 9-9, each port has an interrupt request output line. These are labeled $\overline{IRQA}$ (pin 38) and $\overline{IRQB}$ (pin 37). The lines connect to open drain transistors, so they are usually wire-Ored together as shown.

To study the operation, suppose bits 0 and 1 of control register A were both set by the programmer. Next, an interrupting device drives line $CA1$ (pin 40) HIGH. Since the interrupts are enabled, pin 40 going HIGH causes bit 7 to set and simultaneously drives IRQA (pin 38) LOW. The LOW signal at pin 38 pulls the $\overline{IRQ}$ (pin 4) input of the MPU LOW. The interrupt sequence then begins.

Part of the interrupt service routine should contain an instruction to READ from port A. This will clear the interrupt flag (bit 7).

Incidentally, if side B requests an interrupt, bit 7 of control register B will be set, just as occurs in side A. Part of the B side service routine must include a READ from port B to clear bit 7. This *dummy* READ is necessary, even though side B is being used as an output. A READ (LDAA 2006) is the only way to clear the interrupt flag without resetting the entire chip.

---

* Handshaking refers to some method of acknowledging a transaction.

Table 9-1 Control of Interrupt Inputs CA1 and CB1 [a]

CRA-1 (CRB-1)	CRA-0 (CRB-0)	Interrupt Input CA1 (CB1)	Interrupt Flag CRA-7 (CRB-7)	MPU Interrupt Request IRQA (IRQB)
0	0	↓ Active	Set high on ↓ of CA1 (CB1)	Disabled—IRQ remains high
0	1	↓ Active	Set high on ↓ of CA1 (CB1)	Goes low when the interrupt flag bit CRA-7 (CRB-7) goes high
1	0	↑ Active	Set high on ↑ of CA1 (CB1)	Disabled—IRQ remains high
1	1	↑ Active	Set high on ↑ of CA1 (CB1)	Goes low when the interrupt flag bit CRA-7 (CRB-7) goes high

Notes: 1. ↑ indicates positive transition (low to high).
2. ↓ indicates negative transition (high to low).
3. The interrupt flag bit CRA-7 is cleared by an MPU read of the A data register, and CRB-7 is cleared by an MPU read of the B data register.
4. If CRA-0 (CRB-0) is low when an interrupt occurs (interrupt disabled) and is later brought high, IRQA (IRQB) occurs on the positive transition of CRA-0 (CRB-0).
5. CRA-0 is bit 0 of control register A, CRA-1 is bit 1 of control register A, etc.

[a] Courtesy of Motorola.

Fig. 9-9. Interrupt control of PIA.

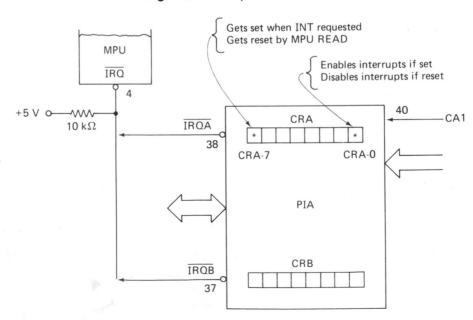

There is also another reason for reading the control registers. Since there is only one $\overline{IRQ}$ pin on the MPU, there is no hardware way for the MPU to determine whether side A or side B actually generated the interrupt request. The *program* must then determine the source. It does so by first reading the side A control register. If bit 7 was not set, the MPU should then read the side B control register. Whichever control register has bit 7 set is the one that generated the interrupt request. The appropriate service routine is then followed.

Here is one way to test bit 7 of control register A using a *masking* technique:

B6	LDAA 2005	Read CR A
20		
05		
84	ANDA	AND ACCA (IMMED) with bit pattern 10000000
80		
27	BEQ	If Z flag is set, b_7 must have been cleared
--		Go to port B service routine
B6	LDAA 2006	If Z flag was not set, b_7 must have been set
20		Begin port A service routine
06		
--		

First, the control byte from CR A is loaded into ACC A. Then, since b_7 is the only bit of interest here, the rest of the bits are *masked out* by the bit pattern 10000000 (80H). This operation causes the Z flag to clear if b_7 was set and to set if b_7 was not set. The BEQ instruction then directs the MPU to branch to the port B service routine or to fall through to the port A service routine, depending on whether the Z flag was set or cleared. [The service routines are not shown here, of course. Only the bit test (polling) sequence is shown.]

Consider the following initialization sequence for the PIA wired to respond to addresses 2004–2007:

```
RESET
86      LDAA        (IMMED)
05                  (control byte)
B7      STAA 2005   (store in CRA)
20
05
73      COM 2006    (invert all bits in 2006)
20
06
86      LDAA        (IMMED)
04                  (control byte)
B7      STAA 2007   (store in CRB)
20
07
```

The system RESET clears all registers. Then storing the byte 05 in 2005 sets bit 2 and bit 0 of CRA. Setting bit 0 enables interrupts; resetting bit 1 makes the interrupt request respond to an active LOW signal at $CA1$. And, of course, setting bit 2 gives the MPU access to output register A through address 2004.

The instruction COM 2006 complements all the 0 bits to 1s in data direction register B, thus making port B an output port. Is port B interrupt-enabled?

We shall go into detail in setting up and handling the interrupt service routines in a later chapter.

9-4 Serial I/O

Regardless of the actual hardware that is used, parallel I/O techniques transfer all 8 bits of a byte simultaneously from one device to another. Parallel I/O techniques work well as long as the two devices communicating with each other are close together, say within a foot or so. But if the devices must be placed farther apart, say several feet, or in different rooms, or perhaps in different parts of a large manufacturing plant, problems arise that didn't show up before.

For one thing, wires running long distances are subject to electrical noise pickup. These noises can act like signals at the receiving end and thus alter the data being sent.

In addition, the rise and fall times of the logic signals being transmitted are very short. In other words, the signals have some very high-frequency components. When high frequencies are transmitted over wires, strange things begin to happen, such as time delays due to capacitance and inductance of the wires. Higher-frequency components of the rectangular pulses are affected more by these time delays than are the lower-frequency components. As a result, the received waveform actually has a different *shape* than it would if the wires were shorter.

In fact, the long wires are subject to all the phenomena of transmission lines. As you might know from the study of communications theory, every transmission line has a certain characteristic impedance depending on its physical construction. If a transmission line is not properly terminated in its characteristic impedance, reflections will occur at the receiving end. Some part of the transmitted signal reflecting back along the transmission line interferes with the signal being sent, either adding to or subtracting from its amplitude. The net result is that the actual signal seen by the receiver can be so drastically distorted that it doesn't even resemble the original transmitted pulse. Obviously, the distorted signal can be interpreted incorrectly, so that the data latched into the receiver can be erroneous.

To overcome these problems, when it is necessary to send data over long distances, a technique known as *serial* communications is often used. In serial communications, each byte is transmitted 1 bit at a time over a

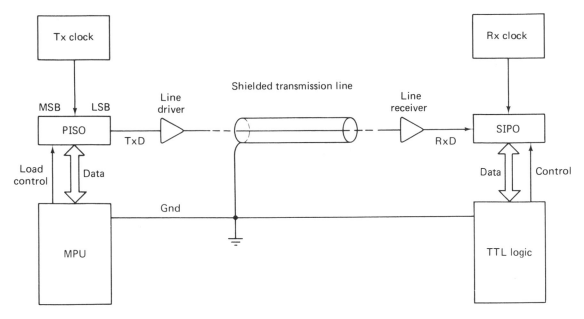

Fig. 9-10. Simple one-way serial communications link.

single transmission line. The transmission line is properly shielded from noise pickup. Also, the rate of data transmission is purposely made slower, so the problems of fast rise and fall times are reduced. And most importantly, a *line driver* is used at the sending end, and a *line receiver* is used at the receiving end of the line. These drivers and receivers are not TTL chips with fast rise and fall times but rather linear amplifier circuits whose rise and fall times (slew rates) are much slower than TTL. Often the driver and receiver input and output impedances are low (about 100 Ω) and thus match the transmission line much better than TTL, thereby reducing reflections to a negligible amount.

Figure 9-10 shows how a simple one-way serial communications link can be built. The MPU, at the left, has its 8-bit data bus feeding a parallel in–serial out (PISO) shift register. When the MPU wants to send a byte to the TTL logic circuit at the right, the MPU places the byte on the data bus and then parallel loads the byte into the shift register. Next, the transmitter (Tx) clock pulses the shift register eight times to shift the byte out, LSB first. This action is just like that of the arithmetic shift registers you studied earlier.

The entire 8-bit byte is fed, one bit at a time, to the line driver. The line driver then drives the transmission line feeding the line receiver. The line driver and line receiver round off the leading and trailing edges of the pulses to prevent distortions, as mentioned earlier.

The output of the line receiver feeds the input to a serial in–parallel out (SIPO) shift register. This register is clocked by the TTL logic circuits at the right, by the receiver (Rx) clock, at precisely the correct times, to shift in each new bit as it arrives at the receiver.

Finally, after all 8 bits are clocked into the SIPO register, a control signal is generated by the TTL logic circuits to dump the byte onto the data bus and latch it into the TTL circuits. In this way, the entire 8-bit byte is transmitted over a single-wire transmission line, which is shielded against noise pickup and properly terminated by the driver and receiver to minimize reflections.

The advantage of serial transmission over parallel transmission is that much less hardware is needed to do the job. Only one driver, receiver, and shielded line are needed. The obvious disadvantage is that serial data transmission is much slower than parallel transmission.

Since no clock signals are sent with the data, this method of communication is referred to as *asynchronous*. Of course, the transmitter and receiver registers must be shifted at the same times, so they must agree on the rate at which the bits are clocked out of the transmitter. To make asynchronous communications feasible with a wide variety of equipment, certain more or less standard bit rates are used. The number of bits per second being transmitted is commonly referred to as the *baud rate*. Typical rates are 75, 110, 150, 300, 600, 1200, 2400, 4800, 9600, and 19.2K baud.

Teletypes commonly use 110 baud, whereas higher-speed printers often run at 300 baud. Digital cassette recorders may operate at 1200 baud, and communication between computers or programmable controllers often runs at 9600 baud.

In addition to clocking the transmitter and receiver shift registers at the same rates, we have an additional problem. Remember that the incoming data timing is asynchronous to the receiver clock. That is, transmission of data from the sender may begin at any instant. For example, suppose the data are coming from a typewriter keyboard. The operator may happen to hit a key or series of keys at any instant. How does the receiver know when the first bit of a byte is coming?

To handle this problem, certain formatting of transmitted characters is necessary. The most commonly used format is shown in Fig. 9-11.

Fig. 9-11. Transmitter data at serial output pin for asynchronous transmission of data byte 45 hex.

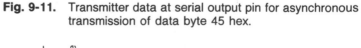

First, while no data are being sent, the transmitter output remains at a logic HIGH, and the transmitter is said to be *marking* time. In serial communications terminology, a *mark* is a logic 1, and a *space* is a logic 0.

When a byte is transmitted, the first bit sent is a logic 0 *start bit*. This change from the HIGH marking level to the LOW start bit signals the receiver that a data byte will follow.

Immediately following the start bit come the data bits. The data byte shown here contains 8 bits. Note that the LSB is received immediately after the start bit.

Often, to check for good transmission and reception, a parity bit is sent following the MSB. The parity may be even or odd, depending on the user's choice, but must, of course, be agreed upon prior to transmission.

Last, following the parity bit, one or two *stop bits* (logic 1s) are sent. Usually 2 stop bits are used for 110 baud and 1 stop bit for all other rates.

Each and every character transmitted asynchronously must have the same format: a LOW start bit, data bits, optional parity bit, and finally a stop bit or bits.

Obviously, more circuitry is needed than is shown in Fig. 9-10 in order to insert start bits, stop bits, and parity bits at the transmitter and to check for these bits at the receiver. A considerable amount of hardware would be needed if all this was done with SSI circuits. Fortunately, manufacturers make LSI devices called *UARTs* (universal asynchronous receiver transmitters), which automatically take care of the formatting and checking for you. One such UART is Motorola's asynchronous communications interface adapter (ACIA), which we shall study in the next section.

9-5 Asynchronous Communications Interface Adapter (ACIA)

The asynchronous communications interface adapter, MC6850, is to serial data I/O what the PIA is to parallel data I/O. The ACIA connects to the MPU via the 8-bit data bus, and it interfaces with the outside world through a transmit data (TxD) pin and a receive data (RxD) pin. The ACIA performs all necessary parallel-to-serial and serial-to-parallel conversions internally. In addition, it generates and monitors control lines used with *modems*. A modem (contraction for <u>mo</u>dulator-<u>dem</u>odulator) is a device used in serial data systems for communications over long distances, for example, via phone lines. The modem control signals, $\overline{CTS}$, $\overline{RTS}$, and $\overline{DCD}$ will be discussed in the chapter on applications. For now we shall concentrate on the transmitter and receiver.

Figure 9-12(A) shows all inputs and outputs of the ACIA, the left side being the MPU side and the right side being the peripheral side. Pinouts for the ACIA are shown in Fig. 9-12(B).

Note that there are four internal registers shown. These are the registers that the MPU can communicate with. The transmitter data register and control register can be written into from the MPU but not read. The receive

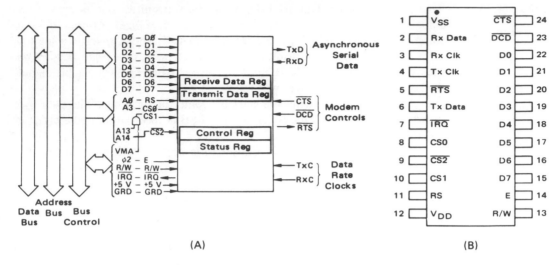

Fig. 9-12. MC6850 ACIA: (A) bus interface; (B) pin assignments.

data register and status register are read only registers. Only one register select pin is needed, along with the $R/\overline{W}$ control pin to select any particular register. Register selection is accomplished as follows:

$R/\overline{W}$	RS	Register Selected
0	0	Control register
0	1	Transmit data register
1	0	Status register
1	1	Receive data register

Just like the PIA, the ACIA must be programmed on power up to tell it how to operate. The ACIA must be told the *clock divide ratio* (more on this later), the *word length, parity, number of stop bits,* and *interrupt conditions.* It is told all these things by a single byte which the program writes into the control register prior to using the ACIA.

Table 9-2 gives the complete description of register contents. The transmitter data and receive data registers are self-explanatory. The control register byte configures the ACIA as follows:

CR1	CR0	Function
0	0	÷ 1
0	1	÷ 16
1	0	÷ 64
1	1	Master reset

Table 9-2 Definition of ACIA Register Contents[d]

Data Bus Line Number	Buffer Address			
	$RS \cdot \overline{R/W}$ Transmit Data Register (write only)	$RS \cdot R/W$ Receive Data Register (read only)	$\overline{RS} \cdot \overline{R/W}$ Control Register (write only)	$\overline{RS} \cdot R/W$ Status Register (read only)
0	Data bit 0[a]	Data bit 0	Counter divide select 1 (CR0)	Receive data register full (RDRF)
1	Data bit 1	Data bit 1	Counter divide select 2 (CR1)	Transmit data register empty (TDRE)
2	Data bit 2	Data bit 2	Word select 1 (CR2)	Data carrier detect ($\overline{DCD}$)
3	Data bit 3	Data bit 3	Word select 2 (CR3)	Clear to send ($\overline{CTS}$)
4	Data bit 4	Data bit 4	Word select 3 (CR4)	Framing error (FE)
5	Data bit 5	Data bit 5	Transmit control 1 (CR5)	Receiver overrun (OVRN)
6	Data bit 6	Data bit 6	Transmit control 2 (CR6)	Parity error (PE)
7	Data bit 7[b]	Data bit 7[c]	Receive interrupt enable (CR7)	Interrupt request (IRQ)

[a] Leading bit = LSB = bit 0.
[b] Data bit is don't care in 7-bit plus parity modes.
[c] Data bit will be zero in 7-bit plus parity modes.
[d] Courtesy of Motorola.

The clock divide ratio can be set at 1, 16, or 64. If a ÷ 16 ratio is used, the transmitted data will be shifted out of the serial shift register at $\frac{1}{16}$ of the Tx clock input. For example, to transmit at 300 baud using a ÷ 16 clock ratio, the actual input Tx clock frequency must be 300 × 16 = 4800 Hz. The reason for dividing the clock down is actually to resolve a *receiver* problem. You will remember that in asynchronous transmission, since no clock signals are sent, the receiver recognizes that a data byte is coming by a negative transition of the signal, indicating a start bit. To not be falsely started by a noise spike, the receiver samples the incoming signal at one-half bit time (eight clock pulses) after the first negative transition. If the signal level is still LOW, the receiver assumes a valid start bit and starts assembling the received byte. Each received bit is sampled at its midpoint in time to prevent the possibility of sampling during a transition. See Fig. 9-13. Since the receiver clock frequency is 16 times the incoming data frequency, the ACIA receiver simply counts 8 of its own clock pulses following the leading edge of the start bit and samples. If a valid start bit is sensed, the receiver then samples the incoming data every 16 clock pulses thereafter.

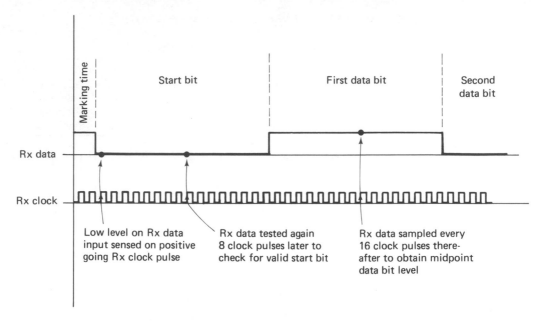

Fig. 9-13. Waveforms of receive data and receive clock with RxC operating at 16 times the RxD bit rate.

The midpoint sampling also corrects for any slight difference, say 1 or 2%, in the transmitter and receiver clocks.

Control bits 2, 3, and 4 define the word format as follows:

CR4	CR3	CR2	Function
0	0	0	7 bits + even parity + 2 stop bits
0	0	1	7 bits + odd parity + 2 stop bits
0	1	0	7 bits + even parity + 1 stop bit
0	1	1	7 bits + odd parity + 1 stop bit
1	0	0	8 bits + 2 stop bits
1	0	1	8 bits + 1 stop bit
1	1	0	8 bits + even parity + 1 stop bit
1	1	1	8 bits + odd parity + 1 stop bit

Bits 5 and 6 of the control register determine the state of the $\overline{\text{RTS}}$ pin and the transmitter interrupts as follows:

CR6	CR5	Function
0	0	$\overline{\text{RTS}}$ = low, transmitting interrupt disabled
0	1	$\overline{\text{RTS}}$ = low, transmitting interrupt enabled
1	0	$\overline{\text{RTS}}$ = high, transmitting interrupt disabled
1	1	$\overline{\text{RTS}}$ = low, transmits a break level on the transmit data output; transmitting interrupt disabled

We shall discuss the $\overline{RTS}$ and other modem signals later.

Finally, bit 7 of the control register enables the receiver interrupt when set. For example, setting bit 7 of the control register will cause an interrupt to be requested by the ACIA when a complete byte has been received and is ready to be read by the MPU. The received byte also sets bit 0 in the status register (receive data register full), as shown in Table 9-2. As an example of how to configure the ACIA, let's set it up to operate as follows: a ÷ 16 clock, 8 bits per byte, even parity, 1 stop bit, $\overline{RTS}$ LOW with Tx interrupt disabled and with receive interrupt enabled. Let's assume that the ACIA is wired as follows: $A14$ to $\overline{CS2}$, $A13$ to $CS1$, $A3$ to $CS0$, and $A0$ to RS. Mapping would show the following:

$A15$	$A14$	$A13$	$A12$	$A11$	$A10$	$A9$	$A8$	$A7$	$A6$	$A5$	$A4$	$A3$	$A2$	$A1$	$A0$
X	0	1	X	X	X	X	X	X	X	X	X	1	X	X	—

The ACIA then would respond to addresses 2008 and 2009.

We first start by writing a master reset into the ACIA control register as follows:

```
86      LDAA        (IMMED)
03                  (reset code)
B7      STAA 2008   (ACIA)
20
08
```

Then we would configure the ACIA by writing a byte into the control register, as shown in Fig. 9-14.

The program steps would be as follows:

```
86      LDAA        (IMMED)
99                  (control byte)
B7      STAA 2008
20
08
```

Fig. 9-14. Control word loaded into ACIA control register.

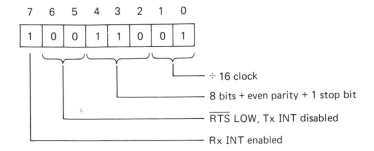

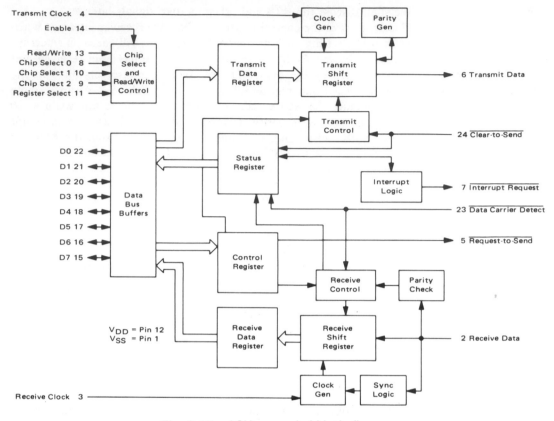

Fig. 9-15. ACIA expanded block diagram.

That's all there is to it. First a master reset and then a control word is written into the control register.

Whenever the MPU wants to transmit a byte, it simply stores the byte into the Tx data register, just as if it were storing it in memory.

Figure 9-15 shows how the internal registers are connected. After the control register is loaded, a byte can be stored into the Tx data register (2009). This byte, coming from the MPU, goes into the data bus buffer. From here it is transferred into the Tx data register, due to the selection of that register by *RS*0. Internal control circuitry automatically adds the proper start, stop, and parity bits to the data byte and then loads the byte from the Tx data register into the transmitter shift register. As soon as this byte is in the shift register, shifting begins at $\frac{1}{16}$ the Tx clock rate. No additional commands are needed from the MPU.

The Tx clock and Rx clock inputs of the ACIA (which are often tied together) come from an external clock, sometimes called a *baud rate generator*. This external clock, which is different from the system ϕ (MPU) clock, is usually crystal-controlled to maintain an exact frequency. The Tx and Rx clocks run continuously, even when no data are being sent or received.

The big advantage of using a UART can be seen here. Once the data byte is stored into the Tx data register by the MPU, the UART takes care of all formatting and shifting. The MPU is free to do other things while the byte is being shifted out.

Now let's consider a received byte, coming from some other transmitter. Remember that we initialized the receiver to generate an interrupt. The MPU can be busy doing other things when an incoming bit stream starts to enter the receiver. The receive shift register recognizes the start bit and, if it is valid, begins shifting in the data byte.

When all bits have been received, the byte is transferred by internal control circuitry into the Rx data register. Here, parity and framing are checked. (Framing refers to the proper number and position of start and stop bits.) If there are no errors, bits 0 and 7 of the status register are set. See Table 9-2. If there is any error, the appropriate status bit is also set. Setting bit 7 generates an interrupt request.

Just as with the PIA, when the MPU receives an interrupt request, it finishes its current instruction, pushes appropriate registers onto the stack, and then jumps to the interrupt service routine.

The interrupt service routine should include a READ from the status register (LDAA 2008). The status word should then be examined by the program to test for any errors in the byte. Once the status has been checked, the MPU should do a READ from the Rx data register (LDAA 2009) to obtain the actual byte. The start, stop, and parity bits are automatically stripped from the byte inside the ACIA, so that only the data byte will be read by the MPU.

In some newer devices now under development by Motorola and other companies, serial channels are being built right on the large-scale chips along with the MPU. However, the same ideas of initializing, formatting, and error checking still apply. So an understanding of the ACIA as a separate UART will aid you in working with more complex newer devices as they become available.

Review Questions

1. Give two reasons why latches are used when outputting data from an MPU.

2. Why must three-state buffers be used when connecting input switches to the data bus, rather than simply tying the switches directly to the data lines?

3. What precaution must be observed when using partial address decoding?

4. What problem might occur if only active HIGH signals are used as inputs to the device select logic gates, such as those in Fig. 9-3?

(*Hint:* Consider what happens to all address and control lines on reset. Also remember what open TTL inputs act like.)

5. The MC6821 PIA has two parallel I/O parts which can be configured as inputs or outputs. How is this accomplished?

6. Name the three registers associated with each port of the PIA, and briefly explain the function of each.

7. The process of an MPU servicing an interrupt can be likened to what takes place when a person reading a book is interrupted by someone ringing the doorbell. The reading of the book is like the computer working on its main task. The ringing of the doorbell corresponds to the interrupt request. When the doorbell rings, the person places a bookmark at the current place in the book. He or she then answers the door (services the interrupt). Finally he or she returns to the previous place in the book to resume the "main task." What operation of the MPU corresponds to placing a bookmark in the book?

8. Referring to Review Question 9–7, what operation of the MPU corresponds to returning to the exact place where the reader left off?

9. The interrupt mask bit can be set or cleared by the program so as to disable or enable interrupts, respectively. Give an example of when you might want to disable the possibility of an interrupt.

10. Give one advantage and one disadvantage of serial communications over parallel data transfer.

Problems

9-1 Refer to Fig. 9-1. New data are transferred from the data bus to the peripherals (a) every machine cycle, (b) only during a WRITE to 0800. At this time, the output of the 7402 goes momentarily (a) HIGH, (b) LOW, (c) high-Z.

9-2 Again referring to Fig. 9-1, once data are strobed into the 74LS75 chips, the Q outputs (a) go to the high-Z state, (b) retain the data until the E inputs are strobed again.

9-3 Referring to Fig. 9-3, new data are transferred from the input switches to the data bus (a) every machine cycle, (b) only during a LOAD from 0400. At this time the output of the 7404 goes momentarily (a) HIGH, (b) LOW, (c) high-Z.

9-4 Again referring to Fig. 9-3, once data are strobed into the 74LS125 chips, the outputs (a) go to the high-Z state, (b) retain the data until the E inputs are strobed again.

9-5 For which of the following addresses will the input buffers of Fig. 9-3 be strobed (list all possibilities): (a) 0400, (b) 0436, (c) F500, (d) 0200, (e) FC00?

9-6 The PIA of Fig. 9-5 is wired to respond to addresses 2004–2007. To which of the following addresses would the PIA respond if the inputs from A_{13} and A_{14} were interchanged (list all possibilities): (a) 2004, (b) 3004, (c) 4004, (d) 5004, (e) 6004?

9-7 What byte should you write into data direction register B to make PB_3, PB_4, and PB_5 inputs and all other bits outputs?

9-8 What bit in CRB must be set to gain access to the output register?

9-9 Refer to Fig. 9-8. Assume that port A was initialized as an input port and port B as an output port. Also assume the switches S_0, S_3, and S_4 are closed. The MPU then executes the following program bytes: B6 20 04 B7 20 06. What hex value will be displayed on the LEDs after execution?

9-10 Referring to Problem 9-9, suppose the MPU executes the following program bytes: B6 20 04 43 B7 20 06. What hex value will be displayed on the LEDs?

9-11 Where must the programmer store the starting address of the interrupt service routine?

9-12 Suppose the programmer erroneously initialized the stack pointer at some ROM location. Would the MPU service the first interrupt? Would the MPU return to the proper place in its main task after servicing an interrupt?

9-13 An interrupt causes all registers to be pushed onto the stack, whereas a jump to subroutine pushes only the program counter contents. What should the programmer do in order to save the contents of a register that might get destroyed in a subroutine? (Review Sec. 8-5 as needed.)

9-14 Assuming the programmer did the correct operation as discussed in Problem 9-13, what should be done after returning from subroutine?

Problems 9-15–9-20 refer to the MC6821 PIA.

9-15 Which bit in the control register must the programmer set to enable interrupts?

9-16 Which bit of the control register must be set to make port A respond to an active HIGH signal on $CA1$?

9-17 Which bit of a control register gets set by an external request for interrupt?

9-18   Referring to Problem 9-17, how is that bit cleared?

9-19   In a polling operation, to check whether or not a port has requested an interrupt, the control register is loaded into the accumulator. Then a logical operation is performed to test the interrupt request bit. The operation could be to AND (IMMED) with a particular bit pattern and then test the *Z* flag to see whether or not the result is zero. What bit pattern (what byte) would you use for the AND (IMMED) operation?

9-20   Referring to Problem 9-19, would the *Z* flag be set or cleared if there had been an interrupt request?

9-21   Draw the bit pattern you would expect to see at the TxD output in Fig. 9-10 if byte 23H were being transmitted at 1200 baud, even parity.

9-22   Draw the bit pattern you would expect to see at the TxD output in Fig. 9-10 if the byte C8H were being transmitted at 300 baud, odd parity.

The remaining problems refer to the ACIA.

9-23   What are the two lowest addresses to which the ACIA of Fig. 9-12(A) will respond?

9-24   What address should you write into to load a byte into the transmit data register? What address should you write into to load a control word?

9-25   What address should you read from to load a word from the receive data register into the accumulator? What address should you read from to load the status byte into the accumulator?

9-26   Refer to Table 9-2. Suppose you are writing a program to transmit a block of data, one byte after another. Of course you must wait until the previous byte is completely sent before loading the next byte into the transmit data register. Otherwise, garbage will be sent. You can set up a test loop to continually load the status word into the accumulator and test a bit. Which bit should you test?

9-27   Assuming that the ACIA is already set up to transmit properly, what program bytes should be executed to take a byte from memory location 1D05 and transmit it? (*Hint:* Six program bytes are needed.) Assume the ACIA is wired as shown in Fig. 9-12(A).

9-28   What Tx clock frequency should you use to transmit at 1200 baud using a clock divide ratio of ÷ 16?

9-29   You want to configure the ACIA as follows: receiver interrupt enabled, $\overline{\text{RTS}}$ LOW, Tx INT disabled, 7 bits + odd parity + 2 stop bits, ÷ 16 clock. What control word should you write into the control register?

9-30 Write a short program sequence to load the control word of Problem 9-29 into the ACIA wired as in Fig. 9-12(A). Remember to first write a reset code into the ACIA. (A total of 10 program bytes are needed.)

9-31 Suppose you have configured the ACIA as in Problem 9-29 to communicate with a teletypewriter. Whenever the teletypewriter operator presses a key, the code for that key will be received by the ACIA and generate an interrupt. Your interrupt service routine should first test the status word to check for any received errors. What 3 bits of the status word should be tested?

9-32 All 3 error bits can be tested simultaneously by loading the status word into ACCA and then performing an ANDA (IMMED) operation with a test pattern. After the test, the Z flag will be set or cleared accordingly. Write a short program sequence to load the status word into the accumulator and then perform the test. (Only 5 program bytes are needed.)

9-33 If the error test of Problem 9-32 caused the Z flag to be set, no receiver errors would be present. Your program should then branch to a routine that loads the received character into the accumulator. Write a short program sequence to load the received character into the accumulator and then store it into memory location 0100 for later use. (Use only 6 bytes.)

9-34 Modify your program of Problem 9-33 so that the first character received will be stored in memory location 0100; then each character received thereafter should be stored in successive locations, 0101, 0102, etc. Use the index register as your memory location pointer. Assume that the index register has already been initialized at 0100. (Your program sequence should take only 6 bytes.)

CHAPTER 10

Program Languages, Formats, and I/O Devices

In Chapter 3 we learned about different programming languages. We shall look at these again here. More specifically now, we shall study an assembly language listing of an MC6800 MPU's program. It is important that a modern digital and computer technologist understand the format of such listings. Assembly language listings will often be the only source of information about what a given MPU-based system is doing and specifically how it does it. The format described here is *very* similar to the assembly language formats of other types of MPUs and minicomputers.

We shall also learn ways that computers are programmed, that is, how programs are developed and loaded into a computer and how the results of executed programs are made available to the human operator. The hardware devices, described here, that enable us to program computers and to read their results are called I/O (input/output) devices or peripherals.

10-1 Machine Language

In our studies of the J-100 (Chapter 7), we learned that this basic computer was told what to do by means of a program. A program contains instructions, each of which has its own op code. Op codes are groups of logic HIGHs and LOWs that are understandable (decodable) by the computer. Likewise, all numerical information (data) and address locations must be in a binary format; refer back to the program of Fig. 7-3 for an example. The HIGHs and LOWs in successive memory locations are called *machine language;*

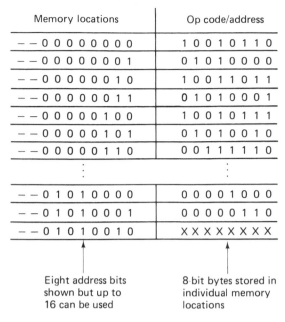

Memory locations	Op code/address
− − 0 0 0 0 0 0 0 0	1 0 0 1 0 1 1 0
− − 0 0 0 0 0 0 0 1	0 1 0 1 0 0 0 0
− − 0 0 0 0 0 0 1 0	1 0 0 1 1 0 1 1
− − 0 0 0 0 0 0 1 1	0 1 0 1 0 0 0 1
− − 0 0 0 0 0 1 0 0	1 0 0 1 0 1 1 1
− − 0 0 0 0 0 1 0 1	0 1 0 1 0 0 1 0
− − 0 0 0 0 0 1 1 0	0 0 1 1 1 1 1 0
⋮	⋮
− − 0 1 0 1 0 0 0 0	0 0 0 0 1 0 0 0
− − 0 1 0 1 0 0 0 1	0 0 0 0 0 1 1 0
− − 0 1 0 1 0 0 1 0	X X X X X X X X

Eight address bits
shown but up to
16 can be used

8-bit bytes stored in
individual memory
locations

Fig. 10-1. Machine language program for the
MC6800 MPU; equivalent to the pro-
gram of Fig. 8-5.

the only language computers and MPUs, by themselves, can understand. The program of Fig. 8-5, written for the MC6800 MPU, is again shown here, this time in machine language; see Fig. 10-1.

The J-100 and the MC6800 are called 8-bit machines because each reads 8 bits at a time from memory when executing a program. Some of the early MPUs were 4-bit processors, and now, at the opposite end of the spectrum, there are 16-bit MPUs. The 8-bit MPUs, however, having many advantages, will continue to hold a large share of the MPU applications market. The 8-bit MC6800 has 16 address lines, which can access up to 2^{16} or 65,536 (65K) memory locations, including peripherals (I/Os). Most MPU applications require far less than 65K of memory, and all address lines need not be used.

Machine language programs can be entered (loaded) into some types of computers through their front-panel switches; see Fig. 7-10 and Fig. 10-2. Figure 10-2 shows the front panel of a typical 16-bit minicomputer. The toggle switches can be used to load or examine any one of 65K memory locations. The front-panel indicators also allow the computer operator to read the results of an executed program and the contents of some major registers. Trends are toward fewer switches and indicators on front panels of modern mini- and microcomputers—they simply are not necessary for most applications.

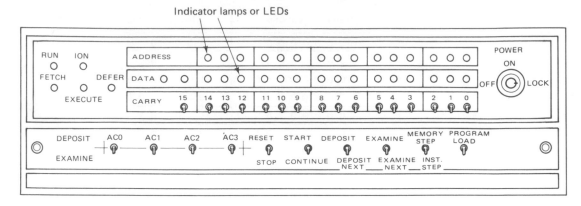

Fig. 10-2. Typical front panel of minicomputer; a 16-bit machine.

10-2 Hexadecimal Keyboards

There are many MPU development and training kits available; see the example in Fig. 10-3. With these kits, programs can be loaded and run through the keyboard. Each instruction and data byte is loaded in hexadecimal format,

Fig. 10-3. Typical MPU trainer with hexadecimal keyboard and seven-segment display. (Courtesy of Heath Company.)

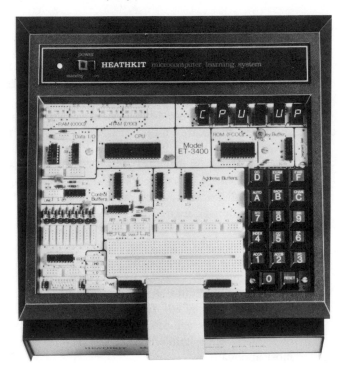

which is much more convenient than binary format. The contents of any memory location and of the major registers, which include the results of a program, can be observed on the seven-segment displays. Most of these kits have ROM that contains a *monitor program*. The monitor program, generally, causes the MPU to scan and accept information via the keyboard and to output the MPU registers' and memories' data to the seven-segment display. These kits, with residing monitor programs, are indeed among the most convenient and effective tools to help us learn how MPUs work and to develop and debug relatively short programs.

10-3 Assembly Language

As we already know, MPU manufacturers provide us with an instruction set (Table 9-1) that lists each instruction's mnemonic. Mnemonics are easier to remember and work with than are bit patterns of machine language or op codes in hex. With a computer, teletypewriter, or similar terminal and an assembler program, a programmer can develop software by typing mnemonics—never concerning himself or herself with specific op codes. Programming with mnemonics is called *assembly language programming*. A program typed in assembly language is called a *source program*. The computer, with its assembler program, translates the source program into an object program. This object program consists entirely of machine language which is executable by the computer.

If a computer is to assemble programs for itself or the same type of computer, it requires an assembler. On the other hand, if a computer is to assemble programs for another type computer or MPU system, it requires a *cross-assembler* program. A cross assembler is generally much lengthier. The computer doing the assembly for another computer is called a *host computer*.

If an assembled (object) program is intended for an MPU-based system, say a system that monitors an engine's temperature and then determines fuel mixture, the program can be tested before the system is completely built. If this system is to be MC6800 MPU based, a similarly based computer, called an EXORciser, can be used to behave like the system to be built. The EXORciser is then said to *emulate* the system that does not yet exist. Similar hardware is available to emulate systems based on other types of MPUs. A host computer, having an entirely different type of MPU, can also be used to behave like the MC6800-based system provided the host has appropriate I/O. In such cases, the host also requires a *simulator* program and is said to be *simulating* the MC6800 system. Of course, host computers can likewise simulate systems that use other types of MPUs provided each such host contains an appropriate simulator program and has the proper I/O.

10-4 Assembly Language Format

Assembly language is also called symbolic language because symbols can be used to represent branch addresses and operands. A partial listing of an assembly language program is shown in Fig. 10-4. It is the program of Fig. 8-8, discussed previously. As shown, the assembly list consists of a sequence of horizontally printed statements (lines). Each line can include some or all of the following:

1. Sequence number

2. Instruction/data address

3. Instruction

4. Label

5. Mnemonic

6. Operand

7. Comment

As shown in Fig. 10-4, the sequence numbers are in decimal. They simply serve to number the lines.

The instruction/data address field (column) indicates locations in which the op codes are stored. Note that address 0000 contains the op code 96.

Fig. 10-4. Typical assembly language listing; equivalent to the program of Fig. 8-8.

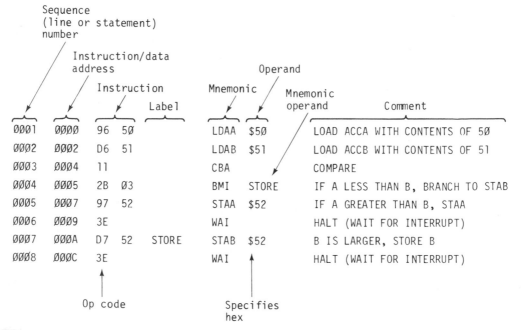

Similarly, op codes D6 and 11 are in locations 0002 and 0004. Address locations 0001 and 0003, not listed, contain the second bytes of the LDAA and LDAB instructions. Generally then, the instruction/data address field lists numbers that increase by 1, 2, or 3 depending on whether the succeeding instructions are 1-, 2-, or 3-byte instructions.

The instruction field simply lists the op code followed by the operand address, data, or nothing depending on the mode of addressing.

The label field can be used by the programmer to identify a memory location. He or she can then use the label instead of the actual address when branching from one location to another in the program. For example, in Fig. 10-4, the label STORE identifies address 000A. Thus the BMI instruction causes a branch to location STORE if the result of the previous instruction, CBA in this case, is negative. Note in line 0004 that BMI is followed by STORE in the mnemonic and operand columns.

The mnemonic field, obviously, contains the mnemonics of the instructions being used in the program.

The meaning of each number or symbol in the operand field is dependent on the mnemonic in the same line. The operand field tells us the mode of addressing. If the operand field is empty, as in lines 0003 and 0006 of Fig. 10-4, the addressing mode is inherent. If the operand field contains an expression, numerical or symbolic, the addressing mode is direct, extended, immediate, or relative. Lines 0001, 2, 5, and 7 are examples of direct mode addressing. Statement 0004 contains a relative mode instruction and a label for the operand. Generally, it is very convenient to use address labels with branch instructions. A # sign prefix on an expression in the operand field identifies immediate mode addressing. Also, prefix $, @, or % or no prefix identify hexadecimal, octal, binary, or decimal numbers, respectively. A comma and then an X following an expression in the operand field specifies index mode addressing.

The last column in the assembly listing is the comment field. This field is optional and is used by the programmer to *document* (explain the operation of) the program. The comment field is ignored by the assembler.

Figure 10-5 shows how the program of Fig. 10-4 appears as it is being developed by the programmer.

Fig. 10-5. Assembly language source program as it is being developed by the programmer.

```
LDAA    $50 LOAD ACCA WITH CONTENTS OF 50
LDAB    $51 LOAD ACCB WITH CONTENTS OF 51
CBA     COMPARE
BMI     STORE IF A LESS THAN B, BRANCH TO STAB
STAA    $52 IF A GREATER THAN B, STAA
WAI     HALT (WAIT FOR INTERRUPT)
STORE   STAB $52 B IS LARGER, STORE B
WAI     HALT(WAIT FOR INTERRUPT)
```

An assembly language program can also contain labels to represent addresses of memory locations that are used to temporarily store data. For example, a programmer can use equate (EQU) statements in the source program as shown in (A) of Fig. 10-6. The first three statements of this program show that the label DATA1 is made equivalent to address location 0050_H, DATA2 is made equivalent to location 0051_H, and symbol ANS is equivalent to location 0052_H. Note that these labels are then used in the remaining statements of the source program.

Use of EQU statements simplifies editing and debugging programs—especially long programs. For example, a given memory location, say 0050_H, might be used many times to temporarily store data in a large program. Should a change of this address location become necessary during editing or debugging and the EQU statement were not used, the programmer would

Fig. 10-6. (A) Source program containing equate (EQU) statements to assign labels to address locations; (B) assembled program listing of program using labels DATA1, DATA2, and ANS to represent memory locations used to store data temporarily.

```
DATA1 EQU $50
DATA2 EQU $51
     LDAA DATA1 LOAD ACCA WITH CONTENTS OF 50
     LDAB DATA2 LOAD ACCB WITH CONTENTS OF 51
     CBA  COMPARE
     BMI STORE IF A LESS THAN B, BRANCH TO STA B
     STAA ANS IF A GREATER THAN B, STA A
     WAI  HALT(WAIT FOR INTERRUPT)
STORE STAB ANS  B IS LARGER, STORE B
     WAI  HALT(WAIT FOR INTERRUPT)

              (A)

     DATA1     EQU  $50
     DATA2     EQU  $51
     ANS       EQU  $52
0001 0000 95 50         LDAA DATA1     LOAD ACCA WITH CONTENTS OF 50
0002 0002 D6 51         LDAB DATA2     LOAD ACCB WITH CONTENTS OF 51
0003 0004 11            CBA            COMPARE
0004 0005 2B 03         BMI  STORE     IF A LESS THAN B, BRANCH TO STA B
0005 0007 97 52         STAA ANS       IF A GREATER THAN B, STA A
0006 0009 3E            WAI            HALT(WAIT FOR INTERRUPT)
0007 000A D7 52 STORE   STAB ANS       B IS LARGER, STORE B
0008 000C 3E            WAI            HALT(WAIT FOR INTERRUPT)

              (B)
```

have to search for each statement that references the operand address 0050_H and change it—a time-consuming task. If, on the other hand, statement DATA1 EQU $0050 were used, the programmer could simply retype this EQU statement specifying the new address. The assembler then does all the work and reassigns this new hex address to all statements referencing address DATA1.

Usually, programmers try to select descriptive terms for symbolic addresses that make the assembly listing easier to read. See Fig. 10-6(B) for such a listing.

As a computer hardware technologist or engineer, you must know programming, at least on the machine and assembly language levels. When designing, troubleshooting, and repairing computers and their I/Os, you will often have to load instructions and entire *diagnostic programs.* Diagnostic programs make computer systems routinely check themselves and can also provide you, the operator, with a printout specifically identifying a defective board or part. Also, as a technologist, you may have to examine the contents of an MPU's registers. Here, too, correct interpretations of such examinations depend on understanding software. As a hardware technologist, you will usually not be expected to develop long and complicated programs, though often you will be expected to read them. Commonly, hardware people repair MPU-based equipment while armed with little more than a manual containing the engineering drawings and a listing of the ROM's program.

10-5 Higher-Level Languages

Although modern computer hardware specialists are required to know software, users of computers, including most programmers, need know little about computer hardware. For example, banks, department stores, and consulting engineering firms use computers and the services of programmers but rarely do such programmers have any detailed knowledge of how their computers actually work. These programmers use high-level languages that make the hardware's activity *transparent* (not apparent). As mentioned in Chapter 3, common high-level languages are COBOL, FORTRAN, and BASIC. PASCAL is another high-level language that is becoming popular with MPU based systems.

10-6 Input/Output and Storage Media

Both front-panel switches and hex keyboards are inefficient means of loading lengthy programs or blocks of data into a computer. A number of alternatives are the following:

Punched cards Source programs, or data, can be placed on cards via a keypunch machine. A keypunch has a typewriter-type keyboard on which the program is typed. The result is a stack of punched cards; see Fig. 10-7(A), which in turn can be run on a card reader. The card reader's output

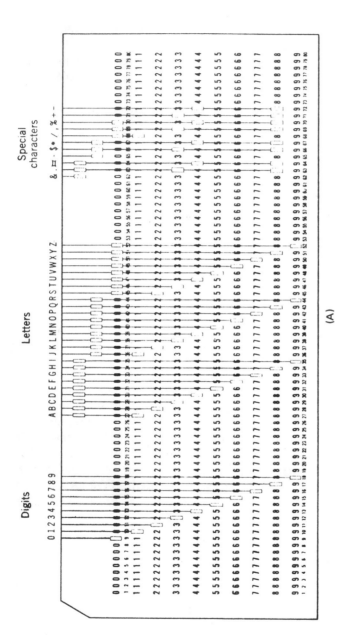

(A)

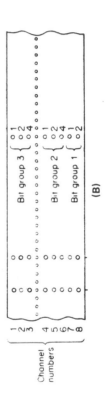

(B)

Fig. 10-7. (A) IBM's 80-column punched card code; (B) paper tape for 8-channel ASCII code.

is then the input to the computer. Punched cards were once a major way of storing programs and data. Cards, however, are relatively bulky and require considerable storage space. Also, card readers are quite slow by current standards.

Paper tape   Paper tape, Fig. 10-7(B), is similar to punched cards in that the storage medium is paper with holes. Punched tape has advantages of less bulk and lower cost—the punching and reading hardware is usually less expensive. Although relatively slow, paper tape is still used for loading programs, such as compilers and interpreters, into computers.

Cassettes   Audio cassettes can store programs and data and are very popular with microcomputer users. An ordinary general-purpose audio cassette recorder can serve to load and store programs, though more sophisticated reader/recorders are available; see Fig. 10-8(A). Often, computer service people use cassettes to load diagnostic programs into a computer of a malfunctioning system. Although inexpensive and very portable, cassettes are still relatively slow.

Magnetic tapes   Magnetic tapes are similar to cassettes in that bits of information are stored in the form of magnetized areas along the length of a tape. Magnetic tapes, however, are larger and capable of storing much larger programs and/or blocks of data. Also, magnetic tape drives are much more sophisticated than cassette readers [see Fig. 10-8(B)] and are able to rapidly load the tape's information into the computer.

Disks   Programs and data can be loaded from or stored on circular disks coated with magnetic material that is similar to a tape's material. In a disk drive, a disk rotates continuously and a read/write head scans its surface. Disks are able to store a large amount of information. A full-sized disk can typically store several million bytes. The smaller, less expensive floppy disks (see Fig. 10-9) can typically store a few hundred thousand bytes. Floppy disks are popular with microcomputer users.

Disks enable programmers to efficiently utilize a computer's memory (RAM). In a typical disk operating system, the MPU's RAM is divided—including sections called resident and nonresident areas. Programs that are used frequently, or with which execution time is important, are loaded into the resident area from the disk. Programs that are called infrequently, or with which execution time is not as important, reside on the disk. Then when needed, these programs are *rolled into* the nonresident area from the disk. When no longer needed, they are *rolled out*. Thus the nonresident section of the read/write memory (RAM) can serve to temporarily hold occasionally needed programs. The result is a system that can function with much less RAM than would be needed if the disk were not part of the system. A computer uses a disk as we use a handbook. We don't have to memorize a

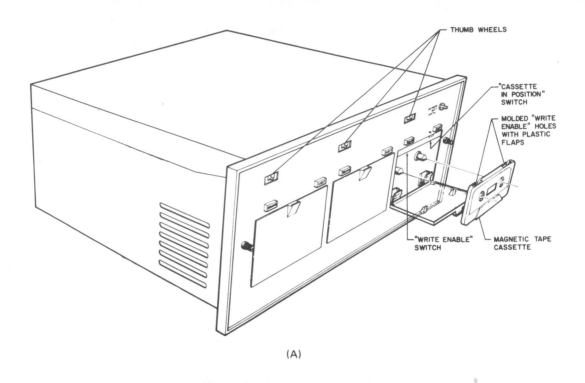

THUMB WHEELS

"CASSETTE IN POSITION" SWITCH

MOLDED "WRITE ENABLE" HOLES WITH PLASTIC FLAPS

"WRITE ENABLE" SWITCH

MAGNETIC TAPE CASSETTE

(A)

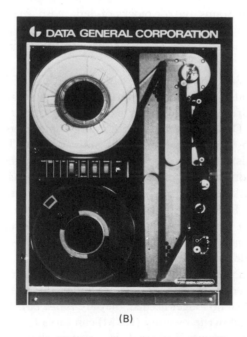

DATA GENERAL CORPORATION

(B)

Fig. 10-8. (A) Cassette chassis; (B) tape drive. (Courtesy of Data General Corporation.)

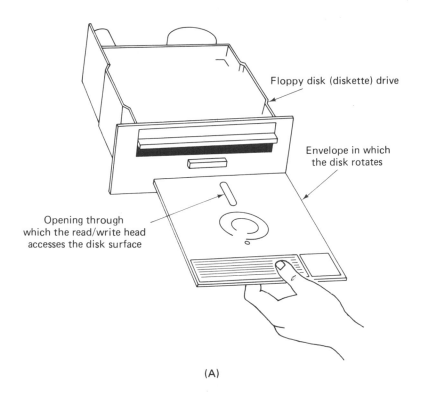

Floppy disk (diskette) drive

Envelope in which
the disk rotates

Opening through
which the read/write head
accesses the disk surface

(A)

(B)

Fig. 10-9. Diskette (floppy disk) and diskette drive. (Courtesy of Data General Corporation.)

seldom-used formula or information. We can simply read it when needed. Likewise, a computer reads temporarily needed information from the disk.

10-7   Terminals

Programs are usually developed and inputted through a typewriter-like terminal; see Fig. 10-10. Also, the computer is usually controlled by commands issued through such a terminal. Thus the terminal serves as an input device.

Fig. 10-10.   Typewriter-type keyboards with printer for hard copy and video terminal. (Courtesy of Data General Corporation.)

Fig. 10-11. Typical video terminal with keyboard. (Courtesy of Digital Equipment Corporation.)

It also serves as an output device through which the computer can type *hard copy*. Line printers, without keyboards, are also available for the purpose of producing hard (typed or printed) copy. Hard copy is not always needed, and in such cases, keyboards with video displays (see Fig. 10-11) are very common. The television-like screen can rapidly display data or programs for the operator's inspection. These video terminals are much faster and generally less expensive than hard-copy printers and are popular with microcomputer users. In the latter chapters of this text, where printed program listings are illustrated, the number zero is represented by the symbol ϕ. This symbol also appears in figures and text where zero and the letter O are more apt to be confused.

Review Questions

Answer Review Questions 10-1–10-5 comparing machine and assembly languages.

1. What is an advantage of assembly language?

2. With which do we need the hexadecimal or octal op codes of the various instructions? With which do we need the mnemonics?

3. Which language does the computer itself understand?

4. A source program can be in which of these languages?

5. The object language is in what language?

6. What is a host computer?

7. What is an assembler?

8. What is a cross assembler?

9. What is an emulator?

10. What is a simulator?

11. What is the purpose of a mnemonic label in the label field of an assembler listing?

12. What do the prefixes $, @, or % mean if they appear in the operand field of an assembly listing?

13. What does the prefix # mean if it appears in the operand field of an assembly listing?

14. By their mnemonics, list the instructions used in the program of Fig. 10-12 that are (a) direct mode, (b) extended mode, (c) inherent mode, (d) immediate mode.

```
0000     8E 00 FF            LDS    $00FF
0003     86 01       LOOP    LDAA   $01
0005     B7 10 00            STAA   $1000
0008     BD 00 20            JSR    DELAY

  .         .                  .
  .         .                  .
  .         .                  .

0020     CE FF FF    DELAY   LDX    $FFFF
0023     01          REPEAT  NOP
0024     01                  NOP
0025     01                  NOP
0026     01                  NOP
0027     09                  DEX
0028     26 F9               BNE    REPEAT

002A     39                  RTS
```

Fig. 10-12. Partial assembly language listing; sequence numbers omitted.

15. Referring to the program of Fig. 10-12, what address location does the label DELAY represent?

16. In the program of Fig. 10-12, what address location does the label REPEAT represent?

17. What program in Chapter 8 does the program of Fig. 10-12 represent?

18. Name three high-level languages.

19. What address locations do the labels DATA1, DATA2, and ANS represent in the program of Fig. 10-6?

20. What effect does the comment field have on how the program runs?

21. Name six hardware devices that are used to load (enter) programs into a computer.

CHAPTER 11

Microprocessor Applications

Microprocessors are used in a wide variety of applications. But all applications have some features in common. They all involve some means of transferring data to and from the MPU.

In this chapter, we shall study the three major categories of data handling in a microprocessor system. We shall see how analog (nondigital) signals are handled by means of A/D and D/A converters. Next we shall look at parallel data transfers in a typical industrial control system. And finally, we shall study serial data transmission, such as is used in a typical computer or communications link.

Once these three applications are understood, you should be able to analyze and understand almost any use of microprocessors.

11-1   Digital-to-Analog (A/D) Converters

Often, information in a digital format must be converted to analog equivalent signals. In such applications, the data output port (data lines) drives the data input port of a digital-to-analog converter (DAC). The circuit of Fig. 11-1 shows an application of an MPU and two DACs that generate signals for analog devices. Typical analog devices receiving such signals are oscilloscopes, XY plotters, chart recorders, servomotors, etc.

DAC packages are available commercially, as we shall see later. For the present, we can note that a basic DAC can be constructed in a *resistive*

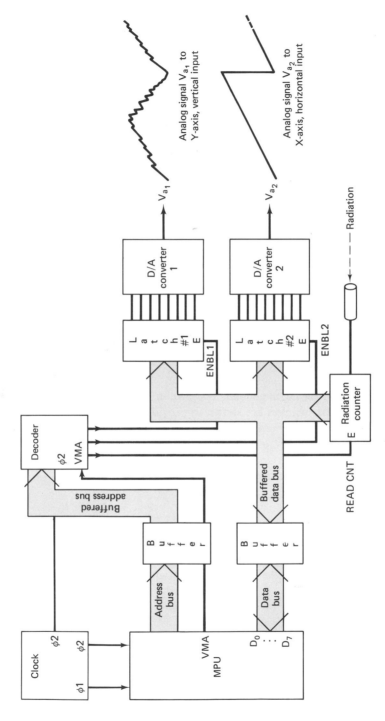

Fig. 11-1. Application of digital-to-analog converters in MPU-based system; although not shown, ROM and RAM are necessary.

307

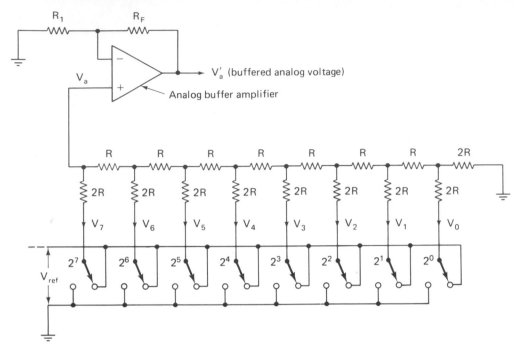

Fig. 11-2. Eight-input resistive (R–$2R$) ladder converts 8-bit binary inputs to analog equivalent signals V_a.

ladder arrangement, as shown in Fig. 11-2. For illustrative purposes, mechanical switches are shown to provide the digital input signals. In practice, these digital inputs, V_0–V_7, would come from a latch, as shown in Fig. 11-1. In the circuit of Fig. 11-2, each signal, V_0–V_7, is HIGH (the V_{ref} voltage) or LOW (ground potential) depending on the position of its respective switch. Generally, an R–$2R$ ladder's analog output

$$V_a = \frac{V_0 + 2V_1 + 4V_2 + 8V_3 + \cdots}{2^n} \qquad (11\text{-}1a)$$

where n is the number of digital inputs and V_0 represents the LSB. Specifically, for the eight-input R–$2R$ ladder,

$$V_a = \frac{V_0 + 2V_1 + 4V_2 + 8V_3 + 16V_4 + 32V_5 + 64V_6 + 128V_7}{256} \qquad (11\text{-}1b)$$

Example 11-1

If $V_{ref} = 5\,\text{V}$ in the circuit of Fig. 11-2, find the analog output V_a and the buffered analog output V_a' with each of the following hexadecimal equivalent inputs: (a) 00_H, (b) 02_H, (c) 10_H, (d) 80_H, (e) $4E_\text{H}$, (f)

FF_H. Assume that the buffer amplifier's voltage gain is 2; the buffer prevents loads on this DAC from affecting its accuracy.

Answers

(a) $V_a = 0$ V, $V_a' = 0$ V. (b) $V_a = 39$ mV, $V_a' = 78$ mV. (c) 312.5 mV, 625 mV. (d) 2.5 V, 5 V. (e) 1.523 V, 3.047 V. (f) 4.98 V, 9.96 V. For part (e), the input $4E_H = 01001110_2$. Thus the signals V_7–V_0 are 0 V, 5 V, 0 V, 0 V, 5 V, 5 V, 5 V, and 0 V, respectively. Substituting these into Eq. (11-1b), we can show that

$$V_a = \frac{2(5\text{ V}) + 4(5\text{ V}) + 8(5\text{ V}) + 64(5\text{ V})}{256} = 1.523 \text{ V}$$

Then $V_a' = 2(1.523 \text{ V}) = 3.047 \text{ V}$

If we replace the switches in the circuit of Fig. 11-2 with logic signal outputs of an 8-bit binary counter, the analog output voltage will be a staircase waveform, as shown in Fig. 11-3(A). Each $\overline{\text{CLOCK}}$ pulse increments the counter, and the signals V_a and V_a' will increase one step. An 8-bit counter driving an eight-input R–$2R$ DAC will generate a 256- (2^8-) step waveform. After state 255, the counter *overflows*, and V_a drops to 0 V—the first step of another upward staircase. A down counter decrements with each $\overline{\text{CLOCK}}$ pulse, and if used to drive an eight-input R–$2R$ ladder, the resulting V_a waveform is a downward staircase; see Fig. 11-3(B). However, it is not practical to drive an R–$2R$ ladder directly with the outputs of a counter because the resulting accuracy of the V_a signal is usually poor. That is, the HIGH outputs of, say, a TTL counter or latch can be in the range of 2.4 V (minimum) to 3.3 V (typical) if $V_{CC} = 5$ V. This kind of range cannot provide consistent heights (amplitudes) of the steps in the V_a waveform. A better arrangement is to use a voltage reference and analog switches, as shown in Fig. 11-4.

The AH0146 analog switches in the circuit of Fig. 11-4 actually contain FETs that serve as the voltage-operated switches. In this application, if a

Fig. 11-3. The V_a and V_a' waveforms of the R–$2R$ converter being driven by (a) a binary upcounter; (b) a binary down counter.

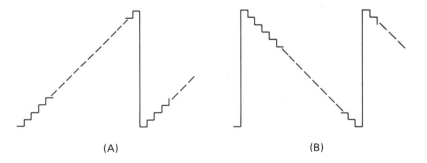

(A)   (B)

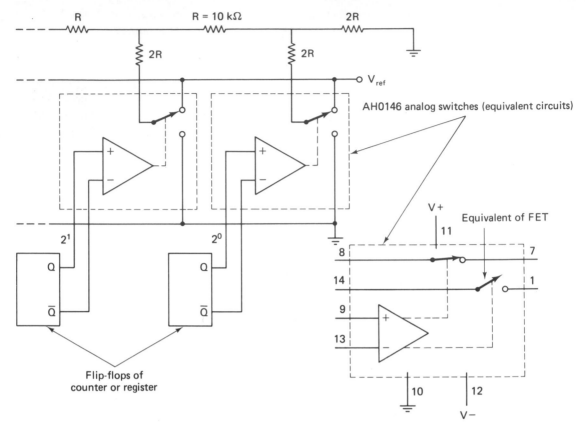

Fig. 11-4. Analog switches used to apply either the reference voltage V_{ref} or ground to the inputs of the R–$2R$ ladder.

flip-flop (FF) is set, the AH0146 places the reference voltage V_{ref} to its respective $2R$ resistor. When the FF is reset, the $2R$ resistor is pulled down to ground potential. The FETs (switches) have about 10-Ω on resistance, and therefore, if a well-regulated V_{ref} is used, the analog output V_a of the R–$2R$ ladder is an accurate equivalent of the applied digital input.

A typical packaged DAC is shown in Fig. 11-5. Since this is a 12-bit DAC, it can output staircase waveforms with as many as 4096 steps; that is, $2^{12} = 4096$. Compared to the eight-input R–$2R$ ladder, such smoother output waveforms are said to have better *resolution*. As shown in Fig. 11-5, the DAC1280 is a ". . . current mode D/A." This means that the transistors in $A3$ sink more or less total current depending on the value of the 12-bit digital input on pins 1–12. Thus, if we use a 12-bit counter to drive pins 1–12, a 4096-step staircase current waveform is available at pin 20. This output current can swing in the range of 0–2 mA. A current-to-voltage converter amplifier $A4$ is available in this chip. Also, a 6.3-V reference is *on board* this package. Since a reference is internally provided, the digital inputs

Block diagram

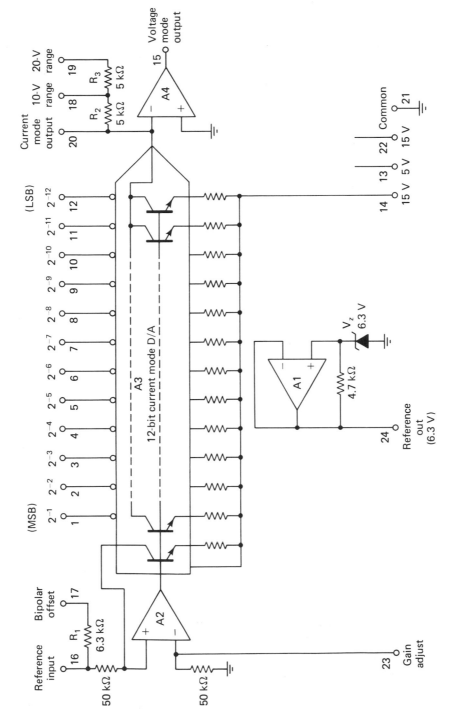

Fig. 11-5. Block diagram of packaged digital-to-analog (DAC) converter; a DAC1280 or DAC1285.

311

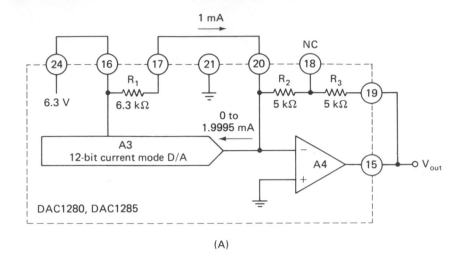

(A)

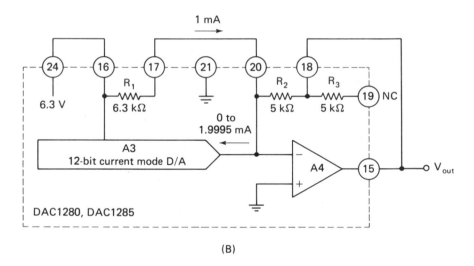

(B)

Fig. 11-6. DAC1280 in (A) wired to have V_{out} swing from -10 V to about $+10$ V and in (B) wired to have V_{out} swing from -5 V to about $+5$ V.

can be driven by typical TTL or MOS devices with no need of analog switches. The amplifier $A2$ applies a base voltage to all switching transistors and enables each to conduct a constant current, when on, over a wide range of temperatures. Although not shown in Fig. 11-5, the individual transistors are turned on or off by the logic inputs applied to the emitters.

The DAC1280 of Fig. 11-6(A) is wired to provide an analog output V_{out} that can swing from -10 V to about $+10$ V. The inverting ($-$) input of $A4$ is at virtually ground potential; therefore, the 6.3-V reference is across $R1$. The resulting current in $R1$ is 1 mA. $A3$ sinks more or less current, up to 2 mA, depending on the value of the 12-bit digital input. The difference between the current $A3$ sinks and the current in $R1$ is forced through $R2$ and $R3$. The resulting drop across these resistors *is* V_{out}. Thus if $A3$ sinks 0 A, then 1 mA flows from left to right through $R1$ and $R2$, causing a $V_{out} = (R1 + R2)(-1 \text{ mA}) = -10 \text{ V}$. On the other extreme, if $A3$ sinks 2 mA, then 1 mA must flow from right to left through $R1$ and $R2$. In this case, $V_{out} = (R1 + R2)(1 \text{ mA}) = +10 \text{ V}$.

Example 11-2

Modify the circuit of Fig. 11-6(A) so that its output swing is ±5 V instead of the ±10 V.

Answer

See Fig. 11-6(B).

11-2 Analog-to-Digital (A/D) Converters

Often, when an MPU is to receive and process information from the *outside world,* it does so via an analog-to-digital converter, which is also called an ADC. An ADC is able to receive a smoothly changing voltage, called an analog signal voltage V_a, and convert it to a series of digital equivalent signals. For example, an engine block's temperature can be monitored with thermistors. The thermistors are mounted on the block, and their resistances vary as the temperature of the block varies. A couple of thermistors in a bridge circuit, as shown in Fig. 11-7, will cause the voltage across the bridge, signal V_s, to change with changes in temperature. As shown, such signal changes can be amplified and applied to the input of an ADC. The ADC's output can then be read by an MPU, as directed to do so with appropriate software.

There are many types of ADCs. They differ in speed, accuracy, stability, etc. We can expect many changes, improvements, and cost reductions in packaged ADCs, especially for MPU-based applications. We shall therefore consider ADCs from the functional block point of view.

A typical ADC is shown in Fig. 11-8(A). It has an 8-bit output port, D_7–D_0, though ADCs with more or less output bits are common. The 8-bit output signal is a digital equivalent of the analog input V_a. This type of ADC works in a *continuous mode.* This means that a change in V_a causes the ADC to respond by adjusting its digital output to a value equivalent to the new V_a. The adjustment (conversion) takes more or less time depending on the type of ADC, clock frequency,* amount of change in V_a, etc. The

---

* The clock of the ADC is not necessarily the clock of the MPU.

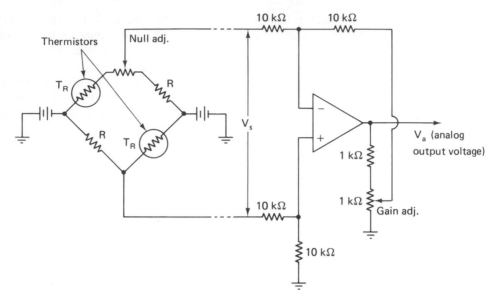

Fig. 11-7. Typical source of analog signal V_a.

Fig. 11-8. Block diagrams of analog-to-digital converters: (a) continuous mode, (b) start/stop mode.

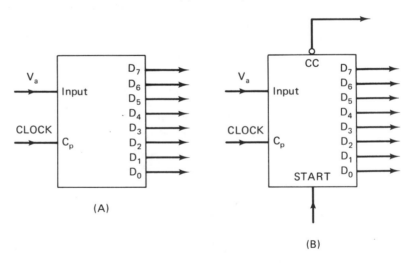

ADC of Fig. 11-8(B) is intended for *start/stop mode* of operation. A START pulse applied to this ADC causes it to start converting the V_a input to a digital equivalent. When this conversion is completed and the digital equivalent is settled and available at the output port, the ADC outputs a $\overline{CC}$ (conver-

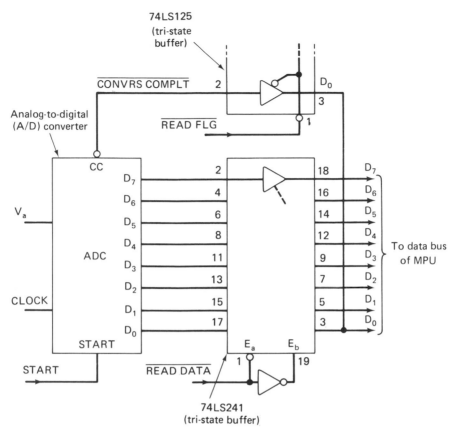

Fig. 11-9. Analog-to-digital converter (ADC) interfaced with a 6800 MPU.

sion complete) pulse. After the $\overline{CC}$ signal pulses LOW, the ADC stops and waits for another START pulse.

Referring to the circuit of Fig. 11-9, the START, $\overline{\text{READ FLG}}$, and $\overline{\text{READ DATA}}$ signals are generated by the MPU and a decoder. A flowchart for an appropriate program is shown in Fig. 11-10. The START pulse starts the A/D conversion process. The $\overline{\text{READ FLG}}$ pulse reads the $\overline{CC}$ bit into the MPU. If this $\overline{CC}$ bit is HIGH, the ADC is not finished, and the program branches back to generate another $\overline{\text{READ FLG}}$ pulse. The MPU stays in this loop until the ADC is finished converting its V_a input to a digital equivalent output, at which time its $\overline{CC}$ output goes LOW. This causes a $\overline{\text{READ DATA}}$ pulse, which reads the digital equivalent, D_7–D_0, data into the MPU's accumulator. From here, the MPU would typically proceed with a program that processes this inputted data. A decoder and typical 6800 MPU program are shown in Fig. 11-11.

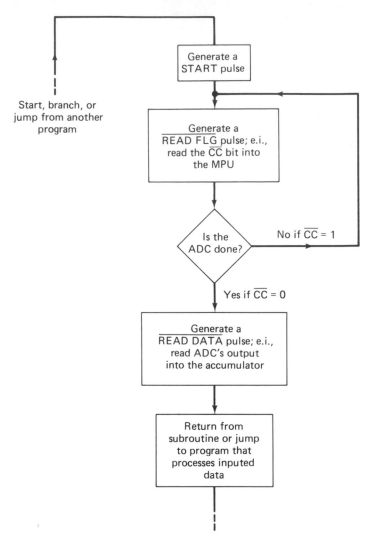

Fig. 11-10. Flowchart for a program that controls the circuit of Fig. 11-9.

11-3 Industrial Controller

A common application of a microprocessor is as an industrial process controller. Figure 11-12 shows the setup for an automatic parts counter and box filler. Each box moves along a conveyor line until it arrives beneath a hopper which is loaded with parts. The parts in this example are pellets. When the box gets under the hopper, the conveyor stops, and a door opens on the hopper, allowing pellets to fall out in single file. The pellets are counted

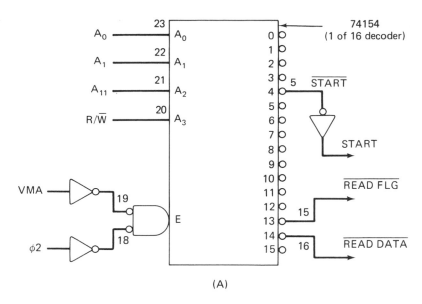

(A)

Mem. loc.	Op code/address	Mnemonic	Comments
0000	B7	STAA	Start the ADC
0001	08		
2	00		
3	B6	LDAA	Read flag; the $\overline{CC}$ signal, into the MPU's accumulator A
4	08		
5	01		
6	84	ANDA	Mask out unwanted bits D_7–D_1; retain bit D_0
7	01		
8	26	BNE	Branch to location 0003 if not zero; $\overline{CC}$ is not LOW
9	F9		
A	B6	LDAA	MPU reads digital equivalent of V_a into accumulator A
B	08		
C	02		
D	39	RTS	Return from subroutine

(B)

$$\overline{START} = VMA \cdot \phi2 \cdot \overline{R/\overline{W}} \cdot A_{11} \cdot \overline{A_1} \cdot \overline{A_0}$$

$$\overline{READ\ FLG} = VMA \cdot \phi2 \cdot R/\overline{W} \cdot A_{11} \cdot \overline{A_1} \cdot A_0$$

$$\overline{READ\ DATA} = VMA \cdot \phi2 \cdot R/\overline{W} \cdot A_{11} \cdot A_1 \cdot \overline{A_0}$$

(C)

Fig. 11-11. (A) Decoder for the circuit in Fig. 11-9; (B) typical program for the ADC interfaced with the 6800 MPU; (C) Boolean expressions for the decoder's output signals.

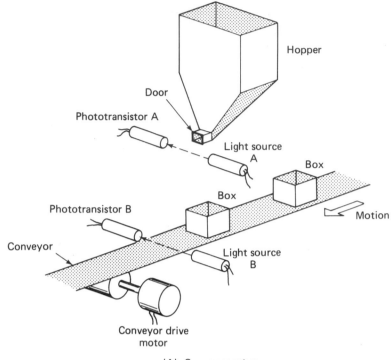

(A) Conveyor setup

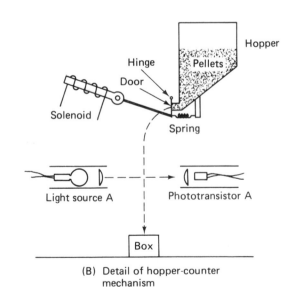

(B) Detail of hopper-counter
mechanism

Fig. 11-12. Automatic parts counter and box filler.

as they fall. When the correct amount has fallen into the box, the hopper door closes, and the conveyor starts again, bringing the next box into position for filling.

Here's how it works:

1. The operator keys in the number of parts he or she wants in each box by means of a keyboard. This number is stored in RAM in a location we shall call PRESET.

2. The operator then throws a switch, allowing the conveyor drive motor to start. The microprocessor has been programmed to keep the motor running until a beam of light from light source B to phototransistor B is broken by a box moving between the two.

3. When the box breaks the beam, the power to the motor is turned off, stopping the conveyor.

4. A solenoid, shown in Fig. 11-12(B), is then energized, opening the hopper door.

5. By mechanical funneling, the pellets fall out in single file. As they fall, each pellet breaks a beam of light from light source A to phototransistor A.

6. The output pulses from phototransistor A are counted by the microprocessor and compared to the PRESET value stored in RAM.

7. When the parts count equals the PRESET value, the solenoid is de-energized. A spring return pulls the hopper door closed.

8. The conveyor drive motor is then energized again, moving the full box out and keeping the conveyor moving until the next empty box breaks the beam from light source B.

The process can continue indefinitely, as long as there are pellets in the hopper and boxes on the conveyor. Any time he or she wishes, the operator can stop the conveyor and key in a different number of parts and then start up again. This is where the programmable feature of the microprocessor demonstrates its value. No wiring changes are necessary to change the count.

Now let's take a look at the interface circuitry.

Figure 11-13 shows how we could construct a decimal keyboard encoder. Note that all outputs, *DCBA,* are HIGH when no key is pressed. When any key is pressed, the BCD code for that key will appear on the output lines. Examine the diode matrix for yourself to see how the proper code is produced.

Also note that the 7420 four-input NAND gate generates an active HIGH KEYSTROBE signal whenever *any* key is pressed. KEYSTROBE can be used to generate an interrupt request.

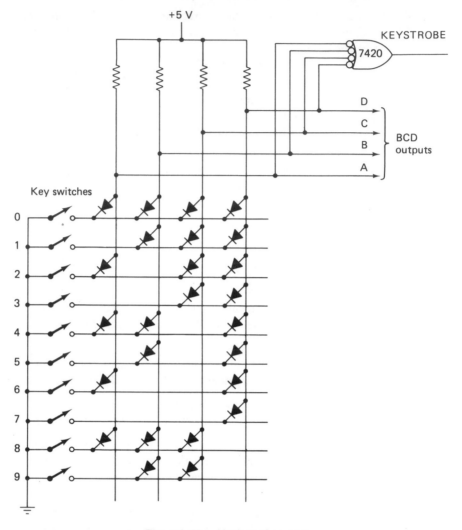

Fig. 11-13. Keyboard encoder.

Figure 11-14 shows the keyboard encoder output feeding into port B data lines on the PIA and the signal line labeled **KEYSTROBE** connected into $CB1$, the interrupt request input. As you can see, port B must be configured as an input port. No switch debouncing is shown in the figure. Either some hardware debouncing or a time delay in the program must be used to eliminate the bounce.

Since only a single BCD digit can be input at a time, the port B service routine must take in the first digit, store it in RAM, and wait for the second digit. For simplicity, let's assume that we can fill each box with any number of parts from 1 to 99. The MPU will then read the most significant digit when it is entered and then shift it left four times and store it in RAM.

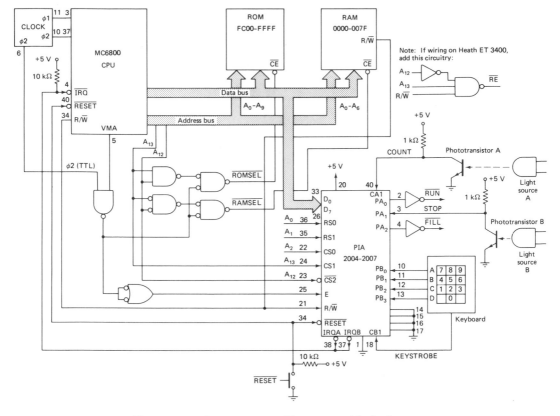

Fig. 11-14. Parts counter-filler system block diagram.

Then when the second digit is entered, the MPU will read the digit in from port *B* and then OR it with the most significant digit. The accumulator will then contain *both* BCD digits.

Port *A* of the PIA is used to control the conveyor motor, the solenoid, and the COUNT and STOP lines. First, PA_0, configured as an output line, drives an inverter which generates the $\overline{RUN}$ signal.

$\overline{RUN}$ is fed to the input of the optoisolator shown in Fig. 11-15(A). Note that when $\overline{RUN}$ is active LOW, the LED in the optoisolator will light. The light from the LED shines onto a photoconductive cell inside the optoisolator, making its resistance low.

The triac acts as a switch in series with the motor, *S*1, and ac line. When the resistance between the GATE and T_2 of the triac is HIGH (no light), the triac acts like an open switch, so the motor does not run, even though *S*1 is closed. But when the LED shines on the photoconductive cell, the cell's resistance goes low enough to turn on the triac. The motor then runs.

Rather than go into detail about the complete operation of the triac,

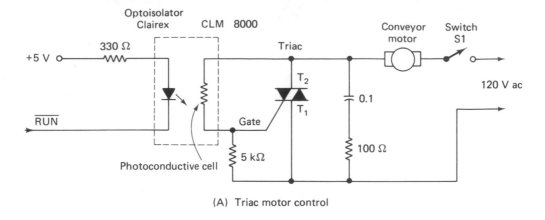

(A) Triac motor control

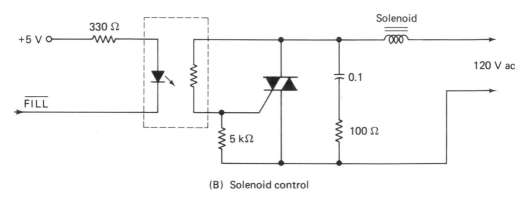

(B) Solenoid control

Fig. 11-15. ac power control circuits.

we can say that it essentially acts as a closed switch as long as the LED is on, that is, as long as $\overline{RUN}$ is active. But when $\overline{RUN}$ goes inactive HIGH, the triac turns off, stopping the motor.

The *R-C* network across the triac is necessary to ensure proper turn off of the triac when working into an inductive load, such as a motor.

Similarly, the solenoid will be energized whenever $\overline{FILL}$ is active LOW, as shown in Fig. 11-15(B).

The reason for using the optoisolators is to provide electrical isolation between the ac line circuitry and the low-power digital circuitry.

Getting back to Fig. 11-14, note that after the operator keys in the desired number of parts and closes the motor start switch, the program must make PA_0 HIGH and PA_2 LOW. This will make $\overline{RUN}$ LOW, turning on the triac in Fig. 11-15(A), and will also make $\overline{FILL}$ HIGH, de-energizing the solenoid.

When a box breaks the beam from light source *B*, phototransistor *B* turns off. The collector of the transistor then goes HIGH, making STOP active HIGH. The signal STOP is connected to PA_1, which is configured as an *input* pin on initialization. Here we see the flexibility of being able to configure any pin as an input or output.

Of course, when STOP goes HIGH, no interrupt will be generated. So how does the microprocessor know when it goes HIGH? To keep track of the input level on PA_1, the program must continually poll (read) port A and test PA_1 while the motor is running. That is, the program must contain a loop, which is repeated over and over, which continually reads and tests bit 1 of port A. (The flowchart and program listing for the counter-filler are shown in Figs. 11-16 and 11-17.)

When bit 1 goes HIGH, indicating a box in position, the program falls through the NEXBOX loop and causes $\overline{\text{RUN}}$ to go HIGH and $\overline{\text{FILL}}$ to go LOW. Then the temporary storage location, labeled PARTS, is cleared. PARTS is used to keep track of the number of parts that have fallen into a box.

Next the loop from line 46 to line 48 continually loads ACCA from PARTS and compares it to PRESET until PARTS = PRESET.

Here's how PARTS gets updated: As pellets fall out of the hopper, COUNT pulses are received from phototransistor A and fed to $CA1$. (When counting small objects, the signal at the collector of phototransistor A must be amplified to get a sufficiently large signal to activate $CA1$.) Each pulse received at $CA1$ generates an interrupt request.

The interrupt service routine, starting at line 57, begins with a *dummy read* to clear the interrupt request flag, bit 7 of CRA.

Then a value of *one* is added to ACCA, because one part has fallen into the box. (Remember, ACCA was loaded from PARTS in the TEST loop. So ACCA contains a total of the parts in the box.)

The next instruction, decimal adjust accumulator (DAA), is used to convert the count in PARTS into BCD code. If this were not used, PARTS would contain a *binary* equivalent of the total number of parts in the box. But remember, the operator initially loaded PRESET using a *decimal* keyboard. We must be consistent so that our comparisons will be valid.

The DAA instruction simply causes the MPU to examine the ACCA contents after an ADD instruction. Then if the value indicated by the four LSBs exceeds 9, the MPU adds 6 to that group, thus converting it back to a BCD number. The addition of 6 also produces a *half-carry,* that is, a carry from the four LSBs to the four MSBs, thus setting the H flag.

For example, suppose the ACCA contents were 09, and then the MPU added 01 to it. The ACCA contents would go to 0A. But when the DAA instruction is executed immediately after the ADD, the ACCA contents will be adjusted to 10 or *ten* in BCD.

Getting back to the program, line 60 shows that the new value for the total number of parts in the box is stored into PARTS, and the MPU returns from the interrupt routine to where it left off in the TEST loop.

When PARTS finally equals PRESET, the program falls through the TEST loop and makes $\overline{\text{FILL}}$ HIGH and $\overline{\text{RUN}}$ LOW, thereby closing the hopper and starting the conveyor again. The process is then repeated.

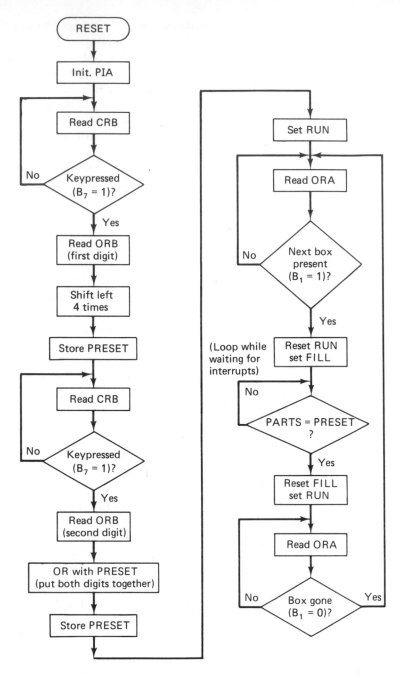

Fig. 11-16. Flowchart for parts counter-filler.

```
 1                              NAM      FILLER REV 0.1
 2                              OPT      NOP
 3                              ORG      $FC00
 4            007E       PARTS   EQU      $007E
 5            007F       PRESET  EQU      $007F
 6            2004       PIAOUT  EQU      $2004
 7            2005       CRA     EQU      $2005
 8            2006       PIAIN   EQU      $2006
 9            2007       CRB     EQU      $2007
10                              ** INITIALIZATION
11   FC00     0F         INIT    SEI               DISABLE INTERRUPTS DURING INIT
12   FC01     8E  007D           LDS      #$007D   INIT STACK POINTER
13   FC04     86  05             LDAA     #05      LOAD ACCA WITH DATA DIR BYTE
14   FC06     B7  2004           STAA     PIAOUT   STORE IN DDRA
15   FC09     86  07             LDAA     #07      LOAD ACCA WITH CONTROL BYTE
16   FC0B     B7  2005           STAA     CRA      STORE IT IN CRA
17   FC0E     86  06             LDAA     #06      LOAD ACCA WITH CONTROL BYTE
18   FC10     B7  2007           STAA     CRB      STORE IT IN CRB
19                              ** KEYBOARD ROUTINE
20   FC13     B6  2007   GET1    LDAA     CRB      POLL CRB
21   FC16     84  80             ANDA     #$80     KEY PRESSED? (BIT 7 = 1?)
22   FC18     27  F9             BEQ      GET1     NO—POLL AGAIN
23   FC1A     B6  2006           LDAA     PIAIN    YES—GET IT
24   FC1D     48             ASLA              SHIFT LEFT 4 TIMES
25   FC1E     48             ASLA                 TO FORM MSD
26   FC1F     48             ASLA
27   FC20     48             ASLA
28   FC21     B7  007F           STAA     PRESET   STORE MSD IN PRESET
29   FC24     B6  2007   GET2    LDAA     CRB      POLL CRB
30   FC27     84  80             ANDA     #$80     KEY PRESSED? (BIT 7 = 1?)
31   FC29     27  F9             BEQ      GET2     NO—POLL AGAIN
32   FC2B     B6  2006           LDAA     PIAIN    YES—GET IT
33   FC2E     BA  007F           ORAA     PRESET   OR IT WITH PRESET TO FORM 2 DIGITS
34   FC31     B7  007F           STAA     PRESET   STORE IT BACK IN PRESET
35                              ** MAIN TASK—START CONVEYOR
36   FC34     0E             CLI               ENABLE INTERRUPTS
37   FC35     86  01             LDAA     #01      SET RUN, RESET FILL
38   FC37     B7  2004           STAA     PIAOUT
39   FC3A     B6  2004   NEXBOX  LDAA     PIAOUT   POLL PIAOUT
40   FC3D     84  02             ANDA     #02      BOX PRESENT? (BIT 1 = 1?)
41   FC3F     27  F9             BEQ      NEXBOX   NO—POLL AGAIN
42   FC41     86  04             LDAA     #04      YES—RESET RUN, SET FILL
43   FC43     B7  2004           STAA     PIAOUT
44   FC46     7F  007E           CLR      PARTS    CLEAR TEMP STORAGE
45                              ** LOOP WHILE WAITING FOR INTERRUPT
46   FC49     B6  007E   TEST    LDAA     PARTS    GET CURRENT PARTS COUNT
47   FC4C     B1  007F           CMPA     PRESET   PARTS = PRESET?
48   FC4F     26  F8             BNE      TEST     NO—LOOP AGAIN
```

Fig. 11-17. Program for counter-filler.

49				** START CONVEYOR AGAIN		
50	FC51	86	01	LDAA	#01	YES—RESET FILL, SET RUN
51	FC53	B7	2004	STAA	PIAOUT	
52	FC56	B6	2004	BOXGON LDAA	PIAOUT	POLL PIAOUT
53	FC59	84	02	ANDA	#02	FILLED BOX GONE YET? (BIT 1 = 0?)
54	FC5B	26	F9	BNE	BOXGON	NO—POLL AGAIN
55	FC5D	20	DB	BRA	NEXBOX	YES—LOOK FOR NEXT BOX
56				** INTERRUPT SERVICE ROUTINE		
57	FC60	F6	2004	LDAB	PIAOUT	DUMMY READ
58	FC63	8B	01	ADDA	#01	ADD 1 TO CURRENT PARTS COUNT
59	FC65	19		DAA		CONVERT TO BCD
60	FC66	B7	007E	STAA	PARTS	UPDATE PARTS COUNT
61	FC69	3B		RTI		
62				END		

FFF8	FC		START OF INTERRUPT SERVICE
FFF9	60		ROUTINE[1]
FFFE	FC		START OF MAIN PROGRAM
FFFF	00		AFTER RESET[2]

Notes: 1. To run program on Heath ET3400, load starting address of interrupt service routine into 00F7, 00F8. To run program on MEK D2 kit, load starting address of interrupt service routine into A000, A001.

2. To run program out of RAM in either of above kits, simply change two most significant digits of all addresses to 00 instead of FC.

Fig. 11-17. (Cont.)

The unused pins of port *A* are simply left unconnected. Some engineers prefer to tie unused outputs or inputs to ground or V_{CC} through 10-kΩ resistors to prevent possible static damage to the MOS device. Inputs PB_4–PB_7 should be grounded.

11-4 Video Terminal Interface

In Chapter 9 we discussed some serial I/O techniques. Serial I/O is commonly used between a computer and a video terminal or hard-copy printer. One popular video terminal, used both in industry and by computer hobbyists, is the Lear-Siegler ADM-3A, shown in Fig. 11-18.

For computers to be able to interface easily with these terminals as well as with a variety of other peripherals, such as cassette tape units and telephone modems, there must be some standardization of the interface. That is, various pieces of equipment must use the same signal levels, driver and source impedances, connector pinouts, etc. The problem was recognized years ago, and a recommended standard was proposed by the Electronic Industries Association (EIA) called RS-232-C, which is the most commonly used serial interface specification today. The ADM-3A has RS-232-C-compatible ports.

Fig. 11-18. Video terminal. (Courtesy of Lear-Siegler, Inc., Data Products Division.)

The RS-232-C specification describes the electrical, mechanical, and functional characteristics of the data interchange.

Briefly, RS-232-C specifies that the driver circuits on the interchange must be able to withstand open circuits or shorts without damage. The receiver must be able to withstand an input signal of up to ±25 V without damage. And the input impedance of the receiver must not be less than 3 kΩ or more than 7 kΩ. There are a few other restrictions, but since RS-232-C-compatible integrated circuits (line drivers and receivers) are available off the shelf, most users need not be concerned with the fine points.

RS-232-C provides good-quality communications over single-wire transmission lines up to 50 ft at data rates up to 20K bits per second. To be able to communicate well in a noisy atmosphere, RS-232-C recommends using large-signal voltage swings. Actually the signal must swing positive and negative with respect to ground. Typically ±12- or ±15-V signal levels are used. The negative voltage is considered the logic 1 (mark) and the positive voltage is logic 0 (space). Figure 11-19 shows the details.

Two commonly used ICs are shown in Figs. 11-20(A) and (B). Normally, the threshold controls of the 75154 receivers are tied to pin 15 (V_{CC}). This ensures that the input signal must pass more than 1 V or so beyond ground in either direction before output switching will occur.

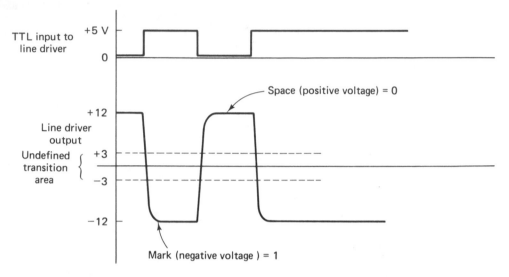

Fig. 11-19. Signal details for RS-232-C interchange.

RS-232-C even specifies which pins to use for various signals on a standard 25-pin D-shell connector, made by several connector manufacturers. So you can plug any terminal into any computer, and if they are both RS-232-C compatible, they will work together.

Some of the important pinouts are the following:

Pin	Function	Abbreviation
1.	Protective ground	
2.	Transmitted data	TxD
3.	Received data	RxD
4.	Request to send	RTS
5.	Clear to send	CTS
6.	Data set ready	DSR
7.	Signal ground	
8.	Received line signal detector	DCD
20.	Data terminal ready	DTR

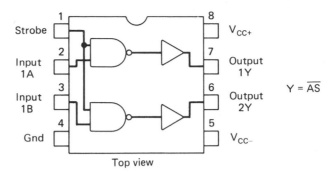

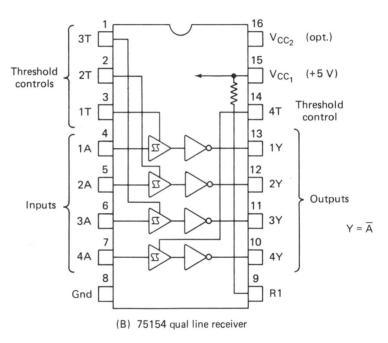

(A) 75150 dual line driver

(B) 75154 qual line receiver

Fig. 11-20. Typical RS-232-C interface chips.

See Fig. 11-21 for the connector layout. The control lines, such as pins 4, 5, 6, 8, and 20, are used for handshaking where necessary, such as in a modem. Most often, the only connections that must be made between a terminal and computer are pin 2 (TxD), pin 3 (RxD), and pin 7 (ground).

Sometimes, as is the case with the TI Mod 743 printer, the printer outputs a +12 level on its DTR output (pin 20) on power up to signal the modem or computer that it is ready. Similarly, it looks for a +12-V level from the external device on its DCD input (pin 8) before it will receive any signal. *Always read the specifications of any device before attempting to use it!*

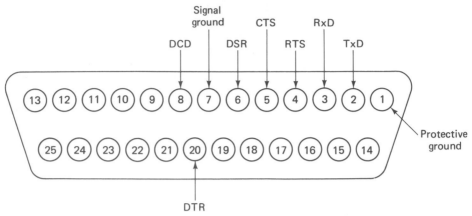

Fig. 11-21. Front view of standard 25-pin connector (receptacle) compatible with RS-232-C.

The designations such as transmitted data, etc., refer to the *terminal*. Of course the terminal's TxD output becomes the computer's RxD input, etc.

A diagram of the complete hookup of a video terminal to an ACIA is shown in Fig. 11-22. The line drivers and receivers should be mounted close to the ACIA, within inches if possible. The connection of the ACIA to the microprocessor is as shown in a previous chapter.

Assuming that a video terminal is connected as shown in Fig. 11-22 and assuming that the ACIA is initialized as described in Chapter 9, two simple program routines are necessary for two-way communications. We shall call them TTYIN (for inputting characters to the CPU from the terminal) and TTYOUT (for sending characters from the CPU to the terminal). Let's assume that the receiver interrupt enable (bit 7 of the ACIA control register) was set HIGH on initialization and that the CPU interrupt flag has been cleared. An incoming character from the terminal will then generate an interrupt request when the character has been completely received, that is, when RDRF (bit 0) of the ACIA status register goes HIGH.

The interrupt service routine is as follows:

TTYIN	LDAA	STATUS	Look at status word
	ANDA #$70		Test for error bits
	BNE	ERROR	If error, go to error routine
	LDAA	DATA	If no error, read data
	STAA, X		Store character in RAM
	INX		Point to next available RAM location
	RTI		

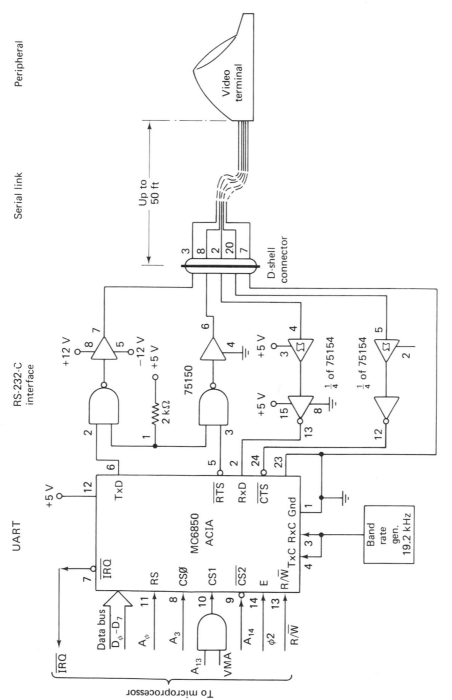

Fig. 11-22. Hookup of a video terminal to a microprocessor via an RS-232-C port through an ACIA.

The first two instructions read and examine the receiver STATUS word. If any error exists, the CPU is directed to branch to ERROR routine (not shown), which would flag the operator of the error.

However, if no error exists, the Rx data register is read, thus loading the data byte into the accumulator. Reading the data register also clears the IRQ (bit 7 of the status register). DATA, of course, represents address 2009, the ACIA data register.

The received character is then stored in memory for later use. The routine assumes that the index register has been previously loaded with the location in which to deposit the first character. It then gets incremented after each character is stored, thus pointing to the next available RAM location.

Finally, the RTI instruction restores all MPU registers to what they were prior to the interrupt, and the CPU continues what it was doing.

When the MPU wants to send characters to the terminal, it simply jumps to the TTYOUT subroutine.

Let's suppose that we want to transmit a message which is stored as ASCII characters in contiguous (adjacent) memory locations. The last stored character (indicating end of message) is 00. Before jumping to the subroutine, we first load the index register with the address of the first character of the message to be sent. Then we execute the jump to the TTYOUT subroutine, which runs as follows:

TTYOUT	LDAA, X	Load ACCA indexed
	BNE SEND	Last character?
	RTS	Yes, return
SEND	LDAB STATUS	If not last character, check
	ANDB #$02	if Tx buffer empty
	BEQ SEND	If not empty, check again
	STAA DATA	If buffer empty, send character
	INX	Point to next character
	BRA TTYOUT	Repeat

Other routines, such as ASCII-to-hex and hex-to-ASCII conversion, are often included in the character-handling routines in order to save memory space. However, these routines show generally how the MPU can communicate with either a TTY or a video terminal.

Problems

11-1 If in the circuit of Fig. 11-2, $V_{ref} = 10$ V and the buffer amplifier's gain is 1 (unity), what is the analog output voltage V'_a with each of the following inputs: (a) 255_{10}, (b) 168_{10}, (c) 300_8, (d) 125_8, (e) 33_H, (f) CC_H?

11-2 Referring to the circuit of Fig. 11-6(B), if the connections across pins 24 and 16 and across 17 and 20 are removed (pin 20 is open), over what range can voltage V_{out} swing with all possible combinations of 12-bit inputs?

11-3 Referring to the circuit of Fig. 11-6(B), if a 6.3-kΩ resistor is placed across pins 17 and 20 while all other connections are left intact, over what range can voltage V_{out} swing with all possible combinations of 12-bit inputs?

11-4 With a block diagram, show how to interface the MPU with two DACs using a PIA instead of the buffers, decoder, and latches shown in Fig. 11-1.

11-5 Referring to the ADC of Fig. 11-8(A), if the digital output $(D_7–D_0)$ is FF_H when $V_a = +10$ V and 00_H when $V_a = -10$ V, about what digital output can we expect when (a) $V_a = 0$ V, (b) $V_a = -5$ V, (c) $V_a = +5$ V?

11-6 In the circuit of Fig. 11-9, can the $\overline{CC}$ and D_0 outputs of the ADC communicate via the data bus at the same time? Why? Refer also to Fig. 11-11.

11-7 Which instruction in the program of Fig. 11-11(B) generates the START pulse?

11-8 Referring to the decoder and program of Fig. 11-11, the second and third bytes of the STAA instruction specify address 0800. What other hex addresses will work as well with this instruction and decoder? List at least 10.

11-9 Which instruction in the program of Fig. 11-11(B) generates the $\overline{\text{READ DATA}}$ pulse?

11-10 Which of the instructions in the program of Fig. 11-11 are extended mode?

11-11 Which of the instructions in the program of Fig. 11-11 are direct mode?

11-12 Which of the instructions in the program of Fig. 11-11 are (a) inherent mode, (b) relative mode?

11-13 Refer to the keyboard encoder of Fig. 11-13. How many diodes are forward-biased (conducting) when switch 4 is closed? List the condition of the outputs at this time: $D =$ _____, $C =$ _____, $B =$ _____, $A =$ _____, KEYSTROBE = _____.

Problems 11-14–11-20 refer to Fig. 11-14.

11-14 What size ROM is indicated?

11-15 What size RAM is indicated?

11-16 Give two reasons why RAM is needed for this application.

11-17 What is the address of PIA control register *A?*

11-18 What address must the CPU read from when inputting numbers from the keyboard?

11-19 What address must the CPU read from in order to see whether STOP is high?

11-20 STOP will be HIGH whenever phototransistor *B* is (ON, OFF).

Refer to Figs. 11-14 and 11-17 for Problems 11-21–11-24. For purposes of troubleshooting, several manufacturers make a test instrument called a *logic analyzer.* The logic analyzer allows the user to sample and observe the logic levels on various address, data, and control lines at the precise instant of a memory READ or WRITE operation. By using this instrument, along with a program listing, the user can see whether the intended sequence of events is occurring.

11-21 List the logic levels (H or L) that you would expect to see on the following PIA pins in Fig. 11-14 at the instant the MPU executes the STAA instruction on line 14 of the program of Fig. 11-17:

38 __   21 __   25 __   23 __   24 __   22 __   35 __   36 __
26 __   27 __   28 __   29 __   30 __   31 __   32 __   33 __

11-22 As in Problem 11-21, list the levels you would expect to see while the MPU is executing the instruction on line 23. Assume that the operator has just pressed key 7 on the keyboard.

38 __   21 __   25 __   23 __   24 __   22 __   35 __   36 __
26 __   27 __   28 __   29 __   30 __   31 __   32 __   33 __

11-23 List the logic levels you would expect to see on the following pins at the instant the MPU is executing the instruction at line 39. Assume that the conveyor is running and that a box has just moved in front of phototransistor *B.*

4 __   3 __   2 __   40 __
38 __   21 __   25 __   23 __   24 __   22 __   35 __   36 __
26 __   27 __   28 __   29 __   30 __   31 __   32 __   33 __

11-24 List the levels you would expect to see while the MPU is executing the instruction at line 57.

38 __   21 __   25 __   23 __   24 __   22 __   35 __   36 __
26 __   27 __   28 __   29 __   30 __   31 __   32 __   33 __

Problems 11-25–11-27 refer to Fig. 11-23.

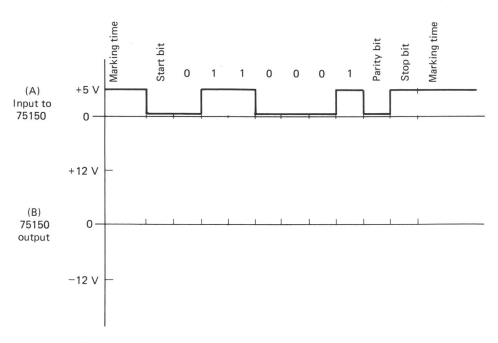

Fig. 11-23. Waveforms for Problems 11-25, 11-26, and 11-27.

11-25 The input waveform shown is applied to a 75150 line driver. Draw the output waveform on the axis provided. Assume ±12-V power supplies.

11-26 What 7-bit ASCII character does this waveform represent?

11-27 Does this waveform use odd or even parity?

Refer to Fig. 11-22 for Problems 11-28–11-33.

11-28 When $\overline{\text{RTS}}$ is active, what voltage will be present on pin 8 of the *D*-shell connector?

11-29 If the ACIA is set up for a ÷ 16 clock, what will be the actual output baud rate at the TxD pin?

11-30 To be able to output the waveform of Fig. 11-23(A) from the ACIA, what control word would you write into the control register (2008)? Give all bits and disable Tx interrupts. (Refer to the ACIA setup tables in Chapter 9.)

11-31 What byte would you write into 2009? (Refer to Problem 11-30.)

11-32 Assume that when the video terminal is powered up it outputs a DTR signal of +12 V. On what connector pin would this signal appear?

11-33 The signal on the $\overline{\text{CTS}}$ input to the ACIA (pin 24) is used as a handshake signal to indicate to the ACIA that a terminal is connected and ready to receive. With the line receiver wired as shown (pin 2 floating), an unconnected input (pin 5) will cause the output (pin 12) to go HIGH. The HIGH signal on the $\overline{\text{CTS}}$ input will prevent transmission from the ACIA. Connecting pin 5 of the 75154 to the DTR output of the terminal will make $\overline{\text{CTS}}$ (HIGH, LOW) when the terminal is powered up. However, if the *D*-shell connector should accidentally become disconnected, the ACIA will be informed of the fault by a (HIGH, LOW) on the $\overline{\text{CTS}}$ input.

Problems 11-34–11-36 refer to the TTYIN service routine.

11-34 The label STATUS represents the status register of the ACIA. When entering the assembly language program on a minicomputer, STATUS would have to be EQUated to the hex address value corresponding to the status register. What is the location of the status register, that is, what would you EQUate STATUS to?

11-35 Assuming no communication errors and that the Tx data register is empty, what byte would you expect to read into the accumulator after executing the instruction LDAA STATUS?

11-36 DATA, which represents the Rx data register, also represents a location that the CPU can read from. What is the location of DATA?

Refer to the TTYOUT subroutine for Problems 11-37–11-39.

11-37 How does the CPU know when the last character of a message has been transmitted?

11-38 What is the purpose of polling STATUS?

11-39 Is DATA in the same location as in the TTYIN routine? Explain.

CHAPTER 12

The 8085A and the Z80 MPUs

Having become familiar with the MC6800 MPU, we are in a position to quickly adapt to other types. Two other types are discussed in this chapter. These are the 8085A and the Z80; both are popular 8-bit processors. By studying these MPUs and their applications here, we gain reinforcement of the materials covered in previous chapters, a clearer picture of the fact that all MPUs generally work the same way, and a confidence that still other MPUs can easily be mastered too.

12-1 The 8085A Microprocessor Unit

The 8085A is an 8-bit MPU that Intel Corporation has evolved from its popular 8080 MPU. Not long ago, a basic MPU-based system required about 60 ICs—memory chips, buffers, clocks, latches, etc.—and often more than one supply voltage. Now a comparable, but faster, 8085A-based system can be built with just three chips and a single +5-V dc supply. These include the 8085A MPU* chip, a ROM (8355) or EPROM (8755A), and a RAM (8155 or 8156). Both the ROM and RAM chips also include I/O ports, and the latter includes a programmable timer; see Fig. 12-1. Such a system has plenty of power for most dedicated industrial control applications. As mentioned before, the ROM or EPROM is necessary for storage of permanent

---

* Intel Corporation refers to its microprocessors as CPU (central processor unit) chips.

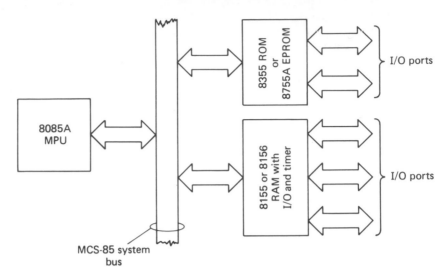

Fig. 12-1. Functional block diagram of a three-chip system using MCS-85 family components.

programs. The RAM is necessary for scratch-pad memory, that is, to temporarily store data.

The architecture of the 8085A is shown in Fig. 12-2. Although it is beyond the scope of this chapter to discuss all aspects of the 8085A, we can look at some of them thoroughly, especially those comparable to the MC6800's already described. The 8085A has one accumulator, which we shall call the A register. This seeming disadvantage, compared to the MC6800's two accumulators, is offset by the 8085A's register array. This array consists of a group of general-purpose registers, some of which can be used as single 8-bit registers or as 16-bit register pairs. We shall learn to appreciate the power of these registers as we study some 8085A applications in later sections.* Note that the 8085A has a 16-bit program counter and stack pointer, as does the MC6800. The flag register has a function very similar to the function of the condition code register discussed previously. The 8085A's clock is on the chip—no separate clock chip or circuit is necessary. As shown in Fig. 12-3, a crystal or RC circuit is used to drive the X_1 and X_2 inputs of the 8085A. Of course, where precise timing and clock frequency are necessary, the crystal is used. If the 8085A is to be synchronized with other MPUs or associated circuits, a central clock can drive its X_1 input; X_2 is left floating as shown.

Like the MC6800, the 8085A is housed in a 40-pin package. To make more of these pins available for control signals, Intel uses a multiplexed

---

* The reader should not assume that the authors are recommending any one type of MPU over another. A given MPU can, comparatively, have advantages in a specific application but then have as many disadvantages in different applications.

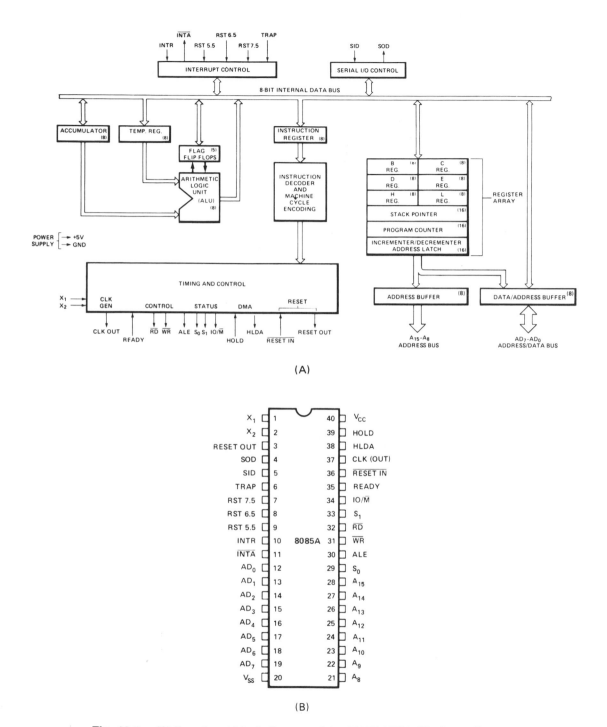

Fig. 12-2. (A) Functional block diagram of the 8085A MPU; (B) pin configuration of the 8085A. (Reprinted by permission of Intel Corporation, copyright 1978.)

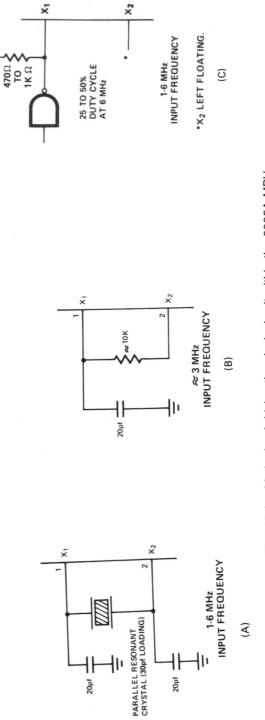

Fig. 12-3. Methods of driving the clock circuit within the 8085A MPU.

bus scheme on their 8085A. As shown in the pinout diagram of Fig. 12-2, pins 12–19 are identified as AD_0–AD_7, respectively. This means that the MPU uses these pins as address outputs A_0–A_7 when addressing a RAM or ROM location. When reading 8-bit bytes into or writing them out of its accumulator, the MPU uses these same pins for data, D_0–D_7. If the 8085A is used with support chips from the MCS-85 component family, as in the minimum system of Fig. 12-1, the user need not be concerned with this address/data multiplexing action. The MPU system manages it.

The 8085A communicates with the outside world a little differently from the MC6800. The latter, we learned, communicates with I/O devices as it does with memory. That is, the MC6800 uses memory-mapped I/O, which means that its I/O devices are assigned addresses that must not overlap ROM or RAM locations; review Figs. 6-23 and 6-24 as needed. This means that instructions like LDA and STA perform a read (input) and write (output)

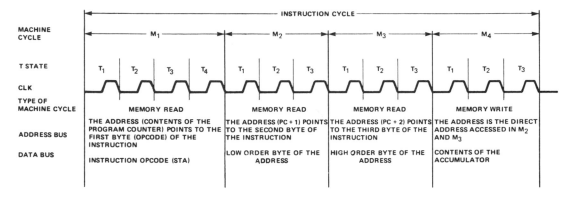

Fig. 12-4. The 8085A's timing for the 3-byte STA instruction. (Reprinted by permission of Intel Corporation, copyright 1978.)

operation, respectively, on either memory or I/O devices. The 8085A, on the other hand, uses what Intel calls *standard I/O technique*. This I/O technique provides separate INput and OUTput instructions to input and output data from and to I/O devices. The import of this will become clear when we analyze a typical I/O application later.

Each read or write operation is referred to as a *machine cycle*. Each instruction of the 8085A requires a sequence of one to five machine cycles. A machine cycle consists of a minimum of three to as many as six *clock cycles* called *T states*. For example, as shown in Fig. 12-4, a 3-byte LDA instruction requires 4 machine cycles $(M_1$–$M_4)$ consisting of 13 clock cycles (*T* states). The number of cycles or states each instruction requires is listed in the instruction set and enables the designer to predict the time it takes a given program to run. The number of clock cycles per second is half the frequency driving the X_1 and X_2 inputs of the MPU.

12-2 The 8155 and 8156 RAM with I/O Ports and Timer

As shown in Fig. 12-5, the 8155 and 8156 are 40-pin devices. These chips are identical except that the 8155 has an active LOW chip enable ($\overline{CE}$), whereas the 8156 has an active HIGH chip enable (CE). Note that the 8155/8156 contains a 256-byte RAM. When the MPU accesses RAM, it places the RAM address on the AD_0–AD_7 lines and loads it into the latches of the 8155/8156. The MPU also outputs the ALE (address latch enable) signal that strobes the address into the latches. This action is very similar to the action of the transparent latches of Fig. 5-12, described earlier. The MPU then reads from or writes to the addressed location via the same AD_0–AD_7 lines. When the MPU performs a read, it outputs a LOW $\overline{RD}$ signal. When performing a write operation, it outputs a LOW $\overline{WR}$. When accessing memory, the MPU pulls its $IO/\overline{M}$ output LOW. When communicating with I/Os (peripherals), the MPU outputs a HIGH $IO/\overline{M}$ signal.

The three I/O ports—an 8-bit port A (PA), an 8-bit port B (PB), and a 6-bit port C (PC)—can be individually programmed to be either input

Fig. 12-5. (A) Functional diagram of the 8155/8156; (B) its pin configuration. (Reprinted by permission of Intel Corporation, copyright 1978.)

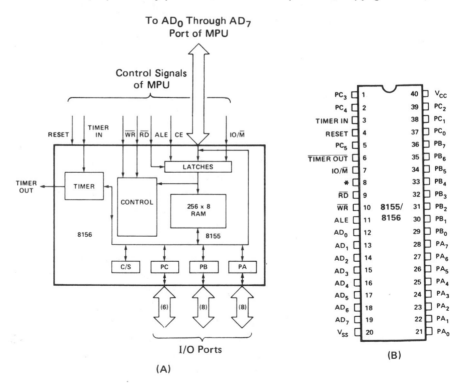

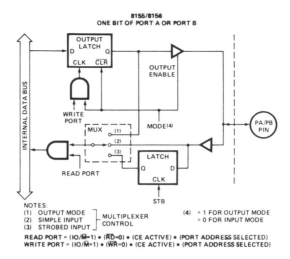

NOTES:
(1) OUTPUT MODE ⎫
(2) SIMPLE INPUT ⎬ MULTIPLEXER CONTROL
(3) STROBED INPUT ⎭

(4) = 1 FOR OUTPUT MODE
= 0 FOR INPUT MODE

READ PORT = (IO/$\overline{\text{M}}$=1) • ($\overline{\text{RD}}$=0) • (CE ACTIVE) • (PORT ADDRESS SELECTED)
WRITE PORT = (IO/$\overline{\text{M}}$=1) • ($\overline{\text{WR}}$=0) • (CE ACTIVE) • (PORT ADDRESS SELECTED)

Fig. 12-6. Diagram of how I/O ports *A* and *B* are structured within the 8155/8156. (Reprinted by permission of Intel Corporation, copyright 1978.)

or output ports. Each port has its own register that can latch data that are to be inputted or outputted. Figure 12-6 shows how each bit of *PA* and *PB* is managed.

The command/status (C/S) register is actually two registers in one. There is the command register with an 8-bit latch. This latch is loaded by the program and, as shown in Fig. 12-7(A), serves to configure the ports *PA* and *PB* as input or output. The significance of this is much easier to understand while analyzing a program of a typical I/O routine. This will be done later, and we shall refer back to this figure at that time. The other register is called the status register. It consists of a 7-bit latch that can be used to receive interrupts for *PA* and/or *PB*, via *PC*, and to monitor the status of the *PA* and/or *PB* latches. The command register can be altered by a *write* operation with the I/O address XXXXX000$_2$, and the status register can be polled by a *read* operation using the same address. The *PA* and *PB* registers' addresses are XXXXX001$_2$ and XXXXX010$_2$, respectively.

The timer is a 14-bit down counter that decrements with each pulse applied to the TIMER IN input. The timer's bits T_{13}–T_0 can be loaded (preset) by the program, and thus the $\overline{\text{TIMER OUT}}$ signal frequency can be made a fraction of the TIMER IN frequency. Also, the $\overline{\text{TIMER OUT}}$ signal can be either a square wave or a pulse when terminal count (TC) is reached. Either output waveform, like frequency, is selected by the programmer. Figure 12-8 shows the timer's format and modes of operation. As shown in the table, the M_2 and M_1 bits can select one of four modes of operation. The timer's M_2, M_1, and T_{13}–T_8 bits are loaded by a write operation to address XXXXX101$_2$. The T_7–T_0 bits are loaded by a write to address

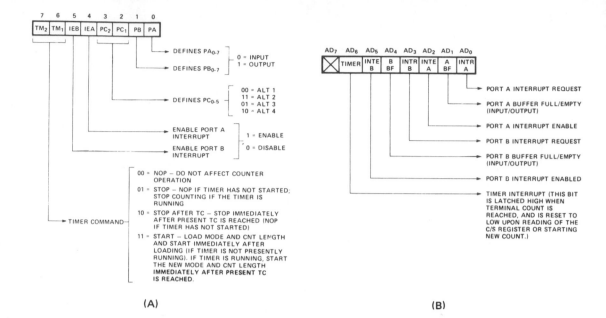

(A)   (B)

TABLE OF PORT CONTROL ASSIGNMENT.

Pin	ALT 1	ALT 2	ALT 3	ALT 4
PC0	Input Port	Output Port	A INTR (Port A Interrupt)	A INTR (Port A Interrupt)
PC1	Input Port	Output Port	A BF (Port A Buffer Full)	A BF (Port A Buffer Full)
PC2	Input Port	Output Port	A $\overline{\text{STB}}$ (Port A Strobe)	A $\overline{\text{STB}}$ (Port A Strobe)
PC3	Input Port	Output Port	Output Port	B INTR (Port B Interrupt)
PC4	Input Port	Output Port	Output Port	B BF (Port B Buffer Full)
PC5	Input Port	Output Port	Output Port	B $\overline{\text{STB}}$ (Port B Strobe)

The set and reset of INTR and BF with respect to $\overline{\text{STB}}$, $\overline{\text{WR}}$ and $\overline{\text{RD}}$ timing is shown in Figure 8.

To summarize, the registers' assignments are:

Address	Pinouts	Functions	No. of Bits
XXXXX000	Internal	Command/Status Register	8
XXXXX001	PA0-7	General Purpose I/O Port	8
XXXXX010	PB0-7	General Purpose I/O Port	8
XXXXX011	PC0-5	General Purpose I/O Port or Control Lines	6

When PC is programmed to either ALT3 or ALT4, the control signals for PA and PB become initialized as:

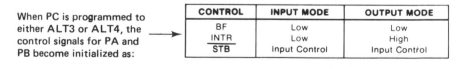

CONTROL	INPUT MODE	OUTPUT MODE
BF	Low	Low
INTR	Low	High
$\overline{\text{STB}}$	Input Control	Input Control

(C)

Fig. 12-7. (A) Command register bit assignment; (B) status register word format; (C) table of port control assignments. (Reprinted by permission of Intel Corporation, copyright 1978.)

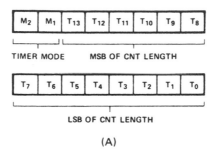

M_2	M_1	T_{13}	T_{12}	T_{11}	T_{10}	T_9	T_8

TIMER MODE   MSB OF CNT LENGTH

T_7	T_6	T_5	T_4	T_3	T_2	T_1	T_0

LSB OF CNT LENGTH

(A)

M_2 M_1 defines the timer mode as follows:

M_2	M_1	
0	0	Puts out low during second half of count.
0	1	Square wave, i.e., the period of the square wave equals the count length programmed with automatic reload at terminal count.
1	0	Single pulse upon TC being reached.
1	1	Automatic reload, i.e., single pulse everytime TC is reached.

(B)

Fig. 12-8. (A) Timer format; (B) modes of operation. (Reprinted by permission of Intel Corporation, copyright 1978.)

$XXXXX100_2$. Control, such as starting and stopping the timer, is available by way of the command register, as shown in Fig. 12-7(A).

12-3 The 8355 ROM

This MCS-85 family chip is in a 40-pin package, contains 2048 bytes of ROM, and has two I/O ports; see Fig. 12-9. To access ROM or I/O ports, both chip enables, CE and $\overline{\text{CE}}$, must be active. The ROM locations are selected with an 11-bit address input. While executing a memory reference instruction, the MPU first latches the address into the 8355 on the falling edge of the ALE signal. The MPU transports the lower-order bits via AD_7–AD_0 and the higher-order address bits via A_{10}–A_8. After the address is secured into the 8355's address latch, the MPU reads from the addressed location, now using AD_7–AD_0 for data. The MPU outputs LOW IO/$\overline{\text{M}}$ and $\overline{\text{RD}}$ signals during a memory read. The MPU can also read from or write to port A or port B via AD_7–AD_0. When doing so, it outputs a HIGH IO/$\overline{\text{M}}$.

The I/O ports of the 8355 are similar to ports A and B of the PIA. As with the PIA, some pins of either port can be programmed (configured)

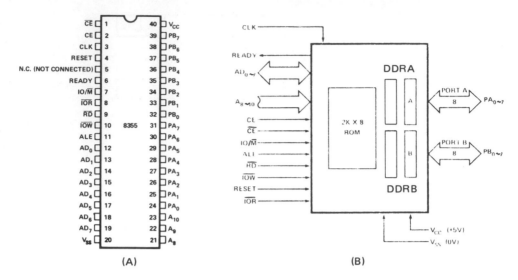

(A)   (B)

Fig. 12-9. (A) Functional diagram of the 8355; (B) its pin configuration. (Reprinted by permission of Intel Corporation, copyright 1978.)

Fig. 12-10. (A) Diagram of how each bit of port *A* and port *B* is structured within the 8355/8755A; (B) summary of port and DDR designations. (Reprinted by permission of Intel Corporation, copyright 1978.)

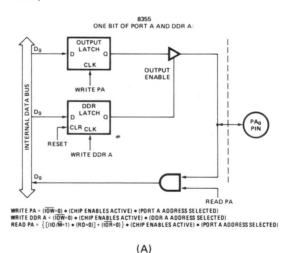

WRITE PA = ($\overline{\text{IOW}}$=0) • (CHIP ENABLES ACTIVE) • (PORT A ADDRESS SELECTED)
WRITE DDR A = ($\overline{\text{IOW}}$=0) • (CHIP ENABLES ACTIVE) • (DDR A ADDRESS SELECTED)
READ PA = {[(IO/$\overline{\text{M}}$=1) • (RD=0)] + ($\overline{\text{IOR}}$=0)} • (CHIP ENABLES ACTIVE) • (PORT A ADDRESS SELECTED)

(A)

AD$_1$	AD$_0$	Selection
0	0	Port A
0	1	Port B
1	0	Port A Data Direction Register (DDR A)
1	1	Port B Data Direction Register (DDR B)

(B)

as inputs and others on the same port as outputs. Note in Fig. 12-9 that the 8355 has data direction registers A and B (DDRA and DDRB) that serve the same purpose here as DDRA and DDRB do in the PIA; review Sec. 9-2 as needed. The DDRA or DDRB are loaded by a write operation to address $XXXXXX10_2$ or $XXXXXX11_2$, respectively. An 8-bit byte loaded into DDRA or DDRB specifies the I/O status of each pin of its corresponding port. A logic 1 specifies an output mode; a 0 specifies an input mode. Port A is read from or written to with the address $XXXXXX00_2$. Port B's read or write address is $XXXXXX01_2$. Figure 12-10 shows the 8355's structure for each bit of ports A and B.

The 8755A is an EPROM and is almost identical to the 8355. The 8755A is different only in that it is field programmable and erasable. As with EPROMs mentioned before, the 8755A is erased by exposure to ultraviolet light.

12-4 The 8085A Instruction Set

Before we can start analyzing programs intended for 8085A-based systems, we must become familiar with this MPU's instruction set. As with the MC6800, the 8085A's instruction set includes 1-, 2-, and 3-byte instructions. It also includes the ability to *move* data from one register to another within the register array. Intel's designations for these registers is shown in Table 12-1. Note that each register has a bit pattern designation shown in the "DDD or SSS" column. DDD and SSS refer to destination and source registers, respectively. The significance of these designations can be seen by examining a relevant instruction, such as MOVr1,r2, the first instruction of Table 12-2. We can see that this instruction has the general binary op code 01DDDSSS. This means that if the programmer *moves* the contents of the accumulator (A register) to the C register, the op code is 01001111_2. This op code, when decoded by the MPU, causes a move of the contents of the

Table 12-1 The Bit Pattern Designating One of the Registers A,B,C,D,E,H,L[a]

DDD or SSS	Register Name
111	A
000	B
001	C
010	D
011	E
100	H
101	L

[a] DDD = destination, SSS = source.

Table 12-2[a]

8085A INSTRUCTION SET SUMMARY

Mnemonic	Description	D7	D6	D5	D4	D3	D2	D1	D0	Clock[2] Cycles
MOVE. LOAD. AND STORE										
MOV r1,r2	Move register to register	0	1	D	D	D	S	S	S	4
MOV M r	Move register to memory	0	1	1	1	0	S	S	S	7
MOV r M	Move memory to register	0	1	D	D	D	1	1	0	7
MVI r	Move immediate register	0	0	D	D	D	1	1	0	7
MVI M	Move immediate memory	0	0	1	1	0	1	1	0	10
LXI B	Load immediate register Pair B & C	0	0	0	0	0	0	0	1	10
LXI D	Load immediate register Pair D & E	0	0	0	1	0	0	0	1	10
LXI H	Load immediate register Pair H & L	0	0	1	0	0	0	0	1	10
LXI SP	Load immediate stack pointer	0	0	1	1	0	0	0	1	10
STAX B	Store A indirect	0	0	0	0	0	0	1	0	7
STAX D	Store A indirect	0	0	0	1	0	0	1	0	7
LDAX B	Load A indirect	0	0	0	0	1	0	1	0	7
LDAX D	Load A indirect	0	0	0	1	1	0	1	0	7
STA	Store A direct	0	0	1	1	0	0	1	0	13
LDA	Load A direct	0	0	1	1	1	0	1	0	13
SHLD	Store H & L direct	0	0	1	0	0	0	1	0	16
LHLD	Load H & L direct	0	0	1	0	1	0	1	0	16
XCHG	Exchange D & E H & L Registers	1	1	1	0	1	0	1	1	4
STACK OPS										
PUSH B	Push register Pair B & C on stack	1	1	0	0	0	1	0	1	12
PUSH D	Push register Pair D & E on stack	1	1	0	1	0	1	0	1	12
PUSH H	Push register Pair H & L on stack	1	1	1	0	0	1	0	1	12
PUSH PSW	Push A and Flags on stack	1	1	1	1	0	1	0	1	12
POP B	Pop register Pair B & C off stack	1	1	0	0	0	0	0	1	10
POP D	Pop register Pair D & E off stack	1	1	0	1	0	0	0	1	10
POP H	Pop register Pair H & L off stack	1	1	1	0	0	0	0	1	10
POP PSW	Pop A and Flags off stack	1	1	1	1	0	0	0	1	10
XTHL	Exchange top of stack H & L	1	1	1	0	0	0	1	1	16
SPHL	H & L to stack pointer	1	1	1	1	1	0	0	1	6
JUMP										
JMP	Jump unconditional	1	1	0	0	0	0	1	1	10
JC	Jump on carry	1	1	0	1	1	0	1	0	7/10
JNC	Jump on no carry	1	1	0	1	0	0	1	0	7/10
JZ	Jump on zero	1	1	0	0	1	0	1	0	7/10
JNZ	Jump on no zero	1	1	0	0	0	0	1	0	7/10
JP	Jump on positive	1	1	1	1	0	0	1	0	7/10
JM	Jump on minus	1	1	1	1	1	0	1	0	7/10
JPE	Jump on parity even	1	1	1	0	1	0	1	0	7/10
JPO	Jump on parity odd	1	1	1	0	0	0	1	0	7/10
PCHL	H & L to program counter	1	1	1	0	1	0	0	1	6
CALL										
CALL	Call unconditional	1	1	0	0	1	1	0	1	18
CC	Call on carry	1	1	0	1	1	1	0	0	9/18
CNC	Call on no carry	1	1	0	1	0	1	0	0	9/18
CZ	Call on zero	1	1	0	0	1	1	0	0	9/18
CNZ	Call on no zero	1	1	0	0	0	1	0	0	9/18
CP	Call on positive	1	1	1	1	0	1	0	0	9/18
CM	Call on minus	1	1	1	1	1	1	0	0	9/18
CPE	Call on parity even	1	1	1	0	1	1	0	0	9/18
CPO	Call on parity odd	1	1	1	0	0	1	0	0	9/18
RETURN										
RET	Return	1	1	0	0	1	0	0	1	10
RC	Return on carry	1	1	0	1	1	0	0	0	6/12
RNC	Return on no carry	1	1	0	1	0	0	0	0	6/12
RZ	Return on zero	1	1	0	0	1	0	0	0	6/12
RNZ	Return on no zero	1	1	0	0	0	0	0	0	6/12
RP	Return on positive	1	1	1	1	0	0	0	0	6/12
RM	Return on minus	1	1	1	1	1	0	0	0	6/12
RPE	Return on parity even	1	1	1	0	1	0	0	0	6/12
RPO	Return on parity odd	1	1	1	0	0	0	0	0	6/12
RESTART										
RST	Restart	1	1	A	A	A	1	1	1	12
INPUT/OUTPUT										
IN	Input	1	1	0	1	1	0	1	1	10
OUT	Output	1	1	0	1	0	0	1	1	10
INCREMENT AND DECREMENT										
INR r	Increment register	0	0	D	D	D	1	0	0	4
DCR r	Decrement register	0	0	D	D	D	1	0	1	4
INR M	Increment memory	0	0	1	1	0	1	0	0	10
DCR M	Decrement memory	0	0	1	1	0	1	0	1	10
INX B	Increment B & C registers	0	0	0	0	0	0	1	1	6
INX D	Increment D & E registers	0	0	0	1	0	0	1	1	6
INX H	Increment H & L registers	0	0	1	0	0	0	1	1	6
INX SP	Increment stack pointer	0	0	1	1	0	0	1	1	6
DCX B	Decrement B & C	0	0	0	0	1	0	1	1	6
DCX D	Decrement D & E	0	0	0	1	1	0	1	1	6
DCX H	Decrement H & L	0	0	1	0	1	0	1	1	6
DCX SP	Decrement stack pointer	0	0	1	1	1	0	1	1	6
ADD										
ADD r	Add register to A	1	0	0	0	0	S	S	S	4
ADC r	Add register to A with carry	1	0	0	0	1	S	S	S	4
ADD M	Add memory to A	1	0	0	0	0	1	1	0	7
ADC M	Add memory to A with carry	1	0	0	0	1	1	1	0	7
ADI	Add immediate to A	1	1	0	0	0	1	1	0	7
ACI	Add immediate to A with carry	1	1	0	0	1	1	1	0	7
DAD B	Add B & C to H & L	0	0	0	0	1	0	0	1	10
DAD D	Add D & E to H & L	0	0	0	1	1	0	0	1	10
DAD H	Add H & L to H & L	0	0	1	0	1	0	0	1	10
DAD SP	Add stack pointer to H & L	0	0	1	1	1	0	0	1	10
SUBTRACT										
SUB r	Subtract register from A	1	0	0	1	0	S	S	S	4
SBB r	Subtract register from A with borrow	1	0	0	1	1	S	S	S	4
SUB M	Subtract memory from A	1	0	0	1	0	1	1	0	7
SBB M	Subtract memory from A with borrow	1	0	0	1	1	1	1	0	7
SUI	Subtract immediate from A	1	1	0	1	0	1	1	0	7
SBI	Subtract immediate from A with borrow	1	1	0	1	1	1	1	0	7
LOGICAL										
ANA r	And register with A	1	0	1	0	0	S	S	S	4

Table 12-2 (Cont.)

8085A

8085A INSTRUCTION SET SUMMARY (Cont.)

Mnemonic	Description	D7	D6	D5	D4	D3	D2	D1	D0	Cycles	Mnemonic	Description	D7	D6	D5	D4	D3	D2	D1	D0	Cycles
XRA r	Exclusive Or register with A	1	0	1	0	1	S	S	S	4	RAL	Rotate A left through carry	0	0	0	1	0	1	1	1	4
ORA r	Or register with A	1	0	1	1	0	S	S	S	4	RAR	Rotate A right through carry	0	0	0	1	1	1	1	1	4
CMP r	Compare register with A	1	0	1	1	1	S	S	S	4	**SPECIALS**										
ANA M	And memory with A	1	0	1	0	0	1	1	0	7	CMA	Complement A	0	0	1	0	1	1	1	1	4
XRA M	Exclusive Or memory with A	1	0	1	0	1	1	1	0	7	STC	Set carry	0	0	1	1	0	1	1	1	4
ORA M	Or memory with A	1	0	1	1	0	1	1	0	7	CMC	Complement carry	0	0	1	1	1	1	1	1	4
CMP M	Compare memory with A	1	0	1	1	1	1	1	0	7	DAA	Decimal adjust A	0	0	1	0	0	1	1	1	4
ANI	And immediate with A	1	1	1	0	0	1	1	0	7	**CONTROL**										
XRI	Exclusive Or immediate with A	1	1	1	0	1	1	1	0	7	EI	Enable Interrupts	1	1	1	1	1	0	1	1	4
ORI	Or immediate with A	1	1	1	1	0	1	1	0	7	DI	Disable Interrupt	1	1	1	1	0	0	1	1	4
CPI	Compare immediate with A	1	1	1	1	1	1	1	0	7	NOP	No operation	0	0	0	0	0	0	0	0	4
ROTATE											HLT	Halt	0	1	1	1	0	1	1	0	5
RLC	Rotate A left	0	0	0	0	0	1	1	1	4	**NEW 8085A INSTRUCTIONS**										
RRC	Rotate A right	0	0	0	0	1	1	1	1	4	RIM	Read Interrupt Mask	0	0	1	0	0	0	0	0	4
											SIM	Set Interrupt Mask	0	0	1	1	0	0	0	0	4

NOTES 1 DDD or SSS B 000, C 001, D 010, E 011, H 100, L 101, Memory 110, A 111
2 Two possible cycle times. (6/12) indicate instruction cycles dependent on condition flags

*All mnemonics copyright ●Intel Corporation 1977

source register (SSS = 111) to the destination register (DDD = 001). In an assembly language listing, this op code, in hex, and mnemonic would be

$$4F \qquad \text{MOV C,A}$$

Similarly, then, if the E register's contents are to be moved to the B register, the op code must be 01000011_2. In an assembly language format, this move would be

$$43 \qquad \text{MOV B,E}$$

Example 12-1

Describe the moves that are executed by each of the following instructions:

(a) 47   MOV B,A
(b) 57   MOV D,A
(c) 67   MOV H,A
(d) 6F   MOV L,A

Answer

(a) Moves data of A register to B register. (b) Moves data of A register to D register. (c) Moves data of A register to H register. (d) Moves data of A register to L register. These register-to-register moves do not affect the contents of the source register.

The H and L registers of the 8085A MPU, as a pair, serve as a 16-bit *pointer register*. This means that with memory reference instructions the H-L register pair points to the referenced memory location, which can be any 1 of up to 65,536. For example, if the accumulator's data are to be added to the contents of location $20E3_H$, the H and L registers would have to contain 20_H and $E3_H$, respectively, and then the instruction ADD M would perform this arithmetic operation. We can describe this action as follows: When the MPU decodes the op code 86_H, the code for ADD M, it loads its incrementer/decrementer address latch (equivalent of the memory address register of the J-100) (see Fig. 12-1) with the 16-bit address residing in the H-L register pair. Thus the operand is read out of the memory location whose address ($20E3_H$ in this case) is in the address latch. The arithmetic logic unit (ALU) then performs the addition. After the addition is executed, the sum is in the accumulator. The H-L register pair can be loaded before the ADD M instruction with a load immediate instruction: LXI H. Thus in assembly language format we could have

```
21E320      LXI   H, 20E3H
86          ADD   M
```

A pointer register, like the H-L register pair, allows for 1-byte memory reference instructions and, therefore, shorter program execution times in certain applications. Equally as important, the H-L register pair can be incremented or decremented; see the INX H and the DCX H instructions of Table 12-1. This gives the programmer indexing capability.

12-5 Number Crunching

We can get a better feel for the 8085A by analyzing programs that perform familiar functions. For example, in Chapter 8 (Fig. 8-6), we studied an MC6800 program that added two numbers; obtaining them from RAM locations and stored the sum in RAM. Here, in Fig. 12-11(A), we have an 8085A program doing a very similar thing. As mentioned before, LXI H is a 3-byte instruction that loads the H and L registers with 20_H and $A1_H$, respectively. Next, the 3-byte LDA instruction loads the accumulator from location 20A0. ADD M then adds data 2, from location M, to data 1 already in the accumulator—remember that the H-L register pair points to M. The resulting sum is then in the accumulator. Finally, INX H increments the H-L register pair, causing it to point to location 20A2 during the MOV

Mem. loc.	Op code/address	Mnemonic	Comments
2000	21	LXI H	Load H-L reg. pair with $20A1_H$
2001	A1		LSBs of operand address
2002	20		MSBs of operand address
2003	3A	LDA	Load acc. from mem. address 20A0
2004	A0		LSBs of operand address
2005	20		MSBs of operand address
2006	86	ADD M	Add contents of 20A0 with contents of acc.
2007	23	INX H	Increment H-L reg. pair
2008	77	MOV M, A	Move contents of acc. (sum) to location 20A2
2009	CF	RST 1	Jump to monitor progm restart; address 0008*
20A0	Data 1		
20A1	Data 2		
20A2	Sum		

(A)

```
2000    21A120    LXI    H, 20A1H
2003    3AA020    LDA    20A0H
2006    86        ADD    M
2007    23        INX    H
2008    77        MOV    M, A
2009    CF        RST 1
  .
  .
  .
```

(B)

Fig. 12-11. (A) 8085A program that adds the contents of locations 20A0 and 20A1 and stores the sum at 20A2; see comparable program in Fig. 8-6; (B) typical assembly listing.

M,A operation. The last instruction could be a HLT instead of the RST 1 instruction shown.*

Note that the second and third bytes of the LXI H and LDA instructions specify the LSBs and MSBs, respectively, of the operand address. This se-

* RST 1 is preferred in place of HLT if the reader has Intel's SDK-85 system design kit available. With this kit, the RST 1 instruction causes a jump to ROM where the monitor program resides. The monitor allows the kit operator to observe unaltered contents of all registers after programs are executed.

quence is opposite of the MC6800's, with its 3-byte instructions. Our attention is required on this matter only if we are loading programs via a hex keyboard or register switches. Programming via an assembler would relieve us of such concerns. An assembly listing of this program is shown in Fig. 12-11(B); sequence and comment fields are not shown.

At this point we should note that the 8085A instruction set includes IN and OUT instructions, under the INPUT/OUTPUT heading in Table 12-2. These are 2-byte instructions. The IN instruction followed with the second byte, XX_H, inputs data from the I/O device that has the address XX_H and places these data in the accumulator. The OUT instruction, followed by a byte, XX_H, outputs the contents of the accumulator to the I/O device whose address is XX_H. Since the second byte has 8 bits, the 8085A can access up to 256_{10} I/O devices or functions through the IN and OUT instructions. During data transfers by the IN or OUT instructions, the 8085A's output $IO/\overline{M}$ goes HIGH. This disables all ROM and RAM so that I/O addresses on AD_7–AD_0 are never confused with memory locations having the same addresses.

12-6 Digital-to-Analog Converter Application

An MPU can be used to output data to a digital-to-analog converter (DAC), as shown in Fig. 12-12. The 8156 chip serves as the interface and as RAM. The waveshape and frequency of V_{out} can be selected and controlled by software. In the example here, V_{out} is a sawtooth waveform as might be required by the X input of a chart recorder or the horizontal input of a scope. For illustrative and experimental purposes, the program of Fig. 12-13 is shown in RAM locations, though typically such programs would be stored in ROM. By driving the CE input of the 8156 with A_{13} out of the MPU, 256_{10} bytes of RAM can be accessed with addresses 2000_H–$20FF_H$.

Referring to Fig. 12-13, we shall call the information in locations 2000–200F the *main* program. The time delay subroutine resides in locations 2020–202D.

At location 2000, MVI A is a 2-byte immediate mode instruction that loads the accumulator with 01_H. Next, OUT 20_H outputs the contents of the accumulator, 01_H in this case, to the I/O device that has the address 20_H. We recall that the command register (CR) has the address $XXXXX000_2$, and since $20_H = 00100000_2$, the CR is loaded with 01_H. Note in Fig. 12-7(A) that this defines port A *(PA)* as an output port. Next, LXI SP is a 3-byte instruction that loads the stack pointer (SP) with $20BF_H$. As with the MC6800, the SP points to the current location of the stack. The 1-byte INR A instruction simply increments the contents of the accumulator. The 2-byte OUT 21_H instruction then outputs the accumulator's contents to the I/O device whose address is 21_H. We recall again that *PA* has the address $XXXXX001_2$ and therefore responds to 21_H. Thus *PA* outputs the data of the accumulator to the DAC, and therefore V_{out} is an analog equivalent of

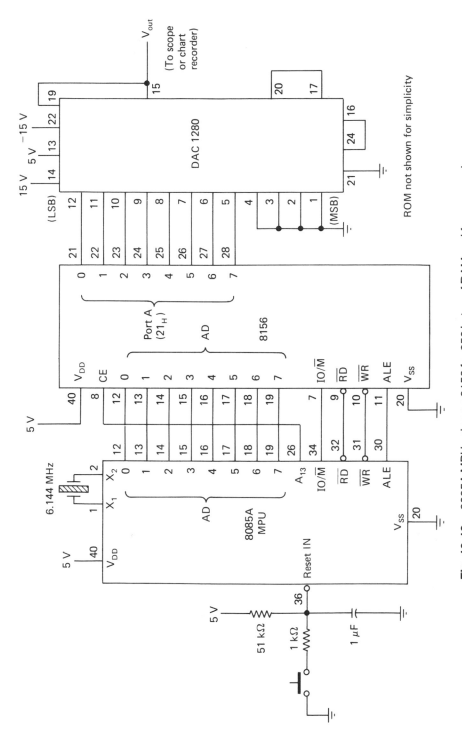

Fig. 12-12. 8085A MPU using an 8156 for 256 bytes of RAM and for communicating with a digital-to-analog converter, via port A, to synthesize waveforms for scope or chart recorder.

353

Memory address	Hex code	Mnemonic	Comments
2000	3E	MVI A, 01H	MOVE IMMEDIATE 01 INTO A-REGISTER
2001	01		
2002	D3	OUT 20H	OUTPUT A-REGISTER TO PORT 20; THE COMMAND REGISTER, MAKES PORT A AN OUTPUT PORT
2003	20		
2004	31	LXI SP, 20BFH	LOAD STACK POINTER
2005	BF		
2006	20		
2007	3C	INR A	INCREMENT THE A-REGISTER
2008	D3	OUT 21H	OUTPUT A-REGISTER TO PORT 21
2009	21		
200A	CD	CALL 2020H	CALL TIME DELAY SUBROUTINE, PUSHES PROGRAM COUNTER ONTO STACK
200B	20		
200C	20		
200D	C3	JMP 2007H	JUMP BACK TO INR A AFTER RET
200E	07		
200F	20		
. . .			
2020	F5	PUSH PSW	PUSH PROCESSOR STATUS WORD ONTO STACK
2021	D5	PUSH D	PUSH D-E REGISTER PAIR ONTO STACK
2022	11	LXI D, 4FFFH	LOAD IMMEDIATE D-E REGISTER PAIR; SET DELAY TIME
2023	FF		
2024	4F		
2025	1B	DCX D	DECREMENT D-E REGISTER PAIR
2026	7A	MOV A, D	MOVE D-REGISTER TO A-REGISTER
2027	B3	ORA E	LOGIC OR E-REGISTER WITH A-REGISTER
2028	C2	JNZ 2025H	JUMP IF NOT ZERO TO LOCATION 2025
2029	25		
202A	20		
202B	D1	POP D	POP D-E REGISTER PAIR OFF STACK
202C	F1	POP PSW	POP PROCESSOR STATUS WORD OFF STACK
202D	C9	RET	RETURN TO MAIN PROGRAM FROM SUBROUTINE

Fig. 12-13. 8085A program that generates sawtooth voltage V_{out} for the circuit of Fig. 12-12.

those data. The CALL instruction calls the time delay subroutine, which means that the program jumps to the starting address of the subroutine. It does this by first pushing the current contents of the PC, 200D (location of JMP) in this case, onto the stack and then places the second and third bytes of the CALL in the PC. Thus when RETurning from the subroutine, the MPU pops the address 200D off the stack and puts it back into the PC. The main program thus resumes with the JMP instruction, which causes a jump back to location 2007. At 2007, INR A again increments the accumulator, and the process of OUTputting its contents and CALLing the subroutine is repeated over and over. The resulting V_{out} waveform is a staircase, like that of Fig. 11-3(A).

The time delay subroutine starts with a PUSH PSW. This instruction pushes the processor's status word (PSW) onto the stack. The PSW includes the contents of the accumulator and the flag register. Saving the contents of the accumulator is very important in this application. Next, the PUSH D instruction pushes both D and E registers onto the stack too. This is done because these registers are being used in this subroutine, and it is generally good practice to save their contents, which would otherwise be lost. This could possibly affect other subroutines or programs not shown here. The immediate mode LXI D loads the D-E register pair with $4FFF_H$, which sets the time delay and is equivalent to $20,479_{10}$. This causes the delay routine to go through $20,478_{10}$ time-delaying loops. That is, the DCX D decrements the D-E register pair and then MOV A,D moves the contents of the D register to the accumulator. ORA E logically ORs the contents of the E register with those of the accumulator; the result resides in the accumulator. If this result of the ORA E operation is not zero, the JNZ instruction causes a jump back to 2025, the location specified by this instruction's second and third bytes. In this way, the D-E register pair is repetitively decremented until its contents becomes 0000_H. At that time, the program falls through the loop and reads the POP D and POP PSW instructions. These pop the previously pushed information off the stack and restore the D and E registers and the processor status word to their status prior to the CALL of the delay routine. Finally, the RET pops the 200D off the stack and places it in the PC. The operation thus RETurns to the main program which OUTputs another byte to the ADC.

12-7 Analog-to-Digital Converter Application

The way an 8085A MPU can be interfaced with an ADC (analog-to-digital converter) is shown in Fig. 12-14. This is essentially equivalent to the MC6800-based circuit of Fig. 11-9. As before, the MPU outputs a START pulse that causes the ADC to start converting the analog input V_{analog} to a digital equivalent. Since it takes time for the ADC to complete its conversion, the MPU polls the $\overline{CC}$ (conversion complete) output, labeled $\overline{DONE}$/BUSY in this case, and thus waits for this ADC output to go LOW. While HIGH,

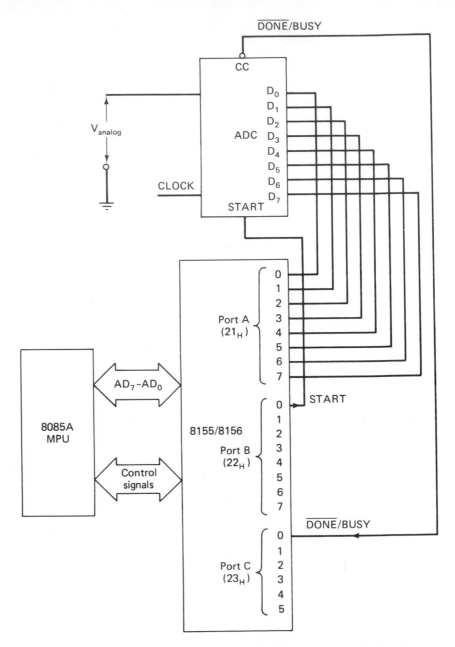

Fig. 12-14. Typical ADC (analog-to-digital converter) interfaced with an 8085A MPU.

Memory address	Hex code	Mnemonic		Comments
2000	21	LXI	H, 20A0H	LOAD H-L REGISTER PAIR WITH 20A0; THE
2001	A0			STARTING ADDRESS OF RAM LOCATIONS THAT
2002	20			WILL STORE EACH BYTE RECVD FROM THE ADC
2003	3E	MVI,	02H	LOAD ACCUMULATOR WITH 02H
2004	02			
2005	D3	OUT	20H	OUTPUT 20 TO COMMAND REGISTER; DEFINES PA AS
2006	20			INPUT, PB AS OUTPUT AND PC AS INPUT PORT
2007	3E	MVI,	01H	LOAD ACC WITH 01
2008	01			
2009	D3	OUT	22H	OUTPUT A START PULSE TO ADC
200A	22			
200B	DB	IN	23H	POLL PORT C; READ STATUS OF DONE/BUSY SIGNAL
200C	23			
200D	E6	ANI	01	MASK OUT UNWANTED BITS
200E	01			
200F	C2	JNZ	200BH	IF DONE/BUSY IS HIGH, JUMP TO 200B
2010	0B			
2011	20			
2012	DB	IN	21H	READ DIGITAL EQUIVALENT OF ANALOG SIGNAL
2013	21			FROM THE ADC
2014	77	MOV	M, A	STORE DIGITAL EQUIVALENT IN RAM
2015	23	INX	H	INCREMENT TO NEXT RAM LOCATION
2016	CF	RST 1		JUMP TO MONITOR PROGRAM RESTART

Fig. 12-15. Program that polls ADC of Fig. 12-14 and stores each byte in successive memory locations.

the $\overline{\text{DONE}}$/BUSY signal informs the MPU that the ADC is still busy converting. When done with its conversion, the ADC outputs a LOW $\overline{\text{DONE}}$/BUSY signal, and the MPU reads the now valid digital equivalent of V_{analog} from the ADC's outputs D_7–D_0. When reading, the MPU first INputs the ADC's output byte into the accumulator and then *moves* it to RAM. The program that causes the MPU to perform this function is shown in Fig. 12-15.

In Fig. 12-15, the LXI instruction loads the *H-L* register pair with the starting address of RAM in which successively read bytes from the ADC will be stored. MVI 02_H loads, immediate, the accumulator with 02_H. Then OUT 20_H places this 02_H in the command register. This defines *PA* as an input port, *PB* as an output port, and *PC* as an input port. Next, MVI 01_H loads the accumulator with 01_H, and then OUT 22_H outputs it to port *B*. This causes the ADC to start because the MPU outputs a START pulse. The MPU now enters a polling loop. IN 23_H polls the $\overline{\text{DONE}}$/BUSY signal; that is, it reads *PC* and places the result in the accumulator. The ANI 01_H performs a logic AND function with 01_H and the contents of the accumulator. This masks out all but the LSB in the accumulator; that is, all bits of the accumulator except the LSB definitely go LOW. The LSB goes HIGH or LOW depending on whether $\overline{\text{DONE}}$/BUSY is HIGH or LOW, respectively. If the LSB (the $\overline{\text{DONE}}$/BUSY bit) in the accumulator is HIGH, then the result of the ANI is a nonzero value, and the MPU jumps to location $200B_H$ as instructed to do by JNZ. Thus the MPU polls $\overline{\text{DONE}}$/BUSY until this signal goes LOW. When it does, the result of the ANI instruction is a zero in the accumulator. The MPU then falls through the loop and proceeds to IN 21_H. This instruction reads the valid digital equivalent (D_7–D_0) output of the ADC. The MOV M,A then moves it to memory. Next, INX H increments the pointer (*H-L* register pair) so that the next byte from the ADC is stored in the next higher RAM location. If this program were in ROM, the last instruction would not likely be RST 1.* Instead, an RET or an appropriate jump instruction would more likely be used.

12-8 The Z80 Microprocessor

Having been designed by some of the same people who designed Intel's 8080, the Z80 incorporates all the 8080 instructions as a subset of its own. But many new instructions were added as well as some hardware features that will be described here.

The Z80 requires only a single +5-V power supply, and although it needs an external clock, it need only be a single-phase clock of 5-V amplitude. The Z80 operates with clock frequencies up to 2.5 MHz, and a faster but otherwise identical version, called the Z80A, operates up to 4 MHz. Control signals are easily handled and don't require any demultiplexing.

The Z80 incorporates several features found in the MC6800, such as a nonmaskable interrupt, indexed addressing, relative addressing, extended addressing, and direct addressing.

In addition to these addressing modes, a new mode called *bit addressing* is available. Bit addressing allows the CPU to test, set, or reset any bit in any register or memory location with one instruction. (Remember that a masking operation was used in polling a particular bit in previous examples. The polling of a specific bit can be done with a single instruction with the Z80.)

A new BLOCK MOVE instruction allows you to move a large contiguous block of memory bytes from one memory location to another or to an I/O port. And a BLOCK COMPARE instruction lets you search a large block of memory for a specified bit pattern.

All in all, the Z80 has 80 more executable instructions than the 8080; however, we shall not study Z80 programming, since it is very similar to 8080/8085 programming.

There are a few additional internal hardware features that should be pointed out at this time.

* As mentioned before, RST 1 makes the program more convenient for experimental work on Intel's SDK-85 system design kit.

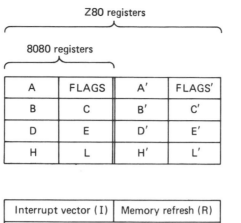

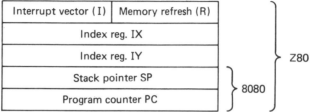

Fig. 12-16. Internal Z80 registers.

As shown in Fig. 12-16, in addition to containing all the 8-bit registers found in the 8080/8085, the Z80 contains a duplicate set, identified as the *primed* set $A'-L'$. This duplicate set allows a rapid saving of the program *environment* (all registers) by just two instructions. One instruction (EX AF,AF') swaps A' and F' with A and F, respectively,* and the other instruction (EXX) exchanges the contents of register pairs *BC, DE, HL* with *BC', DE', HL'*, respectively. Thus, when jumping to a subroutine, or to an interrupt service routine, all registers can be saved quickly without having to push each pair onto the stack.

Note in Fig. 12-16 that besides the *PC* and *SP*, the Z80 has two independent index registers, *IX* and *IY*, which are used just like the MC6800 index register. It also has an interrupt vector *(I)* register and a memory refresh *(R)* register.

You will remember that in the MC6800 system the programmer must load the starting address of the interrupt service routine into FFF8 and FFF9. In the Z80 system, the *program* loads the most significant byte of a *table* of interrupt service routine starting addresses into the *I* register. This is similar to the table of starting addresses stored in the highest memory locations, i.e., FFF8–FFFF, in the Motorola system. In this way, any one of *several* different routines can be quickly jumped to, depending on the contents of the *I* register. In fact, if the table is stored in RAM, the *I* register contents can be modified during program execution.

* *F* represents the flag register.

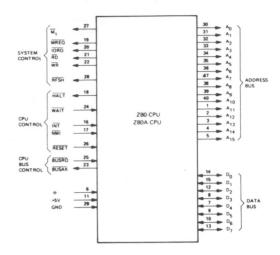

Fig. 12-17. Z80, Z80A CPU pin configuration. (Courtesy of Zilog, Inc. Z80 is a copyright of Zilog, Inc.)

The least significant byte of the interrupt vector (starting address of the routine) is obtained from the data bus while the CPU does an interrupt acknowledge. This will be explained later.

The final internal register is the memory refresh *(R)* register. It was mentioned in the chapter on memories that dynamic memories need periodic refreshing. The Z80 automatically outputs (onto the address bus) the address of the memory location to be refreshed following each op code fetch. This is accompanied by an active LOW MEMORY REQUEST ($\overline{\text{MREQ}}$) signal while the READ ($\overline{\text{RD}}$) and WRITE ($\overline{\text{WR}}$) are held inactive HIGH. This combination of signals is used to refresh any dynamic memories. The *R* register sequentially outputs new addresses after each op code fetch, eventually scanning through all possible addresses.

Figure 12-17 shows the pin assignments for the Z80/Z80A.

A description of the pins and controls of the Z80/Z80A* follows:

A_0–A_{15} (address bus)	Tri-state output, active HIGH. A_0–A_{15} constitute a 16-bit address bus. The address bus provides the address for memory (up to 64K bytes) data exchanges and for I/O device data exchanges.	D_0–D_7 (data bus)	Tri-state input/ output, active HIGH. D_0–D_7 constitute an 8-bit bidirectional data bus. The data bus is used for data exchanges with memory and I/O devices.

* Reprinted by permission of Zilog, Inc. Z80 is a copyright of Zilog, Inc.

$\overline{M_1}$
(machine
cycle one)

Output, active low. $\overline{M_1}$ indicates that the current machine cycle is the op code fetch cycle of an instruction execution.

$\overline{MREQ}$
(memory
request)

Tri-state output, active LOW. The memory request signal indicates that the address bus holds a valid address for a memory read or memory write operation.

$\overline{IORQ}$
(input/
output
request)

Tri-state output, active LOW. The $\overline{IORQ}$ signal indicates that the lower half of the address bus holds a valid I/O address for an I/O read or write operation. An $\overline{IORQ}$ signal is also generated when an interrupt is being acknowledged to indicate that an interrupt response vector can be placed on the data bus.

$\overline{RD}$
(memory
read)

Tri-state output, active LOW. $\overline{RD}$ indicates that the CPU wants to read data from memory or an I/O device. The addressed I/O device or memory should use this sig-nal to gate data onto the CPU data bus.

$\overline{WR}$
(memory
write)

Tri-state output, active LOW. $\overline{WR}$ indicates that the CPU data bus holds valid data to be stored in the addressed memory or I/O device.

$\overline{RFSH}$
(refresh)

Output, active LOW. $\overline{RFSH}$ indicates that the lower 7 bits of the address bus contain a refresh address for dynamic memories and the current $\overline{MREQ}$ signal should be used to do a refresh read to all dynamic memories.

$\overline{HALT}$
(halt state)

Output, active LOW. $\overline{HALT}$ indicates that the CPU has executed a HALT software instruction and is awaiting either a nonmaskable or a maskable interrupt (with the mask enabled) before operation can resume. While halted, the CPU executes NOPs to maintain memory refresh activity.

$\overline{WAIT}$
(wait)

Input, active LOW. $\overline{WAIT}$ indicates to the Z80

CPU that the addressed memory or I/O devices are not ready for a data transfer. The CPU continues to enter wait states for as long as this signal is active.

$\overline{INT}$
(interrupt request)

Input, active LOW. The interrupt request signal is generated by I/O devices. A request will be honored at the end of the current instruction if the internal software controlled interrupt enable flip-flop (IFF) is enabled.

$\overline{NMI}$
(non-maskable interrupt)

Input, active LOW. The non-maskable interrupt request line has a higher priority than $\overline{INT}$ and is always recognized at the end of the current instruction, independent of the status of the interrupt enable flip-flop. $\overline{NMI}$ automatically forces the Z80 CPU to restart to location 0066_H.

$\overline{RESET}$

Input, active LOW. $\overline{RESET}$ initializes the CPU as follows: Reset interrupt enable flip-flop, clear PC and registers I and R, and set interrupt to 8080A mode. During reset time, the address and data bus go to a high-impedance state and all control output signals go to the inactive state.

$\overline{BUSRQ}$
(bus request)

Input, active LOW. The bus request signal has a higher priority than $\overline{NMI}$ and is always recognized at the end of the current machine cycle and is used to request the CPU address bus, data bus, and tri-state output control signals to go to a high-impedance state so that other devices can control these buses.

$\overline{BUSAK}$
(bus acknowledge)

Output, active LOW. Bus acknowledge is used to indicate to the requesting device that the CPU address bus, data bus, and tri-state control bus signals have been set to their high-impedance state and the external device can now control these signals.

12-9 Interfacing the Z80

Figure 12-18 shows how a minimum Z80 system can be built. As is usual with most MPUs, a ROM is needed as well as some sort of I/O device. In this case, the system can be used for some dedicated control application, such as a sequence controller. The control program is burned into the 2704 EPROM. Then after reset, the program is run, occasionally outputting bit patterns at the 74LS75 latch outputs. The latched outputs can be fed to optoisolators which drive lamps, motors, pumps, or whatever.

The timing loops and output bit patterns are all stored in the EPROM and are normally repeated over and over. However, should it become necessary to modify the sequence slightly, either to change the timing or operation, the EPROM can be erased and a new program burned in.

Note that $\overline{\text{MREQ}}$ and $\overline{\text{RD}}$ are gated together to enable the EPROM. As described earlier, $\overline{\text{MREQ}}$ goes active LOW whenever a memory READ or WRITE is executed. The output latch, on the other hand, is enabled when $\overline{\text{WR}}$ and $\overline{\text{IORQ}}$ both go active LOW, which occurs whenever the MPU does an OUT instruction. Since the EPROM and the latch are the only two devices being used here, no address decoding is necessary.

The clock can be any astable multivibrator, operating at a frequency up to 2 MHz. However, it must have an output swing from 0 to +5 V, with rise and fall times less than 30 nsec.*

All unused input pins (not shown), such as $\overline{\text{WAIT}}$, $\overline{\text{INT}}$, etc., should be pulled up to V_{CC} through pull-up resistors of 10K or so.

A more powerful microcomputer system having ROM, RAM, input, and output circuitry is shown in Fig. 12-19. Note that the 2716 EPROM connects to the MPU via the address bus and data bus. Being a 2K × 8 EPROM, it requires 11 address lines. The slash line through the heavy address bus with the number 11 nearby indicates that 11 lines form that part of the bus. Similarly, note that only 8 lines form the part of the address bus going to the 2112A RAM chips, since the RAM contains only 256 bytes.

Getting back to the EPROM, note that the chip enable $\overline{\text{CE}}$ and output enable $\overline{\text{OE}}$ are driven active LOW by gate 4 when $\overline{\text{MREQ}}$ and $\overline{\text{RD}}$ are active LOW, while address line A_{15} is inactive LOW. Thus the EPROM responds to addresses 0000–07FF. Like the 8080/8085, the Z80 program counter is reset to zero by a system $\overline{\text{RESET}}$. The initialization program, then, should begin in ROM at address 0000. The RAM chips are enabled when $\overline{\text{MREQ}}$ and either $\overline{\text{RD}}$ or $\overline{\text{WR}}$ are active LOW, while A_{15} is active HIGH. Thus, the RAM responds to 8000–80FF. Of course RAM space may begin at any address not used by ROM, at the system designer's discretion.

The microcomputer uses a 74LS244 tri-state octal buffer to input data from an external source. The input buffer is enabled by gate 7 during execution

---

* The *rise time* of a waveform is defined as the time it takes for the waveform to change from 10% to 90% of its final value, e.g., 0.5–4.5 V for a 5-V peak signal. The *fall time* is defined as the time it takes to fall from 90% to 10% of its initial value, e.g., 4.5–0.5 V.

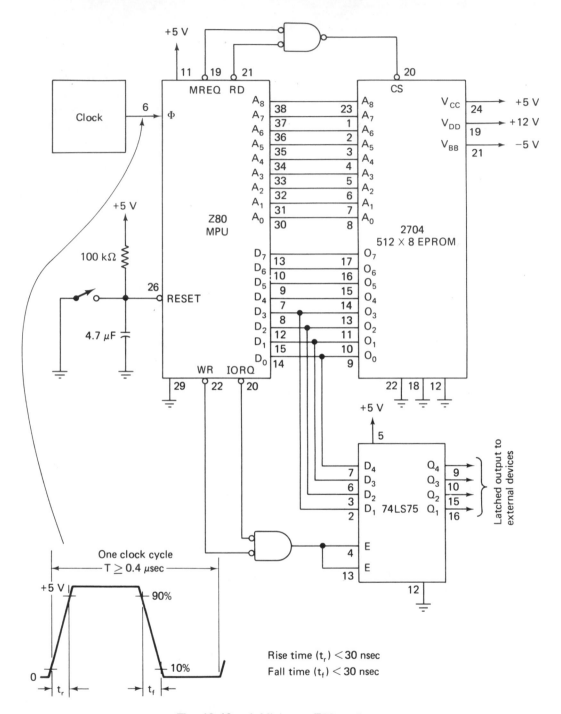

Fig. 12-18. A Minimum Z80 system.

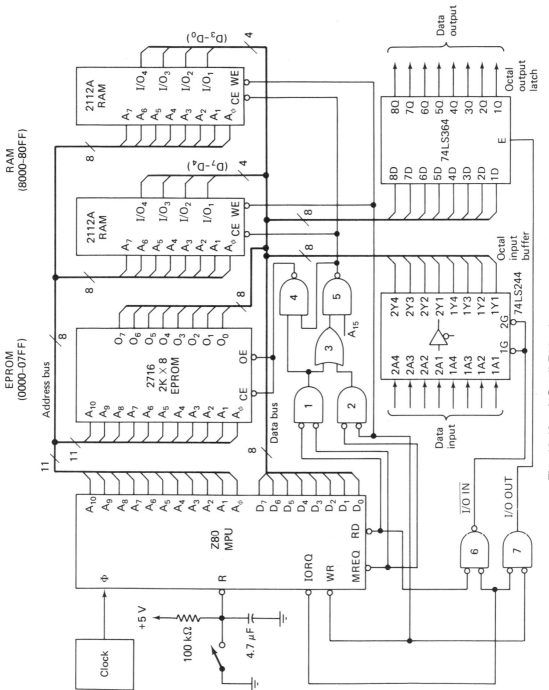

Fig. 12-19. A Small Z80 microcomputer system.

365

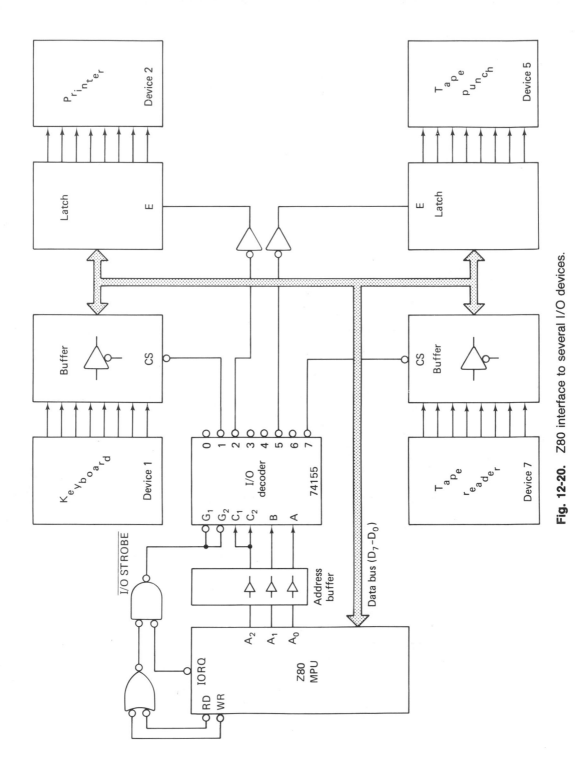

Fig. 12-20. Z80 interface to several I/O devices.

366

of an IN instruction, which causes $\overline{\text{IORQ}}$, and $\overline{\text{RD}}$ to go active LOW. Likewise, the 74LS364 octal latch, which is used to output data from the MPU to an external device, is enabled by the output of gate 8 going HIGH during the execution of an OUT instruction. The MPU drives $\overline{\text{IORQ}}$ and $\overline{\text{WR}}$ active LOW when executing an OUT instruction.

Since only one input device and one output device are shown, no I/O decoding is necessary. However, in a larger system having several I/O devices, some means of selecting the desired device is needed. I/O decoding is accomplished in the same manner as with the 8085A. The address of the selected I/O device is output on the eight least significant address lines at the same time that the MPU executes an IN or OUT instruction.

A program byte following the IN or OUT instruction identifies the device. For example, suppose the MPU interfaces with a keyboard, a tape reader, a printer, and a tape punch, as shown in Fig. 12-20. When the MPU executes the instruction IN 01, an $\overline{\text{I/O STROBE}}$ is generated which enables the 74155, a 1 of 8 decoder. The decoder then decodes address lines A_2, A_1, and A_0, which at this time are at 001, respectively. (The second byte of the instruction, 01H, is output on the address bus.) Output 1 of the decoder goes active LOW, enabling the tri-state input buffer connected to the keyboard (device 1), thus causing the keyboard outputs to be placed on the data bus. The data bus is simultaneously read by the MPU, thereby loading the keyboard data into the accumulator.

Similarly, to output a byte to the tape punch, the MPU executes an OUT 05 instruction. The I/O decoder decodes address lines A_2, A_1, and A_0 (101) and drives its output 5 LOW. This enables the latch connected to the tape punch, while the MPU simultaneously outputs the accumulator contents onto the data bus.

The address buffer, shown between the MPU and the I/O decoder, is used to prevent excessive loading on the address lines. Address buffers are normally used whenever an MPU must interface with several devices, since the loading on any one line must not exceed one TTL load.

Like other MPUs, the Z80 has a parallel interface chip, called the Z80-PIO, which is similar to Motorola's PIA. The PIO has two ports which can be programmed as either inputs or outputs. It also has interrupt capabilities. The Z80 treats the PIO as an I/O device, communicating with it by means of IN and OUT instructions, rather than treating it as memory space, like the M6800 does with the PIA. Figure 12-21 shows the pin configuration of the PIO.

Figure 12-22 shows how two PIOs can be used to interface the same four peripheral devices as in Fig. 12-20.

As shown in Fig. 12-22, each PIO has two address inputs, which are used for register selection. Address line A_0 connects to the $B/\overline{A}$ input and selects port B or port A. Similarly, address line A_1 connects to the $C/\overline{D}$ input which is used to select the control register or data register (output register) of the selected port. These are similar to Mororola's PIA register

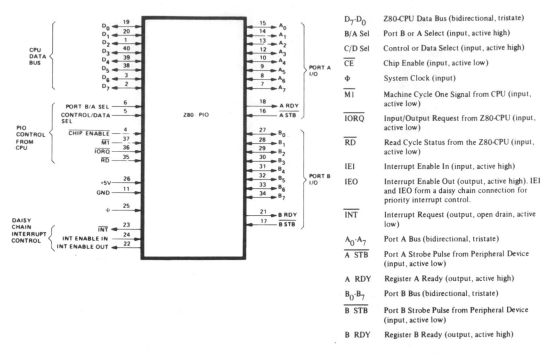

Fig. 12-21. Z80 PIO pin description. (Reprinted by permission of Zilog, Inc. Z80 is a copyright of Zilog, Inc.)

select (RS) inputs. In addition, $\overline{MI}$, $\overline{IORQ}$, and $\overline{RD}$ are connected to each PIO for control purposes.

Although we shall not discuss the complete initialization of the PIO, the procedure is very similar to initializing the MC6821 PIA. Each port is loaded with control bytes which configure it as an input or output port, set up interrupt conditions, etc.

Note that the address lines feeding the I/O decoder, in this case, are A_6, A_5, and A_4. To select PIO 1, A_6, A_5, and A_4 must be 001, respectively. Similarly, to select PIO 2, A_6, A_5, and A_4 must be 010, respectively. Thus, to load a control byte into port A of PIO 1, the MPU first loads the control byte into the accumulator. Next, the MPU executes an OUT 12 instruction. When executing OUT 12, the least significant bits of the address bus are as follows:

A_7	A_6	A_5	A_4	A_3	A_2	A_1	A_0
0	0	0	1	0	0	1	0

Address bits A_6, A_5, and A_4, being 001, respectively, drive output 1 of the I/O decoder LOW, enabling PIO 1. Address line A_0 being LOW selects port A, and A_1 being HIGH selects the control register of that port.

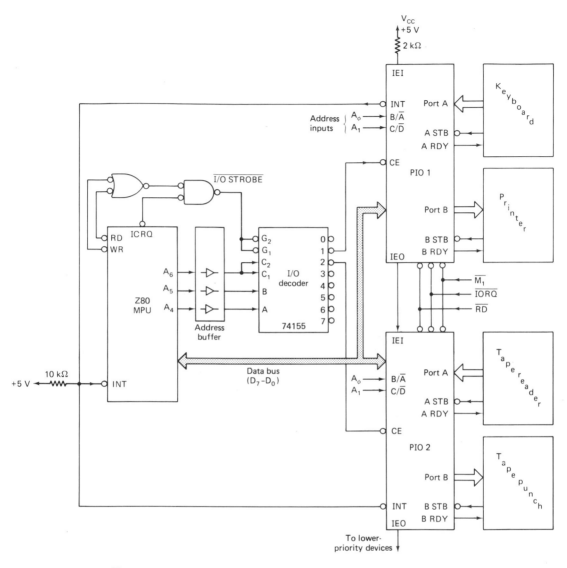

Fig. 12-22. Interfacing I/O devices to the Z80 with PIO chips.

While the I/O address is on the address bus, the MPU simultaneously outputs the accumulator contents onto the data bus, which now connects to the control register of port *A* of PIO 1.

Similarly, once the PIO has been properly initialized, the MPU can output a data byte from the accumulator to the printer by executing an OUT 11 instruction. Examine the addressing for yourself to see why an OUT 11 instruction outputs a byte to the printer.

12-10 Z80 Interrupt Handling

The last topic we shall study is how the Z80 handles interrupt requests. Actually, the Z80 has three different interrupt modes, but we shall look only at MODE 2, which is the most powerful mode.

Note in Fig. 12-22 that the $\overline{\text{INT}}$ outputs from both PIOs connect to the single $\overline{\text{INT}}$ input on the MPU. These are wire-ORed, as was done in the MC6800 system. Either PIO $\overline{\text{INT}}$ going LOW will request an interrupt from the MPU.

Let's assume that any one of the four peripheral devices shown can generate an interrupt request. To drive the $\overline{\text{INT}}$ output of a PIO active LOW, the peripheral device pulls its corresponding strobe ($\overline{\text{STB}}$) line LOW. For example, if the keyboard requests an interrupt, it pulls $\overline{\text{A STB}}$ of PIO 1 LOW. Similarly, if the tape punch requests an interrupt, it pulls $\overline{\text{B STB}}$ of PIO 2 LOW.

Either of these actions drive the $\overline{\text{INT}}$ input of the MPU LOW, thus signaling an interrupt request.

The question now arises as to how does the MPU know which device requested the interrupt? The MPU must know the answer to this question in order to jump to the proper interrupt service routine. (Since there are four peripheral devices, there must be four different interrupt service routines.)

Remember that the MC6800 solves this problem by polling the interrupt request flag bits in each PIA control register. But the Z80 uses a *vectored interrupt* technique, which is much faster.

Here's how it works: As each port of each PIO is initialized, an *interrupt vector* is loaded into a vector register inside that port. The vector is simply the least significant byte of a table of service routine starting addresses. The most significant byte of the table is loaded into the *I* register on initialization. Let's assume the interrupt service routines start at the following addresses.

Keyboard	0420 H
Printer	0510 H
Tape reader	05A0 H
Tape punch	0730 H

Let's also assume that the programmer decided to store this table in ROM, beginning at 07F0H. The table, shown in Fig. 12-23, contains the starting addresses of the service routines.

At time of initialization, the program loads the most significant byte of the table address (07) into the *I* register. It then loads the least significant byte of the table address (vector) into each PIO port vector register. In this case, the bytes F0, F2, F4, and F6 are loaded into PIO 1 port *A*, PIO 1 port *B*, PIO 2 port *A*, and PIO 2 port *B*, respectively.

Assuming that the interrupt vectors have been loaded into the vector registers as described, let's follow through the interrupt sequence for the keyboard.

Starting address pointed to by:

I Reg. (07)	PIO Vector Reg. (FØ)

Mem. loc.

Ø 7 F Ø	2 Ø	} Keyboard routine starting address
0 7 F 1	0 4	
0 7 F 2	1 0	} Printer routine starting address
0 7 F 3	0 5	
0 7 F 4	A Ø	} Tape reader starting address
0 7 F 5	Ø 5	
0 7 F 6	3 Ø	} Tape punch starting address
0 7 F 7	Ø 7	
0 7 F 8	– –	

Fig. 12-23. Interrupt service routine starting address table.

1. The keyboard (in response to a human operator pressing a key) pulls $\overline{\text{A STB}}$ LOW.

2. PIO 1 drives its $\overline{\text{INT}}$ line LOW, thus requesting an interrupt from the MPU.

3. If interrupts have been enabled within the MPU (by the program), the MPU finishes its current instruction and then pushes the program counter onto the stack. (Note that only the PC, not all registers, is pushed onto the stack. This is different from the MC6800.)

4. The MPU acknowledges the interrupt request by driving its $\overline{\text{M1}}$ and $\overline{\text{IORQ}}$ lines LOW, while keeping $\overline{\text{RD}}$ inactive HIGH.

5. PIO 1 responds to the above signals by placing the interrupt vector (F0H) of the requesting port onto the data bus.

6. The MPU reads the data bus at this time, loading the vector (F0H) into the accumulator.

7. Next the MPU combines the least significant byte (F0H) held by the accumulator with the most significant byte (07) held by the *I* register. This forms a pointer to the table of service routine addresses. See Fig. 12-23. The MPU then loads the contents of 07F0H into the lower byte of the PC and the contents of 07F1H into the upper byte of the PC.

8. The MPU now has the starting address of the requested interrupt service routine (0420H) in the PC. It jumps to the first instruction of that routine immediately, without having to poll other devices.

9. Upon completion of the service routine, a return from interrupt, RETI, instruction pulls 2 bytes off the stack and loads them into the PC. Program execution then continues where it left off prior to the interrupt.

As mentioned in step 3, only the PC is automatically pushed onto the stack when the MPU services an interrupt. If the programmer wishes to save the contents of other registers, the first instructions in his or her interrupt service routine must either push those registers onto the stack, or he or she can exchange them with the primed set.

The lines labeled $\overline{\text{A RDY}}$ (A READY) and $\overline{\text{B RDY}}$ (B READY), connecting from the PIOs to the peripheral devices in Fig. 12-22, are handshake lines. These can be programmed to signal the peripheral devices when their interrupt requests have been granted.

The Z80 system also provides a simple hardware solution to another problem that arises when two or more devices have the ability to request interrupt. Suppose two or more devices request service at the same time. Which one should be serviced? The problem here is one of interrupt *priority*. Higher-priority devices should get serviced before lower-priority devices.

The system designer must decide the priority of each device at the time he or she designs the hardware. He or she then simply connects the peripheral devices to the PIOs in the proper order.

Note in Fig. 12-22 that a pin labeled IEI (interrupt enable input) connects from PIO 1 to V_{CC}. Also the pin labeled IEO (interrupt enable output) from PIO 1 is connected to IEI on PIO 2. This forms a "daisy-chain" hardware-prioritized system. The PIO whose IEI is closest to V_{CC} has the highest priority. Port *A* also has higher priority than port *B*.

Here's how it works: Suppose the tape reader requests interrupt. If no higher-priority device (keyboard or printer) is being serviced, the MPU acknowledges the tape reader's interrupt request and begins servicing it. But if a higher-priority device, say the printer, requests interrupt, service to the tape reader will be suspended while the MPU jumps to the printer service routine. When finished with the printer routine, the MPU will automatically resume the tape reader routine. However, if the tape punch requests service while the tape reader is being serviced, the interrupt request will not be granted until the MPU returns from the tape reader routine.

IEO of PIO 1 goes LOW while either PIO 1 device is being serviced, thus disabling any interrupt requests from PIO 2. This daisy-chain connection can be extended to several PIOs in series or to other peripheral chips, such as Zilog's serial interface chip (Z80-SIO), or DMA controller (Z80-DMA), or counter/timer chip (Z80-CTC). These other chips have programmable vector registers like the Z80-PIO and can generate interrupts in the same manner. The starting addresses of their routines are similarly stored in the starting address table.

12-1 Which takes more time, a move instruction that transfers a byte from one register to another within the 8085A or a move that moves a byte from one of the registers to a memory location? Why? *Hint:* See the cycles column of the instruction set.

12-2 Referring to the program of Fig. 12-13, how many T states (cycles) does it take the MPU to execute the instructions in locations 2025–202A, that is, one time-delaying loop? Assume that the jump does occur.

12-3 The contents of what memory locations must we change to change the number of time-delaying loops in the delay subroutine of Fig. 12-13?

12-4 Referring to the program as it is in Fig. 12-13, about how long will it take the MPU to reach the RET instruction after the subroutine is CALLed? Assume that the 8085A's crystal frequency is 6.144 MHz.

12-5 Referring to Problem 12-4, about how long does it take this program and its associated hardware (the circuit of Fig. 12-12) to output one cycle of a sawtooth wave?

12-6 Referring to the circuit of Fig. 12-12, what are this circuit's RAM locations if CE is connected to A_{12} instead of A_{13}?

12-7 What change can we make in the circuit of Fig. 12-13 to cause it to output a negative (downward-sloping) staircase instead of a positive one?

12-8 If the A_{12} output of the MPU is wired to CE of the 8156 of Fig. 12-14, what change(s) must be made in the program of Fig. 12-15 if the function of the circuit and program is not to change?

In the circuit of Fig. 12-24, chip A10 is a 1 of 8 decoder. A_2–A_0 are its address inputs; $\overline{E_1}$, $\overline{E_2}$, and E_3 are its chip enables.

12-9 Referring to the circuit of Fig. 12-24, what logic levels on the A_{15}–A_{11} outputs of the MPU will cause chip A14 to become enabled?

12-10 Referring to the circuit of Fig. 12-24, what logic levels on the A_{15}–A_{11} outputs of the MPU will cause chip A15 to become enabled?

12-11 Referring to the circuit of Fig. 12-24, what logic levels on the A_{15}–A_{11} outputs of the MPU will cause chip A16 to become enabled?

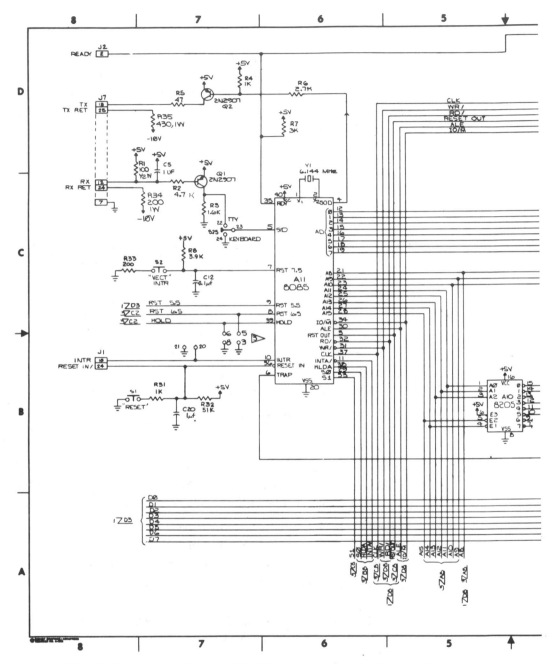

Fig. 12-24. Portion of Intel's SDK-85 system design kit. (Reprinted by permission of Intel Corporation, copyright 1977.)

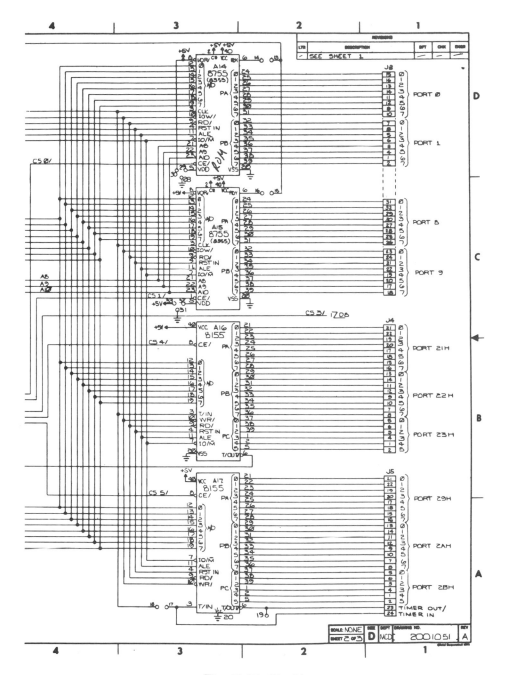

Fig. 12-24. (Cont.)

12-12 Referring to the circuit of Fig. 12-24, what logic levels on the A_{15}–A_{11} outputs of the MPU will cause chip $A17$ to become enabled?

12-13 How many ROM locations are available in the circuit of Fig. 12-24?

12-14 How many RAM locations are available in the circuit of Fig. 12-24?

12-15 Assume that the MPU in Fig. 12-18 is fetching an instruction from 0052H. List the logic levels you would expect to see on the following pins while executing the fetch (write in 1 or 0):

Z80 pins 19 __ 20 __ 21 __ 22 __
38 __ 37 __ 36 __ 35 __ 34 __ 33 __ 32 __
31 __ 30 __
2704 pin 20 __
74LS75 pins 4 __ 13 __

12-16 Assume that the MPU in Fig. 12-18 is executing an OUT instruction and that the accumulator contents are OCH. List the logic levels you would expect to see on the following pins:

Z80 pins 19 __ 20 __ 21 __ 22 __
2704 pin 20 __
74LS75 pins 7 __ 6 __ 3 __ 2 __ 4 __ 13 __
9 __ 10 __ 15 __ 16 __

Problems 12-17–12-20 refer to Fig. 12-19.

12-17 List the logic levels you would expect to see at each of the gate outputs while the MPU is executing an op code fetch from 0350H:

Gate 1 __ 2 __ 3 __ 4 __ 5 __ 6 __ 7 __

12-18 List the logic levels you would expect to see at each gate output while the MPU is storing the accumulator contents into 8032H:

Gate 1 __ 2 __ 3 __ 4 __ 5 __ 6 __ 7 __

12-19 List the logic levels you would expect to see at each gate output while the MPU is executing an IN instruction:

Gate 1 __ 2 __ 3 __ 4 __ 5 __ 6 __ 7 __

12-20 List the logic levels you would expect to see at each gate output while the MPU is executing an OUT instruction:

Gate 1 __ 2 __ 3 __ 4 __ 5 __ 6 __ 7 __

12-21 What instruction must the MPU of Fig. 12-20 execute in order to send a byte to the printer? (Show only the lowest I/O address that will select the printer.)

12-22 What instruction must the MPU of Fig. 12-20 execute to read a byte from the tape reader?

Refer to Fig. 12-22 for Problems 12-23–12-26.

12-23 If the CPU executes an IN 20 instruction, from which I/O device is it inputting data?

12-24 If the CPU executes an OUT 22 instruction, to which register of which PIO is it writing?

12-25 What I/O instruction should be executed to read a byte from the keyboard?

12-26 What I/O instruction should be executed to output a byte to the tape punch?

For the remaining problems, assume that the MPU interrupts have been enabled, that the interrupt vectors have been loaded into the PIO registers of Fig. 12-22, and that the starting address table is as shown in Fig. 12-23.

12-27 When the tape reader requests an interrupt by pulling $\overline{\text{A STB}}$ LOW, assuming no other device is being serviced, the PIO $\overline{\text{INT}}$ pin will go (HIGH, LOW) and IEI of PIO 2 will (go LOW, remain HIGH).

12-28 The MPU acknowledges the interrupt request and simultaneously reads in the interrupt vector on the data bus. What vector (what hex byte) will it read?

12-29 The MPU combines the vector with the contents of the *I* register and points to what location in the starting address table?

12-30 After getting the starting address from the table, the MPU jumps to the interrupt service routine. Where does the tape reader routine begin?

12-31 Suppose while executing the tape reader interrupt service routine, the tape punch requests an interrupt. Will the MPU acknowledge it?

12-32 Suppose while servicing the tape reader, the keyboard requests an interrupt. Will it be acknowledged?

APPENDIX A

Addressing Modes

Microcomputers and computers in general have more than a few addressing modes. We must understand, at least generally, addressing modes if we expect to be able to read a program listing and to determine what an MPU system is doing.

MC6800s, as do other 8-bit MPUs, have the following addressing modes:

> Immediate
> Direct
> Extended
> Index
> Inherent
> Relative

Note that these terms identify various columns in the instruction set of Tables 9-1, 9-2, and 9-3. As shown, some instructions have more than one addressing mode. For example, the op code for instruction ADDA is 8B for *immediate* mode, 9B for *direct* mode, AB for *index* mode, and BB for *extended* mode. Similarly, the LDAA instruction has op codes 86, 96, A6, and B6, respectively, for each of these modes.

Figure A-1(A) shows how the LDAA instruction works with *immediate* mode addressing (op code 86). It is a 2-byte instruction, as indicated under the # sign in Table 8-1. The second byte *is* the operand; that is, the second byte is the data this instruction will operate with. In this case, the value 30_H is loaded into accumulator *A*.

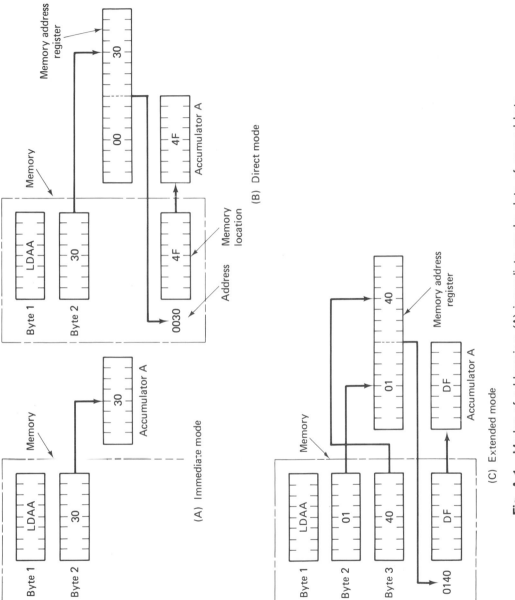

Fig. A-1. Modes of addressing: (A) immediate mode; data of second byte loaded into accumulator A; (B) direct mode; second byte points to 1 of 256₁₀ memory locations from which data are read; (C) extended mode; second and third bytes from a 16-bit address that point to one of 65,536₁₀ locations.

In (B) of Fig. A-1, we see how the LDAA instruction works with *direct* mode addressing (op code 96). As with the immediate mode, a direct mode instruction requires 2 bytes. With direct mode, however, the second byte is the *address* of the operand, not the operand itself. In computer terminology, we say that the second byte *points* to the address of the operand. When the MPU decodes a direct mode LDAA instruction, it places the second byte, 30_H in this case, into its memory address (MA) register. The MA register then applies its contents onto the address bus. In this case, the contents of address location 30_H, the value 4F, is read and loaded into accumulator *A*. Since the second byte has 8 binary bits, it has 256_{10} possible combinations. This means that a direct mode instruction can access from 0_{10} to 255_{10} memory locations or peripherals.

As shown in Fig. A-1(C), an extended mode instruction requires 3 bytes. The second byte identifies the most significant 8 bits of a 16-bit address, while the third byte identifies the 8 least significant bits. Thus the second and third bytes can point to as many as 65,536 memory locations or peripherals. Extended mode instructions must be used to access, ROM or RAM, locations higher than 255_{10}.

Index mode instructions are used when successive memory locations are to be accessed. For example, if a long list of data bytes is to be read and processed, index mode instructions are usually used. Similarly, if a list of data bytes is to be stored in successive memory locations, *index* mode

Fig. A-2. Index mode addressing.

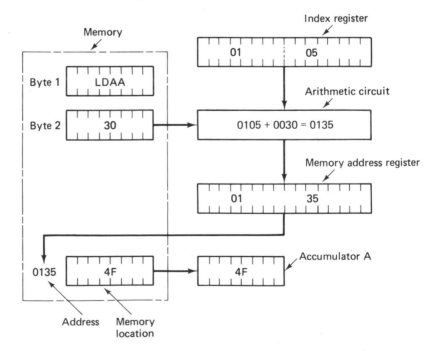

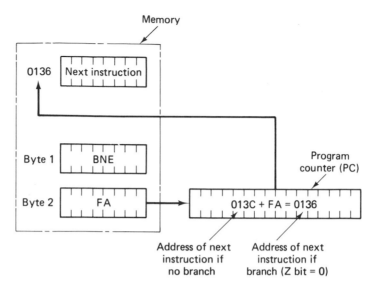

Fig. A-3. Relative mode addressing.

instructions serve the purpose. Figure A-2 shows how the LDAA instruction works with index mode addressing. As shown, it is a 2-byte instruction; the second byte, called the *offset* or *displacement,* is added to the contents of the index register. Their sum becomes a 16-bit address (0135 in this case) that points to the location from which data (4F in this case) are read and loaded into accumulator *A.* The index register is usually loaded by a 3-byte LDX instruction at the beginning of the program. Then after each data byte is read from memory, the index register is incremented (INX instruction) or decremented (DEX instruction), causing it, plus the displacement, to point to the location of the next data byte.

The branch instructions are *relative* mode instructions. For example, as shown in Fig. A-3, the BNE instruction (branch if not equal to zero) is a 2-byte instruction. If the result of the previous instruction is not equal to zero (the Z bit $= 0$ in the condition code register), the second byte (called the displacement or offset) adds to the contents of the program counter (PC). The sum is the new contents of the PC that then points to the location of the next instruction to be executed. If the offset is the value from 00_H to $7F_H$ (a positive number), the program branches to a higher memory location. If the offset is a value from 80_H to FF_H (a negative value), then the branch is to a lower memory location, as shown in Fig. A-3. The offset can add only to the 8 least significant bits of the PC. The 8 most significant bits of the PC are not affected by the offset.

APPENDIX B

TTL Device Numbering and Identifications; Comparisons within the TTL Family

5400 series: Temperature range, −55–125°C (military).
7400 series: Temperature range, 0–70°C (commercial).

Prefixes such as

DM   (National Semiconductor)
SN   (Texas Instruments)
MC   (Motorola)

indicate manufacturer.

Suffixes indicate package type, such as

G: TO–8 metal can—8, 10, 12 pin packages
N: molded DIP—8, 14, 16, 24 pin packages
F: flat package—multilead

383

TTL Device Num-
bering and Identifi-
cations; Compari-
sons within the TTL
Family

Example

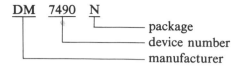

Device No.	Type	Gate Propagation Time (nsec)	Max. Clock Freq. (MHz)	Typical Unit Load	Power Dissipation per Gate (mW)
7400	Standard TTL	10–15	30	10	10
74H00	High-power TTL	6	50	12	20
74L00	Low-power TTL	30–40	3	3	1
74S00	Schottky	3	120	12	20
74LS00	Low-power Schottky	10	40	5	2

APPENDIX C

TTL Devices; Logic and Pin Diagrams

FLATPAK

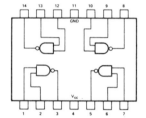

DIP

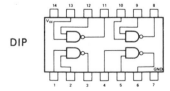

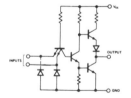

Diagram of each gate

54/7400 Quad two-input NAND gate.

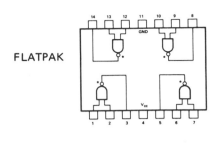

FLATPAK

DIP

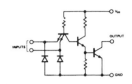

Diagram of each gate

54/7401 Quad two-input NAND gate.

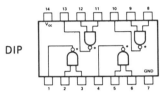

FLATPAK

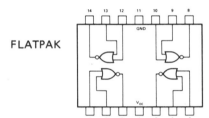

DIP

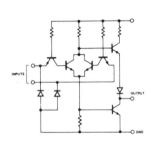

Diagram of each gate

54/7402 Quad two-input NOR gate.

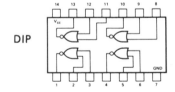

DIP

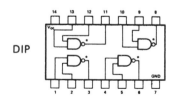

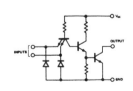

Diagram of each gate

54/7403 Quad two-input NAND gate.

FLATPAK

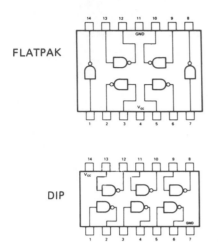

DIP

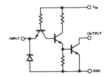

Diagram of each inverter

54/7404   Hex inverter.

FLATPAK

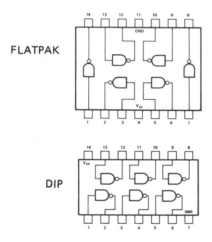

DIP

Diagram of each inverter

54/7405   Hex inverter with open collector.

FLATPAK

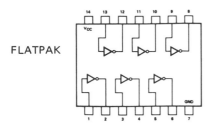

DIP

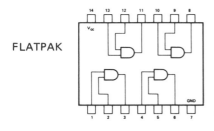

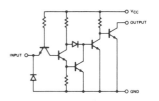

Diagram of each buffer

54/7406 Hex inverter buffer with open collector.

FLATPAK

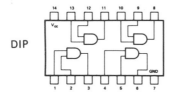

DIP

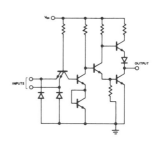

Diagram of each gate

54/7408 Quad two-input AND gate.

387

FLATPAK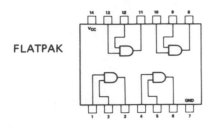

DIP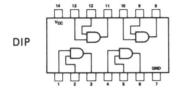

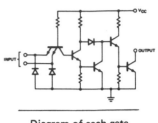

Diagram of each gate

54/7409   Quad two-input AND gate with open collector.

FLATPAK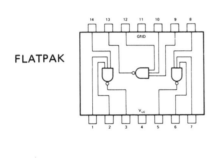

DIP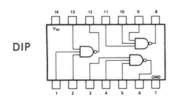

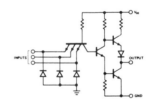

Diagram of each gate

54/7410   Triple three-input NAND gate.

FLATPAK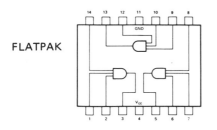

DIP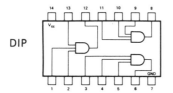

54/7411 Triple three-input AND gate.

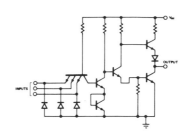

Diagram of each gate

FLATPAK or DIP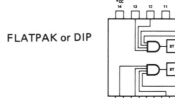

54/7413 Dual four-input Schmitt trigger.

FLATPAK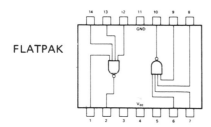

DIP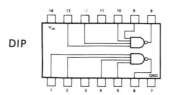

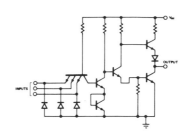

Diagram of each gate

54/7420 Dual four-input NAND gate.

FLATPAK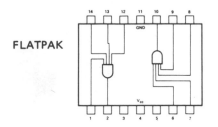

DIP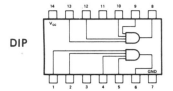

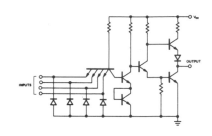

Diagram of each gate

54/7421   Dual four-input AND gate.

FLATPAK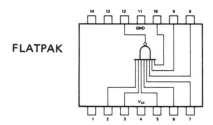

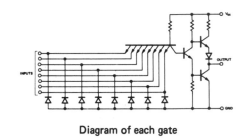

Diagram of each gate

DIP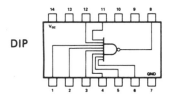

54/7430   Eight-input NAND gate.

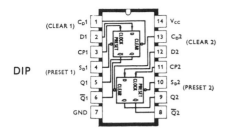
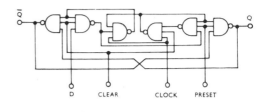

Logic diagram of each flip-flop

54/7474 Dual *D*-type edge-triggered flip-flop.

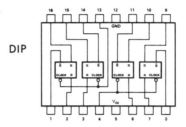

54/7475 Quad bistable transparent latch.

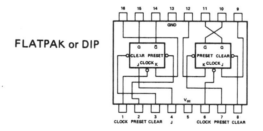

54/7476 Dual *JK* flip-flop.

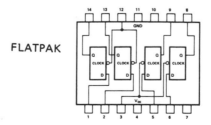

54/7477 Quad bistable transparent latch.

FLATPAK

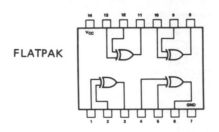

DIP

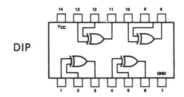

54/7486 Quad two-input exclusive OR gate.

DIP

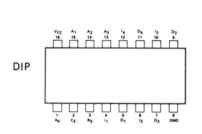

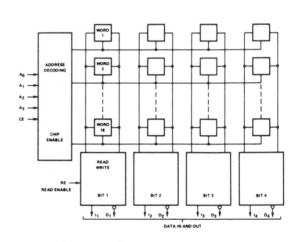

54/7489 16 × 4 read/write memory with open collector outputs.

FLATPAK

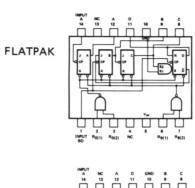

DIP

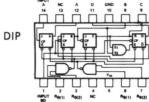

54/7490 Decade ripple counter.

FLATPAK

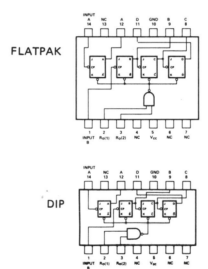

DIP

54/7493 Four-bit binary ripple
counter.

DIP

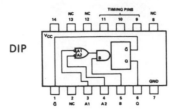

54/74121 Monostable multi-vibrator.

DIP

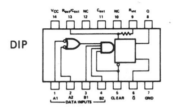

54/74122 Retriggerable monostable multivibrator.

DIP

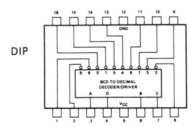

54/74141 BCD-to-decimal de-coder.

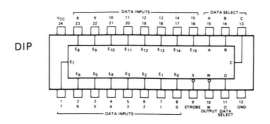

DIP

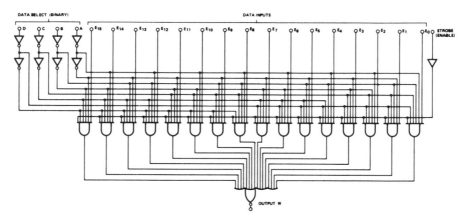

Circuit diagram

54/74150 16-to-1 multiplexer.

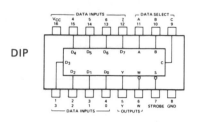

DIP

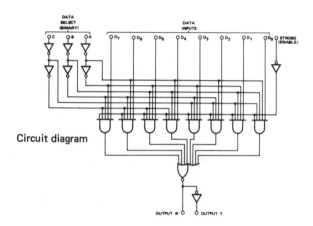

Circuit diagram

54/74151 8-to-1 multiplexer.

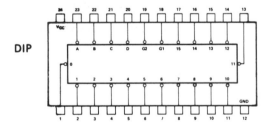

DIP

54/74154 1 of 16 decoder.

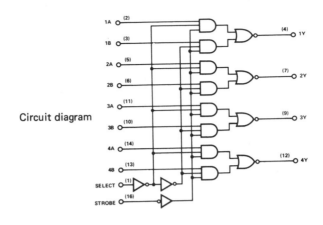

Circuit diagram

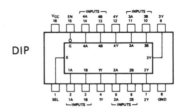

DIP

54/74157 Quad 2-to-1 multiplexer.

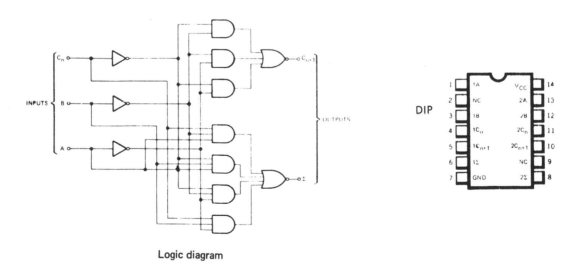

Logic diagram

54/74183 Dual full adder.

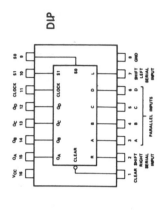

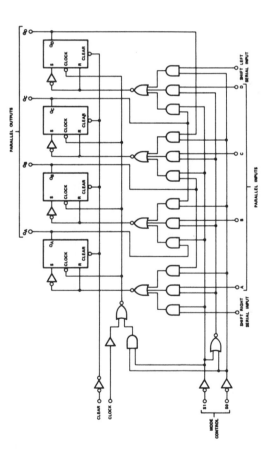

54/74194 Four-bit bidirectional shift register.

APPENDIX D

TTL Family Characteristics

STANDARD (54/74) TTL FAMILY DC CHARACTERISTICS

DC CHARACTERISTICS OVER OPERATING TEMPERATURES (Unless otherwise specified on Data Sheet)

	PARAMETER	TEST CONDITIONS		Min	Typ[1]	Max	UNIT
			LIMITS				
V_{IH}	Input HIGH voltage	Guaranteed input HIGH voltage for all inputs		2.0			V
V_{IL}	Input LOW voltage	Guaranteed input LOW voltage for all inputs				0.8	V
V_{CD}	Input clamp diode voltage	V_{CC} = Min, I_{IN} = −12mA			−0.8	−1.5	V
V_{OL}	Output LOW voltage	V_{CC} = Min, I_{OL} = 16mA				0.4	V
V_{OH}	Output HIGH voltage	V_{CC} = Min, I_{OH} = −800µA		2.4	3.5		V
I_{OH}	Output HIGH current (open collector)	V_{CC} = Min, V_{OUT} = 5.5V				250	µA
I_{OZH}	Output "off" current HIGH (3-state)	V_{CC} = Max, V_{OUT} = 2.4V, $V_{\overline{OE}}$ = 2.0V				40	µA
I_{OZL}	Output "off" current LOW (3-state)	V_{CC} = Max, V_{OUT} = 0.5V, $V_{\overline{OE}}$ = 2.0V				−40	µA
I_{IH}	Input HIGH current[2]	V_{CC} = Max, V_{IN} = 2.4V				40	µA
I_I	Input HIGH current at max input voltage	V_{CC} = MAX, V_{IN} = 5.5V				1.0	mA
I_{IL}	Input LOW current[2]	V_{CC} = Max, V_{IN} = 0.4V				−1.6	mA
I_{OS}	Output short circuit current	V_{CC} = Max, V_{OUT} = 0V	Mil	−20		−55	mA
			Com	−18		−55	mA

HIGH SPEED (54H/74H) TTL FAMILY DC CHARACTERISTICS

DC CHARACTERISTICS OVER OPERATING TEMPERATURES (Unless otherwise specified on Data Sheet)

	PARAMETER	TEST CONDITIONS	Min	Typ[1]	Max	UNIT
V_{IH}	Input HIGH voltage	Guaranteed input HIGH voltage for all inputs	2.0			V
V_{IL}	Input LOW voltage	Guaranteed input LOW voltage for all inputs			0.8	V
V_{CD}	Input clamp diode voltage	V_{CC} = Min, I_{IN} = −8mA		−0.8	−1.5	V
V_{OL}	Output LOW voltage	V_{CC} = Min, I_{OL} = 20mA			0.4	V
V_{OH}	Output HIGH voltage	V_{CC} = Min, I_{OH} = −500µA	2.4	3.5		V
I_{OH}	Output HIGH current (open collector)	V_{CC} = Min, V_{OUT} = 5.5V			250	µA
I_{OZH}	Output "off" current HIGH (3-state)	V_{CC} = Max, V_{OUT} = 2.4V, $V_{\overline{OE}}$ = 2.0V			50	µA
I_{OZL}	Output "off" current LOW (3-state)	V_{CC} = Max, V_{OUT} = 0.5V, $V_{\overline{OE}}$ = 2.0V			−50	µA
I_{IH}	Input HIGH current[2]	V_{CC} = Max, V_{IN} = 2.4V			50	µA
I_I	Input HIGH current at max input voltage	V_{CC} = Max, V_{IN} = 5.5V			1.0	mA
I_{IL}	Input LOW current[2]	V_{CC} = Max, V_{IN} = 0.4V			−2.0	mA
I_{OS}	Output short circuit current	V_{CC} = Max, V_{OUT} = 0V	−40		−100	mA

NOTES
1. Typical limits are at 25°C and V_{CC} = 5.0V
2. The specified limits reflect one unit load for the family. When more than one load is connected internally, the limits must be multiplied by the number of connected loads. See the INPUT AND OUTPUT LOADING AND FAN-OUT TABLE on the data sheets for the guaranteed limit for each input.

a subsidiary of U.S. Philips Corporation

SCHOTTKY (54S/74S) TTL FAMILY DC CHARACTERISTICS

DC CHARACTERISTICS OVER OPERATING TEMPERATURES (Unless otherwise specified on Data Sheet)

PARAMETER		TEST CONDITIONS		LIMITS			UNIT
				Min	Typ[1]	Max	
V_{IH}	Input HIGH voltage	Guaranteed input HIGH voltage for all inputs		2.0			V
V_{IL}	Input LOW voltage	Guaranteed input LOW voltage for all inputs				0.8	V
V_{CD}	Input clamp diode voltage	V_{CC} = Min, I_{IN} = −18mA			−0.65	−1.2	V
V_{OL}	Output LOW voltage	V_{CC} = Min, I_{OL} = 20mA				0.5	V
V_{OH}	Output HIGH voltage	V_{CC} = Min, I_{OH} = −1.0mA	Mil	2.5	3.4		V
			Com	2.7	3.4		V
I_{OH}	Output HIGH current (open collector)	V_{CC} = Min, V_{OUT} = 5.5V				250	μA
I_{OZH}	Output "off" current HIGH (3-state)	V_{CC} = Max, V_{OUT} = 2.4V, $V_{\overline{OE}}$ = 2.0V				50	μA
I_{OZL}	Output "off" current LOW (3-state)	V_{CC} = Max, V_{OUT} = 0.5V, $V_{\overline{OE}}$ = 2.0V				−50	μA
I_{IH}	Input HIGH current[2]	V_{CC} = Max, V_{IN} = 2.7V				50	μA
I_I	Input HIGH current at Max input voltage	V_{CC} = Max, V_{IN} = 5.5V				1.0	mA
I_{IL}	Input LOW current[2]	V_{CC} = Max, V_{IN} = 0.5V				−2.0	mA
I_{OS}	Output short circuit current	V_{CC} = Max, V_{OUT} = 0V		−40		−100	mA

LOW POWER SCHOTTKY (54LS/74LS) FAMILY CHARACTERISTICS

DC CHARACTERISTICS OVER OPERATING TEMPERATURES (Unless otherwise specified on Data Sheet)

PARAMETER		TEST CONDITIONS		LIMITS			UNIT
				Min	Typ[1]	Max	
V_{IH}	Input HIGH voltage	Guaranteed input HIGH voltage for all inputs		2.0			V
V_{IL}	Input LOW voltage	Guaranteed input LOW voltage for inputs	Mil			0.7	V
			Com			0.8	V
V_{CD}	Input clamp diode voltage	V_{CC} = Min, I_{IN} = −18mA			−0.65	−1.5	V
V_{OL}	Output LOW voltage	V_{CC} = Min, I_{OL} = 4.0mA			0.25	0.4	V
		V_{CC} = Min, I_{OL} = 8.0mA (Com. only)			0.35	0.5	V
V_{OH}	Output HIGH voltage	V_{CC} = Min, I_{OH} = −400μA	Mil	2.5	3.4		V
			Com	2.7	3.4		V
I_{OH}	Output HIGH current (open collector)	V_{CC} = Min, V_{OUT} = 5.5V				100	μA
I_{OZH}	Output "off" current HIGH (3-state)	V_{CC} = Max, V_{OUT} = 2.4V, $V_{\overline{OE}}$ = 2.0V				20	μA
I_{OZL}	Output "off" current LOW (3-state)	V_{CC} = Max, V_{OUT} = 0.4V, $V_{\overline{OE}}$ = 2.0V				−20	μA
I_{IH}	Input HIGH current[2]	V_{CC} = Max, V_{IN} = 2.7V				20	μA
I_I	Input HIGH current at Max input voltage	V_{CC} = Max, V_{IN} = 10V[3]				0.1	mA
I_{IL}	Input LOW current[2]	V_{CC} = Max, V_{IN} = 0.4V				−0.4	mA
I_{OS}	Output short circuit current	V_{CC} = Max, V_{OUT} = 0V		−15		−100	mA

NOTES

1. Typical limits are at 25°C and V_{CC} = 5.0V.
2. The specified limits reflect one unit load for the family. When more than one load is connected internally, the limits must be multiplied by the number of connected loads. See the INPUT AND OUTPUT LOADING AND FAN-OUT TABLE on the data sheets for the guaranteed limit for each input.
3. The following LS devices are limited to a 5.5V input breakdown voltage: All inputs of the LS181; clock inputs of LS90, LS92, LS93, LS196, LS197, LS290, LS293, LS390, LS393 and LS490.

Signetics
a subsidiary of **U.S. Philips Corporation**

Courtesy of Signetics Corporation

APPENDIX E

Rules for Using CMOS Devices

1. The leads of CMOS devices should be in contact with conductive material, such as the conductive foam in which they are inserted during shipping, except when being used.

2. Metal parts, such as soldering iron tips and tools, should be grounded before being placed in contact with a CMOS pin. Grounding straps on the wrists of persons handling a CMOS are also recommended.

3. CMOS ICs should never be removed or inserted in a circuit while the power is on.

4. Input signals should never be applied while the supply power is off.

5. All unused inputs must be connected to either the V_{DD} supply or to ground.

Answers to Selected Odd-Numbered Problems

Chapter 2

2-1 (a) 7, (b) 52, (c) 73, (d) 129, (e) 255, (f) 170, (g) 85, (h) 256

2-3 (a) 1100, (b) 11111, (c) 100000, (d) 1101001, (e) 11111110, (f) 100101100, (g) 11111111111, (h) 1000 0000 0000, (i) 1010 0110 0000, (j) 100 0000 0000 0000 0000

2-5 (a) 07, (b) 64, (c) 111, (d) 201, (e) 377, (f) 252, (g) 125, (h) 400

2-7 (a) C, (b) 1F, (c) 20, (d) 69, (e) FE, (f) 12C, (g) 7FF, (h) 800, (i) A60, (j) 4000

2-9 (a) 00001000, (b) 00010101, (c) 00011111, (d) 00111111, (e) 01000000, (f) 10011011, (g) 11101110, (h) 11111111

2-11 (f)–(h)

2-13 (a) 00001010, (b) 11000001, (c) 11101011, (d) 01111111, (e) 10001101, (f) 00110101

2-15 (b), (c), and (e)

2-17 (b) $11000001_2 = -63_{10}$
(c) $11101011_2 = -41_{10}$
(e) $10001101_2 = -115_{10}$

2-19 (a) $1111_2 = 15_{10}$, (b) $1111_2 = 15_{10}$, (c) $1010_2 = 10_{10}$, (d) $10000_2 = 16_{10}$, (e) $11110_2 = 30_{10}$, (f) $10000101_2 = 133_{10}$

2-21 (a) 1000, (b) 00 1010, (c) 1011 0110, (d) 0111 1110,
(e) 0000 0000, (f) 0101 0101, (g) 1010 1010, (h) 0 1111 1111

2-23

	Binary	Two's Complements	Octal	Hexadecimal
(a)	00101011	11010101	325	D5
(b)	11010100	00101100	054	2C
(c)	00000000	00000000	000	00
(d)	11111111	00000001	001	01

2-25 (a) 0001 0010, (b) 0011 0001, (c) 0011 0010,
(d) 0001 0000 0101, (e) 0010 0101 0100, (f) 0011 0000 0000,
(g) 0010 0000 0100 0111, (h) 0010 0000 0100 1000,
(i) 0101 0010 1000 0000, (j) 0001 0110 0011 1000 0100

2-27 (a) 0000 1000 or 08_H, (b) 0001 0100 or 14_H, (c) 1111 1110 or
FE_H, (d) 1100 1001 or $C9_H$

2-29 Answers to 27(c) and 27(d) are -2_{10} and -55_{10}, respectively.

2-31 (a) 0000 0010, (b) 1111 1110, (c) 0011 1111, (d) 1100 0001,
(e) 0111 0100, (f) 1000 1100

2-33 (a) 000011, (b) 001100, (c) 001010, (d) 001101, (e) 001111,
(f) 011000, (g) 011010, (h) 101011, (i) 111101

2-35 (a) 1000011, (b) 1001100, (c) 1001010, (d) 0001101, (e) 100111,
(f) 1011000, (g) 0011010, (h) 1101011, (i) 0111101

Chapter 3

3-1
00	LDA	0A
01	ADD	0B
02	ADD	0C
03	ADD	0D
04	ADD	0E
05	STO	0F
06	HLT	

3-3
00	LDA	0A
01	MUL	0A
02	PRT	
03	LDA	0A
04	ADD	0B
05	STO	0A
06	SUB	0C
07	BMI	00
08	HLT	

09
0A   2
0B   2
0C   50

3-5   (a) 2, (b) 6, (c) 10, (d) 20, (e) 25, (f) 25, (g) 25

3-9   (a) Yes, (b) no, (c) yes

3-11   00000   10101010
           00001   11101011
           00010   00100110
           00011   10101010
           00100   00001110
           00101   01100000
           00110   10101011
           00111   00001110
           01000   01100000
           01001
           01010
           01011

3-13   X = 1
                      I = 2
                      F = 99
           BEGIN   LDA X
                    MUL X
                    PRT
                    LDA X
                    ADD I
                    STA X
                    SUB F
                    BMI BEGIN
                    HLT

3-15   COMP 2   LDA A
                     SUB B
                     BMI BLARGE
                     LDA A
                     PRT A
                     HLT
           BLARGE   LDA B
                     PRT B
                     HLT

3-17   3

3-19   10   LET   A = 2
           20   LET   B = 3

```
30   LET  C=4
40   LET  X=5
50   Y = A * X ↑ 2 + B * X + C
60   PRINT Y
70   END
```

3-21
```
00   AA
01   CB
02   EC
03   OF
04   60
05
06
07
08
09
0A   07
0B   06
0C   08
0D
0E
0F   XX
```

3-23
```
A = 7
B = 6
C = 8
LDA  A
ADD  B
SUB  C
STO  R
HLT
```

Chapter 4

4-1 (a) $I = 10.9$ mA, (b) 24 V, (c) 0 V

4-3 (a) $I \cong 0$, (b) about 0 V, (c) about 24 V

4-5

X	V_{D_1}	V_{D_2}	V_{D_3}	V_R
0 V	0 V	0 V	0 V	5.5 V
0 V	0 V	0 V	5 V	5.5 V
0 V	0 V	4 V	0 V	5.5 V
0 V	0 V	4.5 V	5.2 V	5.5 V
0 V	4.4 V	0 V	0.2 V	5.5 V
0 V	5 V	0 V	5 V	5.5 V
0.1 V	3.9 V	3.7 V	0 V	5.4 V
3.8 V	0 V	0.2 V	1.5 V	1.7 V

4-7 (a) $I_C \cong 0$, $V_{CB} \cong V_{CC}$, (b) $I_C \cong V_{CC}/R_C$, $V_{CB} \cong 0$

4.9 $R_C = \dfrac{5\text{ V} - 1\text{ V}}{20\text{ mA}} = \dfrac{4\text{ V}}{20\text{ mA}} = 200\ \Omega$

4-11 $I = \dfrac{5\text{ V} - 0.6\text{ V}}{2\text{ k}\Omega} = 2.2\text{ mA}$

4-13 Yes, a standard TTL gate is able to sink and source 16 and 0.4 mA, respectively.

4-15 $\overline{D_0}$–$\overline{D_2}$ are LOW.

4-17 Outputs of inverters 5, 6, and 7 are LOW, HIGH, and LOW, respectively.

4-19 No, because a single standard TTL input requires a 1.6-mA sink capability of the device driving it

4-21 Yes, because Q_2, Q_4, and Q_5, working in parallel, will likely sink enough current to drive one standard TTL input

4-23 (a) About 3.5 V or higher, (b) about 1.5 V or less

4-27 Erratic switching at the output of the 7413

4-29 About 2.5 times that of a standard TTL gate or 25 standard TTL inputs

4-31 HIGH is 5 V for practical purposes. LOW is 0.5 μV or 0 V for practical purposes.

4-33 The STOP indicator lights, and the $\overline{\text{INHIBIT}}$ signal becomes active.

4-37 X_3–X_0 are 0000, Y_3–Y_0 are 1010, and Z_3–Z_0 are 1010.

4-39 Four two-input NAND gates (7400 chips)

4-41 Identical

4-43 Between times 2 and 3, 13 and 14, and 15 and 16

4-45 D_3–D_0 are 0000.

4-51 $I = \dfrac{5\text{ V} - 1\text{ V}}{220\ \Omega} \cong 18.2\text{ mA}$

4-53 $X_{C_1} = \dfrac{1}{2\pi f C_1} \cong 1.33 \times 10^9\ \Omega$; no significant coupling through this high reactance

4-59 A_3–A_0 must be $0000_2 = 00_8 = 0_{\text{H}}$ or $\overline{A_3}$–$\overline{A_0}$ must be $1111_2 = 17_8 = F_{\text{H}}$.

5-1 The Q output is **HIGH** between times 2 and 4, 6 and 9, 13 and 17, and after 18. $\overline{Q}$ is **LOW** in those same times.

5-3

CLOCK	A	B	C	D
0	1	1	0	0
1	0	1	1	0
2	0	0	1	1
3	1	0	0	1
4	1	1	0	0
5	0	1	1	0
6	0	0	1	1

5-5 The $\overline{\text{PRESET}}$ signal should go to the $\overline{S_D}$ (direct set) inputs of flip-flops A and B and to the $\overline{C_D}$ inputs of flip-flops C and D.

5-7

	D_7	D_6	D_5	D_4	D_3	D_2	D_1	D_0	Octal	Hexadecimal
After 1,	1	0	0	0	0	0	1	0	202	82
2,	0	0	0	1	0	1	0	0	024	14
3,	0	1	1	1	0	1	1	0	166	76
4,	1	1	1	0	1	0	0	0	350	E8
5,	1	0	0	0	1	0	1	0	212	8A
6,	0	0	0	1	1	1	0	0	034	1C

5-9

	D_7	D_6	D_5	D_4	D_3	D_2	D_1	D_0	Octal	Hexadecimal
After 1,					Indeterminate					
2,	0	0	0	1	0	1	0	0	024	14
3,	0	0	0	1	0	1	0	0	024	14
4,	0	0	0	1	0	1	0	0	024	14
5,	1	1	0	0	1	0	0	1	311	C9
6,	1	1	0	0	1	0	0	1	311	C9

5-15

$\overline{\text{CLOCK}}$	ABC	Dec. Equivs
0	LHH	6
1	HHL	3
2	LLH	4
3	HLH	5
4	LHH	6
5	HHL	3
6	LLH	4
⋮		

5-17 See answer for 5-15.

5-19 All the *JK* flip-flops and FF *A*, FF *B*, and FF *C* are cleared.

5-23 All are HIGH, and the LED lights.

5-27 Connect pin 12 to pin 14, CLOCK applied to pin 14, pins 2 and 3 grounded.

5-31 All applications (a)–(d)

5-33 The *CP* (CLOCK) input

5-35 Both $\overline{CE}$ and $\overline{PL}$ must be LOW.

5-37 A_{12}, A_{11}, and A_{10} must be 1, 1, and 0, respectively.

5-43 $031E_H$ or 001466_8

5-45 (a) D_2 and D_c are forward-biased; outputs $\bar{a}$, $\bar{b}$, $\bar{d}$, $\bar{e}$, and $\bar{g}$ are LOW, (b) D_6, D_7, and D_f are forward-biased; outputs $\bar{a}$, $\bar{c}$, $\bar{d}$, $\bar{f}$, and $\bar{g}$ are LOW, (c) D_{13} and D_i are forward-biased; all outputs $\bar{a}$–$\bar{g}$ are LOW.

5-49

	ERROR	NO ERROR
(a)	H	L
(b)	H	L

5-51

	The *S*-word
Row 1	E9
2	1E
3	6A

5-55 Pin 5, because it outputs a TTL-compatible signal; 74154 is a TTL device.

Chapter 6

6-1 4096

6-3 148

6-5 0; 1

6-7 0; 1

6-9 (c)

6-11 1024; 128; 8; 128; 8

6-13 LOW; HIGH; disables; enables; LOW; HIGH

6-17 7; 2; 1

6-19 One; . . . only the core at the intersection of the two lines

6-21 HIGH

6-23 No; yes; an open input on a TTL gate floats HIGH, thus acting as though A_{12} were HIGH.

6-25 Yes; it would also be selected for some incorrect addresses, possibly causing bus contention with another selected device.

6-27 (c) and (d)

6-29 HIGH; LOW; LOW

6-31 LOW; remains LOW

6-33 HIGH; HIGH; the alarm will be set, and the counter will be reset.

6-35 The $0.1\text{-}\mu\text{F}$ capacitor at the output of gate 9

Chapter 7

7-1 7 bits

7-3 14 bits

7-5 111

7-7 B

7-9
PC	00011
MAR	00011
MBR	XXXXXXXX
OP	000
ACC	00000101
B	00000111

7-11 (c)

7-13 (a)

7-15 (d)

7-17 (d)

7-19 (b)

7-21 (b)

7-23 (e)

7-25 (a)

7-27 (b)

7-29 (b)

7-31 (d)

7-33 (a)

7-35 (e)

7-37 (c)

7-39 (b)

Chapter 8

8-1 57H

8-3 2 sec

8-5 0, 0

8-7 08H

8-9 14H

8-11 B6 80 20 B0 41 25 B7 10 00

8-13 27H

8-15 0B

8-17 0100

8-19 0100

8-21 0101

8-23 100_{10} (64H)

8-25 0164

8-27 Bit 0 of memory location 1000 will be set, lighting lamp *A*.

8-29 0020

8-31 FFFF

8-33 *Z* flag; 0

8-35 000B; 00FF

8-37 0003

8-39 The program will branch back to 0005. The program would continue looping, but the byte in location 1000 would always be 02. Hence lamp *B* would always be lit.

9-1   (b); (a)

9-3   (b); (c)

9-5   (a), (b), (c)

9-7   C7

9-9   E6

9-11 High byte in FFF8, low byte in FFF9

9-13 Push the desired register onto the stack prior to jumping to the subroutine.

9-15 Bit 0

9-17 Bit 7

9-19 80H

9-21 S 0 0 1 1 0 1 0 0 P ST

9-23 2008 and 2009

9-25 2009; 2008

9-27 B6 1D 05 B7 20 09

9-29 85H

9-31 Bits 6, 5, 4

9-33 B6 20 09 B7 01 00

Chapter 10

10-1 The programmer is able to use easy-to-remember terms (mnemonics) while developing programs in assembly language.

10-3 Machine language

10-7 It is a program that converts mnemonic statements to their equivalent machine language codes. The assembler is loaded into a computer that assembles the source program and then runs the resulting object program.

10-11 Identifies the mnemonic of the instructions specified in each statement of an assembly list

10-13 # identifies immediate mode addressing.

10-15 0020

10-17 Program of Fig. 8-12(B)

10-19 DATA1, DATA2, and ANS are assigned locations 50_H, 51_H, and 52_H, respectively.

10-21 Front-panel switches, punched cards, paper tape, magnetic tape, cassettes, disks, diskettes, keyboards, etc.

Chapter 11

11-1 (a) $V_a = 9.96$ V, (b) $V_a = 6.5625$ V, (c) $V_a = 7.3828$ V, (d) $V_a = 3.32$ V

11-3 From -5 V to $+15$ V

11-5 (a) About $0111\ 1111_2$ ($7F_H$) or $1000\ 0000_2$ (80_H)

11-7 The 3-byte instruction, STAA $0800

11-9 LDAA $0800

11-11 ANDA

11-13 3; $D = \underline{0}$, $C = \underline{1}$, $B = \underline{0}$, $A = \underline{0}$, KEYSTROBE = $\underline{1}$

11-15 128 bytes

11-17 2005

11-19 2004

11-21

38	H	21	L	25	H	23	L	24	H
22	H	35	L	36	L				
26	L	27	L	28	L	29	L	30	L
31	H	32	L	33	H				

11-23

4	L	3	H	2	H	40	L		
38	H	21	H	25	H	23	L	24	H
22	H	35	L	36	L				
26	L	27	L	28	L	29	L	30	L
32	H	33	H						

11-27 Odd

11-29 19.2 kHz $\div$ 16 = 1200 baud

11-31 46. This is the hex code for the ASCII character to be transmitted, and location 2009 is the Tx data register.

11-33 LOW . . . the ACTIVE DTR signal thus tells the ACIA that a terminal is ready to receive, so the ACIA may send; HIGH

11-35 8B; see Table 9-2.

11-37 The zero flag will be set when the last character (00) is loaded.

11-39 Yes; when receiving, DATA is read; when sending, DATA is written into.

Chapter 12

12-1 A move from one of the MPU's registers to memory (MOVr,M) or from memory to a register (MOV M,r) requires seven cycles (T states), whereas a register-to-register move (MOVr$_1$r$_2$) requires only four.

12-3 2023_H and 2024_H

12-5 About 41 sec

12-7 Change the instruction at 2007_H from INR A to DCR A.

12-9 A_{15}–A_{11} are 00000.

12-11 A_{15}–A_{11} are 00100.

12-13 4096

12-15 Z80 pins 19 ___0___ 20 ___1___ 21 ___0___ 22 ___1___
38 ___0___ 37 ___0___ 36 ___1___ 35 ___0___ 34 ___1___
33 ___0___ 32 ___0___ 31 ___1___ 30 ___0___
2704 pin 20 ___0___
74LS75 pin 13 ___0___

12-17 Gate 1 ___1___ 2 ___0___ 3 ___1___ 4 ___0___
5 ___1___ 6 ___1___ 7 ___0___

12-19 Gate 1 ___0___ 2 ___0___ 3 ___0___ 4 ___1___
5 ___1___ 6 ___0___ 7 ___0___

12-21 OUT 02

12-23 Tape reader

12-25 IN 10

12-27 LOW, go LOW

12-29 07F4H

12-31 No

Index